W9-AKB-047

The Tapestry of Culture

An Introduction to Cultural Anthropology

FOURTH EDITION

Abraham Rosman and Paula G. Rubel

Barnard College, Columbia University

McGRAW-HILL, INC.

New York   St. Louis   San Francisco   Auckland   Bogotá
Caracas   Lisbon   London   Madrid   Mexico   Milan
Montreal   New Delhi   Paris   San Juan   Singapore
Sydney   Tokyo   Toronto

The Tapestry of Culture
An Introduction to Cultural Anthropology

Copyright © 1992, 1989, 1985, 1981 by McGraw-Hill, Inc. All rights reserved. Printed in the United States of America. Except as permitted under the United States Copyright Act of 1976, no part of this publication may be reproduced or distributed in any form or by any means, or stored in a data base or retrieval system, without the prior written permission of the publisher.

2 3 4 5 6 7 8 9 0 HAL HAL 9 0 9 8 7 6 5 4 3 2

ISBN 0-07-053718-6

This book was set in Meridien by The Clarinda Company.
The editors were Phillip A. Butcher, Lori Bittker, and Laura D. Warner.
The cover was designed by Wanda Siedlecka.
The photo editor was Anne Manning.
Arcata Graphics/Halliday was printer and binder.

Cover photo: Section of a palepai (ceremonial textile), sumatra. Courtesy of the Royal Tropical Institute, Tropenmuseun-Amsterdam.

Library of Congress Cataloging-in-Publication Data

Rosman, Abraham.
    The tapestry of culture: an introduction to cultural anthropology
/ Abraham Rosman and Paula G. Rubel. — 4th ed.
      p.   cm.
    Includes bibliographical references and index.
    ISBN 0-07-053718-6
    1. Ethnology.   I. Rubel, Paula G.   II. Title
GN316.R67   1992
305.8—dc20   91-35143

About the Authors

Abraham Rosman received the Ph.D. in anthropology from Yale University. His first fieldwork was with the Kanuri of Bornu Province, in northern Nigeria. He has taught at Vassar College and at Antioch College and is now professor of anthropology at Barnard College, Columbia University.

Paula G. Rubel has a Ph.D. in anthropology from Columbia University. She carried out fieldwork on the Kalmyk Mongol refugees who settled in New Jersey and Philadelphia in 1950. Her Ph.D. dissertation was published as *The Kalmyk Mongols: A Study in Continuity and Change*. She is at present professor of anthropology at Barnard College, Columbia University.

Abraham Rosman and Paula Rubel began their collaboration in 1971 when they published a comparative study of the potlatch in six northwest coast societies entitled *Feasting with Mine Enemy*. They have done fieldwork together in Iran, Afghanistan, and Papua New Guinea, and in 1978 they published *Your Own Pigs You May Not Eat: A Comparative Study of New Guinea Societies*. They have also published many articles on their fieldwork and comparative research. Their most recent article, "Structural Patterning in Kwakiutl Art and Ritual," was published in 1990 in *Man*.

To the memory of Daniel

Contents

PREFACE   *xi*

1   THE ANTHROPOLOGICAL POINT OF VIEW   *1*

Basic Concepts   *5*
The Anthropological Method   *11*
The Discipline of Anthropology   *15*
The Biological Basis for Culture   *16*
Anthropological Theory   *17*

2   RITUALS IN SMALL-SCALE AND COMPLEX SOCIETIES: A CONTRAST   *25*

Marriage in a Small-Scale Society   *26*
Marriage in a Complex Society   *32*
Funeral Rites in a Small-Scale Society   *36*
Funeral Rites in a Complex Society   *40*

3   LANGUAGE AND CULTURE   *45*

The Structure of Language   *45*
Linguistic Relativity   *48*
Language and Cognition   *49*
Ethnosemantics   *50*
Sociolinguistics   *52*
Language Change   *54*

4   SYMBOLIC SYSTEMS AND MEANINGS   *57*

The Symbolism of Food   *59*
Social Groups and Their Symbols   *62*

Symbols, Politics, and Authority   *67*
The Symbolism of Sports   *70*
Universal Symbols   *72*

**5   FAMILY, MARRIAGE,
AND KINSHIP   *73***

Marriage   *74*
Postmarital Residence   *79*
Family Types   *81*
Descent Groups   *84*
The Structure of Descent Groups   *88*
Kindreds   *92*
Relations between Groups through Marriage   *93*
Kinship Terminology   *98*
Fictive Kinship   *102*
Kinship in Complex Societies   *104*

6   GENDER AND AGE   *109*

Male and Female   *109*
Age Grades   *114*
Associations Based on Age   *117*

**7   PROVISIONING SOCIETY:
PRODUCTION, DISTRIBUTION,
AND CONSUMPTION   *121***

Production   *122*
Distribution   *134*
Consumption   *151*

**8   POLITICAL ORGANIZATION:
POLITICS, GOVERNMENT,
LAW, AND CONFLICT   *155***

Concepts Used in Political Anthropology   *157*
Types of Political Organization   *159*
Law and Social Control   *171*
War and Peace   *174*
Politics in the Contemporary Nation-State   *178*

9 RELIGION AND THE SUPERNATURAL *183*

Religion, Science, and Magic *187*
Conceptions of the Supernatural *188*
Ritual Approaches to the Supernatural *193*
Religious Specialists *198*
Aims and Goals of Religious Activity *205*
Latent Functions of Religious Behavior *206*

10 MYTHS, LEGENDS, AND FOLKTALES *209*

Myths *210*
Legends *215*
Folktales *216*
Legends and Folktales in American Culture *219*

11 THE ARTISTIC DIMENSION *225*

The Visual Arts: Sculpture and Painting *226*
Music and Dance *242*

12 CULTURE AND THE INDIVIDUAL *247*

Culture and Personality Studies *249*
Socialization of the Child *251*
The Relationship of Personality to Culture and Social Structure *254*
Culture and Mental Illness *255*
Rebels and Innovators *257*
The Person and the Self *258*

13 FOURTH WORLD PEOPLES IN THE COLONIAL AND POSTCOLONIAL PERIODS *263*

Concepts in the Study of Culture Change *264*
Contexts of Culture Change *265*
The Study of Culture Change *268*
New Ireland: An Example of Increasing Incorporation into the World System *280*
Directed Culture Change *288*
Assertion of Cultural Identity *292*

14   THE ANTHROPOLOGY OF CONTEMPORARY LIFE   *297*

Peasants   *297*
Migration: The Mines and the City   *302*

EPILOGUE: END OF A JOURNEY   *311*

CITED REFERENCES   *313*

SUGGESTED READINGS   *321*

GLOSSARY   *331*

PHOTO AND ILLUSTRATION CREDITS   *339*

INDEX   *341*

Preface

Anthropology in the nineties has become increasingly concerned with a number of issues. Although some of these have been with us since the beginnings of the discipline, contemporary commentators and critics within and outside of anthropology have compelled us to confront them anew. These issues include how anthropologists collect their data, particularly how fieldwork is conducted; how societies conceptualize gender differences and the relationship between males and females; and lastly, how to comprehend and translate into our culture's terms the ideas and behaviors of others.

In this fourth edition of *The Tapestry of Culture,* we have devoted attention to these issues. We have examined the concerns of anthropologists regarding the implications of power and status differences between anthropologists and informants. We have considered problems raised by feminist scholars concerning the relationship between cultural constructions of gender and the anthropological concepts and categories used to study such constructions. We have attempted to treat, in depth, the concern with meaning which pervades anthropology today. This edition of *Tapestry* is characterized not only by increased attention to these matters but also by a general updating of discussions and examples in accord with current thinking in the anthropological literature.

To many anthropologists today, ethnographies are seen as the heart of the discipline. One of the best ways for students to learn about anthropology is by reading ethnographies. Seeing the Trobriand Islands through Bronislaw Malinowski's eyes as he describes them in *Argonauts of the Western Pacific* conveys enthusiasm and a sense of discovery to the student. However, in order to understand and appreciate ethnographies, the student must be provided with concepts and theories which anthropologists have developed. This book was written to give our students a concise and up-to-date conceptual framework with which to understand an ethnography. We have chosen a range of ethnographic works, from those depicting small-scale societies, like the Yanomamo of the South American tropical forest, to those describing aspects of industrialized societies, like the subculture of San Quentin prison. However, an instructor can select ethnographies which suit his or her interests. While we want the student to capture Malinowski's sense of adventure while he was in the Trobriands, we also feel it is necessary to provide a framework for critical evaluation of such an ethnography. Although every ethnographic description is of a society which could be considered unique, anthropology also goes beyond the description of unique characteristics to the level of comparison in order to make generalizations about human behavior.

The title of our book refers to culture metaphorically as a tapestry, composed of many interconnected threads, but the whole is more than the sum of its parts. Standing back from the tapestry, one no longer sees the individual threads but an overall design. The anthropologist doing fieldwork does not see "culture," though, the overall design of the tapestry. Rather he converses with individuals around him and observes their actions; this is the equivalent of the threads. From this the anthropologist builds a picture of the culture when he or she writes the ethnography. Culture is therefore an analytical concept, an abstraction from reality; but, like a tapestry, it can be taken apart and examined. And, like a tapestry, culture has an overall design, even though we take it apart and study it by using analytical categories such as kinship, economics, and religion.

This new edition could not have been written without assistance from many people. First of all, we would like to thank the students in our introductory anthropology classes who, over the years, have asked us many penetrating questions. We are continuously in their debt. We are particularly grateful to the professors who have used *Tapestry of Culture* in their introductory anthropology courses and have given us their pithy comments and observations. Jerome Handler, Southern Illinois University, has continued to give us criticisms in his own refreshing manner; Ira Buchler, University of Texas, provided us with his thoughtful and helpful critique; Jay Powell, University of British Columbia, helped us to reorganize some of the text by spiritedly telling us his own approach to the material; Elvin Hatch, University of California at Santa Barbara, gave us many constructive suggestions; Jack Potter, University of California at Berkeley, frankly told us which parts of the text he liked; Luther Gerlach, University of Minnesota, described how he used the text to introduce anthropology to his students; and Mario Zamora, College of William and Mary, urged us to pay more attention to Third World peoples. To these individuals and all the others who have helped us in the past we owe a debt of gratitude for raising questions which have contributed to a significant improvement in the organization and clarity of this book.

Over the past two years, while they were students majoring in anthropology in our department at Barnard College, Meg Rheingold and Ruthie Cushing provided us with a quality of research assistance for which we are eternally grateful. Finally, our thanks to Phil Butcher and Lori Pearson Bittker, our sponsoring editors, for their help in making the transition from one publisher to another a relatively painless one, and for all of their assistance in launching this, the fourth edition of *Tapestry of Culture*.

Abraham Rosman
Paula G. Rubel

CHAPTER 1

The Anthropological Point of View

 Anthropology teaches us about other peoples, and in the process it teaches us about ourselves. The anthropologist's method is different from that of other social scientists, and this influences the nature of the discipline—its theories, concepts, and procedures. Anthropological research involves a journey, a journey in space, a journey through time, a psychological journey into an alien world. It resembles Alice's trip through the looking glass into another universe where the "rules" may be turned on their heads and people may behave in very different ways. Anthropological investigation of a way of life or a culture other than one's own may seem at first like a trip into Alice's wonderland. However, like the world through the looking glass, different cultures have an underlying logic of their own. The behavior of people makes sense once we understand the basic premises by which they live. The anthropologist's task is to translate that culture and its premises into something we can comprehend.

Some centuries ago, people in Europe who considered themselves civilized viewed the ways of life in "faraway places" as uniformly the same and therefore of no interest. When Boswell presented Samuel Johnson, the eighteenth-century compiler of a dictionary, with a copy of Captain Cook's *Voyages to the South Sea,* Johnson remarked, "These voyages, who will read them through? . . . There can be little entertainment in such books; one set of Savages is like another." Samuel Johnson, so wise in other ways,

1

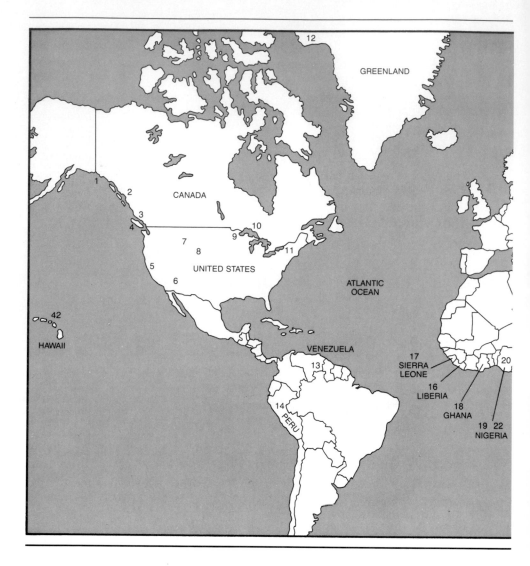

shared with many people of his time, armchair philosophers and the like, the view that "all savages are alike." For Johnson, the label "savages" was used for any people not his kind (civilized Western society). But Samuel Johnson was proved wrong. Many people did indeed read accounts by great voyagers such as Bougainville, Malaspina, Vancouver, and Cook, in which they graphically described the different people they encountered and their "exotic" customs. Explorers and voyagers like Captain Cook were struck by the cultural differences they encountered, sometimes of an extreme sort. Their accounts and illustrations depict some of these differ-

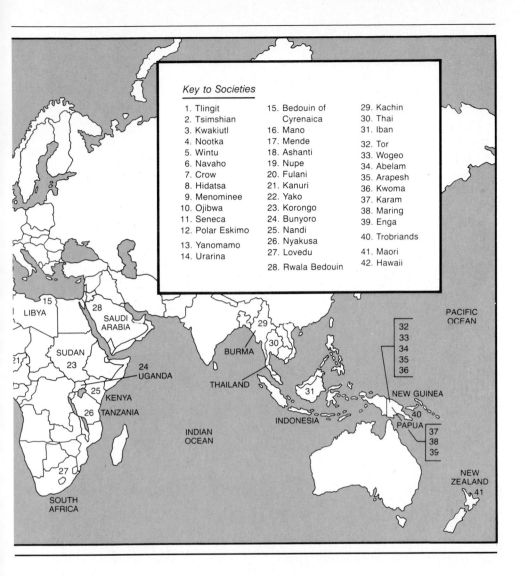

Key to Societies

1. Tlingit
2. Tsimshian
3. Kwakiutl
4. Nootka
5. Wintu
6. Navaho
7. Crow
8. Hidatsa
9. Menominee
10. Ojibwa
11. Seneca
12. Polar Eskimo
13. Yanomamo
14. Urarina

15. Bedouin of Cyrenaica
16. Mano
17. Mende
18. Ashanti
19. Nupe
20. Fulani
21. Kanuri
22. Yako
23. Korongo
24. Bunyoro
25. Nandi
26. Nyakusa
27. Lovedu
28. Rwala Bedouin

29. Kachin
30. Thai
31. Iban
32. Tor
33. Wogeo
34. Abelam
35. Arapesh
36. Kwoma
37. Karam
38. Maring
39. Enga
40. Trobriands
41. Maori
42. Hawaii

ences, although sometimes fancifully. Webber, the artist who accompanied Captain Cook on his third voyage, depicts a human sacrifice on Tahiti (see the illustration). On an earlier voyage, Cook had brought Omai, a Tahitian, back with him to England as a "specimen" who illustrated these cultural differences. Omai returned to Tahiti on Cook's third voyage, and he is depicted in European dress, along with Cook, in the right-hand corner of the picture. The appearance of people like Omai and the numerous publications of voyagers' accounts of people from other parts of the world made eighteenth-century social philosophers like Voltaire and Diderot more aware of cultural differences. They used these accounts to raise questions about the "God-given nature" of their own societies' practices, such as the divine right of kings to rule and the patriarchal position of fathers within the family. Cultural differences were more systematically studied as the field of anthropology developed, and it soon became apparent that "all savages" were not alike.

Even today, despite the worldwide distribution of Pepsi-Cola and McDonald's, a visitor to another culture will still be impressed with cultural differences. People in China may eat sea cucumbers, while people in North America will refuse to eat them. People in every culture think that what they eat is "the right stuff" and healthful for everyone. The way in which families are formed also differs from one culture to the next. In the village of Lesu, in Papua New Guinea, after marriage the couple goes to live with the wife's parents; in Morocco the couple goes to live with the husband's parents, while in our own culture the couple moves off to start a new family, independent of either set of parents. The belief that one's own culture represents the natural and best way to do things is known as *ethnocentrism*. Anthropology opens up the world of cultural differences to overcome this point of view.

If the first thing one notices is that there are cultural differences, the second is that all cultures have a degree of internal consistency. We have called this book *The Tapestry of Culture* because the imagery of a tapestry well conveys the integrated nature of culture. Many strands, many colors,

A human sacrifice on Tahiti, as depicted by the artist John Webber, who accompanied Captain Cook on his voyage around the world in 1776–1780.

many patterns contribute to the overall design of a tapestry, just as many items of behavior and many customs form patterns that, in turn, compose a culture. The patterns and regularities of culture do not remain the same in an eternal, unchanging fashion. Anthropologists view cultures as more or less integrated in relatively distinct ways.

Anthropology goes beyond the description of single cultures to the comparison of cultures with one another in order to identify similarities and differences of patterning. This comparative approach looks beyond cultural differences to seek out what cultures have in common. For example, the Rwala Bedouins of the Saudi Arabian desert depend primarily on their camel herds for subsistence, while the Kazaks of Central Asia rely on their herds of horses in the grassland steppe environment in which they make their home. Anthropologists characterize both these peoples as *nomadic pastoralists*. Despite the fact that the environments in which they live are totally different, they share a number of cultural features. They both move with their animal herds from place to place over fixed migration routes during the year in order to provide pasture for their animals. They live in similar sorts of communities—nomadic encampments consisting of several related groups of people, each with its own tent. In each case, the nomads must depend on exchanging the products of their herds with sedentary communities for commodities like flour and tea which they cannot provide for themselves. Cultures may be grouped together on the basis of similarity in many different criteria, such as type of economic organization, family system, religion, language, political organization, and so on.

Basic Concepts

In order to analyze cultures in terms of their similarities and differences and to group them together into types based on these features, a set of basic concepts is necessary. These basic concepts are commonly agreed upon heuristic tools developed within the discipline that help us to organize the data and make comparisons. The goal ultimately is to formulate generalizations about culture.

Culture

The central concept of anthropology is *culture*. This term, as we have indicated, is used to refer to the way of life of a people. It emphasizes the integrated totality of that way of life—including the people's behavior, the things they make, and their ideas. Other disciplines study the different kinds of human activity universally carried out in all societies, but each discipline studies a different sector of this activity. Thus, economics studies economy; political science studies government; art history, music, and religion each study particular activities of humans as if those activities were largely autonomous. All these fields are investigated by the anthropologist, but the emphasis is on their interrelationship. By focusing on culture as the organizing concept, the anthropologist stresses the relationship between economics, politics, art, religion, etc.

While we stress the integrated nature of culture, we do not mean to imply that all cultures are well-integrated wholes. Integration is a matter of degree. Often there are internal inconsistencies and contradictions in cultures, as we will illustrate in later chapters. Nor should culture be thought of as a single monolithic entity. When we refer to American culture, for example, we recognize that there are many American subcultures based on occupation, social class, region, etc. The subculture of jazz musicians differs from that of truck drivers, but all these subcultures belong to a larger American culture. That American culture is what all Americans have in common.

Culture is learned and acquired by infants through a process referred to by anthropologists as *enculturation.* It has a transgenerational quality, since it continues beyond the lifetime of individuals. Culture therefore has continuity through time. This does not imply that cultures never change. Rather, there is a consistency of pattern through time, despite the fact that culture is continually being reworked. The changes may be brought about as a result of changes in environmental conditions or contact with other cultures. Anthropologists study this process of culture change through time by examining historical, archival, and archaeological data derived from the excavation of prehistoric sites. The process of culture change can also be examined when a culture is studied for the second time years after the first study.

Some anthropologists focus upon culture as primarily a set of ideas and meanings that people use based on the past and that they construct in the present. The role of the anthropologist is then to grasp, understand, and translate those ideas and meanings. Other anthropologists see culture as the means by which human beings adapt to their environment. This perspective emphasizes what humans have in common with other animal species. The concept of culture is so broad that it encompasses both of these points of view. The differences between them represent differing theoretical perspectives, which will be explored later in this chapter.

Cultural Rules

What is learned and internalized by human infants during the process of enculturation are *cultural rules.* For example, cultural rules govern what one eats, when one eats, and how one eats. We drink milk and the Chinese do not. We eat with knife and fork; the Chinese and Japanese eat with chopsticks; and the Kanuri of West Africa eat with the fingers of the right hand only, since eating with the left hand is forbidden. Rules also govern sexual behavior in terms of with whom it is allowed, as well as when, where, and how. For example, in Lesu it is acceptable for sexual intercourse to take place before marriage. The marriage relationship is symbolized by eating together. When a couple publicly shares a meal, henceforth they can eat only with one another. Even though husband and wife may have sexual relations with other individuals, they may not eat with them. Fifty years ago, in our society, couples engaged to be married could eat together, but sexual intercourse was not permitted until after marriage. The act of sexual intercourse symbolized marriage. If either of the spouses had intercourse with other individuals after marriage, this was considered a criminal act, though either spouse could have dinner with someone of the opposite sex. From the perspective of someone in our society, the rules governing marriage in Lesu appear like our rules "stood on their heads." The more extended meaning of eating together and of sexual intercourse in these two societies must be seen in relation to the underlying logic characterizing each society.

For human beings, all biological drives are governed by sets of cultural rules. The enormous variety of cultural differences is due to differences in cultural rules. Frequently people from a particular culture can tell the anthropologist what the rules are. At other times, they may behave according to sets of rules that they cannot verbalize. Defining these cultural rules is like trying to identify the rules on which a language is based. All languages operate according to sets of rules, and people follow these rules in their speech. However, they may be unable to state the rules that govern the way they speak. Just as it is the linguist's job to determine the rules of grammar (which the speakers of the language use automatically and are usually not aware of), it is the anthropologist's job, working with informants, to determine the cultural rules of which the people may also be unaware.

Cultural Rules and Individual Behavior

Anthropologists also explore the relationship between culture and the individual. Though cultural rules exist, it is individuals who interpret them and either act according to these rules or violate them.

Each person speaks his or her unique version of a language, which linguists refer to as one's idiolect. The vocabulary, syntax, and pronunciation one uses represent one's interpretation and use of the sets of rules underlying the language being spoken. In the same manner, individuals act according to their interpretation of the rules of their culture. This frequently involves choosing from among a number of cultural rules that present themselves as options or alternatives.

Individuals may also on occasion violate the cultural rules. All cultures have some provision for sanctioning the violation of cultural rules as well as rewards for obeying them. Both rewards and sanctions differ from one culture to another, in the same way that the sets of cultural rules differ.

Cultural rules can and do change over time. When many individuals consistently interpret a rule differently than it had been interpreted before, such as the change that has come about in our society now that sexual intercourse is no longer a symbol of marriage, the result will be a change in the rule itself.

Society and Social Structure

A second concept, paralleling culture, is that of society. While culture is distinctive of humans, all animals that live in groups, humans among them, may be said to have societies. Thus a wolf pack, a deer herd, and a baboon troop constitute societies. As in a human society, the individual members of a wolf pack are differentiated as males and females, immature individuals and adults, and mothers, fathers, and offspring. Individuals in each of these social categories behave in particular ways. Insects, such as ants and bees, also live in societies. In certain respects, these insect societies may be considered even more complex than the wolf pack. In a beehive, there are a queen bee, worker bees, and drones, and bees in each of these categories have highly specialized roles to perform. The entire bee society depends upon the performance of these different roles. Resemblances between wolf and human societies should not be surprising since both the wolf and the human are social animals. But human societies not only are more complex; they also have culture, that body of learned, symbolic behavior that is transmitted transgenerationally and is infinitely expandable.

In human societies not only are there the minimal distinctions between the sexes and individuals of different ages, but there are also differences in behavior according to the position, or *social status*, that the individual occupies in the society. In human societies, individuals act as fathers, mothers, chiefs, headmen, shamans, priests, etc. The behavior associated with a particular social status in a society is known as the *social role*. Societies, of course, vary in the number and the kinds of social roles. Social roles involve behavior toward other people, as a father to his children, a foreman to his crew, or a headman to his followers. A headman will lead his followers to attend a ceremony sponsored by another headman and his followers. This represents the interaction of two social groups. When the headman orates on such an occasion, he speaks for his group, and he is carrying out the social role of headman. The interaction of people in their social roles and the interaction between groups define *social relationships*.

The particular patterns of social relationships that characterize a society are referred to as its *social structure*. These patterns of social structure are based on cultural rules. Social structure includes the social groupings that the society recognizes, which may be organized on the basis of family, kinship, residential propinquity, or common interest. These groupings have continuity through time and relate to one another in a patterned fashion.

The entire network of social roles constitutes another aspect of social structure. The concept of social structure may be distinguished from *social organization* (Firth, 1951). While structure emphasizes continuity and stability, organization refers to the way in which people act out social roles. Individuals perceive the structure and context of any situation in their own way and make decisions and choices from the alternative courses of behavior. Organization refers to variations in individual behavior and emphasizes flux and change. At this level of individual behavior, culture and its rules are continually being reworked by social action.

Interchanges or interactions between individuals may also be seen in terms of *exchange*. Such exchanges may be verbal exchanges, exchanges of goods or services, or even behavioral exchanges, such as deference. Anthropologists study exchanges in order to gain information concerning the pattern of social relationships between groups and between individuals as they carry out social roles. In other words, data on exchanges provide information on the social structure. Focusing upon exchanges also provides information on cultural meanings and what people in a culture value.

Structure and Function in Anthropological Analysis

The term *structure,* which we used above in defining the social structure, is opposed to another widely used term—*function.* Structure is a description of form, like the term *pattern,* used earlier, while function tells what the parts do and how they operate. Both terms are borrowed from biology. Structure corresponds to anatomy, function to physiology. The structure of the heart consists of a four-chambered entity connected by valves to arteries and veins, while its function is to pump blood throughout the body. In anthropology, analogously, structure consists of a description of parts in their relationship to one another, while function is concerned with how the structure operates, what it does, and what its purpose is. From another perspective, the meaning of something is its function. One may pose the question: What is the political structure of a society like? This is an anatomical sort of question. If talking about the political structure of Trobriand Island society in the South Pacific when it was first studied, at the beginning of the twentieth century, one could state that there are villages with headmen, and that a number of these villages together form a district that is headed by a chief. This constitutes the Trobriand political structure. If one asks what its functions are, the answer would be government. The village headman organizes and directs village ceremonies and collects tribute to be given to the chief of the district. The chief of the entire district maintains order in his district by punishing wrongdoers, and he uses his wealth and tribute to reward those who have performed services for him. In similar fashion, one can describe the economic structure, the religious structure, and the kinship structure of any society, including one's own. In Trobriand society, as in all other societies, an interrelationship exists between the political, religious, economic, and kinship structures, as shall be demonstrated in the later chapters of this book. Anthropological analysis is, in a way, a kind of dissection, in that anthropologists seek to determine the structure. At the same time they are concerned with the function, which is revealed by the political or economic process—how the structure operates.

The Unit of Analysis

In the earlier period of anthropological research, fieldworkers investigated societies that were small in scale and in population, where all spheres of human activity could be encompassed by a single investigator. They frequently selected small islands for study, where the unit of analysis was bounded in a most distinct manner. For example, Raymond Firth, the British anthropologist, studied the island of Tikopia in the Pacific. Not all anthropologists examined island societies; others went off to study societies in Africa and elsewhere. These anthropologists selected a natural grouping, such as the village of Tepoztlan in Mexico or a camp among Australian native peoples, as the unit of analysis on which to concentrate and from which they could generalize about the culture. This unit, sometimes referred to as a *community*, has a name, and the people within recognize themselves as members of it. It is bounded, in that its members concentrate their interactions within it, and it has an internal social structure that can be discerned. The community interacts with other communities, and these connections are also the subject of study for the anthropologist. It should be noted, however, that even in these small-scale societies there is a degree of cultural variation from one community to the next. This is an issue that the anthropologist must consider when making generalizations about the culture as a whole.

Beginning in the 1930s, anthropologists increasingly turned to the study of complex societies. A single community could no longer be considered representative of the culture of a complex society such as India or France, and anthropologists found it extremely difficult to analyze the entire culture without being simplistic in their conclusions. The culture plainly could not be encompassed in its totality at the level of detail at which the anthropologist works. Complex societies are very heterogeneous as a result of regional, social-class, religious, and ethnic differences. People in complex societies belong to different groups based upon occupation, such as railroad engineers and professional athletes, or social movements, such as Greenpeace. Each of these has a subculture of its own, but is not necessarily coterminus with a particular territory. These groups have sometimes become the units of analysis.

Anthropologists working in complex societies also focus on particular problems, such as rural-urban migration, the effects of the closing of a mine or factory in a company town, or the way kinship operates as an adaptive mechanism in an industrialized society. The unit of analysis here is dictated by the problem. It may be a farming community, a labor union, a corporation, or a social movement. These units cannot be studied as isolates, and the anthropologist must attend to how they are related to a larger whole, the nation-state or sometimes even the international community.

As noted above, anthropologists used to look at the small-scale societies they investigated as if they were autonomous entities, though some paid attention to relations with neighboring societies. After contact with Europeans these small-scale societies were increasingly brought under the jurisdiction of larger political entities, typically European colonial empires. Sometimes colonial administrators imposed a structure that they created of "tribes" and districts in order to govern more easily. Some of the entities that anthropologists in the past assumed were "natural groupings" were in reality colonial constructs. In the early days of anthropology, for the most part no attention was paid to the nature of the articulation of the small-scale societies to the colonial empire. Anthropologists today pay attention to the process of incorporation of these societies into the newly formed nation-states of which they are now a part. Modernization and industrialization made small-scale societies part of a world system, and anthropologists now investigate how they have responded to these changes. The effect of missionary activity, the introduction of new political ideology, and the connections with world economic trends are now topics of research.

The Anthropological Method

How does one gain perspective on another society? The answer for the anthropologist has always been to step outside of the web of his or her own world in order to closely examine another, often vastly different, way of life. This is what anthropologists do when they carry out *fieldwork*. Over the years, we have separately carried out fieldwork, Rosman with the Kanuri in northern Nigeria and Rubel with a Kalmyk Mongol émigré community in New Jersey, and we have jointly carried out fieldwork in Iran, Afghanistan, and Papua New Guinea. Fieldwork involves *participant observation*. This means living with other people, learning their language, and understanding their behavior and the ideas that are important to them. It usually includes living in their kind of house, be it the black goat-hair tent which we lived in when we did fieldwork in Afghanistan or the mud-brick house used by Rosman in the Nigerian town of Geidam; donning their dress on ceremonial occasions (see Rosman in Kanuri garb in the illustration); and eating their cuisine—nan, or flat bread of Iran, or the roast pig and taro of a New Ireland funerary celebration. Fieldworkers celebrate the birth rites of the people with whom they are living and mourn with them at funerals.

A participant in another culture often will don its clothing while doing fieldwork. This is Abraham Rosman doing research among the Kanuri.

The fieldworker is always an intruder and at the beginning of fieldwork is often seen as intent on prying loose peoples' innermost secrets. The individuals (government officials, missionaries, members of other communities, etc.) who help the anthropologist gain entry into the group may, by their very actions as outsiders, set community members against the anthropologist. Sometimes the fieldworker gains entry through a community leader only to find out that the individual has his or her own friends and enemies. Developing close relationships with some individuals sometimes precludes developing a relationship with others.

The anthropologist, in addition to learning the language, is also learning the culture of the people. When first immersed in a different culture, the fieldworker experiences culture shock, which is similar to the experience of plunging into an ice-cold bath. As the anthropologist learns the culture, he or she is in the position of a child in that new culture. American anthro-

pologists, who have learned as children to eat with knives and forks, frequently must learn to eat with their fingers from a common bowl, as
Rosman did during fieldwork with the Kanuri. When, because of inexperi-
ence, bits of food fell from his hands and soiled his clothing, people dis-
creetly turned away so that their laughter would not embarrass him. It
was the fate of Rubel to eat boiled lamb (the Mongolian dish served on
festive occasions) and steaks of horsemeat when they could be acquired in
New Jersey. Learning to eat in new ways or accustoming oneself to new
foods places the anthropologist in the uncomfortable role of a child.

Participant observation involves an inherent contradiction. A participant
operates inside a culture, while an observer looks on from outside. As one
learns how to participate as a member of a culture, he or she becomes
engaged in that culture and identifies with it. On the other hand, the
observer is expected to remain detached and to report objectively what he
or she sees and hears. Participant observation is therefore difficult since it
involves a basic paradox.

When an anthropologist goes to do fieldwork, he or she brings along his
or her own cultural categories or ways of seeing things. However, participation in another culture means learning how to view things from what is
called "the natives' point of view." This requires the anthropologist to sus-
pend the categories of his or her own culture. Participant observation
requires interaction with informants. Under the tutelage of the anthropologist, informants begin to think about their own culture in a different way.
As the informants present their own world to the anthropologist, they
begin to reflect about their own behavior and life. They attempt to explain
their culture as they never had to before, in response to the anthropologist's questions.

The personal relationship between anthropologist and informant is a
complex one. Key informants often become intimate friends of as well as
mentors to the anthropologist. When doing fieldwork among the Kanuri,
the key informant for Rosman was the District Head, a titled aristocrat (pictured in the illustration), much older than the fledgling anthropologist,
whom he adopted. This relationship was crucial since many doors opened
as a result of it; however, because of this connection, other sources of
information remained closed.

Often, anthropologist and informant use one another. The anthropologist may be at the mercy of the informant's desires, sometimes being used
to further the political ambitions of the informant. An informant may
become jealous when the anthropologist shifts to questioning other people,
which is inevitable in the course of fieldwork. All these factors involved in
the interaction influence the nature of the information that is obtained,
and these must be taken into account when the data are being analyzed.

At the beginning of fieldwork, things appear chaotic and unintelligible,
and the anthropologist usually records concrete and fairly obvious infor-

mation such as types of houses and economic activities that he or she believes may not be mediated by language or cultural categories. Frequently this assumption proves to be incorrect once the anthropologist learns more about the culture, since even these concrete features are imbued with cultural meaning.

In the field, the anthropologist observes and records peoples' actions and then with the help of informants seeks to understand the meanings of those actions. The observations of the anthropologist are a very important component. Discussions with informants about cultural behavior alone are not sufficient. When the informant attempts to explain his or her culture to the anthropologist, the informant is objectifying his or her own cultural experiences. At the same time the anthropologist is attempting to go beyond his or her own cultural categories to understand the informant's experiences and thereby grasp the natives' point of view. In their inter-action, the two are, in a sense, operating in an area between their two cultures. The data are thus produced through the mutual efforts of anthro-pologist and informant. This process is repeated with other informants. The data are checked against the anthropologist's own observations, as well as with other individuals with whom contacts are more limited. Ultimately, the problem for the anthropologist is to translate the cultural categories of the society being studied into the language of anthropology.

Anthropologists may also utilize other techniques to collect data such as census materials and historical and archival information. As anthropo-logists study new kinds of problems and the unit of analysis is no longer nec-essarily a community, they supplement the central methodology of anthro-pology—participant observation—with a variety of additional techniques, such as questionnaires and statistical analysis. These newer methodologies have often been borrowed from other social sciences, such as sociology and economics, and have been adapted by anthropologists for use in their own research. The anthropologist translates these data into the language of anthropological concepts discussed above. This process begins in the field, continues through the analysis of the data, and ends as an ethnographic account.

Fieldwork must involve reciprocity on the part of the anthropologist, though the nature of what the anthropologist returns in the field situation varies. Sharing of tobacco, which seems to be culturally universal, is one of the ways the anthropologist can make a return, and in Papua New Guinea we always presented tobacco to people with whom we talked. In rural as well as urban areas, the anthropologist with a vehicle often reciprocates by becoming chauffeur for the entire community, as Rubel did for the Kalmyk Mongols with whom she worked in New Jersey. Frequently anthropolo-gists identify with the people among whom they have lived and worked. They become partisans and take on the causes of the community as advo-cates in the media or become expert witnesses for them in the courts.

Fieldwork involves the anthropologist in a moral dilemma. It could be said that anthropologists use informants for their own ends, since they return to their own societies with the information gathered. The publication of this information helps the career of the anthropologist, but in what way does it help the people whose way of life has been recorded? As we have indicated above, the anthropologist tries in a variety of ways to make a return for all that has been given. As we will point out later in this book, the findings of anthropology also may have useful applications for the people who have been studied. In a more general way, the product of the anthropologist's work also makes a contribution to the wider understanding of human behavior.

The Discipline of Anthropology

Anthropology as a discipline comprises four subfields that share not only the single unifying concept of culture but also many of the other basic concepts described above. *Anthropological linguistics* focuses upon the study of languages that in some respects has been considered the most important part of culture. We referred to linguistics earlier when we pointed out how rules of culture operate in the same manner as the rules that underlie the grammar of a language. Like the cultural anthropologist, the linguist is concerned with the analysis of meaning. Similarly, how infants acquire language, another problem investigated by anthropological linguists, parallels the way culture is acquired and passed from generation to generation. *Archaeology* provides information about cultures for which there are no historic, written records and tells us how these cultures were organized. Archaeologists share an interest with cultural anthropologists in how cultures have changed through time. *Physical anthropology* views humans as biological organisms. The biological basis for culture and the evolution of the human being's capacity for culture are of central interest to the physical anthropologist. The fourth subdiscipline of anthropology is *cultural anthropology,* which is the focus of this book.

Today, some of the distinctions between these subdisciplines are blurred. New fields of specialization, such as medical anthropology and nutritional anthropology, address themselves to concerns that bridge the gap between physical and cultural anthropology. Sociobiologists place much greater emphasis on the biological determination of culture and examine cultural behavior in terms of the degree of reproductive success it confers. This is their way of explaining the presence of one cultural trait, and not another, in different societies. The study of black English and its effect on the progress of black students in American schools draws upon both linguistics and cultural anthropology. Educational anthropology applies the methods of the discipline to the study of educational institutions, analyzing the classroom and the interaction of student and teacher, etc. The "practice of anthropology" is a new subfield in which anthropologists are hired by governments and companies to apply their knowledge in an attempt to solve social problems.

The Biological Basis for Culture

We have pointed out that culture is the central concept for anthropology. Human beings are cultural beings. It is the possession of culture that distinguishes them from all other animal species. While animals may be said to live in societies and carry out social roles, they do not have culture as humans do. The social behavior of ants and bees is determined, by and large, by instinct. The differentiated social roles of queens, drones, and workers are completely biologically programmed, as is their system of communication. This is in sharp contrast to human cultural behavior, which is not biologically programmed but rather learned and transmitted from one generation to the next. Social behavior and the communication system in animal societies are uniform throughout each species. However, human cultural behavior and the meanings assigned to it, as well as communication by language, vary from one society to the next, although all *Homo sapiens* are members of a single species.

Today anthropologists are very interested in the evolutionary process of how humans developed their capacity for culture. The evolution of the human species from proto-human and early human forms involved a number of significant physical changes. These included increase in brain size and development of bipedal erect locomotion. Though primates have a significant level of intellectual capacity when compared with other animals, the evolution of humans was marked by a rapid expansion of this faculty. The use of rudimentary tools by some apes was greatly surpassed by even early humans. This was facilitated by the retention of the hands as organs for grasping, combined with the new characteristic of erect posture. The increased sophistication of the tools that were manufactured by early human beings occurred simultaneously with increase in brain size and intelligence. The early archaeological record shows the widespread geographical distribution of the same pattern or style of tool types, indicating the presence of the features that characterize culture. Though tools are made for particular purposes, they also exist in the minds of individuals living over a wide area as common cultural concepts of that particular tool type.

Human communication by language depends on the increase in human intellectual capacity noted above. Unlike the limited call systems of other animal species, every human language has the capacity to enable its speakers to produce new sentences that convey innovative ideas never before voiced. Though no concrete evidence exists on how language and language capacity evolved in human beings, it is apparent that increase in brain size and in the sophistication of tool types was accompanied by a parallel evolution of language and the development of the use, creation, and manipulation of symbols. The central role of language in culture will be explored more fully in Chapter 3.

Still another feature distinguishes human cultural behavior from animal behavior. Human behavior is governed primarily by rules, not the need for immediate gratification. The capacity to defer gratification was increasingly built into the evolution of the human species. This leads to the development of personality characteristics that distinguish human beings from the rest of the animal world—humans have developed the ability to internalize rules of behavior, and they depend upon other humans for approval.

Anthropological Theory

Thus far we have introduced a number of basic concepts that anthropologists use to organize and systematize the information they gather. These include the concepts of culture, subculture, society, social status, social roles, social relationships, social structure, exchange, cultural rules, enculturation, the relationship between culture and the individual, structure, and function. The final stage in the communication of information involves theory construction. Current anthropological theory has been shaped and influenced by theories of the past.

Cultural Evolution

The nineteenth century was a period of colonial expansion and the development of great empires by European powers. The domination and suppression of native peoples as well as the exploitation of the underclass in industrial societies was justified by a particular ideology, Social Darwinism, in which the "survival of the fittest" was said to dictate the fate of these people. It was within this period that the discipline of anthropology developed, and the dominant theory of the time was *cultural evolution.*

The major figures in nineteenth-century cultural evolutionary theory, such as Sir Edward B. Tylor and Lewis Henry Morgan, did not do formal anthropological fieldwork, though Morgan carried out observations on the Iroquois and on the native peoples of the Plains. Generally they utilized the accounts of missionaries; explorers, such as Captain Cook; travelers, such as Prince Maximilian, who explored the area of the Louisiana Purchase (see page 118 for a picture by Karl Bodmer, the artist who accompanied him); and others who described the native peoples they encountered. Tylor and Morgan conceived of cultural evolution in terms of stages through which all societies progressed, with the simple developing into increasingly more complex forms, culminating in their own Victorian society. However, in their view not all societies evolved into complex forms; some remained cases of arrested development, contemporary "survivals" of earlier stages.

The evolutionists organized their data and carried out what is clearly recognizable as the comparative approach. They looked for similarities and differences in cultures, classified them into types, and ordered the types from simple to complex. They tended to be ethnocentric in their evaluation of other societies in comparison with Western civilization; that is, Western religion and family life were all assumed to be the apogee of evolutionary development. Morgan's emphasis on the economic base to define stages of cultural evolution caught the attention of Friedrich Engels. Engels's *The Origin of the Family, Private Property and the State* contains a reinterpretation of Morgan's *Ancient Society* (1877). Both Marx and Engels were taken with the work of Morgan, because, like Morgan, they were interested in the evolution of culture.

The weaknesses of the nineteenth-century evolutionary approach to culture began to be recognized when ethnographic and archaeological data began to accumulate at the beginning of the twentieth century, and it was superseded by other theories. In the 1940s, it was resurrected by Leslie White (1949, 1959), who dealt with the evolution not of particular societies, but of culture as a single entity throughout the world. White, a technological determinist, saw culture evolving and becoming more complex as human beings developed increasingly more efficient ways of capturing energy from the environment.

In contrast, Julian Steward (1955) felt that White's approach to the evolution of culture was too general and could not be used to discuss the ways in which particular societies were transformed. He was interested in the relationship between the environment and economic subsistence activities, which, together with associated social and political institutions, formed what he called the "cultural core." Steward investigated the way in which each society adapted to its particular environment in order to develop a system of cultural types. In his theory of multilinear evolution, each cultural type was seen as having a different line of evolutionary development.

In 1960, Marshall Sahlins and Elman Service attempted to reconcile the theories of White and Steward. They proposed a distinction between specific evolution, concerned with the adaptation of particular societies to their environments as they develop through time, and general evolution, concerned with the emergence of higher forms of culture regardless of historical sequence and based upon progress in terms of energy capture. The adaptation of different societies to their environments became the focus of the ecological approach, which saw the society and its environmental setting as a single, interrelated system.

Though all anthropologists today would agree that complex forms of society have evolved from simpler ones, contemporary cultural anthropological theory, by and large, is not very concerned with evolutionary questions, though these remain central to archaeology.

American Historical Approach

At the beginning of the twentieth century, there was a strong reaction against nineteenth-century evolutionary thinking, particularly the view that all societies had gone through the same series of stages, and alternative anthropological theories began to appear. Though Franz Boas, the founder of the American Historical approach, started out as a supporter of the evolutionary viewpoint, his fieldwork with and long-term study of the Kwakiutl Indians of the Pacific Northwest Coast led him to abandon it. Boas not only learned the Kwakiutl language; he also made the language one of the central objects of his investigation. As a result, he came to respect the significant differences between the way the Kwakiutl viewed the world and the way we view it. He moved away from attempts to range societies from simple to complex, considering all cultures and languages to be distinctive and complex in different ways. Boas's approach emphasized the unique and incommensurable aspects of each culture. The emphasis on these aspects came to be referred to as *cultural relativism*. Boas saw cultures as symbolic systems of ideas rather than as entities adapting to environments. His work stressed the gathering of texts, that is, accounts in the native language concerning all the aspects of the life of the people. Boas trained George Hunt, a native Kwakiutl speaker, in phonetic transcription so that Hunt could collect and send texts back to Boas. He was particularly interested in art, mythology, and language because they reflected the mental processes of the people whose culture he was studying. Boas did not deny that cultures evolved; however, he felt that anthropologists should first concentrate on learning about the history of the development of particular societies, such as the Kwakiutl and other Native American Indian societies, before attempting to theorize about the process of cultural change and evolution. The American Historical approach, which was predominant up to World War II, grew out of Boas's conception of culture.

The interest in the history of particular cultures also led to a concern with *diffusion*, the movement of traits from one culture to another. It was found that culture traits diffused within particular areas, and so a number of societies shared a single repertoire of traits that resembled one another and formed a single culture area. Alfred L. Kroeber related the culture areas of the native peoples of North America, which he had delineated on the basis of cultural traits, to geographical areas, in *Cultural and Natural Areas of Native North America* (1939). By the time Boas and Kroeber began their studies of Native American societies, these societies had already undergone considerable change. The two anthropologists were carrying out a type of "salvage" anthropology, working with a few old people to record what their cultures had been like earlier, rather than studying the kinds of monumental cultural changes these people were experiencing.

Functionalism

The British reaction to nineteenth-century evolution took a somewhat different form from the American approach. At the beginning of the twentieth century, as British anthropologists began to reject the theoretical framework of cultural evolution based upon Darwin's theory, they supplanted it with a different model, also derived from biology. This was the model of society as a living organism. The basic organizing concepts they used were structure and function, which have been discussed above. They rejected the speculative nature of nineteenth-century evolutionary stages and substituted the empirical field observations of the anthropologists who had spent a year or two in the field learning the language and doing participant observation.

Bronislaw Malinowski, a major theorist in the development of functionalism, spent an extended period of time doing fieldwork in the Trobriand Islands off New Guinea. His method of analysis of the field data involved identifying the institutions that made up the skeleton of society and then describing in detail how these institutions functioned. For example, in his two-volume work, *Coral Gardens and Their Magic* (1935), he describes that part of the economic institution of the Trobrianders concerned with horticulture. Not only does he describe the process of planting and cultivating yams, but he also goes into great detail about the magic involved in yam cultivation, the texts of the spells used, and finally the way these yams are used in a complex exchange system of fulfilling obligations to kinsmen and chiefs. Malinowski ultimately saw cultural institutions and their functioning as related to basic human biological needs, which existed for people in all societies, as well as to what he called culturally derived needs.

Though coupled at times with Malinowski as a British Functionalist, A. R. Radcliffe-Brown moved in a somewhat different direction in his anthropological theorizing. His theory derived less from his fieldwork among the Andaman Islanders in the Indian Ocean and depended more on his attempts at comparative research, in which he tried to develop typologies to sort and categorize different kinds of societies (1952). He was more concerned with the "anatomy" of societies than with how they functioned to satisfy biological needs. When Radcliffe-Brown talked of the function of a part of the social structure, such as a clan, he used the term *function* to mean the contribution made by the clan to the ongoing life process of the society. He emphasized the concept of social structure. The next generation of British anthropologists became experts in the delineation of different kinds of social structures and those aspects of culture such as law, political organization, land tenure, and religion that are most directly connected with the social structure. The central organizing concept for them was society and its patterns of interrelationship, rather than culture. As long as Malinowski and Radcliffe-Brown dominated British anthropology, there was no research related to how societies evolved. Radcliffe-Brown strongly opposed what he referred to as conjectural history. Real history, he argued, existed only where there were written records. The effect of Radcliffe-Brown's attitude was to inhibit true historical research.

In the face of culture change and the breakdown of colonialism after World War II, the functionalist theoretical framework, which emphasized the static equilibrium of societies, came under attack. British anthropologists such as A. L. Epstein and Philip Mayer began to follow the tribal people whom they studied as they moved into the cities and went to work in the mines. Others such as E. E. Evans-Pritchard and M. G. Smith turned to the historical investigation of societies based on archival material, rejecting Radcliffe-Brown's injunctions against the study of "conjectural" history.

Structuralism

The fourth theoretical approach that we shall consider is structuralism. It is most closely associated with the work of the French anthropologist Claude Lévi-Strauss. He has taken the way in which a linguist analyzes data as a model and applied it to the analysis of culture. Like the sounds in a language, which by themselves have no meaning but are part of a larger structure that conveys meaning, the elements of a culture must be seen in their relationship to one another as they form a structure. Through such structures, meanings are conveyed. The structural anthropologist looks for the underlying structure of a culture, which corresponds to the grammar of a language produced by the linguist's analysis. It was Boas who first pointed out that the grammar of a language was not in the consciousness of the speaker and, in a similar fashion, that culture had an underlying structure and operated like language, in that the structure was unconscious. Lévi-Strauss makes a connection between his work and that of Boas. Structuralists focus upon cognitive systems, kinship structure, art, mythology, ritual, and ceremony, among other things. Structural anthropologists look for similarities in underlying structures in different cultures. This is not the same kind of typologizing carried out in the other approaches, because the societies grouped together may seem to be very different on the surface.

Other Approaches

Anthropologists today pursue a variety of theoretical approaches. Contemporary approaches are much less unified and do not share a set of assumptions as did the theoretical approaches we have discussed up to this point. In symbolic anthropology, culture is seen as a system of symbols, and the task of the anthropologist is to decipher the system in terms of its meanings. The goal of this approach is the same as that of semantics in linguistics, that is, to ascertain meaning. Edmund Leach, who was directly influenced by the linguist Roman Jakobson, uses the concepts of metaphor and metonym (see Chapter 4) in his analysis of the symbolism of Michelangelo's Sistine Chapel paintings. Mary Douglas (1970) demonstrates how the labels for parts of the body, such as the head and the foot, are used to stand for something else, operating as "natural symbols." David Schneider, in his analysis of American kinship (1980), points out that Americans think of kinship as a connection through blood, in contrast with relations through marriage or in-laws. Thus blood and law are a set of opposed symbols. Clifford Geertz (1973), in his analysis of the Balinese cockfight, shows how layer upon layer of meaning can be uncovered.

Many contemporary anthropologists work within a historic framework. Ethnohistorians use archaeological, archival, and oral history materials to trace the history of cultures where people left no written records. A number of scholars have examined how European economic expansion and political expansion during the colonial period have affected small-scale societies, focusing on the colonial discourse that developed between colonizers and colonized. In contrast, Eric Wolf has been concerned with the impact on Europe during the colonial period of the "people without history" (Wolf, 1982). Marshall Sahlins advocates a theoretical approach that combines history with structuralism. Sahlins points out that when Captain Cook landed on Hawaii, the Hawaiians, perceiving him in terms of their own cultural categories, saw him as the god Lono. When the Hawaiians killed Captain Cook, as they ritually killed the god Lono, this not only affected subsequent events involving Hawaiian-European relations (i.e., history) but also resulted in changes in Hawaiian cultural rules (structure). In this theoretical framework, structure and history are seen as constantly interrelated (1985).

Among the most recent sets of theoretical ideas that have come to the fore in anthropology are those that can be grouped under the rubric of interpretive anthropology. As we noted above, some anthropologists like Geertz, in the 1970s, began to focus on the tangle of interrelated meanings that cultures encoded. The task of the anthropologist then became one of translating the layers of meaning of a "thick description" into our concepts and our language. Some began to feel that the anthropologists' translations of the meanings of others' cultures done in the analysis, as we noted earlier, were not sufficient or adequate to the task. The ethnographer presents his or her analysis on the basis of observations as well as the understandings gained from informants. Some interpretive anthropologists have seen this product as not sufficiently representative of the variety of points of view or ideas held by individuals in the culture. They have even argued that segments of a society may have contested views regarding cultural meanings. They have advocated representing this variety, for example, by including the informants' ideas in their own words in the ethnography itself, as in the Price book, *First Time: The Historical Vision of an Afro-American People,* where Price's picture of the history of the Saramaka is presented along with that of several elders in the culture (1983). In other instances, in order to pay more attention to the views of informants, anthropologists have presented their analyses to their informants for comment, as Steven Feld did to his Kaluli informants to see if they agreed with his conclusions regarding the meanings of sounds in their culture (1987).

There has also been a concern, as we noted above, that more attention be paid to the manner in which the anthropologist operates in the field situation and the effects of this on the resulting fieldwork. A genre of writing concerned with "reflections on fieldwork," which focuses on this aspect of the fieldwork, in contrast to focusing upon the fieldworker's observations and conclusions, is also associated with interpretive anthropology. In these writings, the ethnographer recounts how he or she felt as a person in the fieldwork situation, rather than on the ways, for example, in which a particular people deal with problems, such as birth or death.

These various interpretive perspectives all have in common a focus on trying to better understand and translate the cultures of other peoples, and to better represent those cultures, bridging the gap between us and them by having them talk more directly to us. However, sometimes the comparative aspect of anthropology, which pays attention to what cultures have in common as well as how they differ, has been left by the wayside in the concern to grasp the uniqueness of each culture. Further, in this vein, the legitimate anthropological focus on what can be observed, and sometimes quantified, has been played down in this approach.

Few anthropologists consider themselves to be adherents of a single, theoretical approach. For example, all acknowledge that culture evolved, that one can talk about the functions of institutions, and that all human behavior has symbolic meaning, without calling themselves evolutionists, functionalists, or symbolic anthropologists. Anthropologists usually adopt a theoretical approach and a methodology appropriate to the problem they are investigating. They may refer to themselves as theoretically eclectic.

The journey to another place and another time, which we defined at the beginning of this chapter as the hallmark of anthropology, is recapitulated by fledgling anthropologists as they embark on fieldwork. Lévi-Strauss, in his personal memoir *Tristes Tropiques* (1955), saw his own fieldwork in terms of just such a journey. His journey to the field took him from the Old World to the New World, from the cold North to the tropical South, to a world that contrasted in every respect with his own. His goal was to find a simple form of society, since he felt that in order to understand how societies work it is best to study one that is simple in its organization. As in all fieldwork situations, he was first struck by what appeared to be great cultural differences. However, in time, Lévi-Strauss, the sophisticated French student of philosophy, saw behind the painted faces of the Nambikwara a common humanity that he shared with them. He wrote, "I had been looking for a society reduced to its simplest expression. The society of the Nambikwara had been reduced to the point at which I found nothing but human beings" (Lévi-Strauss, 1961:310). The pages that follow also represent a journey—a journey into the world of anthropology.

CHAPTER 2

Rituals in Small-Scale and Complex Societies: A Contrast

 An examination of rituals in a society illustrates the integrated nature of culture and demonstrates why a tapestry is an apt metaphor for culture. Such events in small-scale societies, which were the traditional focus of anthropologists, involve entire communities, sometimes even the entire society. These rituals have kinship, economic, religious, political, and aesthetic dimensions, a characteristic that led Marcel Mauss, the French anthropologist of the early twentieth century, to refer to them as "total social phenomena" (1925). All these dimensions of social life are simultaneously expressed in the action of the ceremony. In contrast, in complex societies there is much more compartmentalization of institutions. For example, in our own society economics and politics are, to a great extent, separate spheres of activity, separate from each other as well as from kinship and religious institutions. In the twentieth century, art is not usually part of everyday life and is separate from religion and from politics. This was not the case during the Renaissance in Europe, when art, politics, and religion were much more interrelated than they are today.

The term *ritual* refers to an event or performance, often associated with the sacred, which is distinguished from ordinary day-to-day life by the use of special language, music, or dance. Ritual is a form of communication. It is a powerful means of communicating emotion. Ritual involves the use of formulas, stylized speech, and repetition. Therefore, it does not have the capacity for communicating the infinite range of ideas that language has. What ritual, in its stylized form, communicates are important central themes of the culture (Bloch, 1989).

In this chapter, we will present descriptions of rituals from small-scale and from complex societies to illustrate the significance of this difference. The descriptions of these events will also be referred to in later chapters of the book.

Marriage in a Small-Scale Society

As a person moves through the life cycle, there are points, such as birth, puberty, marriage, and death, that mark significant changes in his or her life. These points frequently become the occasions for ceremonies known as *rites of passage*—rites that mark the passing from one stage of life to another. Marriage, one of those rites of passage, is celebrated as a ceremonial event in most societies. How a society celebrates the rite of marriage is integrally related to how it expresses rank and class differences, how it emphasizes links to ancestors, and how it envisions the relationship between husband and wife. Consequently, each society culturally construes this ritual in its distinct way, different from other societies. Here, we will compare marriage among the Kwakiutl with marriage in American society.

In our account of this Kwakiutl ritual, we will be describing it as if it were occurring today, though we know that there have been many changes in Kwakiutl society since the time the description was recorded by anthropologist Franz Boas.* The Kwakiutl are now part of the larger Canadian society.

Boas's research among the Kwakiutl was conducted in the last decade of the nineteenth century. It represents the first extensive anthropological fieldwork carried out with a people in their own language. There is a convention in anthropology, known as the *ethnographic present*, in which the present tense is used to describe a culture, although the description may represent the way the culture was at a much earlier point in time. This description of a Kwakiutl wedding uses the present tense though it describes the way things were in the late nineteenth century. The ethnographic present will also be used in other chapters.

The Kwakiutl are a Native American society who occupy an area along the coast of British Columbia in Canada. They subsist on fishing, hunting land and sea mammals, and collecting wild plants and berries; they do not practice any form of agriculture. They are famous for their expert wood carvings of totem poles and many other items. Because the environment is

---

*This section is based on *Kwakiutl Ethnography* by Franz Boas, edited by Helen Codere, reprinted by permission of The University of Chicago Press.

rich, they are semisedentary and live in winter and summer villages. They build large plank houses that are occupied by many people related to one another. A number of such houses are joined through kinship into a larger family-type grouping, which the Kwakiutl call a *numaym*. The Kwakiutl have chiefs and an elaborate system of rank in which everyone has a different rank position. One of their most distinctive customs is the *potlatch*, a ceremony at which the host distributes large amounts of property to individuals of other groups. By doing this, the host acquires prestige and enhances his rank. Among the Kwakiutl, various rites of passage are the occasions for a donor to hold a potlatch, and the marriage of a child is one of the most important occasions.

This description is of one of the rites involved when the children of chiefs marry. Such a marriage is accompanied by significant transfers of property between the two families of the couple. There are three stages to a marriage. The first stage is the initiation of negotiations and agreement on the size of the bridewealth payment to be made by the family of the groom to the family of the bride. The second stage is the formal wooing and the transfer of the bridewealth payment from the groom's family to

The groom's party arrives by canoe at an early stage of a Kwakiutl marriage. A crest belonging to the groom's numaym *decorates the front of the canoe. Edward L. Curtis took this photograph before 1914.*

the bride's family at a potlatch. The third stage constitutes a repurchase of the bride by her family when goods, names, and privileges go from the family of the bride to that of the groom.

When children of important chiefs marry, invariably two different tribes of the Kwakiutl are involved. In such a marriage, the tribe of the groom needs to come to the village of the bride to symbolically seize or capture her to take her to their village. The bride is "moved" from her village to the village of the groom through the magical power that the chiefs of the groom's group have obtained from their ancestors and through the payment of property by the groom's side in order to "move" the bride. Since the major events of a marriage are accompanied by the distribution of large amounts of property and are witnessed by many people from many tribes, they constitute Kwakiutl potlatches. All the property distributed is eventually reciprocated, and payment is made for the services performed by various chiefs. The giving away of property enhances the prestige of the donor. The advance in social rank that derives from the potlatch aspects of a marriage often entirely overshadows the marriage's primary purpose—the establishment of a family.

The parents of those responsible for the young people arrange the marriage, sometimes without even the knowledge of the young couple. The first messengers are formally sent by the groom's side to the bride's side. They deliver speeches to her father requesting the bride in marriage, and he rewards them with a pair of blankets. When they return to the groom, he too rewards them with a pair of blankets. Then a second group of messengers is sent, this time chiefs, to deliver messages concerning the marriage proposal to the bride's father. He gives them each two pairs of blankets in return for the messages. That night, the groom goes to eat in the bride's house, sitting next to her. The bride's father talks to the groom about the bride's father's expectation of receiving 500 blankets. Then, the groom's father assembles the 500 blankets, and they are piled in front of the door of the bride's father. The groom's father, accompanied by several chiefs, goes to the house of the bride. To one chief he says, "It is your office given to you according to the earliest myths to speak about the blankets given away." As the formal Speaker, this chief receives two blankets for his service from the father of the groom. The blankets are officially counted by the counter from the groom's side and then are handed over to the bride's father by still another officeholder. On receiving the blankets, the father of the bride expresses his thanks.

Several months later, a second ceremony is held at which 550 additional blankets are handed over, this time to "move" the bride. The men of the groom's *numaym* and those of other *numaym* blacken their faces and dress like warriors as they go to the house of the bride with the final payment of blankets, which will "move" her. Often, the bride's doorway is protected by fire against the "invading warriors" of the groom. They may have to run a gauntlet of flaming torches held by men of the bride's side or, as in another

The speaker for the chief distributes blankets at a Kwakiutl wedding potlatch held in 1894.

account by Boas, go through a ring of burning cedar bark soaked in oil. After the groom's men have proved they are not afraid of fire and the fire has burned down, the bride's father "called forth the Devourer of Tribes, who has devoured all those who had tried to woo his daughter. It was a large mask of a sea bear attached to a bear skin (worn by a man). Seven skulls and a number of long bones were hidden under the bear skin. As soon as the man wearing this masked dress came forth, the bride's father poked its stomach with a pole and it vomited skulls and bones."

Now the chiefs from the groom's side make their traditional wedding speeches. In these speeches, the chiefs call upon their supernatural powers, which come from ancient mythological times down through their family lines. These powers are said to be used to "move the bride." For example, Made-To-Be-Tied, chief of the Kwa'wadilikala *numaym*, on being called upon, said, "In the beginning of myth times I was the great supernatural Kwa'wadilikala, the only owner of the great wolf ceremonial that came down to me from heaven. Now I will go and lift the princess." After going out, he returned to the doorway, wearing the great wolf mask of Walking Body, the chief of the wolves. For this he received five blankets from the official Speaker representing the groom's side. At a really great wedding, many chiefs who bear illustrious names make speeches, detailing how their privileges descended to them from ancient times. These privileges include a particular name, the animal designs worn on clothing or in the shape of masks, the songs they sing, and the dances they are privileged to perform.

Each receives a payment of blankets for, as the Kwakiutl say, "the weight of his breath," that is, the speech he has delivered at the wedding. Their combined breath acts as a weight upon an imaginary scale used to move the bride. The metaphor operates such that the greater the names of the bride, the more speeches, or "breath," needed to move her to the groom.

After the last of the chiefs has spoken, the ceremony of giving out the blankets brought by the groom's side for the bride's side takes place. Blankets are counted and ceremonially brought into the bride's house. Then the bride's side piles up 200 blankets with the bride sitting alongside them. A chief from the bride's side says, "Come to your wife and take her into your house with these two hundred blankets as her mat." The groom's side sings the traditional song of thanks while the bride walks between two officials to the groom's side. Then the new wife is led to the seat she is to occupy, and the 200 blankets are distributed to the guests from other Kwakiutl tribes on the groom's side, but not to members of the groom's own tribe. In the evening, all the distinguished young men of the Kwakiutl tribes assemble to sing love songs and lead the groom back to his father's house. The bride's father brings fifty blankets to exchange for food for the young men in order to thank them for bringing the groom. The groom sits alongside his new wife, and this part of the marriage ceremony comes to an end.

Some time later, usually after a child has been born to the couple, the wife's side begins preparations to make a large return payment of goods to the husband's side, a transfer of property that constitutes what Boas refers to as the repurchase of the wife by her own numaym. The Kwakiutl term for this payment means payment of the marriage debt. Since the wife's group has been the recipient of the marriage potlatch given by the groom's group, it is in debt until a return in kind is made. The repurchase at another potlatch constitutes this return. The return does not consist of blankets, but of objects known in Kwakiutl as "trifles, bad things." As we shall see from the list of items included, trifles and bad things mean just the opposite. What is returned is far in excess of what the wife's father received. In one of Boas's examples of a repurchase, the items included were 120 box covers set with sea otter teeth, 100 abalone shells, copper bracelets, horn bracelets covered with dentalia shells, miniature coppers, 1,000 strings of dentalia one fathom long, 200 dressed deerskins, 500 cedar bark blankets, 200 mats, an equal number of wooden boxes, 2 neck rings of twisted copper, and hammered copper objects of great value, "as mast of the marriage debt canoe." A large amount of food was also provided, as well as the horn and wooden spoons with which to eat it. Names and privileges are also given to the son-in-law as part of the marriage payment.

When everything is ready, the wife's father calls together his *numaym* to announce that he is going to hold a potlatch to repay the marriage debt. The song leader of the *numaym* is asked to write a new song to commemorate the occasion, which he does. The song describes the privileges and the

A Kwakiutl wedding party stands before the bride's house. The house posts are carved with the crests of her numaym.

copper that are to be given to the groom. The next morning father-in-law and son-in-law each invite their respective *numayms* to attend. After breakfast, the men of the father-in-law's *numaym* carry the goods to the son-in-law's house. There they arrange the box covers in a square or rectangle, which is called the catamaran because it is supposed to represent the boat upon which the father-in-law comes to repay the debt. All the goods are piled on top, and the *numaym* of the father-in-law "goes on board," where they then sing the song of repayment of the marriage debt. In keeping with the symbolism of warfare, the younger brother of the son-in-law, his face blackened as a warrior, rushes out and splits one of the box covers with an ax, thereby "sinking the catamaran." The box containing the symbols of the privileges to be given to the son-in-law is carried out from the father-in-law's house, and the wife who is being repurchased emerges bearing the copper that is to be transferred. The young wife and her father both dance to the accompaniment of the new marriage repayment song. The father-in-law's Speaker presents the box of privileges to the son-in-law and then presents the copper. The Speaker of the husband's *numaym* expresses his thanks. Then the Speaker of the father-in-law arises and bestows names that traditionally belong to the wife's family upon the husband and his two sisters. These names constitute the final part of the marriage repayment, all the other items having already been transferred. The husband's *numaym* sings songs of gratitude, and this ends the ceremony of marriage repurchase.

Marriage for the Kwakiutl is clearly not a single event, but a series of events that may extend for years, since the repurchase of a wife is normally not held until after the birth of a child. When the wife has been repurchased by her father and her own *numaym,* she is really free to return to her father unless her husband purchases her for the second time. This will also be followed by a second repurchase by her own group. These exchanges of property via potlatches can take place up to four times, after which the wife's rank is so high that she can "stay for nothing." Since the giver of the potlatch feeds the great numbers of guests who come to witness these events and thereby enhances his prestige with each potlatch, the families of both groom and bride respectively increase their standing with each transfer of goods.

The ritual of marriage among the Kwakiutl embodies many of the central ideas in Kwakiutl culture. The Kwakiutl emphasis on rank is reiterated again and again throughout the unfolding process of the marriage potlatch. The high rank of the bride demands that there be high payments for her. At the same time, high payments enhance the rank of the giver, the groom. The importance of making a return for what one has received is reflected in the repurchase payment made by the bride's side. Seating of guests at the potlatch and the order in which they receive gifts reveal their ranking with respect to one another. The political power and legitimacy of sponsoring chiefs is also demonstrated in the potlatch. The claim to rightfully own a title or name is made by a chief at a potlatch when he recites the line of ancestors through whom the title was passed on until it reached him. Lastly, the marriage ceremony is symbolically conceptualized as a form of warfare, in which warriors demonstrate their bravery in capturing the bride, and the return purchase is conveyed by a symbolic war canoe.

Marriage in a Complex Society

At first glance an American wedding appears to be strikingly different from a Kwakiutl wedding. However, there are also some fundamental similarities. Since we have described the marriage of high-ranking children of chiefs, we will compare it to the wedding of two well-known celebrities in American society, rather than an average American wedding, which is an abstraction at best. *Good Housekeeping's Book of Today's Etiquette* contains guidelines on how to conduct an American wedding and can be considered a statement of the ideal pattern. However, weddings nowadays show an enormous amount of variation, depending on social class, ethnicity, religion, or simply individual preference. Using accounts from *Time* magazine, *The New York Times,* and the *Cape Cod Times,* we will describe the wedding of

Maria Shriver and Arnold Schwartzenegger, which was held on April 26, 1986.

Just as the daughter of a Kwakiutl chief belongs to the highest ranks of her society, Maria Shriver, a member of the Kennedy clan, belongs to the moneyed American elite. Her mother, Eunice, is a sister of the late John F. Kennedy. Her father, Sargent Shriver, was the first director of the Peace Corps, a former ambassador to France, and the Democratic nominee for vice president in 1972. The bride is a television celebrity, who, at the time of her marriage, was co-anchor of the *CBS Morning News* television program. The Austrian-born Schwartzenegger, a famous body builder and movie star, is the son of a local Austrian police chief, now deceased. The two first met eight years earlier, a year after her graduation from Georgetown University, at a tennis tournament sponsored by the Kennedy family and named for Maria's late uncle Robert F. Kennedy. At that time she was working for a small television station. She interrupted her own career to work on her Uncle Ted's presidential bid in 1980. In 1981, breaking with the East Coast family tradition, she moved to Los Angeles to continue her career on her own and to be near her boyfriend, Arnold. She worked as a magazine reporter for two years and then returned to television as a reporter for CBS. Schwartzenegger, who has a degree in business and marketing from the University of Wisconsin, became famous as a body builder. He subsequently became a movie star after starring in the movie *Pumping Iron.*

The couple did not marry until she was thirty and he was thirty-eight, eight years after they first met. This may have been due to the demands of their two careers. Career women now tend to marry when they are in their thirties, though this was not the case in American society at an earlier time.

Arnold proposed to Maria during a trip to Austria in August 1985, and they purchased a $3 million house in Pacific Palisades. After their decision to marry, Maria was offered the anchor position at *CBS Morning News,* which required her to move to New York, apart from her future husband.

The wedding was held at the summer residence of the Kennedys in Hyannis, Massachusetts. The Roman Catholic wedding mass, performed by the Reverend John Baptist Riordan, was held at St. Francis Xavier Roman Catholic Church, the Kennedy family's parish church in Hyannis.

Since the couple wanted their wedding to be a "private" affair, details of the wedding were kept from the media, except for information provided by a publicist hired to handle wedding press coverage. Kennedy influence was used to maintain tight security and keep gossip columnists and journalists away from the wedding party. Provincetown-Boston Airline, which flies to Hyannis, was "persuaded" to lock up its computer a day before the wedding so that the guest list would not be revealed. The bride, ever career-oriented, told her viewers she would be off for several days, without mentioning her forthcoming wedding, and the groom arrived the day before the wedding from Puerta Vallarta, where he had been filming a new movie, *Predator.*

The bride wore a muslin, silk, and lace gown in white, with an eleven-foot train, designed by Christian Dior, who had designed the wedding dress of the bride's mother in 1953. The groom wore a classic gray cutaway coat, pleated white shirt, gray vest, and gray-striped ascot. A fellow body builder, Franco Columbu, served as his best man. The thirteen ushers included the bride's four brothers, the bridegroom's cousin and nephew, and body builder friends of the groom. The maid of honor was the bride's cousin, Caroline Bouvier Kennedy, daughter of the late President Kennedy. Among the bridesmaids were several Kennedy cousins. Some sixty women, guests and members of the bridal party, had their hair coiffed at the local beauty salon on the morning of the wedding, but the bride's hair was done by her own hairdresser from Los Angeles. Besides members of the Kennedy family, the more than 450 guests included television celebrities like Diane Sawyer, Tom Brokaw, Barbara Walters, advice columnist Abigail Van Buren, the late pop artist Andy Warhol (wearing a black leather jacket over a black tuxedo and black Reebok sneakers), and actress Grace Jones. Proclaiming the most recent fashions, female guests wore dresses sporting geometric designs from the art deco period and from pop art. Since reporters were barred from the church itself, a viewing stand was erected across the street for them.

The bride and her father walked up the aisle to the familiar wedding march, Wagner's "Bridal March" from the opera *Lohengrin* ("Here comes the bride . . ."). The details of the religious ceremony had been planned by the bride and groom. The couple exchanged traditional Roman Catholic vows, which had been rewritten to remove sexist language, replacing "man and wife" with "husband and wife." Short selections from the New Testament were then read by Senator Kennedy and a friend of Schwartzenegger. Intercessions written by the wedding couple and read by the bride's parents and brother called for an end to terrorism and war, set the bride and groom as a model couple, honored deceased Kennedys, and discussed the meaning of Passover. Oprah Winfrey, the television host, then read Elizabeth Barrett Browning's poem "How Do I Love Thee," a choice of the bride. After a series of musical selections, the ceremony concluded with the bridal couple walking together down the aisle to Rodgers and Hammerstein's "Bridal March" from *The Sound of Music.*

After the ceremony, limousines and buses took the guests to the Kennedy compound for the reception. All air traffic within a two-mile radius of the compound was prohibited from cruising below 2,000 feet for the entire day. The reception was held in two huge white tents, with heavy sidewalls and heaters to keep out the chill winds. Fruit trees in pink and white blossom decorated the tents. The guests danced to music played by Peter Duchin's band, which often plays at society occasions. An elaborate lunch (including cold lobster in the shell and chicken breast with champagne wine sauce) was concluded with the cutting of an 8-tier, 425-pound wedding cake, topped by the traditional figures of a bride and groom, baked by the Shriver family chef and modeled after Shriver's parents' wedding cake.

The couple took a brief honeymoon before returning to work, he to his filming in Puerta Vallarta, she to her anchor position at CBS in New York.

The above account is a description of a single wedding taken from the published sources. Clearly, many things took place that were not reported by the press. When the families of the bride and groom are strangers to one another, there is usually a formal meeting of the two sets of parents. There is no information on whether or how the Shrivers met Mrs. Schwartzenegger. Often, the bride receives an engagement ring, and an engagement party is held. Wedding gifts may be publicly displayed at the bride's home. According to *Good Housekeeping's Book of Today's Etiquette,* "the expenses of the wedding are divided in a time-honored way." The bride's family pays for the following: invitations; reception cards and announcements; the rental of the place where the ceremony is to be held; fee for the organist, choir, and sexton; transportation of the bridal party from house to church or temple and from there to the reception; bridesmaids' bouquets; the bride's gifts to the bridesmaids; the bride's wedding dress and trousseau; and all the expenses of the reception. The groom pays for the engagement and wedding rings, marriage license, contribution to the clergyman, flowers for the bride's mother and groom's mother, and the bachelor dinner. Whether or not one is rich is not the sole factor in determining which of these features of an American wedding are present or absent. Today, couples often live together, sometimes for several years, before getting married. Despite this, they may elect to go through some or all of the ceremonies associated with an American wedding. Though the couple may have lived together for several years, the bride still wears a white gown, a symbol of virginity.

A comparison of Kwakiutl and American weddings reveals that in the American wedding, even that of the member of an important family, the focus is almost exclusively on the bride and groom. The Shriver-Schwartzenegger wedding is an American wedding, but it is not an average American wedding. It is less a matter of two kin groups establishing a relationship, as is the case in a Kwakiutl wedding, and more a matter of bringing together and displaying a personal network of friends and colleagues. Because both bride and groom have established careers and are such well-known celebrities, their personal network is large and studded with stars, making this wedding different from the average American wedding. Also, the bride and groom planned the wedding themselves. They act as the centers of all activity, though other individuals from their respective families as well as friends and relatives play some part. This emphasis on the couple demonstrates the importance in American culture of the newly formed family as autonomous and separate from other families. The Kwakiutl wedding, on the other hand, is a total social phenomenon in which the entire community is involved and in which elements of economics, politics, and political maneuvering concerning transfer of a whole series of privileges as well as property are at issue, to such a point that Boas, the observer, notes that these things overshadow the purpose of the wedding—to establish a new family. In the American wedding economics is involved, in that goods are purchased and there are many expenditures, but in the Kwakiutl marriage, the wedding itself is an institution for transfers of large amounts of property and is equivalent to the institution of the stock exchange. Similarly, though religion is involved in the American wedding, in the Kwakiutl marriage the rights and privileges exhibited demand the recitation of myths linking people to their ancestors, a cornerstone of Kwakiutl religious belief. In sum, in a Kwakiutl marriage the whole underlying structure of the society is played out, whereas this is not the case in American society, where weddings really focus on the couple who are establishing the new family, and other aspects are only tangentially related.

There are some interesting similarities that should not go unnoticed. In both Kwakiutl and American societies, all weddings are public ceremonies witnessed by guests. In both instances, the guests who attend and eat the food at the feast perform the function of publicly witnessing a rite of passage. In the American wedding described, an attempt was made to keep it a private affair, limited to just 450 witnesses. As celebrities, the bride and groom wanted the entire society to witness their wedding, but they wanted to control the information that was made available about it. In both societies, prestige is determined by the size of the outlay, which, in turn, relates to the social status of the families involved. The more lavish the display, the greater the standing and renown.

Funeral Rites in a Small-Scale Society

Death rites constitute the last rite of passage for an individual. The surviving members of the community carry out this ceremonial event in all societies. We will compare funeral rites among the Trobriand Islanders with those of American society.

The Trobriand Islands are located off the coast of New Guinea, in Melanesia. Today they are part of the new nation of Papua New Guinea. The Trobrianders are intensive gardeners, and yams are their staple crop. Fishing is also important. The people live in large, compact villages, with each village controlled by a chief. There is an elaborate system of rank differences. The kinship groupings of the Trobriand Islanders are known as clans, and each man belongs to the clan of his mother. At many rites of passage, a ceremony called *sagali*, a large-scale distribution of goods, is held by the chief of the clan that serves as host. At this ceremony great amounts of food and valuables are distributed to members of other clans who come as guests. The death of a Trobriand chief is the occasion for a large *sagali*. We will describe Trobriand funerary ceremonies as presented by British Functionalist Bronislaw Malinowski* (1929) and more recently by American anthropologist Annette Weiner (1976).

When death is near, all the relatives crowd about the bed. The widow begins to wail at her husband's point of death, and this wail is picked up by the women of the village. At death, the spirit of the deceased leaves the body and goes to the island of Tuma, where the spirits dwell. The mortuary rites have nothing to do with the spirit of the dead person. The corpse is washed, anointed, and covered with ornaments; the legs are tied together, and the arms bound to the sides. It is placed on the knees of a row of women, with the widow holding the head. The corpse is fondled, stroked, and moved while mourners continue to wail. In the meantime, the sons dig the grave, and a few hours after death the body is laid in it and covered with logs. The widow lies on the logs and keeps vigil, while around her the mourners, kinsmen and villagers, sit and wail, singing mourning songs. On the following evening, the body is removed from the grave and examined for signs of sorcery. The corpse is reburied and then exhumed later and reexamined. Then the sons of the deceased remove some of the bones from the corpse to keep as relics. This is considered to be a disgusting duty, but it is done as an act of piety by sons. Some of the bones are turned into ornaments. The skull is turned into a lime pot and the jawbone into a neck ornament worn by the widow. Then the remains are buried a third time. Formerly this took place in the central plaza of the village; now it is done away from the village.

In Trobriand society, a man belongs to the clan of his mother, not that of his father. This is his matrilineal clan. At a funeral, there is a sharp distinction in behavior between the deceased man's matrilineal clansmen and the members of his wife's clan, which includes his children and other in-laws. The matrilineal kinsmen are forbidden to touch the corpse and may not wash, adorn, or bury it. They believe that touching the corpse would cause their death. They weep as a sign of their grief, but must not mourn ostentatiously. The widow, children, and relatives-in-law make more outward displays of their grief and perform all the necessary burial activities. After the body is reburied, mourners disperse, and the widow moves into a small cage built within her house, where she lives for several months while food is brought to her.

The first *sagali* distribution takes place on the day after the third and final burial, when relatives-in-law are repaid for their help by the matrilineal clan of the deceased. Bundles of banana leaves, which are used to

---

*Adapted from *The Sexual Life of Savages in North-Western Melanesia* by Bronislaw Malinowski. Copyright, 1929 by Bronislaw Malinowski. Reprinted by permission of Paul R. Reynolds, Inc., 12 East 41st Street, New York, N.Y. 10017, and Routledge Kegan Paul Ltd.

make women's skirts, are given to women who in some minor way helped with the funerary arrangements and burial. People from other hamlets who came to mourn are given piles of taros and yams. Men who sang mourning songs receive gifts of taros, yams, bananas, and betel; the more important the political status of the man, the larger his gift. Money, clay pots, stone ax blades, and shell valuables are given to relatives-in-law of the deceased who carried, bathed, or dressed the corpse or dug the grave.

Subsequently, a second *sagali* takes place to distribute bundles of banana leaves—women's wealth objects—which releases the widow from some of the extreme taboos she must observe. This is predominantly a women's ceremony. Women of the matrilineal clan of the deceased give the banana leaf bundles to male relatives of the widow, who now shave their heads and continue to mourn publicly for the dead man. The widow herself also receives skirts and bundles of leaves.

Some months later, after the accumulation of large quantities of food-stuffs, pigs, women's skirts, banana leaf bundles, and valuables by the matrilineal clan of the dead man, the third *sagali*, or women's mortuary ceremony, is held. The women of the matrilineal clan of the deceased sit in the central plaza of the village surrounded by bundles of banana leaves and skirts. These are then distributed to the women of the widow's matrilineal clan. The first and largest payment of bundles is made to the widow for

A small display of the taro and yams to be distributed at a Trobriand mortuary sagali. *Malinowski (1914–1918).*

having remained secluded and observing the mourning rituals. Those persons who have shaved their heads and painted their bodies black as a sign of mourning are also given bundles. Those who previously brought cooked and uncooked food during the mourning period are given bundles. Finally, the relatives-in-law of the dead man, who have carried out the public mourning, are given valuables such as clay pots, stone axes, and shell decorations for the services that they have performed. The women of each hamlet present as witnesses at the *sagali* are given raw yams and taro plants by the matrilineal kinsmen of the deceased. Mortuary *sagali* to commemorate the dead continue to be given annually.

This sequence of *sagali* distributions after a death requires the accumulation of large quantities of food, goods, and valuables on the part of the matrilineal clan of the dead man. The chief of the dead man's clan is the organizer of all this activity. He collects the goods from other members of the clan and then redistributes them at the *sagali*. If a chief dies and a series of large *sagali* are required, his successor is the organizer. It is at the mortuary *sagali* for the deceased chief that his heir and successor is recognized and accepted as the new chief.

There is always a suspicion of sorcery when a person dies, and those principally suspect are the wife and children. The ostentatiousness of their grief is to demonstrate to the world that they really cared for the departed and to allay suspicions of sorcery on their part.

Women in mourning perform a dance at a mortuary ceremony. Malinowski (1914–1918).

A number of the central ideas of Trobriand culture are played out in this funerary ritual. Trobriand ideas about kinship are seen in the contrast in behavior between people who are conceptualized as blood relatives of the deceased and people who are defined as affines of the deceased, namely his wife and children. The blood relatives may not deal with the corpse, but they sponsor and pay for the *sagali* ceremony. The affines, who may be suspected of causing the death through sorcery, prepare and bury the body, and mourn in an extravagant way. The successor to the deceased chief sponsors the *sagali*, thereby legitimating his new position. The display of large quantities of food at a *sagali* bears witness to the pleasure Trobrianders derive from seeing lavish displays of food. A chief demonstrates his importance through his generosity in distributing food.

Funeral Rites in a Complex Society

Like a Trobriand funeral, an American funeral involves a series of rituals at this critical rite of passage. We will describe, in general, how American funerals are carried out by Christians, rather than describe the funeral of any particular individual, so that this account will parallel the Trobriand funeral. This description may vary from that of funerals among other religious groups in America that emphasize other details.

Death in present-day American society may occur at home or, often, in a hospital. At an earlier period, the sick and the aged usually remained at home, where they died. The remains were then cared for by relatives. Today, immediately after death, bodies are taken to funeral homes, where a full-time specialist, formerly called an undertaker but now referred to as a funeral director, takes complete charge of preparing the body for burial.

The immediate family of the deceased is the central focus of activity. One member of the family, or a very close friend, takes responsibility for handling all the details. Immediately after death, certain legal papers must be filed, the body is prepared for the funeral, a casket is chosen, a member of the clergy is selected to carry out the religious rites, a cemetery plot is arranged for, neighbors, friends, and relatives are notified of the times for visiting the funeral home and of the time and place of the funeral, organizations to which the deceased belonged are notified of the death, and death notices are placed in the newspapers. The funeral director, who has been selected by the family representative, takes over full responsibility for many of these activities. The family representative must know how much money the immediate family intends to spend on the funeral. The funeral is a reflection of the social status of the family, and the family representative must uphold it.

After these initial arrangements have been made, there are four stages to a funeral. The first of these is the viewing of the body, sometimes called the wake. This custom began with relatives sitting up all night with the body, while friends, acquaintances, and more distant relatives came to pay their respects to the deceased. Viewing the body used to take place at home, but now it is held in the funeral parlor in a room made to appear homelike. The casket is placed in a dominating position in the room and is often surrounded by masses of floral arrangements. Condolences are extended to the immediate family, some members of whom are present throughout this stage of the proceedings. There is no organized ritual or leadership at this event, which is predominantly one of social intercourse. Variations in the range of behavior at wakes reflect ethnic differences. The rules of a wake for some groups involve joking and ribaldry, but the somberness of funeral parlors usually inhibits such rowdy behavior. Some groups bring in food and drink, but this may not be permitted by many funeral parlors.

The second stage is the funeral service, usually a religious rite, which may be held either at the church or at the funeral parlor. If held at the church, ushers and pallbearers, who are close friends or relatives of the deceased, carry out special roles. There are formal seating arrangements for the funeral service. The casket is placed in front of the group, with the closest relatives nearest to it. More distant relatives and friends sit farther back. The pallbearers, if present, sit up front. The minister is in the most prominent position at the altar or pulpit, and he or she conducts the religious service. A eulogy, which emphasizes the virtues and good deeds of the deceased, is frequently given by a friend or prominent person. The demeanor of the group is solemn throughout.

Interment of the body at the cemetery is the next stage. Fewer people attend this event than attend the funeral service, but many may go to the cemetery if the deceased was an important person. The funeral director arranges for the transportation of casket and mourners to the cemetery. A hearse bearing the casket leads the procession. At the cemetery, the minister officiates in a brief religious rite. Though the rite is short, the finality of the event is brought out by the power of the religious formula recited—"Ashes to ashes. . . ." Among certain ethnic groups, a widow may attempt to throw herself into her husband's grave as his casket is lowered.

The final stage occurs when the mourners return home from the cemetery. Food prepared by neighbors and friends is then served to the group. This is an informal gathering.

Somber clothing is worn by the mourners at all the events of a funeral. A widow wears black at her husband's funeral and may continue to wear black as a sign of mourning for some time afterward.

The family representative who has made the arrangements for the funeral assumes responsibility to see that the necessary fees are paid by the family. These fees include the fee to the funeral parlor, which covers the price of the casket and the cost of various services, such as hearse and limousine for transportation to the cemetery; the fee to the minister for performing the religious rites; and the fees to the sexton and organist if the funeral is held in a church.

A tombstone is erected some time later. A specialist who makes tombstones engraves it with the name and dates of birth and death of the deceased. The size and elegance of the tombstone formerly reflected the status of the deceased's family. Some cemeteries no longer use tombstones, only small plaques in the ground, making the cemetery appear like a garden. In other instances, the body of the deceased is placed in a burial vault in an aboveground building containing hundreds of such vaults.

The practice of embalming to preserve the body was introduced by funeral directors in this century. It is forbidden by some religions and has met resistance in other groups. Similarly, cremation has been introduced and is most common in areas where cemetery space is limited. It has met greatest resistance among those religious groups who hold a strong belief in the resurrection of the body.

A number of contrasts emerge as one compares a Trobriand funeral with an American funeral. The Trobriand funeral is a long series of rites and distributions extending over a number of years, while the stages in an American funeral are telescoped into a few days, with the tombstone erected at some indefinite time afterward. Among the Trobrianders, the body is cared for, handled, and dressed by a category of relatives within the Trobriand social structure, while at an American funeral today the body is handled entirely by specialists. The Trobriand funeral is marked by large-scale distributions of economic goods to those relatives who performed mortuary services and to guests who come as mourners. In the American funeral, the family pays the specialists who perform the various specific services, but there is no distribution of goods to guests and mourners. In the Trobriand funeral, memorials to the deceased consist of relics made from the dead person's bones, while the rest of the corpse was traditionally interred in the plaza in the center of the village. The memorial to the deceased at an American funeral is the engraved headstone, and the burial is in a cemetery set apart from the area of the living. A long formal mourning period, during which mortuary rituals continue to take place, is observed by the Trobrianders. In American society there is no formal institutionalized mourning period, though the spouse of the deceased may wear black for a time. Trobriand funeral rites emphasize group-to-group relationships. In the American funeral, the immediate family is involved, while other mourners (more distant relatives, friends, and acquaintances) attend on an individual basis depending on the degree of closeness they personally felt to the deceased.

Fundamental similarities can be seen in Trobriand and American rites of passage at death. The mortuary rites in both societies emphasize the need for the living to reconstitute the social fabric after the death of one of the members of the community, and in both societies there are religious beliefs concerning the continuity of the spirit of the deceased in the afterlife.

Culture molds, elaborates, and transforms universal ideas such as marriage ceremonies and funerals as it weaves them into the "tapestry" of the culture. While there are basic similarities between rites of passage such as weddings and funerals in American, Kwakiutl, and Trobriand societies, there are also significant differences. The descriptions of Kwakiutl and Trobriand rites of passage as total social phenomena illustrate the interpenetration of economic, political, kinship, religious, and artistic institutions and the greater degree of cultural integration in small-scale societies. How the political system operates among the Kwakiutl and the Trobriand Islanders will be discussed in a later chapter. There we will show that the Kwakiutl marriage potlatch and the Trobriand funeral *sagali* are integral parts of their respective political systems. Similarly, in the chapter on economic systems, the production and distribution of goods for the two societies will be related to the Kwakiutl wedding and the Trobriand funeral described in this chapter.

As societies develop more complex political economies, institutional specialization grows. In the accounts we have given of American weddings and funerals, this institutional specialization is apparent. One can even talk about the wedding and funeral industries, each with its own distinctive commodities and specialists.

CHAPTER 3

Language and Culture

From one point of view language is a part of culture, and yet it is more than that. It is central to culture since it is the means through which most of culture is learned and communicated. An infant learns the language and simultaneously learns the culture of the society into which he or she is born. In similar fashion, as we noted in our earlier discussion of fieldwork, an anthropologist carrying out field research learns the language as he studies the culture. Only humans have the biological capacity for language, which allows them to communicate cultural ideas from one generation to the next and to constantly create new cultural ideas. The capacity for language creates a great divide between humans and the other primates. In any language, an infinite number of possible sentences can be constructed and used to convey an infinite number of cultural ideas. Because of this, human language is significantly different from any other system of animal communication.

The Structure of Language

Like culture, language is patterned. However, language is primarily arbitrary in nature. As the Swiss linguist Ferdinand de Saussure (1915) pointed out in his study of language, the units that carry meaning are two-sided.

One side is the physical characteristics that make up the word. These characteristics consist of sounds, or vibrations of the vocal chords, transmitted through the air, which emanate from one person and are received by another. The other side consists of the word's meaning or what it stands for. For example, the word *tree* is made up of a particular series of sounds— t/r/e—and it stands for

The same object is referred to as *arbre* in French and *Baum* in German. Thus the connection between any combination of sounds that make up a word and its meaning is mostly arbitrary—that is, there is no intrinsic and natural connection between the sounds of a word and its meaning. The same meaning—tree—is conveyed by a different combination of sounds in each language. Occasionally, there is some natural connection between sound and meaning, as occurs in words that imitate natural phenomena, such as *buzz* and *hiss*. Language is therefore not completely arbitrary.

Phonemic Structure

We have mentioned that language is patterned. Let us begin at the level of sound, the building blocks of language. Each language has a small number of basic sounds, usually between twenty and forty, which are used in various combinations to make up the units of meaning. These basic sound units are called *phonemes*. All languages are constructed in the same way. From a small number of phonemes, arranged in different ways, an infinite number of words can be produced. For example, the English word *pin* differs in meaning from *pen* since /i/ is a different phoneme from /e/. Add /s/ to *pin* and you get the plural form of *pin*, that is, *pins*. But if the /s/ is added to the beginning of the word, rather than the end, the result is *spin*, a word with a totally different meaning. Thus, the same phonemes in a different order produce a word with a different meaning.

If the reader has been paying close attention, he or she will have noted that the /p/ in *pin* is different from the /p/ in *spin*. If you hold a sheet of paper in front of your mouth and pronounce *pin* loudly, the paper will flutter because the /p/ in *pin* is aspirated (air blows out). Pronounce *spin* and the sheet of paper remains still, because the /p/ in *spin* is not aspirated.

The two /p/'s are said to be *allophones* of the same phoneme. They are variant forms of the single English phoneme /p/, which vary because of their "environments," that is, the contexts in which they are found.

The phonemes of a language form a structure or system. The phonemes of English can be divided into vowels and consonants. For a native speaker, English consonants seem independent and unrelated to one another. However, let us examine the following list of some English consonants:

t	d
p	b
f	v
s	z
k	g

When one makes the sounds /t/ and /d/, the tongue, teeth, and lips, known as the points of articulation, are in the same position for both. This is also true for the other paired sounds on the two lists—/p/ and /b/, /f/ and /v/, /s/ and /z/, and /k/ and /g/. There is a relationship between the group of consonants in the left-hand column and the group of consonants in the right-hand column. The consonants in the column on the left are all pronounced without vibrations of the vocal cords. They are *voiceless* consonants. The vocal cords vibrate when those in the right-hand column are pronounced. These are called *voiced* consonants. The distinction between voiced and voiceless consonants is one of the several kinds of distinctions characterizing English phonemes. All these features organize the set of English phonemes into a structure and serve to differentiate them. If the phonemes of a language are structured, then what is their function? Phonemes serve to differentiate words like *pin* and *pen*. Though phonemes themselves do not carry meaning, their function is to differentiate words in terms of their meanings.

Morphemic Structure

The units of language that carry meaning are called *morphemes.* Morphemes are not equivalent to words, because some words may be broken into smaller units that carry meaning. For example, the word *shoemaker* may be subdivided into three separate morphemes: *shoe, make,* and *-er,* each with its own meaning. Each of these morphemes is in turn made up of phonemes. Some morphemes, like *shoe,* can stand independently. These are called free morphemes. Others, like *-er,* meaning "one who has to do with," are always found bound to other morphemes (as in *speaker, singer,* and *leader*) and are referred to as *bound morphemes.* Sometimes two or more forms, that is, combinations of phonemes, have the same meaning. The form *-er* has the same meaning in English as *-ist* in the word *pianist*. These two forms, *-er* and *-ist*, are known as *allomorphs* of the same morpheme.

Syntax and Grammar

The rules by which larger speech units, such as phrases and sentences, are formed compose the *syntax* of a language. English, like all other languages, has rules about the order of words in a sentence. Word order conveys meaning. Thus, "Man bites dog" has a different meaning from "Dog bites man." In the film *ET*, ET's sentence "Home phone" is undecipherable, until he says "Phone home."

The complete description of a language is known as its *grammar*. This would include the phonology (a description of its phonemic system), the morphology (a description of its morphemic system), and the syntax. In addition, a complete description of a language would also include a lexicon or dictionary that lists all the morphemes and their meanings.

Linguistic Relativity

In the nineteenth century, European philologists discovered that ancient Sanskrit, Latin and Greek, and most of the languages of modern Europe belonged to a single language family—Indo-European, meaning that all these languages had evolved from a single ancestral language—and were basically similar to one another. When early linguists began to encounter the languages spoken by native North Americans, unrelated to Indo-European, they assumed (incorrectly) that these languages could be analyzed in terms of Latin grammatical categories. Like the nineteenth-century anthropologists interested in evolutionary theory, discussed in Chapter 1, these linguists were ethnocentric in their approach and ranged languages as more or less advanced. They termed languages "advanced" if they were spoken by people who were "civilized," while people who were hunters and gatherers were said to speak "primitive" languages.

The intensive study of American Indian languages, spearheaded by Franz Boas at the beginning of the twentieth century, demonstrated the fallacious reasoning behind the nineteenth-century evolutionary approach to language. Boas's own work concentrated on the Kwakiutl, as we noted in Chapter 1, and his students were encouraged to go out and study other American Indian languages. As a result of these studies, it became evident to Boas, and later others, that languages could not be rated on a scale from simple to complex and that there was no one-to-one relationship between technological complexity or cultural complexity and linguistic complexity. All languages known to linguists, regardless of whether the society had writing, are equally complex. Languages spoken by bands of hunters and gatherers are as systematically patterned as English or Latin. As we have mentioned earlier, this was known as *linguistic relativity*. This parallels the concept of *cultural relativity*. Furthermore, Boas convincingly demonstrated that it was necessary to analyze each language in terms of its own structure. This is not to say that there are no universals in language. Indeed there are, since all languages have a phonemic system, a morphology, and syntax. The contemporary American linguist Noam Chomsky has argued that there are a great many other shared characteristics in all languages, which he claims are due to the underlying structure of the human brain.

Language and Cognition

Boas's study of the Kwakiutl language, which led him to his concept of linguistic relativity, includes a discussion of how, in Kwakiutl, the speaker must indicate how he knows about an action individuals other than himself are performing. For example, in the sentence:

The lady was washing clothes

it is necessary in Kwakiutl to make the following distinctions. Did the speaker actually see the lady washing clothes? Did he infer that she was washing clothes from the sound that he heard? Did a third party tell the speaker that she was washing clothes? In the Kwakiutl language, these distinctions must be made as part of the grammar of the language. Some languages have built into their grammars the characteristic that a speaker must specify how he acquired the information he is imparting. English does not have this feature as part of its grammar, though the information can be provided by the speaker, if he wishes to give it, with additional words. Boas made the general point that in all languages, grammatical rules, such as the one in this example, are obligatory. Just as the Kwakiutl speaker is obliged to use a grammatical category that specifies how he knows what he knows, the English speaker must use one tense form or another to indicate whether he is speaking about the past, the present, or the future. Boas also pointed out that such grammatical rules remain unconscious. That is, the speakers of a language are not usually aware of them, though these rules guide all their utterances.

As can be noted from the above example, there is a close and intimate relationship between language and experience. Language organizes experience, and people speaking different languages organize what they experience differently. Thus a Kwakiutl person always attends to how he receives information, because this is necessary in conveying information to others. Since the issue is "how you know what you know," one can imagine the comparison between the precision of a Kwakiutl speaker as a witness at a court trial and the lack of specificity of the equivalent English-speaking witness at the same trial. The relationship between language and how society organizes experience was explored by Boas's student Edward Sapir. He argued that language was a guide to social reality, and that the "real world" was, to a great extent, unconsciously built upon the language habits of a society. This line of argument was carried to what many people considered to be an extreme position by Benjamin Lee Whorf, who considered that the conception of the world by a member of a particular society was determined by the language or "fashion of speaking."

Ethnosemantics

The way in which a particular language organizes experience for its speakers can be seen most clearly by examination of a specific cultural domain, such as the organization and classification of the world of animals, the world of plants, the system of colors, and the realm of relatives or kinsmen.

In all languages, there is a set of terms used to refer to animals. The world of animals is separable from other domains in the world. It is distinct from the domain of plants, though they both share the characteristic of life in contrast to the inanimate world of rocks and soils. People using different languages will sort this world of animals in ways different from our own. For example, the Linnaean system of classification, which we use, groups human beings, bats, and whales as mammals on the basis of criteria such as being warm-blooded, suckling their young, and having hair. Whether these animals fly, live on the land, or swim in the sea is not important. Other peoples use different criteria for their animal classifications. For example, the Karam of Papua New Guinea, studied by Ralph Bulmer, distinguish birds from other animals in their language. However, the cassowary, a flightless bird like an ostrich that stands over five feet tall, is not placed in the category of birds (where we place it). Rather, the Karam place it in an anomalous category.

We have noted above that our category of mammals is distinguished by a series of criteria. These criteria differentiate the category from reptiles, for example. Such criteria, which characterize all kinds of categories, are known as distinctive features or components. When an anthropologist like Bulmer studies Karam language and Karam culture, he not only collects the meanings of all animal terms and the categories in which the Karam place them, but must then determine the Karam basis for the classifications as well. He ascertains the distinctive features the Karam employ when they classify forms such as the cassowary. Each language demonstrates its own cultural logic in making its classifications. The anthropological investigation of this topic is known as ethnosemantics.

In Chapter 5, we will discuss the way in which societies over the world use kinship terms to sort their relatives into different categories. In this chapter, we will examine kinship terminologies from the point of view of their semantic content—that is, as language. A kinship terminology is parallel to a system of animal classification. It is characterized by sets of components or distinctive features and is hierarchically ordered in the same fashion as the system of animal classification. All kinship terminologies may be analyzed in terms of eight features, and specific terminologies employ some of these features but not others. For example, the kinship terminology of the Yanomamo, who live in lowland South America, which we will analyze in Chapter 5, recognizes the features of sex of relative (whether the relative referred to is a male or a female), generation (to which generation the relative referred to belongs), and sex of linking relative (whether the relative is related through one's mother or one's father). It does not take into account the distinction between consanguineal relatives (blood relatives) and affinal relatives (relatives by marriage) or other features that occur in kinship terminologies over the world. In every language there is a kinship terminology that represents a set of terms for relatives and sorts them in a particular way by using certain components and ignoring others. Each kinship terminology is invariably much simpler than it might be if every possible relative were distinguished with his or her own term or label. Thus, in every kinship terminology each kin term represents several different kinds of relatives—the English term *uncle* is a category that includes mother's brother, father's brother, and mother's sister's husband; the Yanomamo term *haya* is a category that includes father and father's brother, and so on.

Still another cultural domain that has been studied in this manner is the set of linguistic terms used for colors. Every language has a set of terms for colors, though the number of these terms varies from one language to another. Viewers looking at a rainbow see an undivided series of colors, one color grading into another, while as speakers of different languages they will divide this spectrum differently. Boas used the example of color categories to illustrate the principle of linguistic relativity mentioned earlier. More recently, Brent Berlin and Paul Kay have done a comparative study of basic color categories in many different languages throughout the world that shows that the classification of colors in different languages is not completely arbitrary. In some languages, there are only two basic color terms, bright and dark (which can be equated to white and black). More common are languages with three terms, and those terms will always be red, bright (white), and dark (black). Still other languages, with four color categories, add either yellow or green. Other groups of languages through time will successively add blue, brown, purple, pink, orange, and gray. What Berlin and Kay have demonstrated is that the color spectrum is not randomly divided. There is order and regularity in the way in which languages add to the number of color terms. This does not mean that people over the world see the color spectrum differently or cannot in a descriptive fashion express in their language the colors they see (without a term for blue they might say "it is the color of a robin's egg"). What it does mean is that the color categories their language possesses will organize their experience in a particular way.

In this general discussion of ethnosemantics we have shown the way in which the concept of distinctive features is used. Sometimes two categories are opposed to one another, such as the categories sorted in terms of differences in locomotion—"creatures that fly" and "creatures that swim." Another, more usual, way of distinguishing two categories from one another is for one of the categories to possess an attribute that the other category lacks. Above, we noted that mammals were distinct from reptiles in the Linnaean classification. Mammals are warm-blooded animals while reptiles are not. Mammals possess an internal mechanism for maintaining a constant warm body temperature that reptiles lack. Thus, one might say that the category of mammals is the "plus" category. The Karam use the same method for classifying animals. They have two categories—one category has wings (the "plus" category) and the other has no wings. The linguist Roman Jakobson identified this principle of classification, where the opposition between two categories was based upon an attribute present in one category but not in the other. The category in which the attribute was present Jakobson called the *marked category,* and the category in which it was absent he referred to as the *unmarked category.* This is known as the *principle of markedness.*

Jakobson pointed out that in linguistics the unmarked category is the more general and inclusive of the two. For example, in English, we have the words *lion* and *lioness.* The marked category is the word *lioness* (*-ess* is added to *lion*—thus marking it). *Lion* includes *lioness,* as in the sentence "Christians were thrown to the lions." The principle of markedness can also be seen in the paired words *actor* and *actress. Actor* is the unmarked form. By adding *-ess, actor* becomes *actress,* which is the marked form. *Actor* is the more general category, and both men and women can belong to the Actors' Guild. But it would be strange for men to join an Actresses' Association. The unmarked category is also often the dominant category, while the marked category is subordinate.

Sociolinguistics

Saussure, the linguist referred to earlier, made a distinction between *langue* and *parole,* that is, between language and speech. Up to this point we have dealt only with language and the differences between languages. To obtain information about a language, the fieldworker observes and records many examples of speech. These examples are analyzed in order to obtain a picture of the grammar, or underlying structure of that language. Sociolinguistics deals with the analysis of parole, or speech, and its social functions. Recently, anthropological linguists have been involved in the ethnography of speech, in which they have examined actual conversations in terms of turn taking, pauses, speech strategies and styles, and variations between speech communities, in order to understand how they operate in the conduct of social life.

In many societies, though men and women are members of the same speech community, distinctions between male and female speech have been noted. In a study of a Malagasy-speaking community of Madagascar, Keenan (1974) has observed that men tend not to express their sentiments openly, are not confrontational, do not show anger, and behave with discretion. This is reflected in men's speech. They favor subtlety in speech and more indirect and circumspect forms of expression. This is particularly characteristic of men's speech on ceremonial occasions. In contrast, women tend to speak in a straightforward manner, directly expressing anger and criticism that may insult the person being addressed. Since direct speech is characteristic of the marketplace, women do much of the bargaining, buying, and selling in this society. Men usually sell goods that are more or less fixed in price. When they do bargain, it is an elaborate and circumspect procedure, in which confrontation is to be avoided. In Japanese there are also marked differences between male and female speech, so strong that some observers talk about a "true" women's language. In contrast to Malagasy, it is the women's speech in Japanese that is characterized by the more frequent use of polite forms. Japanese women's speech is also distinguished from men's speech by the presence of different sets of first- and second-person pronouns and special terms of self-reference and address.

Investigations of male and female speech in American society reveal the same hierarchical pattern of dominance and subordination as was found in the system of marked and unmarked categories discussed above. West and Zimmerman have found that in cross-sex conversations recorded mainly in public places, males accounted for 96 percent of the interruptions. In same-sex conversations, women interrupted one another as often as men interrupted other men (1977). In another study by Fishman, it was found that men do most of the interrupting and talking, and they also often choose what to talk about (1983). Poynton (1989) adds to the list of features distinguishing male from female speech. While women will talk on topics raised by men, men may and do reject women's topics in mixed conversations. When men make commands, they use the imperative form. Women tend to use interrogatives ("Would you mind closing the window?") and declarative forms ("I wonder if you would be so kind as to shut the door."). Poynton argues that men and women use different forms of a common language which encodes an ideological opposition between the sexes. That ideology maintains that males and their activities are of great importance and value, while females and their activities are of less importance and value.

Other kinds of variations in speech within a language correspond to class differences—that is, to vertical differences that structure a society. In *My Fair Lady*, Professor Henry Higgins teaches Liza Doolittle a completely "new" language—upper-class English, so different from her own lower-class Cockney English that the two are almost mutually unintelligible. Such class-correlated linguistic differences can also be found in the United States.

If class differences in speech can be conceptualized as vertical differences, then differences in speech due to geography and region may be conceptualized as horizontal differences. Speakers in different geographical areas speaking different versions of a language are said to speak different dialects. People in different regions of the United States can be identified by their different patterns of speech. One can immediately recognize a Boston accent, a Midwestern accent, or a Southern accent. Dialect differences are found not only in pronunciation but also in vocabulary and in syntax.

Language Change

As we noted in Chapter 1, cultures are continually undergoing some degree of change. Since language is a part of culture, it too is always changing. Of course, during one's lifetime, one is not aware of linguistic change, except for changes in vocabulary, particularly slang words (words like *groovy* and *cool* are no longer used). If we compare our language usage with that of the language in Shakespeare's plays, the extent to which English has changed over the past centuries is obvious.

It is apparent that present-day dialect differences represent development from an earlier form of the language. How do such dialect differences arise in the first place? Speech communities are made up of members of a group within a society who interact and speak frequently with one another. One speech community that is very similar to its neighbor will develop slight differences in pronunciation or vocabulary which will differentiate it from the neighboring speech community. As these differences increase, they become the basis for greater dialect differentiation. Dialect differentiation, over time, leads to divergence and to the development of two separate languages.

If one examines French, Spanish, Portuguese, and Italian, one can immediately recognize a host of similarities. Some languages, such as Spanish and Portuguese, are more closely related than others, such as French and Portuguese. Because of the higher degree of mutual intelligibility between Spanish and Portuguese, one could argue that these two languages are more like different dialects of a single language. These languages, along with other languages like Rumanian, are daughter languages, descendants of the vernacular Latin spoken during the time of Julius Caesar. This was the language spoken by the common people, and it differs from the literary Latin familiar to us from the scholarly works of that time. Dialects of the Latin language spread over large parts of Europe and the Mediterranean world as a result of Roman conquest. These dialects of Latin later developed into separate languages. The vernacular Latin of the Roman period is referred to as the *proto-language,* and the present-day languages descended from it are known as *Romance* languages. In parallel fashion, English, Dutch, German, and the Scandinavian languages compose the Germanic language family—all descended from a common proto-language called Proto-Germanic. Similarly, all the Slavic languages (Russian, Polish, Czech, etc.) are descended from Proto-Slavic. The European languages we have just mentioned, along with other European and Asian languages such as Persian, Hindi, and Bengali, form a large family of related languages called the *Indo-European language family.* All these languages are descended from a common ancestor, Proto-Indo-European.

Not all languages spoken in Europe are part of this family. Finnish and Hungarian belong to the Finno-Ugric family, while Basque is completely unrelated to any other language.

The kinds of languages that anthropologists usually study do not belong to the Indo-European language family. Because of their traditional association with small-scale societies, anthropologists have studied the languages of the indigenous people of North and South America, Africa, and Oceania. These languages can be organized in terms of language families in the same fashion as the European languages discussed above. Some of these language families are very large, encompassing many languages, whereas others may be very small or even isolates, like Basque.

Until studied, these languages had not been recorded in written form. For the languages of Europe, where written records existed for millennia, the historical sequence is known. This enables us to know what Proto-Romance looked like; it was the spoken language, similar to the scholarly language. This study involves the use of the comparative method. Languages thought to be related are systematically compared. Words that have the same or similar meanings are examined. This can be illustrated with a simple example from the Germanic languages. The English word *dance* has as its equivalent the German word *Tanz,* and the English word *door* has as its equivalent *Tür.* The forms that have been paired have the same meaning, and their phonemic structures are similar but not identical. These pairs are referred to as *cognates.* The initial *d* in English regularly corresponds to the initial *t* in German. These two forms represent modern divergences from the original of this phoneme in Proto-Germanic. This correspondence operates throughout the two languages, so that everywhere one finds an initial *d* in English, one would expect to find an initial *t* in German. This is just a single example of the many sound correspondences to be found between German and English.

If one systematically compares cognates in two unwritten languages such as Navajo and Apache, one would also find similar sound correspondences. This not only would demonstrate that the two languages were genetically related to one another and belonged to the same language family, Athapaskan, but would also enable one to reconstruct a tentative picture of the phonemic structure of the proto-language from which these present-day languages have descended. The morphemic structure of the proto-language could be determined through the same comparative approach. This also provides information about what the culture of the speakers of this proto-language was like. Words in the proto-language for plants, trees, and animals can be used to pinpoint the possible location of the speakers' original homeland before they dispersed. This type of research enables us to say that the original homeland of the Navajo and the Apache was in the forest area of northwest Canada, from which they migrated to their present homes in the Southwest.

Still another way in which languages change is as a result of the diffusion or borrowing from speakers of one language by speakers of another language. This may be the borrowing of words, sounds, or grammatical forms. Contact and borrowing come about in a number of different ways, some of them peaceful, others not. An excellent example of this is what happened after the Norman conquest of England, in A.D. 1066. The Norman invaders were speakers of an earlier version of French, while the English spoke Anglo-Saxon, a Germanic language. The effects of that invasion are present today in our own language. The French, famous for their cuisine, introduced a series of terms into the Anglo-Saxon language, referring to different kinds of cooked meat. The *cow* (Saxon), when cooked, became *beef* (*boeuf* in French); *calf* (Saxon) became *veal* (*veau* in French); *sheep* (Saxon) became *mutton* (*mouton* in French); and *swine* (Saxon) became *pork* (*porc* in French).

Since culture is structured, much as language is, procedures and concepts from linguistics have been utilized by anthropologists in their studies of cultural problems. In subsequent chapters dealing with symbolism, mythology, and art, we will be again discussing some of the concepts and ideas we have presented in this chapter.

CHAPTER 4

Symbolic Systems and Meanings

Anthropologists doing fieldwork observe and record what people say and do. Their task then is to understand and interpret the meanings of these actions and words. Anthropologists do this in part by discussing the material with informants and examining these actions in a number of other cultural contexts. People's behavior is framed according to a set of cultural ideas. That set of ideas constitutes the overall design of the tapestry. In order to understand their economic behavior, their political behavior, and their social behavior, one must understand the system of cultural meanings which underlies these institutions. From another perspective, people in their day-to-day actions create and re-create their culture. As they do this, they are also creating and conveying cultural meaning. How they walk, how they dress, how they talk—all convey meaning. Sometimes people change their behavior and then its meaning also changes. In the minds of some anthropologists like Clifford Geertz, in order to understand the meaning of cultural behavior, it must be "read" like a text.

The analysis of symbols deals with the meanings of things in a culture— the meanings of words, the meanings of actions, and the meanings of objects. As we have noted in Chapter 3, language itself is a system made up entirely of symbols. All symbols, like the morphemes of language, operate as if they were two-sided coins. On one side are the physical characteristics, and on the other side is the meaning, or what the symbol stands for.

Metaphor, a kind of symbol, is an important analytical concept used by anthropologists in the study of symbolic systems. A metaphor is an idea that people use to stand for another set of ideas. The meaning of the metaphor is the recognition of the connection between the metaphor itself and the "something else" it represents. In the Kwakiutl marriage ceremony described in Chapter 2, many of the activities we described were also characteristic of warfare, such as blackening the faces, dressing like warriors, and running through a gauntlet of fire in order to capture the bride. Among the Kwakiutl, marriage is metaphorically a form of warfare. The metaphor of warfare among the Kwakiutl is apt, because both involve competition. The competitive aspect of the marriage is seen in the potlatch, which pits one side against the other.

In our society, games are often used as a metaphor for life. Games involve struggle and competition. Sometimes you win and sometimes you lose, but games must be played according to a set of rules. Games demand from the players intelligence, stamina, and courage—virtues in our culture. During Nixon's presidency, White House officials talked about "playing hardball" and used the expression from baseball, "When the going gets tough, the tough get going." The use of the symbol of hardball by White House officials had the meaning of tough, no-holds-barred, dog-eat-dog politics. Baseball is being used to stand for something else—politics— because both have an important characteristic in common, though they may differ in many other respects. Baseball and politics have in common competition, struggle, and some element of danger. These metaphors relate to the competition and struggle in life that is expressed in the symbolism of the game.

Struggle can be physical or mental. The chessboard is a miniature world peopled with a miniature feudal society. In the classic movie *The Seventh Seal,* the White Knight plays against Death, represented by the black pieces. The White Knight plays for his life against death, which represents the Black Death—the plague sweeping Europe. The chess game is used as a medium or metaphor by means of which the moviemaker, Ingmar Bergman, talks about life and death.

Another kind of symbol is a *metonym.* Like a metaphor, a metonym is also based upon a substitution of one thing for another, but in this case the symbol standing for the something else is one of the several things that constitute the something else. Thus the monarch can be referred to as the *head* of state and the capital as the *seat* of government. The crown or the throne can stand as a symbol for the monarch or for monarchy. In each case, a part has been taken and used to stand as a symbol for the whole.

One category of symbols, *public symbols,* constitutes the cultural system for the society. Much of that body of cultural symbols is known, understood, and shared by all the members of the society. However, some of these symbols, often the most important ones, are more esoteric and are known only by religious practitioners. There are also symbols that individuals create out of their own experience, which are not commonly shared by others. They are the symbols of our dream life and fantasies. These are known as *private symbols.* The artist in the creative process also uses private symbols. The process of interpretation of art by the public and the critic involves trying to decipher what the private symbols mean. We will discuss the use of private and public symbols by artists in Chapter 11.

At the beginning of this chapter we referred to the two-sidedness of symbols and the arbitrary relationship between the two sides. The connection between the two for public symbols is culturally, not individually, determined. The connection between the symbol and its meaning may differ from culture to culture, as words do from language to language. Thus there are two ways in which the subject of symbolism may be approached. The first is to examine a symbol and the different meanings attached to it in different cultures. The second is to begin with the other side of the coin—to study the thing symbolized and the different symbols used for it.

Symbols are manifested in behavior as well as in ideas. People's actions are guided by symbols and their meanings. Symbols serve to motivate such actions. Further, people's behavior itself has symbolic meaning to the observers of it.

The Symbolism of Food

As an example of how a symbol may have various meanings attached to it in different cultures, we will examine the symbolism of food. From the utilitarian or materialist perspective, food is what is ingested by the human animal in order to sustain life. It is made up of calories, protein, fats, minerals, and carbohydrates and is introduced into the human animal by eating. This aspect of food is equivalent to the physical manifestations or sounds that make up a word. Not to go beyond this aspect of food in terms of one's investigation would be like analyzing words without considering their meanings. Let us now examine the various meanings that are attached to food and its ingestion in a variety of cultural contexts. Food as a symbol conveys a variety of meanings in different cultures.

Eating is very frequently a metaphor for sexual intercourse in a great many societies, including our own. Why is one a metaphor for the other? What do the two actions have in common? These two acts are completely different physiologically, but nevertheless they are tied together in their symbolic significance. In many societies eating can be used figuratively for sexual intercourse. Sometimes eating as a metaphor is used to signify marriage. In many New Guinea societies, like Lesu mentioned in Chapter 1 and the Trobriand Islanders, marriage is symbolized by the couple eating together for the first time. Adolescent boys and girls freely engage in sexual intercourse without any commitment to marriage or any gossip or criticism from the community. But eating together constitutes a public announcement that they are now married. Eating symbolizes their new status as a married couple. In our society, it is just the reverse. One can take a date to dinner, but engaging in sexual intercourse used to be and frequently still is a sign of marriage. In other New Guinea societies, such as Wogeo, if a man eats with a woman, then she is like his sister and he can't marry her. Here, eating is equally symbolic but has a different meaning. Instead of symbolizing marriage, it indicates a brother-sister relationship—those who cannot marry.

Cultural rules determine every aspect of food consumption. Who eats together defines social units. For example, in our society, the nuclear family is the unit that regularly eats together. The anthropologist Mary Douglas (1972) has pointed out that, for the English, the kind of meal and the kind of food that is served relate to the kinds of social links between people who are eating together. She distinguishes between regular meals, Sunday meals when relatives may come, and cocktail parties for acquaintances. The food served symbolizes the occasion and reflects who is present. For example, only tidbits and snacks—finger foods—are served at a cocktail party. It would be inappropriate to serve a steak or hamburgers. The distinction between cocktails, regular meals, and special dinners marks the social boundaries between those guests who are invited for drinks, those who are invited to dinner, and those who come to a family meal. A similar analysis could be done for American society.

In contrast, in some New Guinea societies the nuclear family is not the unit that eats together. The men live in a men's house, where they take their meals separately from their wives and children. Women live in their own houses with their children, prepare food there, and take the husband's portion to the men's house. The women eat with their children in their own houses. This pattern is also widespread among Near Eastern societies, where men usually eat with other men and women with other women, and husbands and wives do not eat together. Among the Marri Baluch of western Pakistan, where the family arranges marriage between close relatives, husbands never eat with their wives. But in the case of adulterous relationships between a man and a woman, eating together symbolizes their love for one another. In Lesu, on the island of New Ireland in the Pacific, the symbolic meaning of eating is exactly opposite to its meaning among the Marri Baluch. In Lesu, betrothal and marriage are symbolized by a man and woman sitting down and eating together, but a woman never eats with her lover.

Recognition of the metaphoric connection between eating and sexual intercourse can also help to explain some other curious cultural rules that have to do with taboos against eating certain things. In some societies, members of a clan are not allowed to eat the animal or bird that is their totemic ancestor. Since they believe themselves descended from that ancestor, it would be like eating that ancestor or eating themselves. This would be equivalent to sexual intercourse within the group, which is incest. For the Siuai of Bougainville in the Solomon Islands, the supreme taboo is against eating the totemic animal, and they describe intercourse with a person from one's own clan as eating this totemic animal. There is another incestlike prohibition involving food among the Abelam and the Arapesh societies of New Guinea. The Arapesh express it in the form of an aphorism:

Other people's mothers
Other people's sisters
Other people's pigs
Other people's yams which they have piled up
You may eat,
Your own mother
Your own sister
Your own pigs
Your own yams which you have piled up
You may not eat.

The pigs that a person raises are considered to be his children, and the owner of a pig is referred to as its father. The Arapesh explicitly recognize the symbolic connection between eating and sexual intercourse, as evidenced in the prohibition against eating one's own pigs and yams and the prohibition against incest with one's sister and mother. In Abelam and Arapesh, the taboo against eating one's own pigs and own yams compels social groups to exchange their pigs and yams with other groups, resulting in ongoing exchange relationships with those groups.

It would be unthinkable to eat with one's enemies. Even in our own society, one may be compelled to say a polite good morning to one's enemies, but the line is drawn at breaking bread with them. This is generally true in societies over the world. Eating together symbolizes goodwill and peaceful relations. What happens when enemies accidentally find themselves together for one reason or another? In some societies, like the Pathans of Swat, great stress is placed upon the giving of hospitality. Food symbolizes this hospitality. Even if the host learns the guests are enemies, with whom he would normally not share food, the rules of hospitality dictate that as guests they must be fed. When the guests are ready to leave, the host escorts them to the border of his territory. His obligations of hospitality having ended, he is free to treat them like enemies and kill them.

The Maring have elaborated the symbolism of not eating with one's enemy. They have a fire taboo that prevents them from eating food cooked over the same fire as the food of an enemy. This means that they are not allowed to share food, not only with their enemy, but with any third party who has shared food with their enemy.

Food is used to distinguish various social categories of people, as we have described above. It can also be used to distinguish different categories of rank. Among the Trobrianders, the highest-ranked chiefly subclan is not allowed to eat stingaree (a kind of fish) or bush pig, while low-ranking subclans may. Should members of the highest-ranked group eat these things unknowingly and then be told, they would become nauseated and would regurgitate them. The association between food prohibitions and rank is found in the most extreme form in the caste system of India, but there the association is coupled with another idea, that of pollution. A caste system consists of ranked groups, each with a different economic specialization. Members of highly ranked groups can be polluted by coming into contact with the bodily secretions, particularly saliva, of individuals of lower-ranked castes. Because of the fear of pollution, Brahmans and other high-ranked individuals will not share food with, not eat from the same plate as, not even accept food from an individual from a low-ranking caste. In Sri Lanka and southern India, rules about eating as well as rules about sex relations serve to keep castes apart. Higher-caste women do not marry men from lower castes, and people of high caste do not take food from people of lower castes. Once again, rules about eating and rules about sexual intercourse parallel one another in serving to keep social groups apart.

A completely different meaning of food is to be found in the giving of food to the gods. In Hindu ritual in India, various kinds of cooked foods are presented to the gods in the temple, and each kind of food bears a different message or request to the gods. Animal sacrifices represent another form of offering food to the gods. In the Maring ceremonial distribution, the *kaiko*, pigs are sacrificed to the ancestral spirits in return for the help that they have given in previous warfare.

Food has a great many meanings in present-day American society. For example, regions are symbolized by different foods. Grits, fried chicken, black-eyed peas, collards, and mustard greens represent the South. Boiled dinners, clam chowder, and lobster immediately symbolize New England. Over the past few decades ethnic identity has become increasingly important as a component of American identity. Particular dishes distinctive of a national cuisine are used to create an ethnic identity. For example, the principal characters in the *Godfather* films are constantly signaling their Italian-American identities by what they eat.

Social Groups and Their Symbols

In the previous section, we selected something tangible, food, and then discussed the meanings attached to it in different cultures. A social group may be identified with the food that it eats. Its cuisine symbolizes the group, but the group identity is also symbolized in a number of other ways.

A social group such as a clan may be represented by different symbols. A totemic animal may represent the clan, and representations of the animal

A Tsimshian mortuary totem pole, standing today at Gitwinkul, British Columbia, was erected by a family of the Wolf phratry and depicts crests from its origin myth.

are used to signify that clan. This is true of the Kwakiutl, whose wedding potlatch was discussed in Chapter 2, and other tribes of the Pacific coast of Canada, where the specific totemic animal of the group is painted on the facade of the house and carved on the totem pole standing before the house. These tribes are like many other societies of the world in that personal names given to members of the group belong to the entire group. When a person dies, his or her name returns to the pool of names, to be used again when a child is born. There is also the belief that a name carries an identity, and that identity is perpetuated through the names handed down from generation to generation. In this way, individual identity is linked to clan identity, since the name symbolizes membership in the group to the outside world. In general, the clan as a social group may be associated with particular spirits, including spirits of the clan ancestors, who are said to dwell in a specific location in the clan territory. The spirits and the territory represent the clan. Strangers crossing the territory, or hunting in it, are in danger from the spirits that protect it. In such a situation, where the land symbolizes the continuity of the social group (the clan) from mythical times to the present, the land could not be sold for money without destroying the identity of the group itself. Thus, food can stand as a symbol for the group, but so, too, can an animal, a painting, a carving, a name, or a territory.

Fairly common forms used to symbolize social groups are birds, fish, and animals. One may ask why it is that animals are used to stand for people. Though the animal world exists apart from the human world, people use the animal world to talk metaphorically about the human world. The world is seen as a *jungle* or referred to as an *animal farm*. Though the world of animals and the world of people are very different, there are links between them. The world of animals is divided into species and the world of people into social groups. Some animal species are more like others and share a certain number of characteristics: there are those that fly, those that swim, and those that walk or crawl. Societies use these different characteristics to make a system of classification of animals. This classification will differ from one society to the next, because each society may single out a different series of characteristics upon which its classification is based. For example, as we have noted in Chapter 3, among the Karam of New Guinea, the cassowary, an enormous flightless bird like an ostrich, is not classed as a bird, but is in a separate class. In the same manner, human groupings may be closely related, distantly related, or complete strangers. In a society with clans, each clan is different from the others, just as the animal species differ from one another. The differences among animal species are used to express the differences among groups of people.

The animal world may be ordered in still another way. Some animals live very close to humans, even under the same roof; others live under human protection in the barn; still others live in the forest, where humans hunt them; and finally there are the exotic, inedible animals in the zoo. Edmund Leach (1964) has pointed out that this particular series of animal categories corresponds to categories of social distance in English society. Sisters make up the closest category. Next come first cousins. The third category are neighbors who are not kin, and the fourth category are complete strangers with whom one has no social relationship. The significant aspect of Leach's analysis of these corresponding categories is the connection between edibility and permissible sexual relationships. The first category of animals—pets—is equivalent to the first category of females—sisters. Pets may not be eaten, and sisters are not permissible as sex partners. Farm animals make up the second animal category, and these are eaten only if they have been castrated or have not reached physical maturity. The corresponding category of women are cousins, with whom one might have sexual relations but whom one cannot marry. The third category is made up of game animals, which are edible, and they correspond to neighbors who are very marriageable. The fourth category is composed of exotic animals, which are not edible, and, correspondingly, exotic women, who are not marriageable. Leach's analysis demonstrates that the cultural domains of animal classification and of degrees of social distance of females are organized in the same way, and at the same time the parallel between edibility and permissible sex relations becomes apparent.

Arrangements of space also make important symbolic statements about social groupings and social relationships. Among the Nootka of the Pacific coast of Canada, each of the large plank houses in the winter village represents a social group. The floor plan of the house is divided into spaces that are ranked with respect to one another (see Figure 1). The place of honor in the house is occupied by the owner, who is the highest-ranking person in the house and holds the highest title, and his family. This is the right corner of the rear of the house. The next most important man and his family occupy the left rear corner of the house; the third most important man and his family occupy the right front corner of the house; the fourth most important man and his family are in the left front corner; the least important titled man lives with his family on the right-hand side of the house. Untitled commoners and their families live in the remaining spaces along the sides of the house. Each location has its own hearth. Each nuclear family in the Nootka house is ranked with respect to the others, and this rank is symbolized by the location of each family's hearth and its living space in relation to the others. It is like a seating plan according to seniority.

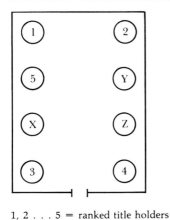

1, 2 . . . 5 = ranked title holders

x, y, and z = commoners

Figure 1
Nootka House Floor Plan.

Social space in a Nootka house symbolizes differences in rank. In a peasant village in northeastern Thailand, space in a house is divided to symbolize not rank, but rules about marriage and sex (see Figure 2). The sleeping room is the most sacred part of the house. First cousins, with whom sexual relations and marriage are not permitted, may enter that room but may not sleep there. More distant relatives, whom one may marry, are not allowed to enter the sleeping room and must remain in the guest room. S. J. Tambiah (1969), who has analyzed the Thai material, also relates categories of animals and their edibility to relatives whom you may and may not marry. First cousins, whom you cannot marry, are equivalent to your own buffalo, oxen, and pigs, who live under the house. You may not eat them and must give them to other people. More distant relatives, whom you can marry, are equivalent to other people's domestic animals, which you can eat. The same logic that connects edible and inedible animals with marriageable and unmarriageable relatives (as pointed out in English society by Leach) is also found in Thai society. Since social space symbolizes degree of social relationship, and edibility also signifies social relationships, then the meaning of social space is also related to edibility.

Another common way to symbolize social groupings and social relationships is to use the human body. Among the Teutonic tribes at the dawn of history, close and distant relatives were symbolized by close and more distant parts of the body, reckoned from the head. The father and mother were symbolized by the head; brothers and sisters were at the neck; first cousins at the shoulders; second cousins at the elbows; third cousins at the wrists; and fourth, fifth, and sixth cousins at the knuckles and finger joints.

Figure 2.   Thai House Floor Plan.

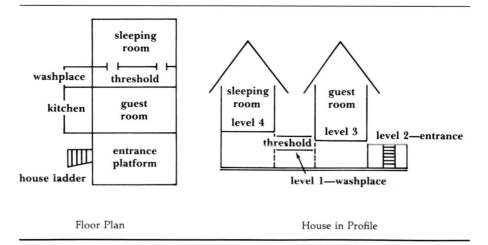

Floor Plan   House in Profile

At the cutoff point of kinsmen were seventh cousins, who were called "nail relatives."

Sometimes, instead of symbolization being based upon a view of the body as made up of articulated parts, the division of the body into right and left sides is used as a point of reference. The society of the Banaro of New Guinea consists of two halves. The two sides of the Banaro men's house, which represents this division into two parts, are referred to as "the left" and "the right." Of course, there are many other ways of symbolizing a dual division where two halves make up the whole: sun and moon, male and female, high and low, etc.

Sometimes the internal structure of the body is used as a metaphor for the internal structure of society. The word *bone* was used for *clan* among the Mongols, and the aristocracy were referred to as *White Bone* to distinguish them from commoners, who were referred to as *Black Bone*. A slightly different metaphor is used by the Riff of Morocco, who refer to their clan as a *vein*. Just as the Mongols used a skeletal metaphor, the Riff use the metaphor of blood vessels to tie together their society.

Americans use the metaphor of blood to represent kinship. In thinking about the biological facts of conception, we can see that the sperm from the father and the egg from the mother, which unite to form the new individual, have nothing to do with blood. Yet Americans say that their father's *blood* flows in their veins and so does their mother's. This is our symbolic way of talking about kinship.

Symbols, Politics, and Authority

Just as clans can be represented by a whole series of things such as totems, houses, and personal names, so too may an entire nation be represented by an array of symbols. The combat between symbolic animals—the eagle and the bear—was used by political cartoonists to portray the conflict between the United States and Russia. Our ancestral spirits, the Founding Fathers, offer philosophical opposition to Marx and Lenin, the ancestral spirits of the U.S.S.R. In the same way that the Nootka house and the Thai house symbolize those who live within it, so also do two buildings represent the United States and the U.S.S.R. The *White House* says this, and the *Kremlin* counters with that. National flags, anthems, and food also represent nations. In a recent presidential election, the candidates spent more time debating the proper relationship between citizens and their flag (whether burning the flag should be tolerated, whether the pledge of allegiance to the flag should be required) than they did discussing vital social and economic issues.

Individuals in positions of authority are associated with particular objects that become symbols of the office they hold. Sometimes the object is something the officeholder wears, such as a crown or imperial regalia or

An Ibo follower performs an act of deference before the Obi, or ruler, of Onitsha in eastern Nigeria. The Obi wears a crown and carries a staff to symbolize his office.

insignia, which the officeholder alone may put on. The installation ceremony for a successor usually involves putting on the garments or insignia of office. Sometimes the officeholder carries a staff, wand, umbrella, or fly whisk. The curved staff of the pharaoh of Egypt was the symbol of office, and so it is seen in the pictures of King Tutankhamen. The vulture and cobra on his headdress symbolized the Upper and Lower Kingdoms of Egypt. Kinds of behavior may be as symbolic of authority as objects. In the accompanying photograph, a follower kneels in deference before the Obi of Onitsha. In our definition of metonym, we pointed out how the crown or the throne could alternatively stand for the monarchy. A parallel is found in the term referring to the leader of an academic department at a college or university. He or she is referred to as either the *chair* or the *head*. These symbols of authority are metonyms. Use of the term "head" draws attention to one end of the human anatomy, while use of the term "chair" draws attention to the opposite end.

If authority is represented by a series of symbols, opposition to that authority is symbolically represented by an inversion of those symbols. In the sixties all men in authority had short hair. Young men created a symbol of opposition when they allowed their hair to grow long. If authorities have short hair, then long hair is a symbol of opposition to that authority. However, today, wearing one's hair long is acceptable. Long hair is no longer a symbol of opposition to society, but dyeing one's hair fuchsia, blue, or orange is. If the established hierarchy wears long hair, then short hair becomes a symbol of opposition. During the seventeenth century, the Cavaliers of Charles I of England wore their hair long, while those who opposed them, the Puritans led by Oliver Cromwell, wore short hair. The Puritans' hairstyle became the focal symbol of their opposition, and so they were called Roundheads (as depicted in a cartoon of the period). These examples relate to the general principle that those who oppose the established authority will select as their symbol something that is the reverse of the symbol of those in authority. Political symbols may seem trivial, but, in reality, people will die rather than deny them or give them up. People's identity as members of a group is powerfully bound up with such symbols. To deny or reject them is to deny one's identity and worth.

The Cavaliers of seventeenth-century England wore their hair long, while their Puritan opposition wore their hair short. In this cartoon of the period both men and their dogs are characterized by their respective hairstyles.

In our society, love poetry is seen solely as the expression of feeling and sentiment toward another person. However, among the Awlad 'Ali Bedouin of Egypt, love poetry, in addition to expressing personal sentiments, is a symbolic means of proclaiming opposition to authority and the social order (Abu Lughod, 1990). This authority is exercised by male elders within the family and the lineage, who make all major decisions concerning such things as resource allocation and the arrangement of marriages. Love poetry, a highly developed art, represents a challenge to that authority since any form of sexuality or desire for marriage outside of what the elders approve of is perceived as a threat to the system of family and lineage. There is an inherent contradiction in Bedouin society between the hierarchical system of lineage and family and the wider sphere of tribal politics with its ideal of autonomy and freedom. Love poetry reflects this fundamental tension. According to Abu Lughod, there is ambivalence and discomfort concerning love poetry, and yet it is also glorified since it represents a refusal to be dominated which echoes the wider tribal ideology. It is a discourse of defiance and rebellion recited by young men and women, those dominated by the hierarchical system, and yet it appeals to both the oppressed and their oppressors and is widely admired by all segments of Bedouin society.

The Symbolism of Sports

As we have noted earlier, games in a culture are often metaphors for life. Sports in American society are children's games played by adults, but they are much more than just games. They make symbolic statements about the society, which explains their enormous popularity. Individual sports, such as tennis, pool, and even chess, whether they are physical or intellectual activities, have certain aspects in common that relate them to American culture. They involve situations of head-to-head competition in which each person relies only on himself or herself to win. This is the "rugged individualism" of American society. In such one-on-one sports, it is important to establish a reputation, which is often not an accurate reflection of the individual's true abilities but rather an attempt to create the impression that one is much better or much worse than one really is. This is either to frighten an opponent or to create overconfidence in the opponent. In pool, this is referred to as one's "speed," and one never should let an opponent know one's true "speed." In many Western films, these same features of individualism and "reputation" characterize the gunfighter. These same symbols, rugged individualism and a reputation that will create fear in others, are also operative in American business, where the people at the top are perceived as having gotten there on their own by beating out their opponents in head-to-head competition.

In American team sports, such as football, individual achievement is subordinated to team effort. Here, the symbolism is different. Football is an exclusively male activity in which male bonding ties individuals together in a collective effort. In this it is similar to male initiations in other societies, in which a ritual separates men from women and binds them together into a male peer group. Like male initiation rites, in professional and college football male players are separated from women during the training period and before games. In his analysis of American football, entitled "Into the Endzone for a Touchdown," Alan Dundes examines the folk speech involved in football and observes ". . . that American football could be a ritual combat between groups of males attempting to assert their masculinity by penetrating the endzones of their rivals" (1978: 86). He likens football, as a form of symbolic homosexual behavior, to the initiation rites of aboriginal Australia, which also have a homosexual aspect. The male bonding of American football sets males, the participants, against females, the outsiders. This would also explain why the New England Patriots had strong feelings that the presence of a female reporter in their dressing room was completely inappropriate. In their eyes, she was intruding into a male ritual. The team aspect of football is also a recapitulation of the value of teamwork, pulling together for a common goal, in American society.

When a sport that originated in one culture spreads to another culture, it may take on a completely different set of symbolic meanings. With the expansion of the British Empire, cricket moved into the colonial areas that the British conquered, and today it is enthusiastically played from the Caribbean to the Indian subcontinent. During the colonial period, it personified the quintessence of British colonialism. In fact, the expression "not cricket" means not acting like a proper Englishman and refers to stretching the rules. Nowhere is it played in a more spirited fashion than in the Trobriand Islands, where it was introduced by English missionaries at the beginning of the twentieth century. Over the years, the Trobrianders transformed the English version of the game, which represented colonial domination, into a cultural creation that has a multiplicity of meanings in their own Trobriand culture. In contrast to English cricket, where all the players wear white, in Trobriand cricket the players dress in the traditional regalia for warfare, and each team may contain up to forty players. The cricket game is usually part of the competition when one village challenges another to a *kayasa,* a competitive period of feasting and exchange of yams. Magic that was used in warfare, which was outlawed by the colonial authorities, is used during the cricket game, since the game of cricket is symbolically like warfare as well as like competitive exchange. When the bowler pitches the ball, he recites the magic formula that was formerly used to make a spear hit its target. In Trobriand cricket, the home team always wins; this is not supposed to happen in Western sports. The symbolism of Trobriand cricket may be seen as more like that of competitive exchange—first *you* "win," then *I* "win"—than the way sports are played in the United States, to decide the "ultimate" winners.

Universal Symbols

It can be argued that certain symbols are found universally and carry similar meanings in all cultures. Colors are frequently associated with emotional states and sometimes with other meaningful messages as well. Some have argued that red brings about emotional arousal on the part of the viewer. In American society red means danger—don't go—and is used for stop signs in traffic control. Green is the complementary color to red and is used to symbolize the opposite of red. Since traffic lights, like all symbols, are arbitrary, the question of whether they might have originally been put forth in reversed fashion, so that red meant go and green meant stop, could be asked. Because these symbols are part of the larger category of color symbolism in our society, in which a red dress symbolizes a prostitute, the red-light district signifies a den of iniquity, and red hair means a fiery temper, it seems likely that the colors could not have been reversed. The question of whether red has the same meaning in other cultures remains to be systematically explored. In our society, black is the color of mourning; at a funeral people wear black clothing. In contrast, white, the color of Maria Shriver's wedding gown, represents purity and virginity. A bride wears white when the relationship is established and black if the relationship is terminated by the death of her husband. In China the color symbolism for death and mourning is exactly the opposite; there white is the color of death and mourning, and mourners wear white clothing. It is clear that the meanings of colors vary from one culture to another.

Other symbols have been suggested as ones that bear a universal meaning. Hair is one of these. As we noted above, long hair can be a symbol of rebellion when everyone else is wearing short hair. However, Edmund Leach (1958) has pointed out that, in a number of widely separate cultures, long hair, especially unkempt long hair, is a symbol of sexuality. Short hair symbolizes restraint, while a shaved head often indicates celibacy. Rituals that involve the cutting of hair are seen as symbolic forms of castration. The symbolism of hair is quite overt. We are not dealing here with private symbols of the type referred to earlier in the chapter, but rather with a culturally accepted and widely understood symbol. It is not a symbol whose meaning is unconscious.

In the chapters to come, we will be discussing different cultural domains such as kinship, economics, political organization, and religion, which are all imbued with symbolic meaning. In order to understand how these institutions work, one must understand the cultural meanings in terms of which they are organized.

CHAPTER 5

Family, Marriage, and Kinship

 In weaving the tapestry of culture, we start with kinship because it plays a fundamental role. In the societies anthropologists first studied, most of daily life was organized on the basis of kinship relationships. In these small-scale societies, all religious, economic, and political behavior was carried out through the structure of kinship. Though many of these societies were shaken to their roots as they were incorporated into colonial empires, and then into new nations, kinship has continued to be very significant in people's lives, whether they have remained in their rural villages or have migrated to look for work in expanding cities like Lagos, Nigeria, or Port Moresby, Papua New Guinea.

Anthropologists who in the past believed that kin relations withered in modern industrial societies have recognized that, although many of the features of kinship structure found in small-scale societies are no longer present, kinship relations in complex societies remain significant in a variety of ways.

In an earlier chapter, we described weddings and funerals in three different societies. In each case, groupings of kin play significant roles in the course of the event. The Kwakiutl have groups based on kinship that they refer to as *numayms*. How does one become a member of a *numaym*? What are one's responsibilities toward other members of the *numaym*? What are one's rights and privileges as a member of a *numaym*? What is one's relationship with people in different *numayms*? Are all of one's relatives in one's own *numaym*? In the Trobriand funeral, people participated in the various activities as members of groups based on kinship. We called these groups *clans,* but the Trobriand word for them is *dala.* The same kinds of questions posed for the Kwakiutl *numaym* can be asked about the Trobriand *dala.* How does one get to belong? What are one's responsibilities? What are one's rights? In contrast to the Kwakiutl wedding and the Trobriand funeral, we described an American wedding and a funeral. Once again we saw groupings of people based on kinship. There are the bride's side and the groom's side, immediate relatives and distant relatives. In addition, there are those who are not relatives at all, but who attend as friends, neighbors, and fellow workers. What are the differences in the ways that relatives are grouped in Kwakiutl society, in Trobriand society, and in our own society? This chapter will present concepts that anthropologists use to answer these questions.

In Chapter 2, we pointed out that a Kwakiutl wedding and a Trobriand funeral were examples of what are called total social phenomena. This means that political, economic, religious, and aesthetic aspects of the society, as well as kinship, are brought into play simultaneously. Despite the interwoven nature of all these aspects of culture in a Kwakiutl wedding or a Trobriand funeral, kinship can be disentangled from the rest for the purposes of analysis. Anthropologists use a set of concepts in order to analyze marriage, the family, and other kinship groupings.

Marriage

All known societies recognize marriage. The ritual of marriage marks a change in status for a man and a woman and the acceptance by society of the new union that is formed. Marriage, like all things cultural, is governed by rules. As the rules vary from one society to another, so does the ritual by which society recognizes and celebrates the marriage. In the American wedding, the bridegroom places a ring on the third finger, left hand, of the bride and repeats the ritual formula, "With this ring I thee wed." In the Kwakiutl wedding, the bridegroom comes as a member of a feigned war party to capture the bride and "move" her from her father's house with the payment of many blankets. These represent just two of the many ways that societies recognize and accept marriage and the formation of a new family. At both Kwakiutl and American weddings, large numbers of guests are present who represent society in serving as witnesses to the marriage. The presence of witnesses signifies that marriage is more than a private affair and that it must be recognized publicly by society.

Marriage Prohibitions

Societies also have rules that state whom one can and cannot marry. Rules about whom one cannot marry are directly related to the *incest taboo*. Like marriage, the incest taboo is found in all societies and is therefore a cultural universal. The incest taboo forbids sexual relations between certain categories of close relatives. Almost universally, forbidden categories include mother and son, father and daughter, and brother and sister. If sexual partners cannot be sought within the immediate family because of the incest taboo, then they must be sought elsewhere. The incest taboo that forbids sexual relations also necessarily forbids marriage, since marriage almost always includes sexual access. Marriage prohibitions are wider in scope than the prohibitions against sexual intercourse, since, in many societies, there are people with whom one can have sexual intercourse but whom one cannot marry. Both the incest taboo and prohibitions against marrying certain close relatives have the effect of compelling individuals to seek sexual partners and mates outside their own group. Beyond the immediate family, there is great variation from one society to another in the rules regarding which categories of relatives one is forbidden to marry. Even within the United States, there is variation between the states in the laws regarding which relatives one may not marry. Some states permit marriage between first cousins, others prohibit it, and still others prohibit marriage between second cousins.

There are a few striking examples of marriage between members of the immediate family that seem to violate the universality of the incest taboo. Among the pharaohs of ancient Egypt, such as Tutankhamen, the Boy King, and the royal lineages of Hawaii and of the Incas in Peru, brother and sister married. In each instance, the ruler had to marry someone equal in rank, and who could be better qualified than one's own brother or sister?

Endogamy and Exogamy

In anthropological terms, marriage within the group is called *endogamy*, and marriage outside the group is called *exogamy*. A rule of exogamy, like the incest taboo with respect to sexual relations, requires that members of the group seek spouses outside of their own group. A rule of exogamy is frequently conceptualized as an extension of the incest taboo in that the same native term is used for both. For example, among the Trobriand Islanders the term *suvasova* is used for the incest taboo and is also extended to forbid sexual relations and marriage with women of one's own larger kin group, or *dala*, who are called "sisters." A rule of endogamy requires individuals to marry within their own group and forbids them to marry beyond it. Religious groups such as the Amish, Mormons, Catholics, and Jews have rules of endogamy, though these are often violated by marriages outside the group. As we noted in the previous chapter, castes in India are also endogamous. Rules of endogamy preserve separateness and exclusivity, and are a means of maintaining boundaries between one group and other groups. In this sense, the brother-sister marriages that we have referred to above reach the absolute limit of endogamy in order to preserve sanctity and power within the ruling families of those societies. More typical are those cases where the immediate family is exogamous, while the larger group is endogamous.

Sister Exchange

Since a rule of exogamy demands that spouses come from outside one's group, the result is that relationships are created through marriage with other groups. If a man cannot marry his own sister, he gives his sister to someone in another group. According to the basic principle of exchange, something given, if accepted by the receiver, must be returned with its equivalent. If a man accepts another man's sister, he must therefore return his own sister as the equivalent. After all, the receiver, too, may not marry his own sister. In fact, in many societies over the world, there is a rule that requires that two men exchange sisters, and anthropologists refer to this as *sister exchange*. Recently, anthropologists who have adopted a feminist point of view have argued that this form of marriage could just as easily be conceptualized as "brother exchange." However, where men dominate the society, this is seen as sister exchange "from the native point of view." When Margaret Mead went to study the Mountain Arapesh in New Guinea, she asked them why they didn't marry their own sisters, expecting a response indicating revulsion at the very thought. Instead, Mead's informant stated, "What is the matter with you anyway? Don't you want a brother-in-law?" (Mead, 1935). This is because one hunts, gardens, and travels with one's brother-in-law among the Arapesh. Thus a marriage creates not only a link between husband and wife but also, through the wife, a link between two men who are brothers-in-law to each other.

Marriage Payments

In many societies marriage involves a transfer or exchange of property. Sometimes, payments are made by the groom and his family to the family of the bride. This payment is known as *bridewealth*. In other instances, the bride brings property with her at the marriage. This is known as *dowry*. When dowry is paid, goods move in the opposite direction from bridewealth payments. In societies that practice sister exchange, there may be an option to give bridewealth if one does not have a sister to exchange. However, it is also common to find sister exchange accompanied by the payment of bridewealth, so that groups are exchanging both women and bridewealth payments. In China both bridewealth and dowry were present. Sometimes the groom exchanges labor for his bride, in lieu of the payment of bridewealth. When the groom works for his wife's family, this is known as *bride service*. It may be recalled that in the Old Testament Jacob labored for seven years in order to marry Leah and then another seven years to marry Rachel, Leah's younger sister, thus performing fourteen years of bride service for his father-in-law.

Shell rings are presented as bridewealth at an Abelam marriage.

Bride service is also practiced by the Yanomamo. During this time, the groom lives with the bride's parents and hunts for them. Since the Yanomamo also have sister exchange, one might say that during this period of bride service, when men move to live with the bride's parents, they really are practicing brother exchange. However, among the Yanomamo, since men control women, they do not conceptualize this as two women exchanging their brothers. After the period of bride service is over, the husband takes his wife back to his group. Yanomamo women prefer to marry within the same village, and not to be exchanged to make an alliance with some distant village; that way they can remain close to their families after marriage so that their brothers can offer them a degree of protection from husbandly abuse.

Numbers of Spouses

Another set of rules concerning marriage is exemplified by the biblical case of Jacob—rules regarding number of spouses. Some societies, like our own, practice *monogamy;* that is, only one spouse at a time is permitted. However, according to the Bible, husbands could have more than one wife. This is known as *polygyny* and is still permitted in many societies in the world. Sometimes, as in the case of Jacob, a man marries several sisters.

This practice is known as *sororal polygyny.* In the societies in which it occurs, it is usually explained by saying that sisters have a good relationship with one another, and this will help to overcome the inevitable jealousy that arises between cowives. On the other hand, there are many societies, such as the Trobriand Islanders and the Kanuri of Nigeria, who explicitly forbid sororal polygyny. The Kanuri explanation for this prohibition is that the good relationship between two sisters should not be allowed to be undermined by the unavoidable friction that arises between two cowives. This simply demonstrates that whatever rules a society has, the people of that society will offer a perfectly rational explanation for their existence. An alternative form of marriage, known as *polyandry,* in which one woman may have several husbands, occurs but is rather rare. In almost all cases, a woman marries several brothers, and this is known as *fraternal polyandry.* Sometimes, anthropologists wish to refer to plural spouses, either husbands or wives. In that case, they use the term *polygamy,* in contrast to the term *monogamy.* Because of the frequency of divorce and subsequent remarriage in the United States, it is sometimes said that American society practices *serial polygamy.* We may not have more than one spouse at a time, but some people have numerous spouses, one after the other.

Levirate and Sororate

The exchange of a woman for another woman or the exchange of a woman for bridewealth is an indication that more than the bride and groom are involved in a marriage. Marriage is even more significantly the concern of the kin groups of the marrying couple. A further demonstration of this is found in the customs of the *levirate* and the *sororate.* Under the levirate, if a man dies, his widow then marries one of his brothers. The brother of the dead man steps into the deceased's place, thereby continuing the relationship between the two kin groups established by the first marriage. In the levirate, a woman marries one brother after the death of another brother; in fraternal polyandry she can be married to two brothers simultaneously. The levirate illustrates what the British anthropologist Radcliffe-Brown has referred to as the equivalence of siblings (1952), where one brother can be substituted for another in certain societies. When a deceased wife is replaced in the marriage by her sister, usually an unmarried younger sister, this is known as the sororate. It is like sororal polygyny, but in the sororate a man marries two sisters, the second after the death of the first.

Dissolution of Marriage

Stability of marriage varies from one society to another. Almost all societies provide a means for the dissolution of a marriage; however, this may be very difficult in some. Divorce is invariably more difficult after children have been born to the couple. Where bridewealth has been paid, it would have to be returned if the wife has left the husband. This may be difficult to achieve if the bridewealth, paid several years before, has been spent, dispersed, or consumed. Some anthropologists have argued that the higher the bridewealth payment, the more stable the marriage, since divorce would require the return of bridewealth which is so difficult in such societies. Others have said that stability of marriage is related not to the amount of bridewealth, but to the degree of incorporation of a wife into her husband's family or kin group. Among the Manchus of Manchuria, who conquered China in the seventeenth century, the wife goes through a "fire ceremony" in front of the hearth in her husband's house, and this ritual serves to conceptually incorporate her permanently into his kin group. In contrast, the Kwakiutl pay bridewealth to the bride's family. At a subsequent ceremony, the bride's family pays a large amount of goods to "repurchase" her, as we noted in Chapter 2, thereby reiterating her membership in the kin group of her birth. The husband must make a new bridewealth payment if he wishes her to continue to be his wife. The bridewealth and repurchase payments of the Kwakiutl, which are integral parts of Kwakiutl marriage, symbolize how two people may be joined together in marriage and yet retain an identity in their own kin groups.

Postmarital Residence

Societies have rules concerning where the new couple should live after marriage. In the North American wedding that we have described, the newly married couple set up their own household. In the case of a couple with two careers in two different cities, two households may be created, though it would appear that the primary residence of the Schwartz-eneggers, whose marriage was described in Chapter 2, is in their Pacific Palisades home. The postmarital residence rule in American society is that the new couple form an independent household. This is referred to as *neolocal residence* (see Figure 1). It is clear that this is a rule in American society, since breaching it brings sanctions. If the newly married couple move in to live for an extended period with the family of either the husband or the wife, this is typically explained in terms of economic hardship or the couple's student status. Gossips will make snide comments about the lack of independence of the couple, since they continue to live as though they were children, and gossip is a strong sanction. If the newly married couple move in with the husband's parents, comments are made about two women in the same kitchen and the "mother-in-law problem"; if they move in with the wife's parents, the result is inevitable difficulties between father-in-law and son-in-law. Americans believe that a couple should not get married unless they are mature, economically independent, and able to set up their own neolocal household. Neolocal residence is found in a number of societies other than our own.

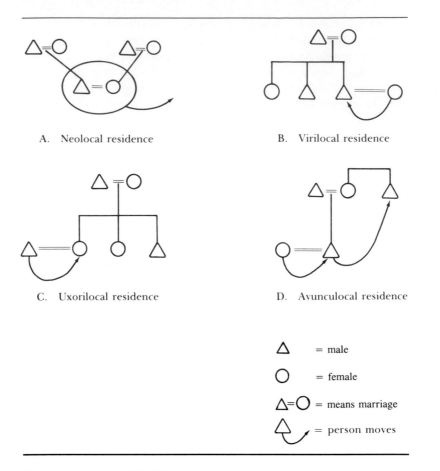

Figure 1.   Rules of Residence.

Probably the most common form of postmarital residence is the situation in which the newly married couple go to live in the household of the groom's parents. This is known as *virilocal residence* (also referred to as *patrilocal residence*). With a rule of virilocal residence for the new couple, the wife is incorporated, to a greater or lesser extent, into the household of her husband's kinsmen, since it is she (the bride) who must leave the family into which she was born and raised. The groom merely stays put.

Less frequent is the case in which the newly married couple go to live in the household of the bride's parents. This is called *uxorilocal residence* (also referred to as *matrilocal residence*). In this instance it is the husband who must be incorporated into his wife's family. In the past, in some Pueblo societies of Arizona and New Mexico which had a rule of uxorilocal residence, the degree of incorporation of the husband into his wife's family was so slight that the wife could divorce him simply by leaving his belongings on the doorstep. When a groom performs bride service for his wife's father, as Jacob did for Laban in the Bible, he lives uxorilocally for the period of the bride service (see page 76). Then, like Jacob, he usually returns with his wife to live virilocally, with his own family.

Still another rule of postmarital residence is the arrangement in which, after marriage, the wife joins her new husband, who is living with his mother's brother rather than his own father. This is called *avunculocal residence*. This rule of residence involves two separate and distinct moves. The earlier move occurs when a man, as an adolescent, leaves his father's house to go to live with his mother's brother, from whom he will inherit later in life. After the marriage, the wife moves to join her husband at his maternal uncle's house. The Trobriand Islanders have an avunculocal rule of postmarital residence.

Sometimes a society will have a rule of residence stating that after marriage, the couple can live either with the bride's family or with the groom's family. Unlike our own society, they cannot establish an independent household. This is called *bilocal residence*. On Dobu, an island near the Trobriands, the married couple spend one year in the bride's village and the following year move to the groom's village, alternating in this manner between the two villages every year. Among the Iban of Borneo, however, a choice must be made at some point after marriage between one side and the other, and this choice becomes permanent.

Lastly, there is a postmarital residence rule in which husband and wife live with their respective kinsmen, apart from one another. This is known as *duolocal residence*. The Ashanti of Ghana, who traditionally lived in large towns, have this form of postmarital residence. Husbands and wives live in the same town, but not in the same household. At dusk, one can see young children carrying the evening meal from their mother's house to their father's house for their father to eat.

Family Types

These rules stating where a couple should live after marriage result in different types of family structures. With neolocal postmarital residence, as exists in American society, the family that is formed is the *nuclear family* (see Figure 2). It consists of the husband, the wife, and children until they marry, at which point those children will establish their own nuclear families. The nuclear family is an independent household that operates autonomously in economic affairs, in the rearing of children, and in other phases of life.

What happens when there are plural spouses, as in societies that practice polygyny or polyandry? Among the Kanuri, who practice polygyny and are typical of a number of African societies in this respect, each wife must have her own house and hearth. The husband must visit each wife in

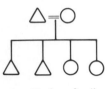

A.   Nuclear family

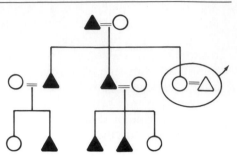

B.   Virilocal extended family

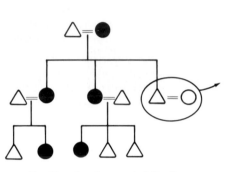

C.   Uxorilocal extended family

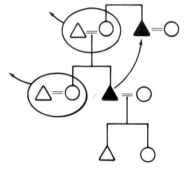

D.   Avunculocal extended family

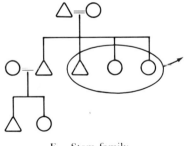

E.   Stem family

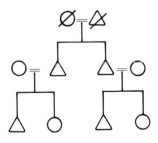

F.   Joint family

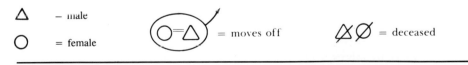

Figure 2.   Family Types.

Members of a large Kikuyu extended family in Kenya all live together as a single household.

turn, at which time she cooks for him and he must stay the night with her. Though he may favor one wife over another, he must treat them equally. A man's house and those of his wives form a single compound or household. In polyandrous societies, like Tibet, a woman and her several husbands, usually brothers, live in the same house.

When several nuclear families live together in the same household, they form an *extended family*. When there is a rule of virilocal residence, the household consists of an older married couple, their married sons and wives, and the unmarried children of both the older couple and their married sons. These all form one extended family. Their married daughters will have left that household to join the households of their husbands. The center of this type of extended family is a core of related men. Their in-marrying wives come from many different places and are not related to each other.

Uxorilocal postmarital residence results in extended families of a very different sort. In this case, a core of related women remains together, and their husbands marry into the extended family. With avunculocal residence there is once again a core of men forming the basis of the extended family, but this core of men is linked through women. Avunculocal residence occurs when a young man moves to his mother's brother's house during adolescence.

Extended families vary in the composition of the core of the family, as discussed above. They also vary in their extent. Some extended families consist only of parents and one married son and his family. Such a family is known as a *stem family* and occurs in parts of rural Ireland. Since the amount of land inherited is small and cannot be profitably subdivided, only one son, typically the youngest one, inherits the land, while his older brothers go off to the cities, become priests, or emigrate to Boston or Hong Kong. Another type of extended family is the *joint family*. This type of family includes brothers and their wives and children who stay together as a single family after the parents have died.

Descent Groups

The kinds of family groups that we have just described are based upon both kinship and common residence. In many societies, there are groups based upon shared kinship or descent where the members need not live in the same place. These groups are usually called *clans* by the anthropologist. Members of a clan believe they are descended from a common ancestor who lived many generations ago. We have previously discussed exogamy, that is, the rule that one must marry outside of one's group. In most societies that have clans, though certainly not in all, clans are exogamous, and one must marry outside of one's own clan. This means that one's mother and one's father come from different clans. A child cannot be a member of both the mother's clan and the father's clan (see Figure 3). Going back two generations, that child has four grandparents, each of them likely to come from four different clans, and eight great-grandparents from as many as eight different clans. Just as the child could only be a member of the clan of one parent, that child's father could only be a member of one of his parents' clans.

Patrilineal Descent and Matrilineal Descent

Societies have rules that state that the child belongs either to the mother's clan or to the father's clan. A rule that states that a child belongs to his or her father's clan is called a *patrilineal rule of descent*. This means that children belong to their father's clan, the father belongs to his father's clan, and so forth, as illustrated in the diagram (see Figure 3). A daughter belongs to her father's clan, but her children do not. Children share common clanship with only one of their four grandparents; however, the other three grandparents are still their relatives and kinsmen. As one goes back through the generations, ties of kin relationships form a web of kinship. A rule of descent carves out of this web of kinship a much smaller segment, which comprises the members of one's own clan. Clans continue to exist

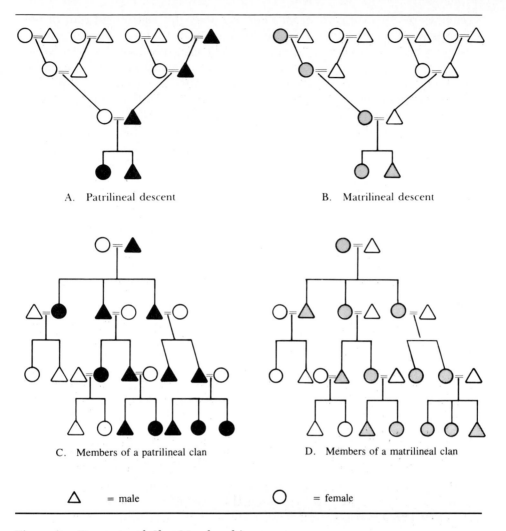

A. Patrilineal descent

B. Matrilineal descent

C. Members of a patrilineal clan

D. Members of a matrilineal clan

△ = male   ◯ = female

Figure 3.   Descent and Clan Membership.

through time, beyond the lifespan of individual members, as new generations continue to be born into the clan.

A *matrilineal rule of descent* states that a child belongs to the clan of his or
her mother and not that of the father. The Trobriand Islanders have such a
rule of descent. Among the Trobrianders, as in all matrilineal societies, the
continuity of the clan is not through a man's own children, but through
those of his sister.

In societies where either matrilineal or patrilineal clans are present, they
have certain functions; that is, they carry out certain activities. Some of the

activities of clans concern rituals. For example, the matrilineal clan of the Trobrianders serves as host at the ceremonial distribution *(sagali)* accompanying a funeral when a member of their clan dies (see the description in Chapter 2). Ritual objects and spells are owned by clans. Clans also have political functions and may compete with one another for power, and even fight with one another. Each clan has some kind of, almost always male, leadership to organize these political activities. The chief (the leader) of a Trobriand clan directs the accumulation of large amounts of food to be given away at a Trobriand *sagali.* Finally, what has frequently been seen as the most important function of the clan is its ownership of land. Members of a clan have the right to use its land by virtue of the fact that they are born into the clan. Clan members may work together at tasks, such as building a communal house or canoe, that benefit the clan as a whole. The common ancestor from whom all the members of a clan believe that they are descended is sometimes conceived of as an ancestral or clan spirit. This ancestral spirit may be thought of as having a non-human form, perhaps that of an animal. In that case all members of the clan are thought of as having a special relationship to that animal, and they may be forbidden to eat it. Such an animal is called the *clan totem,* and as we have noted in Chapter 4, it is a symbol that represents the clan and may be graphically represented as depicted in the totem pole on page 63.

The clan is frequently referred to by anthropologists as a *corporate descent group,* because it has many of the characteristics of a modern corporation. Like a corporation, it has an existence independent of its individual members. Old clan members die and new ones are born, while the clan continues to operate through time. The corporation owns property, and so does the clan. However, anybody can buy stock in a corporation and become an "owner," but membership in a clan is restricted to certain kinds of kinsmen, as defined by the rule of descent.

In the previous chapter we noted the way in which elements of the human body can be used metaphorically to discuss kinship. They can also be used to contrast relationships through the mother and relationships through the father. The way in which the contrast is symbolized differs in patrilineal and matrilineal societies. In many patrilineal societies, the connection between the child and the mother is seen in terms of mother's milk and menstrual blood. In these societies, milk or blood symbolizes the maternal relationship. Connection to the father is seen in terms of semen or bone. The Arapesh of New Guinea believe that a child is created through the semen contributed by the father and the blood of the mother. The Arapesh are patrilineal; the child belongs to the father's clan. The child is seen as linked to the mother's clan through the blood she provided. The mother's clan continues to "own" the blood, and whenever the child's blood is shed through injury or cutting initiation scars, the child's mother's clan must be paid.

Since the Trobrianders are a matrilineal people, one would expect them to conceive of their kinship system in a different way than the Arapesh do. Among the Trobrianders, children belong to the clan of their mother, sharing common substance with their mother and other clan mates. The father is considered an affine, a relative by marriage only. When a child is conceived in the mother's womb, the Trobrianders believe that an ancestral spirit from the mother's clan has entered her womb. The creation of the child is not seen as the result of the merging of substance from mother and father, and therefore sexual intercourse is not seen as having anything to do with the conception of a child. The father, by repeated acts of intercourse, not only makes the child grow but molds the child so that the child resembles him in appearance. The child is like a piece of clay pressed between two palms that takes on the shape of the hands that mold it. But this has nothing to do with the conception of the child in the first place, which is all the doing of the maternal ancestral spirit of the mother's clan. The child cannot be claimed by the father's clan, which had nothing to do with its creation. Though the Trobriand father is a very important relative, he is still an affine, as are all the members of his maternal clan.

Cognatic Descent

Up to now, we have discussed clans based upon either a patrilineal or a matrilineal rule of descent. Anthropologists refer to these as *unilineal descent groups.* There are also societies that have groups based upon descent from a common ancestor, where individuals belong to the group because either their father or their mother was a member of that group. This is called a *cognatic rule of descent.* Individuals have the choice of belonging to either their father's or their mother's group, or they may have rights in both of these groups, though there is usually active membership in only one since a person can live in only one place at a time. Individuals may even have rights in all four kin groups of their grandparents. The type of kin group created by a cognatic rule of descent is based upon descent from a common ancestor, though the links through which individuals trace their descent are through either males or females. The kin group that the Kwakiutl refer to as a *numaym* is a cognatic descent group. A Kwakiutl boy can claim membership in both his mother's and his father's group. He usually becomes a member of the *numaym* of the parent of higher rank, from whom he hopes to inherit the highest titles and the most property. In addition, he inherits rights in the *numaym* of the other parent.

Cognatic descent groups have the same functions as unilineal descent groups (patrilineal and matrilineal clans). For example, the Kwakiutl *numaym* owns houses, fishing sites, berry-picking grounds, and hunting territories. The chiefs of a *numaym* act as political leaders in potlatching and in warfare. The *numaym* acts as a unit on ceremonial occasions, such as the marriage and repurchase of the bride, described in Chapter 2. Kwakiutl

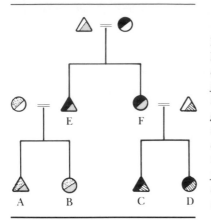

Figure 4
Double Descent. *A and B are brother and sister and belong to the same two descent groups, gray from their father and stippled from their mother. Similarly, C and D belong to the same two descent groups, striped from their father and black from their mother. E and F are also brother and sister and share the two descent groups that they get from their two parents, gray from their father and black from their mother. But their respective children, A and B, and C and D, do not have any descent groups in common.*

myths describe how the supernatural ancestors of present-day *numayms* acquired magical powers that were transmitted down the generations to their descendants.

Double Descent

In some societies in the world, each person belongs to two descent groups, one patrilineal, where descent is traced through the father and father's father, and the other matrilineal, where descent is traced through the mother and mother's mother. Anthropologists call this *double descent* (see Figure 4). The two groups to which an individual belongs do not conflict with one another, since each group has its own distinct functions. For example, the Yako of southeast Nigeria had patrilineal clans called *yepun*, which owned land in common and possessed a single shrine and an assembly house and whose men and their families resided together and farmed together. At the same time, each Yako individual also belonged to the matrilineal clan, or *lejima*, of his or her mother. The matrilineal clans carried out ritual and religious activities, such as funerals and periodic rites during the year aimed at maintaining fertility and harmony. While land is inherited patrilineally, movable wealth, such as valuables and household goods, are inherited through the matrilineal line. Thus, the two types of kin groups, patrilineal and matrilineal, serve different functions.

The Structure of Descent Groups

Though patrilineal clans, matrilineal clans, and cognatic descent groups have the same kinds of functions, they are structured very differently. Because of the rule of descent, the structure of the patrilineal clan is that of men linked through their fathers, along with their sisters who marry out. The patrilineal clan is almost always associated with virilocal postmarital residence. Sisters who marry out and wives who marry in are incorporated in varying degrees into the patrilineal clans of their husbands. In the discussion of marriage and the family in the earlier part of this chapter, we pointed out the degree of variation of the incorporation of the wife into her husband's clan. Matrilineal clans are composed of women related through their mothers and the brothers of these women. The brothers remain members of the clan into which they were born throughout their entire lives. Though they marry out, in matrilineal societies, men are never incorporated into the clans of their wives. Matrilineal clans are usually associated with avunculocal or uxorilocal postmarital residence. With a rule of cognatic descent, both men and women have potential membership in several cognatic descent groups, since they can trace multiple lines of descent. In this situation, husbands and wives, regardless of where they reside, are never incorporated into the descent groups of their spouses, and this is the case among the Kwakiutl.

The way in which political leadership operates also reveals differences in how descent groups are structured. The political functions of descent groups are carried out under the direction of leaders. In patrilineal societies, inherited leadership is usually structured in the following manner: it passes from father to son and from brother to brother (see Figure 5). Leadership in matrilineal societies is handed down from mother's brother to sister's son or from brother to brother. In a matrilineal society, a son can never directly inherit a position of leadership from his father. In such societies, though the line of descent goes through women, the women themselves are rarely the heads of their clans. One may contrast the nature of the relationship of a man to his father and to his mother's brother in patrilineal and in matrilineal societies. In patrilineal societies, a son will replace

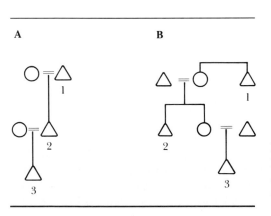

Figure 5
Passage of Political Leadership.
In a patrilineal society (A), and in a matrilineal society (B).

his father in the position of leadership and is perceived as a competitor and antagonist of his father. His mother's brother, who is not in his clan, is a source of support. In contrast, in matrilineal societies, a sister's son will succeed to the position of leadership held by his mother's brother. The relationship between these two parallels that of the father-son relationship in a patrilineal society, while that between father and son in a matrilineal society has all the elements of antagonism and potential conflict between them removed. In societies with cognatic descent groups, a man can succeed to political leadership through his mother or through his father, and thus he can be the heir of his father or of his mother's brother. The contrast between the father-son relationship and the mother's brother–sister's son relationship is therefore of no importance in societies with cognatic descent. An important structural feature of cognatic societies is that brothers are not equivalent. The optional nature of the descent rule permits the possibility that brothers may be in different descent groups. Among the Kwakiutl, it frequently happens that two brothers are in different *numayms,* which can even fight each other. In patrilineal and in matrilineal societies this can never happen, since two brothers are always in the same clan.

Clans and Lineages

Clans come in many shapes and forms. In some societies, one belongs to a clan simply because one's father or one's mother belonged to that clan. Other people belong to your clan, but you may not be able to trace a kin relationship to them. Nevertheless, they are fellow clansmen. Anthropologists say that descent is *stipulated* in such a clan system. Where stipulated descent is found, lengthy genealogies are not kept and people usually remember only back to their grandfathers. Where long genealogies are kept, written or oral, each member of a clan can trace his or her kinship back to the founding ancestor of the clan and by this means to every other member of the clan. Anthropologists call this *demonstrated* descent. In societies where clans include large numbers of people living dispersed over a wide area, each clan may in turn be divided into smaller units. These are referred to as *subclans.*

Anthropologists refer to unilineal descent groups where descent is demonstrated as *lineages.* Sometimes all the people in the society believe themselves to be descended from a single ancestor. This founding ancestor may be historical or mythical, or a little of both. The kin groups of various sizes are related to one another in an extensive genealogy.

The Bedouin Arabs of Cyrenaica in eastern Libya, studied by Emrys Peters, provide us with an example of such a society. They are nomadic pastoralists who keep herds of camels and sheep in the desert areas of their territory and cows and goats in the wooded plateau areas. All the Cyrenaican Bedouin alive today consider themselves to be descended from the single ancestor Sa'ada heading the genealogy (see Figure 6).

Sa'ada was the mother of the two sons who are said to be the founding ancestors of the two largest groups of tribes—Baraghith and 'Aqqara. The genealogy in the diagram provides a set of ideas that the Cyrenaican Bedouin use to talk about how they are related to one another and how their group is related to all other groups. The genealogy is like a branching

Figure 6.   Genealogy of the Cyrenaican Bedouin.   *Diagram illustrating a segmentary lineage system.*

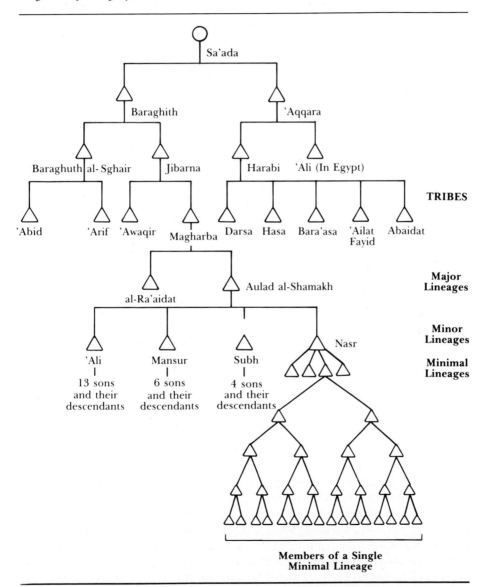

tree, extending out to its many twigs. Several twigs, or lineages, are part of a branch, and several branches, or groupings of lineages, are part of a larger limb. The larger limb represents a still larger grouping of lineages. This kind of descent system is called a *segmentary lineage system*. It is found in societies with patrilineal descent such as the Cyrenaican Bedouin. The constant branching out represents levels of segmentation. The branching out of the genealogy has a close relationship to the occupation of geographical areas. The two groups of tribes, descended from each of the sons of Sa'ada, occupy the eastern and western halves of Cyrenaica. Lineages descended from brothers a few generations back graze their herds on lands adjacent to one another. Lineages that are further away genealogically occupy lands farther apart. In political action, lineages closely related to one another unite to oppose a threat from a more distantly related lineage. This will be discussed more fully in the section on political organization in Chapter 6.

Moieties

Another kind of grouping based on descent is one in which the entire society is divided into two halves, which are referred to as *moieties*. Moieties may be based upon a patrilineal or a matrilineal rule of descent. Sometimes in societies with moieties a village site is divided in half, each half being occupied by the members of one moiety. Among the Tlingit of the Pacific coast of northern Canada and Alaska, the two moieties are known as Raven and Wolf and are based on matrilineal descent. The Abelam of the Sepik River area of New Guinea have patrilineal moieties referred to simply as "us" and "them."

Kindreds

The descent groups that we have examined above are all based on a rule of descent from a single common ancestor and are said to be *ancestor-oriented*. *Kindreds*, on the other hand, are reckoned in an entirely different way. Earlier, we described kinship as a web. Like a spider's web, it extends out from the center. Each person is at the center of his or her web of kinship. Anthropologists refer to the individual at the center as the *ego*, and the relatives who make up that web of kinship constitute the kindred. The kindred includes relatives on both ego's mother's and father's side. Individuals who are descendants of ego, as well as ego's ancestors and everyone descended from those ancestors, are included in ego's kindred. The kindred is *ego-oriented*. The kindred as a unit does not own land or any other property; it only has coherence as a group around the ego at its center (see Figure 7). Societies with kindreds but without unilineal descent groups are known as *bilateral societies*. American society is an example of such a society. In Chapter 2, we described an American wedding. On such an occasion, the kindreds of the bride and groom attend. If any of the first

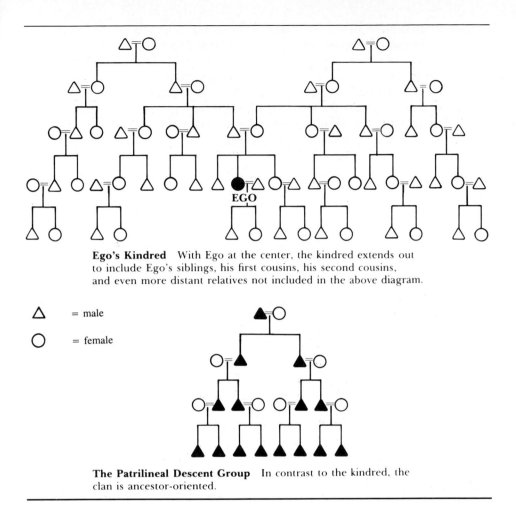

Ego's Kindred   With Ego at the center, the kindred extends out to include Ego's siblings, his first cousins, his second cousins, and even more distant relatives not included in the above diagram.

△   = male

○   = female

The Patrilineal Descent Group   In contrast to the kindred, the clan is ancestor-oriented.

Figure 7.   The Kindred.

cousins of the groom, for instance, his father's brother's son, get married, a different set of relatives will be present, though there will be an overlap with ego's kindred. This overlap occurs since the two egos share a certain set of relatives. Kindreds do not have continuity through generations in the manner of kin groups based on a rule of descent.

Relations between Groups through Marriage

We introduced our discussion of marriage by talking about exogamy, which compelled groups to give their women to someone else, receiving the women of the other group in return. This was called sister exchange.

Arapesh men state that they marry their sisters outside of the group in order to obtain brothers-in-law. In general, marriages not only create links between brothers-in-law but also serve to link their respective kin groups. Groups that give women to and receive women from one another also exchange goods and services such as bridewealth, bride service, and other kinds of services at rites of passage after children are born from the marriage. These links between kin groups established by marriage are called *affinal links*. During warfare, kin groups frequently use these affinal ties and turn to their in-laws for assistance. For this reason, marriage is the basis for what is referred to as *alliance*. Although affines may be in opposition to one another and may even fight one another, the concept of alliance is nevertheless used by anthropologists to refer to linkages between kin groups established by marriage.

In our society, marriage is based upon the decision by the bride and groom to get married. Parents and other individuals are rarely involved in this decision. However, in other societies there are rules stating that one should marry a certain category of relative. These rules have the effect of continuing alliance over time between the groups. When groups continue to exchange sisters over generations, then women of one's own group are always marrying into the group from which wives come. This marriage pattern is referred to as a system of *restricted exchange* (see Figure 8). In such

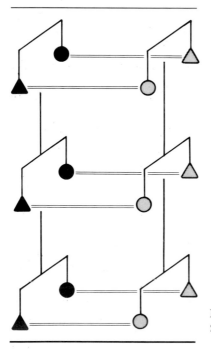

Figure 8
Sister Exchange or Restricted Exchange.

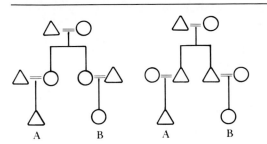
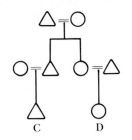

Parallel Cousins   A and B are parallel cousins to each other. They are the children of two sisters or of two brothers.

Cross Cousins   C and D are cross cousins to each other. They are the children of a brother and a sister.

Figure 9.   Types of Cousins.

a system, the prospective husband and the prospective wife will already be related to one another. Since their parents are brother and sister, they will be first cousins. Anthropologists refer to two kinds of cousins: *parallel cousins,* who are the children of the mother's sister or father's brother, and *cross cousins,* who are the children of the mother's brother or father's sister (see Figure 9). When restricted exchange takes place, parallel cousins, who are members of one's own group, are frequently referred to as siblings. Therefore they can't be married. Cross cousins are never in one's own group, but rather are members of the other group with which one has been intermarrying. These cross cousins are known as *bilateral cross cousins,* since they are simultaneously mother's brother's children and father's sister's children. Sister exchange continued over the generations has the same effect as marrying one's bilateral cross cousin. The Yanomamo of southern Venezuela have such a marriage system of restricted exchange. Every Yanomamo man must marry a woman whom he calls by the kinship term for female cross cousin (the Yanomamo term is *suaboya*), and this term is also the term for "wife." Among the Yanomamo, the terms for female cross cousin and wife are identical, as are those for husband and male cross cousin.

There are societies where the two kinds of cross cousins, mother's brother's children and father's sister's children, are referred to by different terms. Either cross cousin is not equally marriageable, as is the case for the Yanomamo. Some societies have a rule that a man may marry the daughter of his mother's brother, but he may not marry the daughter of his father's sister. Ideally, if every man married his mother's brother's daugh-

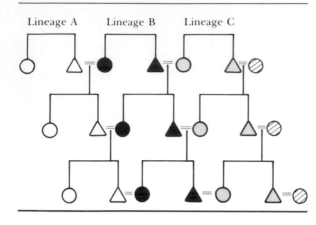

Figure 10
Mother's Brother's
Daughter Marriage, or
Generalized Exchange.

ter, in every generation, the result would be a picture like that in Figure 10. In Figure 10, the groups labeled A, B, and C linked by the marriages are patrilineages. This marriage rule occurs much more frequently in societies with a patrilineal rule of descent, though it also occurs in societies with matrilineal descent. If a man does not have a real mother's brother's daughter to marry, he may marry a classificatory mother's brother's daughter. A classificatory mother's brother's daughter is a woman whom a man calls by the same kinship term as his real mother's brother's daughter, and she is a member of the mother's brother's daughter's patrilineage. As one can see from the figure, lineage B gives its sisters to lineage A, and lineage C gives its sisters to lineage B, in every generation. From the perspective of lineage B, lineage A is always *wife-taker* and lineage C is always *wife-giver*. This system is very different from sister exchange in that you never return a woman to the lineage that gave you a woman. Since wife-giving lineage and wife-taking lineage are always different, a minimum of three groups is required. If there are three groups, then they can marry in a circle, with lineage A giving its women to lineage C. However, it is usually the case that more than three groups are tied together in this kind of marriage alliance. If the royal family of Great Britain gave its daughters in marriage to the royal family of Denmark in every generation, and the royal family of Denmark gave its daughters in marriage to the royal family of Sweden in every generation, and the royal family of Sweden gave its daughters in marriage back to the royal family of Great Britain in every generation, all intermarrying in a circle, then they would have this kind of marriage system. The Kachin of Burma, whose political organization we will discuss in Chapter 8, actually do have this kind of marriage system. It produces a structure of alliance between groups that anthropologists refer to as *generalized exchange*.

In some societies we have the opposite form of the preferential rule of marriage with mother's brother's daughter. In those societies, a man cannot marry his mother's brother's daughter but can marry his father's sister's daughter. If every man married in this fashion, the result would be what is pictured in Figure 11. In the figure, groups A, B, C, and D are matrilineal subclans. This kind of marriage rule always occurs in societies with matrilineal descent. A man marries either his real or his classificatory father's sister's daughter. This marriage rule produces what is, in fact, *delayed exchange*. In the first generation, subclan D gives a woman to C, C gives to B, B gives to A, and A gives to D (if the subclans are marrying in a circle). In the next generation, the flow of women is reversed. Now sub-clan D gives to A, A gives to B, B gives to C, and C gives to D. In the third generation, the flow is reversed once again. Every generation, women move in the opposite direction than they did in the previous generation. This resembles sister exchange in that a woman is returned to the group that originally gave a woman, but the return is made a generation later. Because the return is delayed one generation, there must be more than two groups operating in the system. A minimum of four groups is required. The Trobrianders are an example of a society with a rule for marriage with father's sister's daughter and have this form of delayed exchange.

Each of these two marriage rules produces a different structure of alliances between groups, and both are different from the kind of alliance produced by bilateral cross-cousin marriage. Marrying one's cross cousins, either mother's brother's daughter or father's sister's daughter, begins with a rule of exogamy stating that one must take a wife from outside one's group. By specifying which relatives one should marry, different patterns

Figure 11. Father's Sister's Daughter Marriage, or Delayed Exchange.

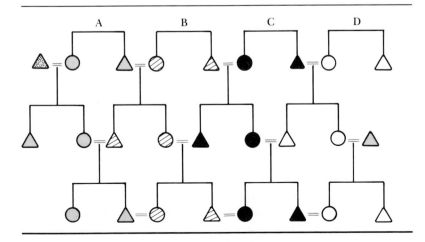

of alliance between groups are created. Figures 8, 10, and 11 represent models of these different patterns to which particular societies conform to a greater or lesser extent.

Some societies, particularly in the Middle East, have a preferential marriage rule that is structurally opposite to this rule of exogamy. The rule states that a man should marry his parallel cousin, in this case his father's brother's daughter. Since the societies of this area, like the Bedouin of Cyrenaica discussed above, are all patrilineal in descent, this marriage rule results in endogamous marriages. The Riff of Morocco, who have this marriage rule, say that they prefer to hold onto their daughters and marry them within their own group to avoid becoming entangled in alliances with other groups.

When one views marriage as an alliance, marriages may be contracted in which the procreative and sexual functions are not relevant. The Lovedu, a Bantu-speaking people of southern Africa, had a queen to whom women were given in marriage. The purpose of such marriages was to create political alliances, and sexual intercourse and procreation did not occur. Among the Kwakiutl, where privileges are transferred as a result of marriage, one man may "marry" the foot of another, become son-in-law to the man whose foot he married, and obtain privileges through this fictive marriage.

Kinship Terminology

Each society in the world has a set of words used to refer to relatives. This set of words or terms is called *kinship terminology.* Of course, the terms differ in every society since all their languages are different. However, anthropologists have been able to sort the terms into a few basic types. Americans accept their own kin terminology as being the natural way of classifying relatives. In our society, you refer to your father's brother and your mother's brother as *uncle. Uncle* is also used to refer to your mother's sister's husband and father's sister's husband. Though the term *uncle* is used for these four relatives, two of them are blood relatives on different sides of the family, while two are relatives by marriage. Each of these four is related to you in a different way, but our kinship terminology ignores these differences and groups them together under one term. Anthropologists diagram kinship terminologies such as our own in the method depicted in Figure 12.

The Yanomamo of Venezuela have a very different way of sorting their relatives. They use the same term for both father's brother and mother's sister's husband, while they use a different term for mother's brother and father's sister's husband. The Yanomamo kinship terminology is pictured in Figure 13.

You can see that the two societies sort the terms for kin in different ways. For the parental generation both the Yanomamo and Americans have four terms. The Americans use *father, mother, aunt,* and *uncle;* the Yanomamo use *haya, naya, yaya,* and *shoaiya.* However, in the Yanomamo

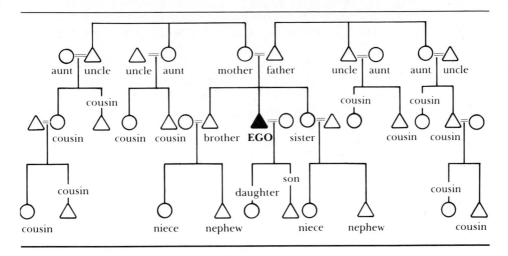

Figure 12. American Kinship Terminology.

system, father's brother and mother's brother have different terms, where-as in our society the same term is used for both. Conversely, the Yanomamo class father and father's brother together, while we use different terms. In your own generation, we have a single term, *cousin,* for all the children of uncles and aunts. This term is unusual in that it is used for

Figure 13. Yanomamo Kinship Terminology.

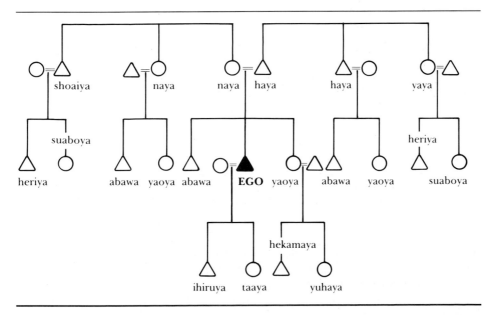

males and females. The Yanomamo are also consistent in their usage. The children of all relatives called by the same term as father and mother are referred to by the term for brother and sister. This means that parallel cousins are grouped with siblings. In contrast, the children of *shoaiya*, that is, one's cross cousins, are referred to by terms different from brother and sister, *suaboya* and *heriya*. Which is more complicated? Neither. Which is more natural? Neither. Each of these kinship terminologies is different because it is related to a different type of social structure. The terms in a kinship terminological system group together some relatives and set apart other relatives in a way that reflects the groupings of these relatives according to the rules of residence, marriage, and descent.

As a result of analysis, anthropologists have recognized that kinship terminologies over the world fall into a limited number of types. The American and Yanomamo kinship terminologies conform to two of these basic types. Strange as it may seem, American kinship terminology is classified as *Eskimo* since it is identical to that of the Eskimos, not in words for the terms, but in the pattern of organization. Its major characteristics are that it distinguishes between the generations and it distinguishes *lineal* relatives from *collateral* relatives (see Figure 14). Lineal relatives are those in the direct line of descent, that is, grandfather, father, son, grandson, grandmother, mother, daughter, granddaughter. The rest of the relatives are referred to as collateral and can be distinguished in terms of *degree of collaterality*, meaning that second cousins are more remote than first cousins. The Eskimo type of terminology emphasizes individual nuclear families, and it is found in societies that have neolocal rules of residence, kindreds, bilateral descent, and the absence of descent groups. Though Eskimo, or Inuit (as they now prefer to be called), society and our own differed in degree of complexity, subsistence pattern, and environmental setting, the pattern of organization of kinship terms is the same.

The kinship terminology of the Yanomamo is classified as *Iroquois*. The Iroquois type of terminology distinguishes between father's side and mother's side. However, the difference between lineal and collateral relatives is ignored; father and father's brother are classed together, as are mother and mother's sister. Generational differences are always recognized, as in Eskimo terminology. The social structure with which this terminology is usually associated is one in which one's own kin group is distinct from the kin group from which one's mother came. The group from which one's mother came is the same group into which one's father's sister marries. In other words, the Iroquois terminology goes with sister exchange, which is the type of marriage pattern the Yanomamo have. This is why, in Yanomamo, the term for father's sister's husband is the same as that for mother's brother, and the term for mother's sister's husband is the same as that for father's brother. Female cross cousin is classed with wife and male cross cousin with brother-in-law. In every generation, "sisters" are exchanged between the two groups, and the kinship terminology reflects

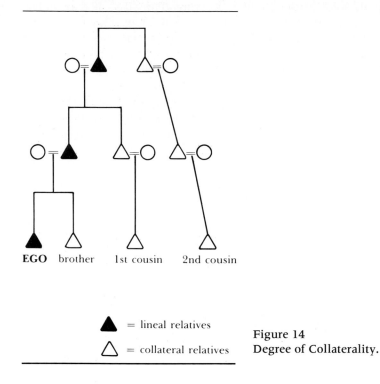

EGO   brother   1st cousin   2nd cousin

▲ = lineal relatives

△ = collateral relatives

Figure 14
Degree of Collaterality.

this. Iroquois terminology is usually associated with virilocal or uxorilocal residence, but not with neolocal residence. Instead of independent nuclear families, extended families are present. This type of terminology is also generally associated with unilineal descent, but not with cognatic descent or bilateral kinship reckoning. Iroquois is by far the most common type of kinship terminology. It should be noted that societies that have Iroquois kinship terminology may not have all these social structural features, but only some of them.

Besides Eskimo and Iroquois terminologies, four other major types of terminologies are distinguished by anthropologists. The *Crow* type, found, for example, among the Trobriand Islanders, is almost always associated with matrilineal descent groups, avunculocal residence, and extended families. Unlike Eskimo and Iroquois terminologies, the same term may be used for members of different generations. *Omaha* kinship terminology is the mirror image of Crow. It is associated with patrilineal descent groups and, like Crow, ignores generational differences in some terms. The simplest terminology having the fewest terms is the *Hawaiian* type, in which only generation and male-female distinctions are made. It is usually associated with cognatic descent groups. Despite its simplicity, it has been found in association with some societies, like the Hawaiian, that had complex political economies. In the last type of kinship terminology, *Sudanese,* every category of relative is distinguished by a different term. It is frequently associated with patrilineal descent and economically independent nuclear families, such as those found among certain nomadic pastoral societies of the Middle East.

A study of kinship terminology can help the anthropologist gain insights into how societies operate where kinship structures social relationships. Kinship terminology is a subject that has a long history in anthropology, and the regularity of its patterning was first noticed by Lewis Henry Morgan (1877). Continued study has revealed the general association of types of terminology with particular kinds of social structure, as we have pointed out. However, some terminologies correspond only in part to the types described above, and sometimes particular terminologies are associated with different social structural features than described above. For example, Iroquois kinship terminology may be found in association with kinship systems that do not have sister exchange but that do have patrilineal segmentary lineage structures, such as the Enga in Papua New Guinea.

With the popularity of interpretive anthropology in recent years and its concomitant emphasis on cultural relativism, some anthropologists like David Schneider (1984) have been critical of the use of the anthropological concepts presented in this chapter for analyzing kinship. They see this set of analytic concepts developed by anthropologists as the imposition of western categories on indigenous ideas. Instead, they prefer to emphasize the native categories that people in each society use to conceptualize kin relationships. In our view, the analysis must begin with indigenous categories, which are then translated into anthropological concepts in order to make cross-cultural comparison and generalization possible.

Fictive Kinship

In peasant communities people rely on social relationships such as *compadrazgo* or *godparenthood,* established on the occasion of ritual observances. Godparenthood creates a set of relationships that are nonkin in their derivation but that utilize a set of terms based on kinship: that is, godparent, godchild. This is not simply an extension of kinship, since it is always possible to extend real kinship in these societies. This kind of relationship is found in many parts of Mediterranean Europe and Latin America. The ritual occasions upon which godparenthood is established are baptism, confirmation, and marriage, at which the godparent serves as a kind of sponsor. Real parents do not carry out the role of godparents. Sometimes more distant relatives may serve as godparents, while in other cases they may not. This *compadrazgo* relationship is frequently established between individuals of different classes for social, political, and economic reasons. In

Baptism in a Latin American community serves to establish the relationship of compadrazgo, *or godparenthood.*

these instances, a patron who is a wealthy or powerful member of the community and probably the landlord may serve as godparent to the children of clients who are economically and politically dependent upon the patron. In such a relationship between parent and godparent, who are defined as *compadres* to each other, and patron and client, the patron receives support from the client when it is needed and the client receives favors from the patron. The relationship between godparent and godchild will parallel this, in that the godparent will be expected to protect and assist the godchild, while the godchild honors the godparent. In still other examples, the compadres may be equal in status to one another. Each may serve as godparent to the other's children.

In Yugoslavia, godparenthood, or *kumstvo,* described by anthropologist Eugene Hammel (1968), which can only be established between nonkin, is continued from one generation to the next. Members of one group (A) stand as godparents to another group (B), and the children of those godparents in A serve as godparents to the next generation of godchildren in B. Godparenthood is not reciprocal since the group of godchildren in B do not return the favor and act as godparents to A, but instead act as god-parents to children in still another group (C). This creates a structure of alliances between groups by means of godparenthood, which is the same as the structure of alliances created by marriage with mother's brother's daughter, described above. Thus, the kinds of relationships that are created through kinship and marriage are paralleled by structures created by other kinds of social relationships, such as godparenthood. The labels for these new relationships use kinship terms such as *father, mother, daughter,* and *son,* but with a special prefix—*god*—differentiating them from real kinship.

Kinship in Complex Societies

In small-scale, face-to-face societies of the type that anthropologists ini-tially studied, kinship provided the basic framework for the social structure. With the appearance of more complex civilizations, cities were established, political structures became transformed into states, and social, religious, and economic hierarchies developed. What became of the role of kinship as these various transformations took place? Clans based upon unilineal descent that had provided the basis for political, religious, and economic activities became less important as state organization grew. Clans were replaced by territorial units, which became the administrative divisions of the state. In the nineteenth century, Lewis Henry Morgan (1877), in his evolutionary work, described the change that took place in ancient Rome as the state developed from a system of clans. With the growth of eco-nomic specialization, social classes based on economic differences devel-oped. Special religious institutions centered on "temples," with hierarchical organizations of specialists controlling ritual knowledge. However, in industrial societies, despite the emergence of separate institutions, which took over functions formerly carried out by groupings organized on the basis of kinship, kinship ties still continue to play an important role.

In fact, there are a number of instances in which clans based on uni-lineal descent continued to exist and assumed a variety of roles, even long after the emergence of complex societies and states. For example, patrilineal clans in prerevolutionary China carried out religious functions in connection with ancestor worship, maintaining ancestral shrines and cemeteries. They also had some economic functions and assisted clan members in obtaining education and other such endeavors. These patri-lineal clans persist in the form of clan associations among overseas Chinese in San Francisco and New York within an urbanized, industrial-ized society.

When peasant societies are incorporated into nation-states, even Communist states, larger-scale kin units may continue to exist. As recently as 1987, ethnic Albanian clans in Kosovo, Yugoslavia, continued to feud with one another, answering one murder with another. As is the case in clan-based societies, all clansmen are held responsible for the actions of a single member. The progress of this feud was reported on Yugoslavian television.

In complex urbanized industrial societies such as our own, kinship ties do not disappear. Studies over the past twenty years have documented the way kin ties beyond the nuclear family are used for economic assistance, help in obtaining jobs, and help in finding a place to live. This goes beyond simple fulfillment of kinship obligations on ritual occasions such as marriages and funerals. Extended kin ties are frequently used when people migrate from rural areas to cities, as well as among urban dwellers. In a study of kinship in the East End of London, British anthropologists Young and Willmot (1962) point out how the mother-daughter tie is reinforced by the mother locating an apartment for the new couple. The mother uses her network of friends and neighbors to find a nearby apartment for her daughter. This postmarital residence pattern, which emphasizes the tie between mother and daughter, resembles in part uxorilocal postmarital residence as described previously.

In recent years, new forms of the family have developed which challenge the definition of marriage and what constitutes a family in American culture. Gay couples and lesbian couples have gone through a ritual they call marriage, and demand legal status as married couples. American society at large does not as yet seem to have accepted the validity of their claim. However, some changes have occurred as a result of this. In California, which has a large homosexual community, the surviving member of a couple can inherit the deceased member's pension. Homosexuals claim that all the functions of marriage are fulfilled, except the production of a child. Some couples have attempted to overcome the latter problem by adoption and, in the case of lesbian couples, by use of artificial insemination.

The work of Carol Stack on kinship among poor black people in the Midwest (1974) demonstrates how relatives, such as aunts and grandmothers, may carry out the role of mother for children. In this situation, relatives form a wide support network within which there is reciprocation of money, child care, food, clothing, shelter, and emotional support. The core of this network is a cluster of linked households. Males are present, but they are usually boyfriends and mothers' brothers, rarely husbands or fathers. If a young couple should marry, the newly formed nuclear family draws the individuals away from their kin in the support networks. Should the young husband lose his job, the marriage has little chance to survive, since the couple fall back on the resources of their respective kin networks which destroy the marriage. In this situation, the ties between brother and sister are stronger than those between husband and wife. In the film *Do the Right Thing,* Spike Lee captures this contradiction when he contrasts the emotional ties between the hero and his sister with the hero's antagonism toward his girlfriend, the mother of his child.

In contrast, the separation and independence of each nuclear family among the American middle class is described in Katherine Newman's recent study of downward mobility in America (1988). Women with teenage children who are divorced after years of marriage are not reintegrated into their natural families, nor do they receive regular financial assistance from their parents. They therefore inevitably experience downward mobility as a result of divorce. When middle-level managers lose their jobs, they rarely seek and cannot expect help from close relatives and often keep the information about loss of job secret. Brothers rarely seek financial help from one another, since the primary responsibility of each is to his own nuclear family. The obligations one has toward a relative are ambiguous in middle-class American society. When asked whether they would prefer to borrow money from relatives or from the bank, one American said, "From the bank! That's what banks are for." Another stated, "From your brother! What are brothers for?"

The family reunion in the United States, which involves kin relations beyond the nuclear family, has been the subject of anthropological research. Neville (1987) recounts how every summer many Southern Protestant families attend such gatherings. The descendants of a male ancestor, now living dispersed over the United States, come together at the same time and place each year (like the Worthy family, which meets at the old camp meeting ground in north Georgia on the third Sunday in July). The descendants of the common ancestor, both male and female, constitute a constantly expanding group of descendants which doubles with each generation. However, not all these descendants choose to come to the reunion. All such reunions include a shared meal cooked and contributed by the women of each family, and visiting and telling of stories about the common ancestor and the kinship connections that bind them all together. They may also include church services, introduction of members, business matters, and the election of officers. When they come together at the reunion, they are reenacting the Protestant biblical ideal of family and kinship. Exchanging food and partaking of a meal together once a year has important symbolic significance. Neville also points out a tendency to emphasize connections through women over those through men in the kinship of her Southern Protestant families. A nuclear family is more likely to attend the reunions of their mother's family than their father's.

The symbolic character of American kinship has also been explored. David Schneider (1980) points out that Americans conceive of two kinds of relatives. There are blood relatives and relatives by marriage. Americans think that a child receives half of his blood from his mother and half from his father, while more distant relatives have smaller shares of that blood, depending on the degree of distance. Such relationships can never be terminated because the symbolic "carrier" of the relationship is the blood. On the other hand, relatives through marriage are different from blood relatives in every respect. They are established by people rather than as the result of a natural process and are thus termed relatives-*in-law*. Relationships that are made by people can also be terminated by people, through divorce. When this happens, the person is no longer a relative.

In complex societies, kinship terms may also be used metaphorically for other kinds of nonkin relationships. Not only is the kin term extended in this way, but so is the emotional content associated with it. In religious communities, kinship terms such as *brother, sister, father,* and *mother* are used, and kinship serves as a model for categorizing and talking to and about people. For example, in the Roman Catholic hierarchy, the Pope is the Holy Father, the world *pope* meaning "papa." Priests are addressed as Father, the head of a convent as Mother Superior, and the nuns as Sisters. Nuns, when they take their vows, are married to Christ. Other religious orders, such as the Shakers, also use kinship terminology. The model of the family, as well as its terminology, is used as a metaphor in ordering social relationships, despite the fact that sexual intercourse and reproduction, one of the functions of the family, is forbidden in both Shaker and Roman Catholic monastic communities. *Brother* and *sister* are also used as metaphors in political settings, as exemplified by the use of the term *brother* in the black community to signify solidarity, as *sister* is used in the feminist movement. Similarly, solidarity is shown in an economic context when a union labels itself the Brotherhood of Teamsters. In all these instances in complex societies, kinship labels are used as metaphors. Even godparenthood, which is itself a system of ritual relations modeled upon kinship, serves as a metaphor. *Godfather* in present-day American society has an ominous connotation because of its association with the Mafia, whereas *godmother* does not have this association.

_____ CHAPTER 6 _____

Gender and Age

 Every society makes social distinctions according to age and sex, and these distinctions form the basis for the differentiation of social roles within a society. Societies always distinguish between male roles and female roles, and the relations between the sexes are also culturally patterned. Gender roles differ from one culture to another, and their patterning forms an important motif in the tapestry of culture.

Male and Female

The relationship between males and females and the way in which each is culturally construed are topics that have received a good deal of attention in recent years. Until recently, anthropologists, male and female, focused primarily on male roles in their field research. In doing so, they were sometimes unconsciously reflecting the cultural bias that emphasized the significance of male roles in their own society and projecting its gender ideology onto the society they were studying. At other times this focus on the primacy of male roles reflected the male bias of the society being studied. Margaret Mead and one or two other female anthropologists were exceptions to this. With the growth of the feminist movement, many anthropologists of both sexes began to pay attention to female as well as male roles and to the female as well as the male point of view of society. They focused attention on the cultural construction of gender roles and how these related to other patterns in the culture. The cultural constructions of what is male and what is female are much more than natural categories based on biological differences. As Errington puts it, "Culture does not lie on the surface of the anatomical and physiological base as decoration, the way icing lies on a cake. If human social life were compared to a cake, we would better say that 'biological givens' are analogous to flour, eggs, and sugar, and the socializing process of human interaction 'cooks' them into their final form: cake" (Errington, 1990:14).

While all societies construct female roles as different from male roles, the nature of the contrast between male and female roles differs from one society to another. The difference between male and female roles in a society like Wogeo, an island off New Guinea, is based on the belief that men and women live separately in two different worlds. But realistically, men and women must come together to reproduce the society as well as to carry out the usually complementary social and economic roles upon which their society depends. Politics and power are controlled by men. Associated with these ideas about the separateness of the sexes is the belief that sexual intercourse is polluting to both sexes and that menstrual blood is harmful to men. While women menstruate naturally, in Wogeo the men incise their penises to rid themselves of the bad "menstrual" blood (Hogbin, 1970).

Some societies, like Wogeo, emphasize the differences, while others downplay the differences. The Wana on the island of Sulawesi, in Indonesia, conceptualize gender relationships very differently from the people of Wogeo. Differences between male and female are minimized; male and female are seen as almost identical anatomically. Husband and wife are equally involved in procreation. The Wana say that the man carries the child for the first seven days of gestation and then puts the child into a woman. It is believed that in the past men menstruated. Men's menstrual blood is said to be "white blood" and to contain the essence of humanity which solidifies in the womb as a fetus (Atkinson, 1990:75, 76). Both the external state organization and the surrounding wilderness lie outside of the Wana communities. These areas are dangerous, but they are also the source of spiritual knowledge and power. The Wana believe that men are braver than women, one area in which there are gender differences. Men obtain knowledge from the spirits of the forest and become shamans. The overwhelming majority of Wana shamans are men. Even in a society where men and women are seen as fundamentally the same, gender does make a difference when it comes to the public realm of politics. Atkinson also reports several cases of gender shifting. In one of them, a woman, who had borne and lost a child, lived like a man "married" to another woman and performed as a shaman (Atkinson, 1990).

In many societies, economic roles are assigned based on cultural constructions of gender. The difference is not an outgrowth of the biological differences between men and women. A specific task may be associated with men in one society and with women in another. Milking herd animals (cows, goats, horses), for example, may be a female task in some societies and a male task in others, as is also the case with making pottery and weaving cloth. Men's economic tasks invariably have greater prestige, even though women's tasks, such as horticulture and collecting plant foods, may provide the bulk of subsistence.

As we have noted earlier, masculinity and femininity are culturally construed concepts. We have pointed out that gender shifting occurs among the Wana. As in the Wana case, women in Western society who carry out masculine roles usually dress and act like men, as did the author George Eliot and Joan of Arc. In other societies, men sometimes consciously elect to carry out female rather than male roles. In such cases, for example among a number of Native American Plains societies, some men, known as *berdache,* dressed like women, performed female tasks, and sometimes lived in homosexual relationships with other men. However, among the Arapesh, men who did not accept the responsibilities of the male role were referred to as "female" men, with no notion of homosexuality implied.

Different spatial areas may be associated respectively with males and females. Because women are identified with mothering, the hearth, and the home, women are usually associated with the domestic realm and men are associated with the public realm. This distinction between domestic and public is an analytical tool that aids us in comparing male and female roles in different societies. However, it is clear that there is not a universal association of males with the public sphere and females with the domestic.

In a number of New Guinea societies, the men's house and the ceremonial plaza are male turf, while women are associated with their own dwelling houses. Women in many Middle Eastern societies are restricted to certain parts of the house and may only come into contact with males who are members of their family. When they leave the house, they must veil their faces. In such societies, the coffeehouse and the market are defined as male domains. However, markets are not universally male domains. As we mentioned in Chapter 3, Malagasy women conduct the haggling in the market, while in some West African societies, women actually control the marketplace.

In our discussion of the island of Wogeo, above, we made note of the fact that menstrual blood and sexual intercourse were seen as harmful to men. Menstrual blood is a substance that, perhaps more than any other, is associated with femaleness and also with pollution. In the course of interaction between male and female, in Wogeo, as in some other societies, men may perceive women as dangerous, and this danger is often projected onto menstrual blood. Among the Mae Enga, a highland New Guinea soci-

A veiled woman walks past the market stalls in a Moroccan town.

ety, men always take wives from enemy groups and consequently wives are seen as dangerous. They believe that a man can be harmed if he has sexual intercourse with a menstruating woman, or when menstrual blood is introduced into food. The belief that menstrual blood is a dangerous substance is found in other societies in the world where wives do not come from enemy groups. A recent comparative study of beliefs about menstruation points out that this idea about the polluting effect of menstrual blood on men tends to be part of a male vision of society (Buckley and Gottlieb, 1988:35). There are few studies of how females in particular societies view menstruation. Menstrual blood symbolically has both positive and negative connotations. In its negative aspect, it can be used in witchcraft. Menstrual blood may be used for its positive qualities in the manufacture of love charms.

In the previous chapter, we pointed out that Americans have their own cultural conceptualizations of kinship based on blood as a "natural symbol." Differences between males and females are also perceived as "natural" differences. Errington (1990) points out that Americans consider the differences in genitalia to be signs of differences in fluids and substances that naturally divide the population into two different, mutually exclusive, categories. Behavior, dress, and demeanor are viewed by Americans as determining membership in one of these two categories. Clearly, this idea of what is considered "natural" by Americans is a culturally constructed category that is continually expressed and enacted.

In our own and other industrial societies, economic, spatial, and behavioral separation of the sexes was true until the beginning of the twentieth century. Ginsburg (1989) points out that in preindustrial America, the home was basically the workplace for both men and women. With increasing industrialization during the nineteenth century, men were drawn into the factories and businesses while women remained in the home, an essentially female domain. Women were identified with an ideology of nurturance and domesticity, despite the fact that some women worked for wages. Politics, the courts, businesses, banks, pubs, and so forth, were male bastions, and so too were the social clubs, where real business was carried out.

At the beginning of the twentieth century, women who questioned the assignment of these male and female roles formed the suffragette movement and began to agitate for the vote, which had been denied them heretofore. Men perceived the pioneers in this movement as very masculine women. World War II brought many women into the work force, and since that time ever-increasing numbers of American women have become part of the labor force. It took the feminist movement of the 1970s and affirmative action legislation to begin to raise both female and male consciousness and bring about the transformations that we see today. As women have moved into occupations like law and medicine, formerly occupied almost exclusively by men, the society at large has come to accept women as well as men in those roles. In this way, women in American society have invaded the public realm of men, and as this has occurred, men have increasingly had more to do in the domestic realm, taking on cooking and child care.

Another example of how gender roles have changed in America concerns childbirth. In the nineteenth century, American women gave birth in the home, which as we noted was identified as a female sphere. At the beginning of the twentieth century with the increasing professionalization and the growth of hospitals, the medical profession, then male-dominated, took control over the process of giving birth, and by the 1930s more births occurred in hospitals than at home. Under these conditions, birth was defined as a medical procedure, and the female reproductive process was taken over and placed in the hands of male physicians. With the significant changes in gender roles in our society, this process is being reversed. There are more female physicians now. Interest in natural childbirth has brought about changes; and home birth is a possibility that some feminists advocate.

The change in gender roles just described is in no way an inevitable progression through which all modernizing societies will pass. Anthropologists have described all sorts of changes affecting gender roles in different parts of the world. In the highlands of New Guinea a women's savings and exchange association, called *Wok Meri*, operates as a social movement to improve the economic position of women who had earlier been completely relegated to the domestic sphere in these patrilineal, male-dominated societies (Sexton, 1986). A contrasting example in which the economic role of women and their position in general has declined comes from Nukumanu Atoll, a Polynesian island north of the Solomons (Feinberg, 1986). Traditionally men and women had separate, clearly defined, but more or less equal roles. As a result of Western contact, there was a shift from a dependence on female cultivation of swamp taro to a dependence on commodities from the outside world. Income to purchase these commodities came from collecting sea cucumbers and sea snails and harvesting coconuts to make copra, which are primarily male activities. This resulted in a decline in the economic importance of women's work. The women have remained culturally separate, but their sphere of influence has been reduced.

Sometimes relations between the sexes swing back and forth, like a pendulum, in response to political changes. In Iran under the Shah, as the country modernized, women began to assume more public roles, gaining higher education and moving into occupations like the civil service. They increasingly wore Western dress and no longer wore the veil. With the rise of Islamic fundamentalism under the Ayatollah Khomeini, there has been a return to the traditional male and female roles as spelled out in the Koran, and women now must veil themselves when they go out in public.

It is clear that gender roles must be viewed in relation to each other. No society can exist solely of males or solely of females. The two are necessary to form a society. But how their roles are culturally defined varies enormously.

Age Grades

Aging is a continuous process, from birth to death. However, the way in which this continuum is divided will vary from society to society, as well as over time within a single society. Every society has terms for different age groups, but the number of terms varies. In our own society, we use such terms as *infant, child, adolescent, adult,* and *old person.* We pointed out earlier how the cultural construction of gender has been changing in North America. A significant change has also taken place in the construction of categories based on age. There is no longer a retirement age and therefore no longer a clearly defined point at which an American moves into the category of senior citizen. However, simply because the law is changed doesn't necessarily mean that people's attitudes and behavior also change. By law, a person need not retire at any age, but individual Americans may still feel that a sixty-five-year-old should retire.

   In some societies, when the age categories are formally named and recognized and crosscut the entire society, they are referred to as *age grades*. In
a number of primarily herding societies in East Africa, from Ethiopia in the
north to Tanzania in the south, formalized male age grades play an important role in the social structure. One such society is the Nandi of Kenya,
studied by G. W. B. Huntingford (1953). The Nandi have a system of seven
age grades that correspond to divisions of a man's life cycle. Every fifteen
years or so, men move from one age grade to the next, more senior, age
grade. This change takes place at a ceremony that is held simultaneously at
several places throughout Nandi territory, and its timing is determined by
the alternate flowering of a bush that comes to flower every $7^1/_2$ years. All
the boys born between one ceremony and the next form a single age set,
which is given a particular name by the Nandi. The age set will keep this
name as it moves through the successive age grades. Since there is a
fifteen-year period between one change in grade and the next, there is a
fifteen-year range in the ages of members of a single set. When the last
man of the oldest set dies, the name that was assigned to that age set is free
to be used again for the age set of male infants being born. There is thus a
set of seven names, each of which is recycled every one hundred five years
(7 grades $\times$ 15 years, the period of time between changes of grade).
   The most junior of the age grades consists of young boys. The second
grade consists of initiates, who will be circumcised at some point while
they are in this grade. The average age at circumcision is about fifteen, and
the ritual involves a lengthy series of ceremonies. Boys, during their time
in this grade, learn the role of warriors, which they will take over when
they move into the next grade. The third age grade is that of the warriors,
the "set in power." They carry out all military actions in Nandi society,
including raids against neighboring peoples. The warriors live in special
bachelor houses and are allowed free sexual access to uninitiated girls.
They have primary responsibility for organizing the circumcision of the
younger age grade of initiates and for testing the younger grade for bravery
and valor. Young men in the initiate group, after their circumcision, take
over the lesser duties of a warrior before the official movement into the
next grade, and the oldest group of warriors takes wives and retires from
active participation as warriors. On leaving the grade of warrior, a man and
his set pass into the first of the four grades of elders. At the ceremony that
marks the change from warrior to the first grade of elder, the retiring warriors remove their clothes and put on old men's fur cloaks.
   There is no elaborate system of age grades, nor age sets, for women.
Instead, women are divided into two categories—girls and married women.
There is a rite corresponding to male circumcision that is performed upon
older girls which involves an operation on the clitoris. Since warriors are
allowed free sexual access to uninitiated girls, girls are seldom virgins when
they are initiated. This elaborate system of age grades among the Nandi
coexists with other kinds of social groupings based on family, lineage, and

clan. The age grade system divides the society like a seven-layer cake and assigns particular functions to each of the grades.

The Nyakyusa of Tanzania, who were studied by Monica Wilson (1951, 1977), use divisions according to age as the basis for a different kind of age grade system. Age mates, as they mature, join together to form a new village. When they are ten or eleven years old, boys build huts and establish a village at the edge of their father's village. They sleep and spend time in their fledgling village, but return to their mothers' huts for meals and assist their fathers in agriculture. The Nyakyusa emphasize that boys at this age should move out because they should not be aware of the sexual activities of their parents. Where other societies, such as the Trobriand Islanders, have the institution of the bachelor house to which adolescent boys must move, the Nyakyusa have extended the idea of the bachelor house to the formation of an entirely new village. When the original founders of the village reach the age of fifteen, the village becomes closed to new members. At about the age of twenty-five, the boys, now young men, marry and bring their brides to live with them virilocally in the new village, and now each wife cooks for her husband. Other East African people, such as the Masai, have temporary warrior villages or barracks, but only the Nyakyusa bring their wives to the living quarters of the age set to form a permanent village. The other peoples all establish their wives with the husband's patrilineal kin. Once in a generation a great ritual is held, at which time administrative power and military leadership are handed over by the older generation to the younger. The men of the retiring generation move to one side, and the new villages of young men are formally established on their own lands. At this ritual the old chief retires, and his sons are recognized as chiefs of the small chiefdoms into which the Nyakyusa are divided. The retiring old chief reallocates all the land and selects a headman for each new village.

All over Nyakyusaland, at any point in time, there are three kinds of age grade villages. There are the villages of the grandfathers, who have retired from leadership positions but who still perform certain ritual functions. There are the villages of the fathers, who rule and are responsible for defense and administration. Finally, there are the villages of the sons, who have not yet "come out," but when necessary fight under the leadership of men of their fathers' generation. Remnants of a fourth great-grandfathers' generation may occasionally be found as a small village of a few very old men. The Nyakyusa have an intense fear of sexual relations between a young man and his father's cowives, who are his stepmothers. Similarly, possible sexual relations between father-in-law and daughter-in-law are dreaded. The age villages are a way of keeping the generations apart and thus avoiding intimate contact between these categories of people. On the positive side, the Nyakyusa stress the friendship and fellowship within one's peer group, which promotes the solidarity of the village. Though the Nyakyusa have a rule of patrilineal descent and patrilineages, the members of a lineage are dispersed over a number of villages. In contrast to the Nyakyusa, most societies with patrilineal descent have villages based on lineage and clan organization, where the lineage or clan owns the land. However, the tension between the generations may undermine the solidarity of the clan. The Nyakyusa say that they prefer to live with people of their own generation with whom they can have easy communication, since relations between members of the same lineage but of different generations are governed by the formal respect required of juniors for their seniors.

We can see a similar situation in our own society. The conflict between generations leads young people in America to move away from their parents to live and relate primarily with people of their own age and generation. Retirement communities in America whose residents must be over fifty-five years of age, which do not allow children to live there, resemble a Nyakyusa village of grandfathers. As American communities move increasingly in the direction of age grading, the Nyakyusa have been moving in the opposite direction, away from their traditional age villages, under the recent pressure of economic change. When men migrate away from their homes for wage labor, they leave their wives with their mothers, thereby negating the traditional value of separating a daughter-in-law from her father-in-law. Furthermore, that individuals seek economic achievement for themselves conflicts with the traditional value of sharing between members of an age village (Wilson, 1977).

Associations Based on Age

A slightly different form of age grade organization occurred among some of the Plains Indians of North America, such as the Hidatsa, Mandan, Arapaho, Blackfoot, and Gros Ventre. Clark Wissler, the ethnographer, tells us that in the past among the Hidatsa, for example, there was a series of ten societies, graded according to age. Unlike the Nandi, where membership in a grade is based solely on age, among the Hidatsa a group of age-mates had to purchase membership collectively from the next oldest group, which currently owned the society. These groupings are called *associations*. One is not born into an association, but he or she becomes a member by voluntarily joining it. Not every male had to join the series of age-graded societies, but practically every boy did join. Having joined, he found himself bound to a set of peers in a social group that existed throughout his entire life.

At the age of ten or eleven, boys would join together, accumulate goods with the help of their fathers and grandfathers, and purchase the rights to certain ceremonial objects and the rights to perform specific ceremonial activities. At this point they became the Stone Hammers, the youngest society. The group that formerly owned the Stone Hammers had to buy the

A member of the Hidatsa Dog Society, one of the age grade societies participating in a ceremonial, wears the traditional dress and insignia of his society. From a painting by Karl Bodmer, who accompanied Prince Maximilian up the Missouri River in 1834.

Lumpwood age grade from the age set that held it. Sometimes a group of age-mates had to wait a long time before being able to buy rights to the next highest society. During this time they had no definite place in the series of age-graded societies. Buyers stood ceremonially in the relation of "sons" to the sellers. An age grade group went together as a unit on warfare expeditions and sponsored rituals such as the Red Stick ceremony, which was held during the winter to bring buffalo herds nearer to the village.

The Hidatsa also had a smaller but parallel series of age-graded societies for women. The mode of purchase was identical to that of the male societies. The women's societies were formally linked to the men's, particularly in celebrating the military achievements of the men. The most senior female societies had a number of magicoreligious functions not present in their male counterparts.

Like the Nandi and the Nyakyusa, the Hidatsa have a fundamental division between male and female. However, the Hidatsa, with their male and female age-graded societies, contrast with the Nandi and the Nyakyusa. The Nandi have a complex age grade system for men and no corresponding system for women, and the age villages of the Nyakyusa are based on the age grading of males, not of females. But the matrilineal Hidatsa emphasize both—a division according to sex and a series of age-graded societies for both sexes.

There are also secret societies that are associations based on age. The Poro Society, an all-male association found among a number of peoples of West Africa—the Mano and Gola of Liberia and the Mende and Temne of Sierra Leone—is an example. The Poro Society was investigated by George Harley (1941), a missionary doctor. The secrets of the Poro Society must be kept from the women and uninitiated boys. Similarly, the secrets of the higher levels of the Poro Society must be kept from members of the lower levels. The Poro Society shares one characteristic of age-graded societies in that all boys go through a series of initiatory rites, which gives them membership in the lowest level of the Poro Society. The boys are separated from the rest of the community at a "bush school," where they live for several months. During this time, they are taught the trades they select to follow as well as how to build houses and how to farm. They learn the tribal lore that an adult should know. As part of the process of initiation, the boys are supposed to be swallowed by the great crocodile spirit (in the case of the Mano) and remain in his belly during the whole time that they are in the bush school. When they emerge, they are said to have been reborn as men from the belly of the crocodile spirit. The most important rite in the course of the initiation is the scarification of the boys' necks, backs, and chests. These scars are said to represent the teeth marks of the crocodile spirit. The boys are also circumcised, but this operation is a minor part of the Poro initiation. The initiate is a boy until he has been scarified and reborn as a man. Boys who pass through initiation together form an age set that thereafter acts as a unit throughout the rest of their lives.

The higher levels of the Poro Society consist of several grades of priests. The whole society forms a kind of pyramid, with the grand master of the Poro at the top. Access to the higher positions is through a combination of hereditary right and the payment of large fees. When acting in their official capacity in the Poro, the priests at the various levels wear carved wooden masks, which represent powerful spirits. These masked priests act as judges and punish wrongdoers, conduct the bush school, and carry out rites that promote the fertility of the fields.

Since the Poro Society is all-male, the basic division between male and female as an organizing principle is also present here. The women have their own secret society, the Sande Society, which parallels the Poro. The Sande Society has its own bush school, for the purpose of teaching and initiating girls. They learn how to take care of the household, cook, sing, dance, and make herbal remedies to cure sickness. They also learn the art of poisoning. Girls have the clitoris removed as part of their initiation. While all girls undergo initiation, only a select few become leaders in the Sande.

The Poro Society does not have the same hold in the multiethnic cities of Liberia and Sierra Leone that it does in the rural areas. The sacred masked spirits no longer make public appearances there. Though there is no Poro bush school in the vicinity of Freetown, initiation goes on upcountry, and membership in the society is important in the new towns near the mines and the railway line.

The ethnographic examples of social units described in this section are groupings based on factors other than kinship and common descent. Age and sex are the most common bases for distinction. Sometimes the groupings according to age differences cut across an entire society. Other times the groupings are not formalized as a set of strata cutting across the entire society, but individuals who are initiated together have a special bond with one another that joins them together for the rest of their lives. There are societies in which each person passes through the stages as an individual, and no social groupings are formed on this basis. In other cases the entire society moves up as an age set is initiated into the next senior grade. In some societies an entire age set has to purchase the privileges of the next higher grade, but in others individuals must make payments in order to move into the next highest grade. Some societies have age grades for men and age grades for women; others have an elaborate age grade system for men and no equivalent system for women. The function of the male age grade is to train and educate adolescent males to carry out adult roles. This is most developed in the Nyakyusa age grade villages, where the functions that are usually performed by unilineal descent groups are performed by age grade villages. Patrilineages among the Nyakyusa are extremely weak. An interesting question that still remains to be answered by anthropologists is: What are the conditions under which age grade systems perform these functions, and what are the conditions under which kin groups perform them?

It would appear, initially, that cultural categories based on age and sex simply build upon biological differences. However, this is not the case in human societies where culture defines these categories and the cultural expression of age and gender varies from society to society. In each case it is one of the central themes that organize the society.

CHAPTER 7

Provisioning Society: Production, Distribution, and Consumption

 The British author and socialist George Orwell characterized capitalist industrial society as one in which the economy dominated all other aspects of life. Paraphrasing Paul the Apostle, Orwell mocked our contemporary life, stating, "Though I speak with the tongues of men and angels and have not money . . . I am nothing. And though I bestow all my goods to feed the poor, and though I give my body to be burned, and have not money, it profiteth me nothing. . . . And now abideth faith, hope, and money, these three; but the greatest of these is money." The point that Orwell was making is that money has become the medium by which all things—labor, land, services, sex, time, art, votes, and even love—have come to be measured, bought, and sold. This increasingly has come to be the case in Western society, as the cultural principle referred to as "market mentality" spreads through every aspect of the society. As Western ideas and industrialization have spread to other parts of the world, so has the Western idea of market mentality. As we shall see, market mentality was not characteristic of the societies that anthropologists studied in the past, nor was it the case in Western society at an earlier point in time.

In this chapter, we will be discussing how societies provision themselves. In the course of it, we will be describing varying systems of distribution like the potlatch and the *kula* ring, in which groups are linked to other groups, and societies are linked to other societies. This interdependence of kinship groups and societies on one another is a demonstration that societies can never be looked at as isolates. Further, the systems of production, distribution, and consumption we will discuss are treated as isolates by anthropologists only for the purposes of analysis. In most cases, even as the anthropologists were doing their research, these societies were encompassed by one or another aspect of the world system, as we shall describe in Chapters 13 and 14.

The economic organization of a society is how that society, in a regularized fashion, goes about providing the material goods and services it needs to perpetuate itself. The economic organization operates according to sets of cultural rules and arrangements that bring together natural resources, human and animal labor, and man-made technology in order to provide for the provisioning of society. Rules relating to economic organization are similar to rules that govern the other aspects of culture. Individuals may interpret the rules to their own advantage—in economic terms, this is known as *maximizing*. In small-scale societies economic behavior operates to a large extent within the context of the kinship structure. In such situations, rules governing who owns the resources, how the work is organized, who uses or eats the product, and so forth, are an aspect of kinship. In this sense, the economy can be said to be embedded in the social structure, within the very tapestry of the culture itself. As societies expand in scale, the separation of economic behavior from the realm of kinship increases, and the economic institution becomes more and more delimited as a separate system.

For purposes of analysis, economic organization may be divided into three parts: production, distribution or exchange, and consumption.

Production

Production is the process whereby a society uses the tools and energy sources at its disposal and the labor of its people and domesticated animals to create those goods necessary for supplying society as an ongoing entity. As will be seen, there are a number of different systems of production.

Hunting and Gathering

For the greatest time of their existence on earth, some 3 to 5 million years, human beings subsisted by means of a combination of hunting wild animals; gathering roots, seeds, and plants; and collecting sea life along the shores. This mode of exploitation of the natural environment is referred to by anthropologists as *hunting and gathering*. We know a good deal about hunting and gathering societies from the work of archaeologists, although today this mode of subsistence continues only as an adjunct to other modes. In what follows, we shall describe hunting and gathering societies as they existed in the past, since at the present time, no groups of people depend primarily upon hunting and gathering as a mode of subsistence.

Societies primarily dependent on hunting and gathering used to be found in a wide range of marginal environments. The Inuit (or Eskimo) of the Arctic region, the Pygmies of the Ituri Forest in Zaire in Central Africa, the San (or Bushmen) of the Kalahari Desert in southern Africa, and the Washo of the Great Basin on the California-Nevada border were all societies that used to depend on hunting and gathering for their subsistence. These hunting and gathering societies occupied very different kinds of environments with very different flora and fauna. However, there are several generalizations that can be made about this mode of subsistence. All these societies had sparse populations with very low population densities. The plants and animals upon which they depended were scarce or abundant according to the seasons. Migratory species were absent for much of the year and then present for a short time in superabundance. Similarly, nuts, fruits, tubers, and seeds ripened during a particular time of the year, at which point they needed to be harvested. At other times, these foods were not available. Hunters and gatherers typically had to exploit all the possible resources available in their environments in order to deal with variations in availability. A migratory cycle during the year is therefore characteristic of these societies. These people had to move because it was necessary to be in different areas so they could harvest what was available in those areas at particular times of the year. While there were regular sites to which they returned every year, they did not have year-round permanent village settlements. Larger agglomerations of individuals came together when greater amounts of food were available in one locale. This was usually the case when some single food resource was in great supply (migratory caribou, spawning salmon, ripening pine nuts, etc.). Religious festivals were frequently held at such times. At other times of the year, small dispersed groups of one or more nuclear families were the migratory units. Julian Steward pointed out that the kind of animal upon which a hunting and gathering society is dependent will determine the organization of the social group or band that hunts it. Societies that concentrated on hunting small mammals, such as rabbits, were organized into patrilineal bands so that the husband could stay in the hunting territory where he had grown up and with which he was familiar. The hunting of large migratory animals, which requires a bigger labor force, was performed by large composite bands with flexibility in affiliation, where membership was acquired through either father or mother.

Technology is that part of culture by means of which people directly exploit their environment. Technology encompasses the manufacture and use of tools according to a set of cultural rules. Therefore, it is possible to identify and type the tool repertoire of a particular society. In fact, archaeologists identify prehistoric cultures primarily through the styles of their tools. The technology of hunting and gathering people is simple in that

*Buffalo hunters, disguised as wolves, stalk their prey on the Great Plains. The "hunter"
on the right is actually the artist George Catlin, sketching the scene in 1832.*

natural materials taken directly from the environment, such as stone,
bone, wood, and sinew, are used and the manufacturing techniques are
relatively simple, involving only a few kinds of operations. Hunters and
gatherers combined intimate knowledge of the environment in terms of
animal behavior and knowledge about the growing patterns of plants with
the development of a variety of techniques for the appropriation of plants
and animals. For example, the Inuit have ten different ways to hunt seal.
Hunters put to use every part of the animals they capture for food and for
the manufacture of a whole variety of goods. Many hunters in Africa and
South America discovered and put to use various kinds of poisons for
fishing or for making the points of their arrows more effective. These poisons affect the prey but not the eaters of the flesh. In hunting and gathering societies, people made the tools they used in subsistence; there were no
specialists who only make tools. The education of a child included the
teaching of tool manufacturing. People who still pursue a hunting and
gathering mode of subsistence today use such modern tools as rifles and
steel traps.

The differentiation of tasks in production is primarily between males and
females. The usual pattern is that men hunt and fish and women gather

plants, collect shellfish, and take care of the domestic tasks, such as clothing manufacture, food preparation, and child care. Children begin to learn tasks at a young age and at puberty assume adult economic roles. Individuals who excel at their tasks (successful hunters or fishers) are accorded respect and prestige, and their advice may be sought. The hunting of certain species of mammals and certain types of fishing are performed by the entire group under an informal leader. Hunting and gathering societies tend not to have social-class divisions. Nor do they rank individuals, that is, distinguish their social statuses as higher or lower. Earlier, many thought that hunting and gathering societies represented a very difficult mode of life, since food acquisition was seen as arduous and time-consuming. Marshall Sahlins (1972) has pointed out, however, that hunters and gatherers spend relatively little time in active pursuit of game, and in their use of leisure they constitute the "original affluent society."

It should not be assumed that the environment remains constant while culture interacts with it. The environment itself changes as a result of human exploitation of it. Ecological balance is altered as people harvest those species they utilize. In some societies, an effort was made to limit exploitation of the environment by imposing some controls in the hunting of certain species or animals of young ages, thereby maintaining the ecological balance. In other cases, the environment became permanently degraded. For example, at an earlier period in New Guinea, because fire was used as an aid in hunting, the primary forests were destroyed and replaced by grassland, totally altering the ecosystem and the fauna of the area.

Some hunting and gathering populations had long-term exchange relationships with agriculturalists and pastoralists. This was particularly true of most, if not all, hunters and gatherers in Africa. The Mbuti of Zaire exchange meat and other forest products with regular exchange partners among their agricultural neighbors. This is an exchange between equals. The Twa of Ruanda are hunters who are part of a hierarchical castelike structure. They exchange with Hutu agriculturalists and Tutsi pastoralists.

The Kwakiutl of British Columbia, whose wedding ceremony was described in Chapter 2, are an interesting exception to what we have said about this mode of subsistence. In the past they were hunters and gatherers, but their environmental resources were so rich, particularly in sea life, that they were able to support a much denser population than is usual in hunting and gathering societies. They had permanent villages with plank houses, though they migrated from these villages at certain times of the year to exploit particular resources. They had craft specialization and elaborate, stationary artwork (totem poles). Inheritance of titles, which were ranked, was also present, and their political system, with chiefly positions that were also inherited, was more complex than was found in other hunting and gathering societies. There are several reasons for this series of differences between the Kwakiutl (as well as other Northwest Coast societies) and other hunting and gathering societies. The rich environment of the Northwest Coast provided game, both mammal and bird, and many species of edible plant life, along with sea resources such as numerous varieties of fish, shellfish, and sea mammals, and lastly but importantly the several species of salmon that annually spawned in the rivers. In addition, the Kwakiutl had highly developed techniques for the preservation and storage of the wide range of products they obtained. This enabled them to produce surpluses, maintain large permanent village communities, and support more complex cultures. This is why the Kwakiutl wedding could be so elaborate. We will discuss how they utilized the surplus for social purposes in the section on distribution below.

The hunting and gathering life as we have described it above no longer exists. Though the Kwakiutl still fish, their catch of halibut or salmon now goes to the cannery or fish market, since they are now an integral part of the Canadian economy. Most of the food they eat is purchased at the store with money they have earned. The Cree of eastern Canada still spend part of the winter season in multifamily communal dwellings in the forest trapping animals with modern steel traps. The skins of the marten, lynx, mink, and weasel they trap end up in the fur markets of New York. When protesters demonstrate against the wearing of fur coats because it represents what they see as the needless killing of fur-bearing animals, this directly affects the livelihood of such Cree families.

Agriculture

The domestication of plants and their use for subsistence beginning some 8,000 to 10,000 years ago represented a significant transformation in human society. This change depended upon the development of a new corpus of information by means of which human beings acquired much greater control of the environment and, in turn, transformed it in a much more significant way than had been done by hunters and gatherers. Social groups were tied to territories differently than was the case with hunting and gathering. Sparsely populated groups of hunters and gatherers moved over wide areas during the course of the seasonal cycle. With a shift to dependence for subsistence upon domesticated plants, social groups utilized a smaller area, population was more dense, and there was a tendency for concentration into hamlets and villages. Agriculturalists are much more in control of their own destiny than are hunters and gatherers. We have noted that the exploitation pattern of hunting and gathering societies was seasonal. Agriculturalists also operate on the basis of a seasonal cycle, especially where there is a marked climate difference between winter and summer or rainy and dry seasons. The year is usually divided into planting time, growing time, and harvest. Audrey Richards (1961), the British social anthropologist, has pointed out that the several months before harvest are known as the "hungry months" for the Bemba of Central Africa, who depend primarily upon their crop of millet. Even when they are under the threat of starvation, agricultural people must restrain themselves from eating their seed or they will have no crop the following year.

How people utilize their labor, how they work the land, how they use water resources, and which crops they grow are the factors to be considered in an examination of different economic systems based on agriculture. Throughout lowland South America and Melanesia, the mode of production is based upon crops that are grown through vegetative propagation, using a part of the plant itself, rather than through the planting of seeds. Since these crops are grown in gardens, this form of cultivation is known as *horticulture*. Systems of production based upon horticulture vary in terms of how the land is used and whether there is a means for controlling water necessary for plant growth.

Horticultural practices among the many New Guinea societies may be ranged on a continuum that reflects greater and greater complexity of techniques for cultivating gardens, which result in higher crop yields and more permanent gardens. The simplest form of horticulture, known as the *swidden* type, or *shifting cultivation*, involves making gardens by burning down the forest and planting the garden in the ashes, which constitute a kind of fertilizer. No other means of fertilizing is used. Because the soil is rapidly exhausted, a new garden in a new location must be planted every few years. Thus, it is called shifting cultivation. Gardens contain many different kinds of plants on a single plot, and a digging stick may be the only tool used for cultivation. This kind of horticulture is supplemented by both hunting and the collection of wild plants. In lowland New Guinea, the sago palm, a wild plant whose pith is used for food, is an important supplement to what is produced in the gardens. For example, as much as 90 percent of the diet of the Tor in western New Guinea may come from wild sago. Their population is almost as sparse as a hunting and gathering society, though they live in villages surrounded by their yam gardens.

An intermediary type of horticulture is characterized by the mode of subsistence of the Abelam of New Guinea. Many varieties of short yams, taro, sweet potatoes, and a range of other plants are grown in gardens that are used several times and then allowed to remain fallow and uncultivated. The Abelam also grow a special species of long yam, which may be eight to ten feet long and which is used in ceremonial exchange. Its cultivation involves special techniques, such as mounding the soil to create a plant bed and erecting trellises for vines. Soil around the growing point may be carefully loosened as the tuber grows. Abelam villages are more or less permanent and much larger than those of the Tor.

The most complex forms of horticulture in New Guinea are found in the mountains of the central highlands. There, people like the Enga use a variety of labor-intensive techniques. The gardens represent a great deal of labor and may be used for a generation or more. Each garden is made up of a regular series of mounds separated by ditches. The mounds are formed from soil and mulch and are used only for sweet potato cultivation. These single-crop gardens are separated from mixed gardens in which most other crops are grown. The yields from the mounded gardens of the Enga are considerably greater than the yields from the other two types of horticulture described above. Enga society numbers over 150,000, so there is considerable pressure for land, and Enga clans may even fight one another for land. The complex exchange system of the Enga, which will be described below, is linked to their great productivity. The horticultural systems described above depend upon rainfall for water. However, root crop cultivation can involve water control. The Dani of the Grand Valley in western New Guinea have used dams, ditches, and drainage systems to turn a natural swamp into a productive cultivation area.

Just as hunting and gathering peoples have intimate knowledge of the plant and animal species that they exploit, horticulturalists display an extensive knowledge of soils, food plants, and cultivation techniques. This practical know-how is frequently combined with magical practices. The Trobrianders are energetic and successful gardeners who believe in the necessity of utilizing gardening magic in addition to their practical knowledge and hard work in order to make yams grow.

The simplest kind of swidden horticulture is practiced by sparse populations living in widely separated villages where villages control access to land. As horticultural techniques become more intensified, gardens become more permanent and population density increases. Land becomes the property of kin groups, such as clans. There is increased competition for good land, and warfare is frequently waged by one clan to drive another from its land, as we noted above for the Enga.

Grain is the focus of swidden agriculture in the more temperate areas of several continents of the world—maize in the New World, millet and sorghum in Africa, and rice in Asia. The same technique of cutting down trees and burning off bush is used in preparing the field for growing grain as for growing tubers in swidden horticulture. There is also a long fallow period after several plantings, as in the swidden cultivation of root crops, and rainfall is the source of water.

Throughout much of Europe and Asia, agricultural societies depend upon a technology involving the use of the plow drawn by draft animals and the use of animal manure as fertilizer. With this type of agriculture, fields become more or less permanent; grains including wheat, rye, and barley are the predominant crops; and there is a dependence upon rainfall for water. The same fields may be used every year if there is crop rotation and the use of fertilizer. Sometimes a system is employed whereby fields are divided, so that some are used while others lie fallow for a year. The use of draught animals and plows requires raising crops such as hay in order to feed the animals.

A form of grain agriculture even more productive per unit of land is dependent upon elaborate irrigation systems. These irrigation systems are much more extensive than the type of water control practiced by the Dani, as described above. This type of agriculture requires an enormous input of labor to create the necessary artificial environment of lakes, ponds, dikes, and terraces. From the Yellow River in China to the Tigris-Euphrates in Mesopotamia, and in the Andean highlands of Peru, irrigation systems were associated with urban civilizations.

A number of factors lead to increased productivity per acre of land. These include various techniques to improve the fertility of the soil, some of which, such as building mounds, require a good deal of labor. The degree to which water for agricultural purposes is controlled is another factor. Elaborate irrigation systems required great outputs of labor initially to establish and a certain amount of labor to maintain. The crops on which people subsist also vary in terms of their storage potential. This affects how crop surplus will be utilized for social purposes and will be discussed more fully in the section on distribution. Of course, the nature of the technology utilized is also an important factor. Steel axes and machetes are more efficient than stone axes. Animal labor is more efficient than human labor, except in places of high population density, like China. Machines and the mechanization of agriculture, as has occurred in the United States, represent a quantum jump in efficiency and therefore in productivity.

The intensification of agricultural production in the world also had unforeseen consequences. Sometimes populations grew beyond the point at which agricultural production could sustain them, resulting in famine. Greater population density resulted in the more rapid spread of infectious diseases. Each technological advance produced its own set of problems. Mechanized agriculture, for example, has resulted in overproduction and the need to store vast agricultural surpluses; the use of chemical pesticides has led to widespread pollution of soil and water. In the United States, fewer farmers are needed to grow the food we eat, and the family farm has become a corporation.

Animal Domestication

The domestication of plants, which brought such a significant transformation in the mode of production, was in most areas accompanied by the domestication of animals. In the Old World, including Asia, Africa, and Europe, a wide variety of animal species was domesticated. Most of these animals furnished meat and milk, and together with domesticated plants, provided subsistence. Some animals, such as the horse, donkey, bullock, and buffalo, were also used for transportation. The hair of others, such as sheep and goats, was woven into cloth. In the New World the only significant animal domesticates were the camelids, such as the llama, alpaca, and guanaco. In addition to variations in the uses to which these animals were put, there was also variation in the nature of animal care. Some domesticated animals foraged in the bush for their food but returned to places of human settlement at night; other domesticated animals were kept in enclosed pens and depended on humans for their entire care and feeding. The mithan, a type of domesticated ox found in southeast Asia among the Nagas and Chin of Burma, is allowed to roam freely, depending completely upon forage for food. Only its meat is used, and then only on ceremonial occasions. In contrast, in Europe, the dairy cow, a relative of the mithan, is kept in a stall or ranges in an enclosed pasture and is milked daily. The dairy cow and the ox are part of the mixed farming complex in Europe and North America.

In New Guinea, the pig is the only domesticated food animal and was introduced there in its domesticated form, since the native fauna includes only marsupials. However, the nature of care varies from society to society. The Tor capture wild piglets, which are tamed and then allowed to forage freely though they are individually owned. They are slaughtered to provide food for feasts. At the other end of the continuum are the Enga, whose pigs are hardly allowed to forage at all. The Enga breed their pigs and completely control their reproduction, care, and feeding.

The productive system of some societies is completely or almost completely dependent upon their domesticated animals, with little or no cultivation of plants. Such societies are referred to as *nomadic pastoralists.* This is a specialized mode of subsistence that developed from an earlier economy that included domesticated plants and animals. Nomadic pastoral societies, with one or two exceptions, are found on the great land mass of the Old World, particularly in arid zones. Sheep, goats, camels, horses, cattle, yaks, water buffalo, and reindeer constitute the basic herd animals for these societies. All these animals are social, not solitary, in their habits. In most cases one or two types of animals form the basis for herds.

The animal species upon which particular nomadic pastoral societies depend is related to the nature of the environment that is exploited. Some species, such as camels, are best adapted to arid desert areas and others, such as horses, to well-watered grassy plains. Some can withstand extremes of temperature, heat or cold, while others cannot. Some, such as goats, do best in steeper mountain environments, while others, such as water buffalo, can live only on flat, swampy lowlands. The way of life of nomadic pastoralists involves seasonal movement or migration in a regular pattern from one place to another. The community and its herds may move from summer to winter pasturage or from wet to dry locations. In their seasonal movements, pastoral nomads resemble hunters and gather ers, particularly those who hunt large herds of migratory animals, such as the caribou. However, there is a crucial difference in that hunters follow the migratory herd wherever the herd goes in its natural migration, whereas the herds that belong to the nomadic pastoralists follow the people who herd them.

The process of domestication involves a shift in the biological characteristics of the animal species, since the animals are selectively bred to enhance those characteristics that make the animal more controllable and more useful to humans and to eliminate characteristics such as intractability. In a sense, humans have shaped these animals through the process of domestication. At the same time, pastoral societies have adapted to the needs of their animals, particularly in the migration cycle followed. Nomadic pastoralists depend upon their herd animals for a range of products. Daily yields of milk and the products made from milk are central to the diet. The wool and hair are also important for making cloth. Nomadic pastoralists never exist as isolates, solely dependent on pastoral products. Live animals, wool, and milk products are used by the pastoralists to exchange with sedentary peoples for essentials such as tea, sugar, and flour. Since wealth is measured in numbers of animals in the herd, pastoralists are loath to kill animals only for their meat. Hence, this is done only on special occasions.

Nomadic pastoralists herd different species utilizing a range of environments. The Marsh Arabs of Iraq, who inhabit the swampy area at the confluence of the Tigris and Euphrates rivers, rely completely on their herds of water buffalo. Since they depend solely on the buffalo, they must trade the dairy products produced from the milk of their buffalo for grain and other foodstuffs from sedentary peoples, who are culturally the same except for mode of subsistence. The watery environment of the Marsh Arab is a sharp contrast to the desert zone of the Arabian plateau inhabited by another Arab-speaking group, the Rwala Bedouin (studied by Alois Musil in the 1920s). They are mainly herders of camels, but they also have some sheep, goats, and Arabian horses. The camels are herded by men and boys, often at some distance from the nomadic camp. The products of the camel include milk and hair, but even more importantly the animal is a mode of transportation. The Rwala also breed camels for sale to sedentary oasis dwellers and transporters who need the animals for long-distance caravan trade. The seasonal cycle of the Rwala involves moving into the desert in the spring, when available water has allowed grass cover to grow. As the year progresses, the climate gets drier, and they move closer to the desert oasis sources of water. Since goats and sheep as well as camels are herded, the Rwala must be mindful of the water requirements of all these animal species.

In the savanna grasslands of West Africa, between the Sahara Desert and the tropical forest area to the south, the Fulani practice still another form of nomadic pastoralism, one that is dependent solely on herds of cattle. The cattle are a long-horned variety of zebu with a humped back. The migration pattern is from the desert fringes in the wet season to the well-watered borders of the tropical forest in the dry season. The availability of grassland is not the only determining factor in the migratory pattern; another consideration is the distribution of the tsetse fly, which is a carrier of sleeping sickness and whose territory they avoid. The Fulani are dependent primarily upon the milk from their herds and milk products such as clarified butter. They migrate within an area containing villages of sedentary grain-growing agriculturalists with whom they trade their milk products for grain in the marketplace.

In the grasslands of Central Asia, nomadic pastoralists such as the Kazak, before the Russian Revolution of 1917, had herds of horses along with sheep, goats, and two-humped camels. The mares were milked, and the milk was made into a fermented drink called *kumis*, a luxury item. The Kazak spent the winter in protected valley areas and migrated to the steppes in summer. Riding horses and the products of the herds were traded to sedentary people in the market towns.

The most widespread form of pastoral nomadism is that which involves the herding of sheep and goats. Excellent examples are the Basseri, Bakhtiari, and Qashqai, pastoral nomads in present-day Iran. Their migration cycle takes them from winter pasturage in the southern lowlands, roughly sea level in altitude, to summer pasturage in the Zagros Mountains, at an altitude of 10,000 feet. The sheep herded by the Basseri are so adapted to the migratory cycle that they could survive neither the cold winters of the mountains nor the torrid summers of the lowlands. In addition to sheep and goats, the Bakhtiari also have in their herds a species of cow that is small and agile and can make the arduous migration. Though

A camp of Pushtun nomadic pastoralists in central Afghanistan in the summer of 1971.

most societies have nomadic pastoralism as their dominant mode of production, combinations are frequently found. For example, the Kazak and the Bakhtiari practice some agriculture and hunting and gathering in addition to nomadic pastoralism.

Many nomadic pastoral societies have undergone great changes under pressure from the governments of their nations and as a result of other contemporary events, such as wars, revolutions, and famines; thus their way of life may no longer be as we have described it above. The homeland of the Marsh Arabs became a major battleground of the recent Iran-Iraq war and was a center of military activity during the Gulf war. The long period of drought in the Sahel has seriously affected the economy of the Fulani and has forced them to sell their herds. The Kazaks in the Soviet Union have been collectivized since the 1930s. Kazaks living in the Peoples Republic of China first underwent an earlier period of collectivization but now, under a more relaxed political regime, again have their own herds of horses. The nomadic groups of Iran were forcibly sedentarized by Reza Shah in the 1920s in order to exercise political control over them, resulting in the loss of their herds and livelihood. Migration was resumed after the abdication of Reza Shah in 1941. Sedentarization was attempted again by Mohammad Shah, Reza's son, in the 1960s, with the same disastrous results. How the nomadic tribes of Iran have fared since the Khomeini revolution is not clear.

Since nomadic pastoral peoples usually occupy marginal lands that are not suitable for agriculture, when they are forced to sedentarize, usually for political reasons, we often find them returning to nomadic pastoralism when political pressure is relaxed.

Organization of Work

The productive tasks performed by males and females are culturally determined. In hunting and gathering societies, there is a division between the female domain of gathering and collecting and the male domain of hunting. Often the gathering activities of women provide the greatest part of the food on which the group subsists. Nevertheless, the products of the hunt brought back by the men represent the most desirable food, and hunting is more prestigious an activity than gathering, reflecting the relative evaluation of male and female roles in the society. The productive tasks assigned to men in one society may be assigned to women in another. In some New Guinea societies, such as Tor, women cut down the sago palm to get its pith, while in other societies, such as the Abelam, men do this.

In both male and female domains, some work tasks are done individually and others in cooperative groups. The hunting of herd animals, such as caribou by the Nunamiut Eskimo and wild peccary by the Mundurucu of Brazil, was carried out communally. Similarly, organized hunting with nets by the Mbuti Pygmies involves group activity. These are cooperative endeavors carried out communally by all the males of the band or village, in the case of the Mundurucu. However, for species in which the animals tend to move individually, for example most of the animal species of the eastern United States, such as the moose, beaver, and porcupine, hunting is done on an individual basis. Gathering and collecting also tend to be done on an individual basis. Though on the northwestern coast of Canada groups of women may go to berrying territories as a group, the berry picking is done individually. The preparation of sago from pith is done in many New Guinea societies on a cooperative basis by women.

In societies whose mode of subsistence involves the cultivation of crops, men tend to be concerned with the preparation of the land for growing, that is, the preparation of the garden plot or field, and also with water-control systems if these are present. Both men and women may be involved in planting, weeding, and harvesting. In some New Guinea societies a clear distinction is made between certain crops, such as bananas and sugar cane, which are grown by men, and other crops, such as sweet potatoes, which are grown by women. When plows and mechanized agricultural implements are introduced, the whole range of agricultural tasks usually becomes the province of men, and women are limited to growing vegetables in gardens, if they are involved in agricultural tasks at all. In nomadic pastoral societies, the task of herding and moving the camp is in the male realm, while women milk the animals and manufacture milk products.

The organization of work in a society relates to the nature of social groupings in that society. Cooperative endeavors in which people work communally serve to reinforce the social solidarity of the group. When the most important subsistence tasks for a society are performed by men acting cooperatively, the residence pattern after marriage tends to be virilocal, whereas when the tasks are performed by women working together, the postmarital residence pattern tends to be uxorilocal. As we shall see in the chapter on political organization, the way that work is organized is often also part of the political system. Chiefs, in societies that have them, are frequently instrumental in organizing certain kinds of production. For example, Trobriand chiefs organize the activities of their clansmen in building a canoe, and Kwakiutl chiefs organize the members of their *numaym* when they build a new house.

Distribution

If production is that part of economic organization concerned with how societies utilize labor and technology to convert environmental resources into cultural products for consumption, then distribution is the manner in which such cultural products circulate through society. What is of concern in discussing systems of distribution or exchange is who gives what to whom, when, where, and how. In every society, the system of distribution can be described in terms of cultural rules. There will be categories of rules concerning the relationship between giver and receiver; the obligations of the giver (for example, mother's brother) to receiver (for example, sister's son); the occasions on which goods are to be given (a birth, a wedding, a funeral); the proper types of goods that are to be given to one category of persons and not to another category; the rules for the behavior involving the giving; and the setting or location where the giving is to take place. These are cultural rules that, like all other cultural rules, have to do with what is considered appropriate behavior for individuals. People use these rules as a guide for behavior, interpreting the rules in their own way. The manner in which goods move in a society is determined both by the operation of cultural rules and by the way in which individuals in the system interpret them. Even in complex societies, where distribution of goods is carried out in markets, cultural rules are operative in addition to supply and demand. The following examples illustrate different kinds of distribution or exchange systems and indicate variations in the cultural rules.

Though systems of exchange may vary, there are certain general principles that apply universally. Exchange may be broken down into three components: to give, to receive, and to return. The offer of a material object initiates a process. It may be accepted or declined. Both the offer and its acceptance or refusal have particular consequences. If the object is accepted, then its equivalent must at some point be returned. The acceptance creates a relationship through time, at least until the return is made. The refusal to accept something offered creates a relationship, but of a negative sort, diametrically opposite to the relationship created by acceptance. From this simple model of exchange, certain observations may be made. Giving, receiving, and returning are a process over time. From the initial offer until the return, two individuals or two groups are linked to each other in a relationship. The acceptance of something offered constitutes the assumption of an obligation to return—recipients place themselves in debt to the givers. If such "indebtedness" continues for a long period of time or if goods go repeatedly in the same direction and are not returned, then the recipients become inferior and the givers superior. The recipients are inferior in the eyes of others as well as in their own eyes. Giving, receiving, and returning therefore create links. The links may be positive, since exchange may be the basis for seeking assistance, recruiting allies, and creating alliances. But there is also an aggressive component in that giving, receiving, and returning usually involve competition. Recipients who cannot return and are in an inferior position may even perceive the initial offer as an aggressive act designed to shame them in the eyes of others. Though exchange, or the distribution of economic goods, may be perceived primarily as an economic phenomenon, in fact it frequently is linked to differences in rank and the political structure; hence the need to view these conjointly as political economy.

Food is universally one of the most significant items of exchange. In many societies, before food is distributed, it is displayed and serves as a source of pride, as it signifies accomplishment and hard work. The display represents the political strength of the group and gives aesthetic pleasure, as we noted for the Trobrianders in Chapter 2. Large-scale accumulations of goods for distribution symbolize the group itself, as was discussed in Chapter 4. This is true even in our own society in the significance placed upon the food, its amount and quality, served at a wedding reception, as is exemplified by the Shriver-Schwartzenegger wedding described in Chapter 2.

Distribution in Egalitarian Societies

Several types of exchange systems characterize egalitarian societies. The simplest type of exchange system involves two sides, of equal status, in continuing exchange with each other. Egalitarian societies are ones in which rank differences are absent. The two sides can be two parts of a village, two clans, or two moieties. This is referred to as *reciprocal exchange* (see Figure 1). It is identical to the concept of restricted exchange applied to the exchange of women in marriage.

Reciprocal exchange is the basis for the exchange system of the Abelam of New Guinea, studied by Phyllis Kaberry (1940), whose mode of production has already been described in this chapter. Their reciprocal exchange system involves only the exchange of goods. They do not have direct sister exchange and bilateral cross-cousin marriage. However, they do have moieties, and the exchange of goods is across moiety lines. The moieties are not named but are referred to as "us" and "them." The Abelam live in patrilineal clan hamlets that are paired with one another across moiety lines. Men in one clan have *tshambura,* or partners with whom they exchange. In our discussion of the cultivation practices of the Abelam, we talked about the special gardens in which men grow long yams solely for purposes of exchange. These yams are of a different species than the yams grown by the women for subsistence and are selected and bred for their

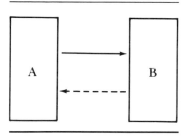

Figure 1
Reciprocal Exchange.

Long yams dressed as men, painted and decorated with feathers and shells, are exchanged at the Abelam yam ceremony.

great length. The gardens of long yams are tended only by men under the leadership of the head of the clan, who uses his special magical knowledge to make the yams grow very long. He himself must abstain from sexual intercourse for the whole growing period of the yams, since sexual contact with women will prevent the yams from growing long. The strength, prowess, and magical power of the group is measured by the length of their yams. The yams are carefully harvested, individually decorated with flowers, feathers, and masks, and then displayed at the ceremony at which they will be distributed to the exchange partners of the group that has grown them. At this ceremony, from which women are barred, all the important men from surrounding hamlets are present as witnesses to the exchange, and they partake of the feast that accompanies it. The giver of the yam keeps a record of the length and circumference of that yam so that the yam given in return can be compared, since it must be the equivalent of what has been given. The leader of the group is in charge of the harvest, decoration, and distribution of the yams. The return is not immediate. It is delayed until sometime in the future, when the group that has received is ready to give. Exchange partners also exchange pigs and perform important services for one another in connection with the initiation of their respective sons.

Reciprocal exchange systems such as that of the Abelam exhibit the following characteristics. They involve two sides that are continually exchanging with one another. Though they may compete to outdo one another, the rule of equivalence in exchange keeps that sort of competition in check. Each side also needs the other, since they perform important services for each other.

More complex systems of economic distribution occur when there are alterations in the rules of exchange. For example, if more than two groups are involved in an exchange system, the pattern becomes significantly different from that of reciprocal exchange described above. Delays in the exchange also operate in these kinds of systems, but in a somewhat different way. The Maring of the New Guinea highlands, who were studied by Roy Rappaport (1984), are an example of a society whose system of economic distribution or exchange involves one host group distributing simultaneously to a number of other groups. This distributive system focuses upon a religious ceremony referred to as the *kaiko,* which extends over many months. The Maring have patrilineal descent; a group of closely related clans serves as hosts of the *kaiko.* The guests who are given pork at the *kaiko* come in groups from the neighboring territories that surround the host group on all sides (see Figure 2). These neighboring groups are groups with which the host group intermarries. Each of these independent groupings of clans has been allied in war to the host group. Each group of guests is invited to come to dance, and they come brandishing their weapons and singing war songs. In the Maring *kaiko,* the dancing involves an aggressive display on the part of guests and hosts. This occurs despite the fact that guests and hosts exchange women with one another, are allied to one another, and distribute food and valuable goods to one another. A great number of pigs are killed by the host, and cooked pork is distributed at the final *kaiko* event. Large amounts of sweet potatoes are grown in order to feed the pigs. It is primarily the task of the Maring women to raise the sweet potatoes and care for the pigs. It takes several years to raise pigs for the *kaiko,* and increasing amounts of sweet potatoes

Figure 2.   *Kaiko* **Exchange.**

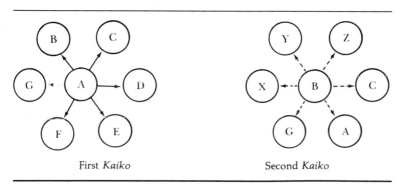

First *Kaiko*   Second *Kaiko*

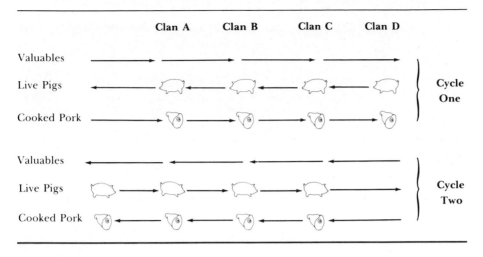

	Clan A	Clan B	Clan C	Clan D

Figure 3.   Enga *Te* Exchange.

must be raised to feed the growing pig herd. Production is therefore directed toward amassing pigs for the *kaiko* distribution. Each of the guest groups will, in the future, hold its own *kaiko,* at which it will fulfill its obligations to make a return. Within a wide area, different groups successively will be holding *kaiko* over a span of years. The Maring distribution system does not involve just two groups, as in reciprocal exchange; rather it involves one group giving to many groups at the same time. The host group is then invited in turn to each of the *kaiko* that the guest groups will hold in the future.

Still more complex systems of exchange link groups together in chains so that goods move from group to group and serve to link an entire region by means of a system of economic exchange. This is an example of generalized exchange, and it is identical to the concept of generalized exchange as applied to the exchange of women. The rules in this kind of system direct the flow of some of the most highly valued goods in the society, upon which great productive effort has been lavished. The distribution system of the Enga, investigated by Mervyn Meggitt (1974), whose system of production we have already described, is of this type. It is known as the *Te* (see Figure 3). Enga patrilineal clans occupy contiguous areas. They fight with their neighbors but also exchange women and goods with them. People who are affines to one another may also become exchange partners, or *Te* partners, to one another. Instead of giving to all one's *Te* partners in many clans at the same ceremony, as is the case for the Maring, an Enga man will have two groups of *Te* partners, one in clans to the east of his group and a second set in clans to the west of his clan. He transmits goods he receives from his eastern partners at their *Te* ceremonies to his western

*Sides of cooked pork are displayed on an enormous platform, ninety feet long, before
they are distributed at an Enga* Te *ceremony held in the summer of 1974.*

partners at the *Te* ceremony that his clan hosts, and vice versa (see Figure
3). The Enga therefore have two different kinds of partners, whereas the
Abelam and Maring have only one kind of partner to whom they give and
from whom they receive. The Enga have one group from whom they
receive and another to whom they give, and they never immediately reciprocate to the *Te* partner from whom they receive. Instead, they have a system of delayed exchange in which goods move from one group to the next
until they reach the end of the chain, when, like a typewriter ribbon, they
must reverse and go down the line in the opposite direction. People who
were givers of valuables such as stone axes, shells, plumes, and small pigs
in the first stage become receivers of live pigs in the second stage. Live pigs
move down the chain as they are distributed at successive *Te* distributions
held in turn by each clan from one end of the chain to the other. At the
end of the chain, there is a second reversal, when the last receiver of live
pigs becomes the first distributor of cooked pork. The pigs are slaughtered,
cooked in earthen ovens, and distributed. The distribution of cooked pork
completes one cycle of the *Te*. It will begin again when initiatory gifts go in
the direction opposite to the pork. Built into the rules of the *Te* is the delay
in the return, since goods must go down the entire length of the chain
through successive *Te* ceremonies before the *Te* partner to whom clan A
has given live pigs gives pork back to clan A.

    Giving and receiving in the *Te* exemplifies the ambivalence seen in the
other kinds of exchanges we have described and in exchange in general.
Clans who are neighbors, though potential enemies to one another, are

dependent upon one another to pass on the objects of the *Te*. If warfare does break out in the middle of a *Te* cycle, the *Te* is disrupted. It is in the interest of *Te* partners in other clans to make peace between the combatants so that goods can continue to move along the *Te* chains. The Enga production system, as has been shown above, is based upon the intensive cultivation of sweet potatoes, which are used to feed the large numbers of pigs used in the *Te* as well as to feed people. The Enga value their pigs greatly; yet their distribution system sends out the pigs that they raise along a line of exchange partners until the pigs eventually come back as roast pork.

The ceremonial distributions that we have described—the Abelam yam exchange, the Maring *kaiko*, and the Enga *Te*—involve the exchange of highly valued goods toward which much productive energy is directed. However, it should be made clear that other kinds of distributions of goods exist in these societies. In all of them, affinal relations demand the distribution of valuable goods to in-laws, particularly at various rites-of-passage ceremonies. Despite significant changes in the economic organization of these Papua New Guinea societies—including the cash cropping of coffee, the production of cattle for market, and the purchase of Western food and other goods—the Abelam, Maring, and Enga continue to hold their ceremonial distributions. Money and cattle have been introduced into these ceremonial exchanges, but the structure of exchange has not been altered.

Systems of Distribution in Societies with Rank

In our general discussion of the principles of exchange we noted that continued indebtedness on the part of the receiver could lead to status differences, with the giver becoming superior and the receiver, who is unable to repay the debt, placed in an inferior position. The kinds of exchange systems in the societies we have discussed up to now stressed the equivalence in status of groups that constitute givers and receivers. There are, however, societies in which rank differences, which are an integral part of the political structure, play a significant role in the exchanges. The Kwakiutl potlatch described in Chapter 2, which took place on the occasion of a wedding, is a kind of distribution in which rank and rank differences are central to the exchanges. The Kwakiutl have cognatic descent groups, the *numayms*. Theoretically, every person in Kwakiutl society holds a rank position that is associated with a name owned by his or her *numaym*, and which is inherited. The rank position of that name can be raised through potlatching. The Kwakiutl use a number of rite-of-passage events as occasions for potlatches, ceremonies at which large amounts of food and property are distributed to assembled guests. Great quantities of food and goods must be accumulated in preparation for a potlatch. This meant, in the past, gathering and storing smoked salmon, olachen grease (oil from the candlefish), berries, and other food, and accumulating blankets and other valuables such as jewelry, masks, and even canoes. These valuables, as described in Chapter 2, are referred to as "trifles." Potlatches may be hosted by one *numaym,* or a group of *numayms* or tribes. At each potlatch, the person whose rite of passage is being celebrated receives a new name. A succession of potlatches is held for a great chief's son as he grows older; at each one he gets increasingly more important titles until at the greatest potlatch he assumes the name that entitles him to the position of chief.

The guests who come to a potlatch serve as witnesses to the event, such as the succession to chiefly power, and receive goods. The guests are seated according to their rank, and they receive goods in that order. These guests are affines of the host, and their group is linked in marriage to the host group. The *numayms* who come as guests are feted and given gifts and must at some future time reciprocate by making a return potlatch. Kwakiutl potlatches are sometimes described as if the motivation for them is competition and the desire to shame one's rivals. As we have pointed out above, all exchange involves some form of competition, and since guests at a Kwakiutl potlatch are also affines, the Kwakiutl potlatch is no more competitive than other kinds of affinal exchanges. Even when coppers were "destroyed" by being cut, as described in Chapter 2, the other chief who is challenged by this act thanks his host for doing this. In order to raise one's rank in the rank scale, it is necessary to hold a potlatch, but one needs equally high-ranking competitors to challenge. Once again, as in all exchange systems, the givers and receivers are dependent upon one another at the same time they compete with one another. The rules governing what must be done when someone assumes a new title or position in effect provide a mechanism, through the potlatch, for redistributing the productive resources of Kwakiutl society.

The potlatch as a form of ceremonial exchange is found in other Native American societies on the Pacific coast of Canada and Alaska. Although all potlatches involve ceremonial distributions, potlatches take somewhat different forms, and the rules differ depending on the nature of the kinship system of the society. This can best be seen by a brief look at the potlatch system of the Tlingit, northern neighbors of the Kwakiutl. In the past the Tlingit were also fishermen, hunters, and gatherers, whose rich environment also enabled them to produce surplus goods. However, while the Kwakiutl have cognatic descent and *numayms*—cognatic kin groups—the Tlingit have a different kind of social structure based on matrilineal descent and matrilineal clans together with avunculocal residence. In addition to the clans, there are also matrilineal moieties, the Wolves and the Ravens. They also have a preference for marriage with father's sister's daughter, which means that each Tlingit clan intermarries with two other matrilineal clans, both of them in the opposite moiety (see Chapter 5, Figure 11).

While the Kwakiutl hold potlatches on the numerous occasions that mark both the growth and increased achievement of a person, the Tlingit have basically only one occasion for a potlatch. It is held when a chief dies and his heir, his sister's son, sponsors the various rites of the funeral and

Chiefs in ceremonial garb wearing their crests at a Tlingit potlatch in Sitka, Alaska, held at the turn of the century.

has a mortuary totem pole erected. By means of this funerary potlatch, the new chief assumes the title, name, and position of his mother's brother. Immediately after the death of the chief, his heir, with the help of the entire clan, begins to accumulate large amounts of goods in preparation for the potlatch. In the past, special food such as olachen grease, preserved berries, and dried fish was gathered and stored. Large quantities of blankets purchased from the Hudson's Bay Company, blankets decorated with buttons, and other forms of property were also accumulated in order to be distributed. The two other matrilineal clans who intermarry with the host clan come as guests and perform important services for the host clan. One clan builds a new house for the heir, and the other clan buries the dead chief and erects the carving in his honor. Both clans also perform the service of witnessing the inauguration of the new chief when he takes on the title of his predecessor. The Tlingit and Kwakiutl potlatches are both systems in which large amounts of goods, in the past produced by a rich economy based upon fishing, hunting, and gathering, are accumulated by chiefs with the help of their kin groups specifically for the purposes of ceremonial distribution to other groups. However, the occasions on which potlatches occur and the manner in which groups are organized and intermarry in cognatic and matrilineal societies differ. This potlatch system of economic distribution operates through the kinship system, which provides the links that channel the flow of goods. Though the potlatch was outlawed by the Canadian government toward the end of the nineteenth century, it continued to be held secretly. The prohibition ended in 1951, and after that, large-scale potlatches began to be held.

Trobriand society, a horticultural society whose staple crop is yams and whose system of production is very different from that of the Tlingit and Kwakiutl, holds *sagali,* or large-scale ceremonial distributions of yams and other foodstuffs, which are structurally identical to the potlatches of the Tlingit. The Trobrianders also have matrilineal clans, avunculocal residence, and father's sister's daughter marriage like the Tlingit (see Chapter 5, Figure 11). An important part of Trobriand funerary rites, described in Chapter 2, is the mortuary *sagali.* The funerary *sagali* is a distribution to the clan of the wife of the dead chief in exchange for all the funerary services provided by clan members. This is the same pattern as in the Tlingit potlatch. The Trobrianders also hold a *sagali* when the chief's sister becomes pregnant. The chief's sister is important since it is her son who will succeed to the position of chief in this matrilineal society. The guests at a pregnancy *sagali* are the father's lineage of the chief and his sister, who have performed services for the chief's sister during her pregnancy and are getting the ceremonial distribution of food, yams, areca nuts, and bananas. In the case of the Trobrianders, the two clans that intermarry with the host clan are guests of two separate *sagali,* a funeral *sagali* and a pregnancy *sagali,* whereas in the Tlingit potlatch these two groups of guests are present at the same time but seated on opposite sides of the house (see Chapter 5, Figure 11).

In addition to *sagali,* the Trobrianders have other types of exchanges. After every harvest, yams are distributed. This is called *urigubu.* The Trobrianders do not pay bridewealth to the bride's family on the occasion of a marriage. Instead, the marriage initiates the annual payment of yams, the *urigubu,* by a man to his sister's husband (see Figure 4). The Trobrianders have three kinds of gardens: the mixed garden and the taro garden for their own use, and the main yam garden to produce the *urigubu* that goes to the sister's husband. So at harvest time, gardeners in sundry Trobriand villages are accumulating piles of yams, which they will display

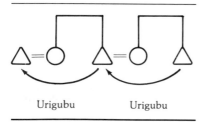

Urigubu   Urigubu

Figure 4
Urigubu **Payments.**

in their own villages. Then, these heaps of yams are ceremonially carried to the house of the sister's husband and presented to him. He will store them in his yam house. In the meantime, the giver of yams will in return be receiving yams from his wife's brother. Yams are the staple crop, and great care and productive effort is given to these yams, though they will eventually be given away. Yams for *urigubu* represent the prestige of the giver as a gardener and as a kinsman fulfilling an obligation. Thus, at harvest time, a great deal of effort is devoted to the display and transportation of yams to be consumed by households other than that of the producer. The most economically efficient system would be for everyone to grow and then eat his own yams. The distribution system of the Trobrianders is different and makes sense only in terms of their matrilineal system. The *urigubu* is paid to the husbands and fathers of the matrilineal lineage for carrying out the important social role, not the biological role, of father. (Trobrianders did not believe that fathers play a role in conception.) Malinowski referred to *urigubu* as economic tribute, and in the case of chiefs it is indeed tribute. A chief takes many wives, up to twenty or more, who are given to him by all the village headmen in his district. The headmen's payments of *urigubu* to the chief are used by the chief to make *sagali*. With so many brothers-in-law, the chief accumulates many yams after each harvest, which he then redistributes as rewards to his followers on the various occasions for feasts.

In addition to *sagali* and *urigubu* distributions, the Trobrianders have a third kind of economic exchange, *kula* exchange. This exchange system links the Trobriand Islands with a circle of other islands that are different culturally and linguistically and are considered dangerous places by the Trobrianders (see Figure 5). The exchange system organizes the islands into an enormous circle. The goods exchanged in the *kula* are two kinds of shell valuables—red shell necklaces, which are exchanged from island to island so that they move clockwise around the circle, and white armshells, which move counterclockwise. Since the islands are separated by stretches of open sea, it is necessary to sail the small native craft to the island of one's *kula* partner. According to the rules of the *kula*, the receivers in the exchange always undertake the voyage to the givers' island. To receive armshells, the Trobrianders would sail in a clockwise direction, east, to the island of Kitava. To receive red shell necklaces, they sail in a counterclockwise direction, south, to the island of Dobu. Thus, *kula* partners are always exchanging red shell necklaces for armshells, and vice versa, but never armshells for armshells or necklaces for necklaces. *Kula* exchange is identical in structure to generalized exchange, that is, the structure of matrilateral cross-cousin marriage described in Chapter 5.

The exchange of shell valuables in the *kula* creates alliances between groups living in potentially hostile areas. While the *kula* exchange, with its elaborate ceremony, is being carried out, at the same time another form of exchange—direct barter of food, pottery, and other manufactured utilitarian objects—is also taking place between the *kula* visitors and their hosts.

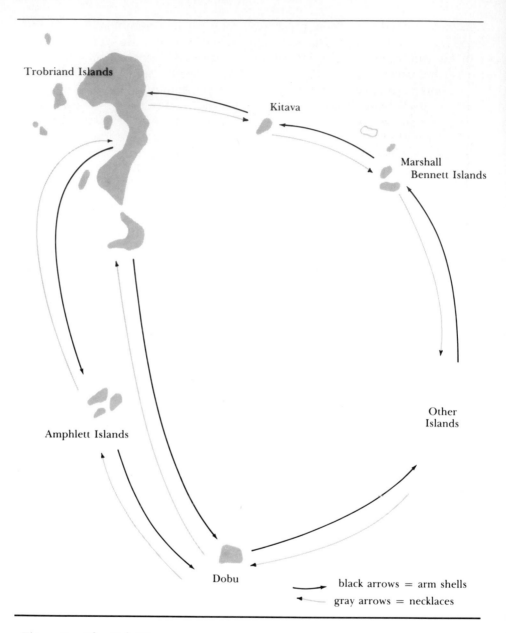

Figure 5.   The *Kula* Ring.

The barter involves the exchange of items that are scarce or absent on one island but not on another. For example, the Trobrianders bring food, plentiful on their island, to exchange for the pottery of the Amphlett Islands. The rules of *kula* exchange require a great deal of ceremonial behavior, while barter is just the opposite. *Kula* exchange is delayed, and barter is

Armshell valuables, which have been brought from the island of Kitava, are to be given to kula *exchange partners on Trobriand Island. Photographed by Malinowski during his 1914–1918 fieldwork.*

direct; *kula* does not involve bargaining, while barter involves trying to get the best deal for oneself. Therefore barter is never conducted with one's *kula* partners but rather with others on the island that one visits.

Each of the three kinds of exchange systems—*sagali, urigubu,* and *kula*—involves a somewhat different range of goods. The social structure serves as the matrix for the exchange systems, in that chiefs are the focal points of all three kinds of distributions. All married men give *urigubu,* but chiefs receive many times more than the ordinary person. Many adult men are involved in *kula* ring exchange, but chiefs own the canoes used, have more *kula* partners, and have in their temporary possession the most valuable objects. The three kinds of exchange systems continue to operate among the Trobrianders despite the fact that they are part of a province of the Papua New Guinea nation-state.

Though the horticultural mode of production of the Trobrianders is markedly different from the fishing, hunting, and gathering mode of the Tlingit and Kwakiutl, all three have rank systems. This means that there are titles and positions of importance that are inherited from one generation to the next. Despite the difference in mode of production, all three societies produce economic surpluses. In these societies, distribution of goods at potlatches and at *sagali* serves to enhance one's rank and prestige. Goods are given to chiefs by their followers in their kin groups as a kind of tribute; the chiefs accumulate these goods and redistribute them on ceremonial occasions. When the chief serves as a host at such a ceremonial redistribution, he thereby validates his claim to high rank. The acceptance of the redistributed goods by the guests means they recognize his claim to high rank. Rank in these societies is flexible, in that the more one distributes, the higher one's rank becomes.

The nature of exchanges is significantly altered when rank differences become fixed. In examples of such systems, aristocrats are separate from commoners, lords from vassals, patrons from clients, and high castes from low castes. These groups differ not only in rank and prestige but also in the economic resources that they control. We also find economic specialization and the division of labor in these societies. The systems of economic distribution and the exchanges that are found in societies with ranked strata always emphasize the inferiority of vassal, client, commoner, and low-caste individual and the superiority of aristocrat, lord, patron, and high-caste individual. When superiors give to inferiors, this is seen as generosity or largess. When inferiors give to superiors, this is seen as tribute. No matter how much tribute the inferiors give, this does not raise their status. It merely further enhances the prestige of their superiors. At the same time, the greater generosity and continual distributions of the superiors also enhance their status and not that of the inferiors. This is not contrary to the general principles of exchange that we have discussed (although it may seem so); rather it is a demonstration of the way in which the social structure determines the meanings of the exchanges. If, in a culture, the lord is defined as superior, his superiority is demonstrated both when he gives and when he receives. The Bunyoro of western Uganda in precolonial times illustrate this kind of an economic system. Among the Bunyoro, studied by John Beattie (1960), the king granted rights over land and over those who cultivated it to chiefs as a reward for service. Chiefs visited the king to give him tribute, consisting of cattle, beer, and grain. The king, on his part, gave frequent feasts. For special services, the king might also give cattle to particular individuals. The chiefs stood in the same relationship to their commoners as the king stood to the chiefs. Commoners brought the chief tribute, and the chief gave feasts. The Bunyoro also illustrate an interesting general point—tribute always seems to be paid in the form of food in its uncooked form, raw or on the hoof, while generosity takes the form of feasts or cooked food.

Not far from the Bunyoro, in neighboring Rwanda, live the Tutsi herders, who in an earlier time dominated the Hutu agriculturalists, whom they controlled within a single political state. Tutsi nobles granted the use of cattle, a strategic resource in this society, to their Hutu clients in exchange for the herding services and some of the pastoral products, as well as the agricultural products of the Hutu. The Tutsi and the Hutu are economically specialized groups of herders and agriculturalists. The groups are hierarchically ranked with respect to one another, and each one is endogamous. As we have noted earlier in this chapter, the Tutsi and the Hutu, together with the Twa hunters, form a caste system like that of India.

In India, castes are endogamous, highly specialized occupational groups. In any particular place, all the castes together form a caste system in which members of the various castes perform their services for one another under the supervision and control of the landholders. The castes are hierarchically ordered, from the Brahmans, who are priests at the top, to the Untouchables, who are tanners, washermen, and sweepers who carry away human excrement. Though Indian castes are relatively fixed in rank, individual castes may disagree on their placement within the system and attempt to change it with respect to other groups.

Where rank differences in the social system are fixed, we find economically specialized occupational groups that are tied together in an interdependent system of economic exchanges. Economic subsistence in these societies is completely dependent upon exchange. The ways in which goods and services are exchanged express the rank differences within the society.

The Market System

The market system is the exchange system with which Americans are most familiar. Its characteristics are different in many respects from those of the exchange systems we have discussed up to now. Perhaps the distinctive feature of market exchange is that the buyer need have no other social relationship with the seller. While one may deal with the same grocer, butcher, or supermarket over many years, one may shift overnight and carry out the same transaction with another store. The relationship between buyer and seller is not dependent upon any other relationship, but has its basis solely in the fact that the seller has something that the buyer wants or needs and is willing to pay for. The relationship can even consist of a single purchase, never to be repeated again. This is in sharp contrast to all the distribution systems we have described up to now. Long yams move back and forth between Abelam exchange partners who are in a fixed social relationship. Kwakiutl chiefs who are affines to one another hold potlatches, taking turns as host and guest. The basic premise of a market system is to make a profit, and the essence of profit is to buy cheap and sell for more than you have paid. Transactions in a market system are governed by bargaining or haggling over price rather than determined by social relationships. In haggling, a buyer tries to buy something as cheaply as possible. This is in contrast to a Trobriand *sagali* or a Kwakiutl potlatch, where the more that is given, the greater the prestige of the giver. The receiver of goods who cannot reciprocate gets the worst of the deal. In the market system, the buyer gives as little as the seller will accept.

A market system is dependent upon the existence of money. Societies that do not have market systems do not have money in the usual sense of that term. Money serves a number of purposes. It can be used as a standard of value because any commodity, service, or labor can be expressed in terms of its monetary worth. Money can be used as a store of value, because it can be hoarded and later used to obtain commodities or services.

But most importantly, money can serve as a medium of exchange whereby one commodity can be transferred in exchange for money and then that money can be used in exchange for any other kind of goods or services. The last use of money is the broadest, and the other purposes, in a sense, can be derived from it. The money used in our society is considered to be all-purpose money, because it can be exchanged for anything in the society and serves all the above uses and others as well. The valuables we have discussed in connection with ceremonial distribution, like the armshells and necklaces in the *kula*, are objects that have value but can be used only for particular ceremonies, such as the *kula*. A Trobriand chief who is obliged to make a *sagali* but has an insufficient supply of yams cannot increase his supply of yams by exchange of *kula* valuables for more yams. *Kula* valuables can only be exchanged with *kula* partners in the *kula* exchange. There are many other societies within which such special-purpose valuables are found. The restricted uses to which such valuables are put is in contrast to the many purposes that money serves.

The term *market* has two meanings. The first refers to the location or site where food commodities and craft items are bought and sold. The second meaning characterizes an entire economic system based upon the determination of prices by the market, that is, in terms of supply and demand. Not all societies with market sites are total market economies. For example, there are societies like the Kanuri in Nigeria, where, in precolonial times, marketplaces were highly developed as the locations where food was sold for fixed prices, while clothing, animals, and artisans' goods imported from other societies were sold for fluctuating prices. However, land and labor were not commodities that could be bought and paid for. Land could be given or taken away only by the king, and labor was provided by the traditional obligations of the social structure. Hence, this was only a partial market economy, since not everything could be bought and sold. The same was true of Europe in feudal times. Markets were periodically held at particular locations where food and other goods were bought and sold, with prices determined by supply and demand. Labor there was carried out by the traditional obligations of the system of serfdom. Land was part of a larger social and political system and could not be freely bought and sold. With the commercial and then the industrial revolutions, all of this rapidly changed to a system in which land, labor, and, in our present-day society, virtually anything can be bought and sold.

Whereas in nonmarket economic systems, the economy is embedded in a larger cultural matrix, the growth of a market economy in an industrialized capitalist society is the development of an economic institution that is separate and independent of other institutions. With this development, the economy now sets the tone and the values for other institutions. The economy influences morality. The axiom "What's good for business is good for the country" illustrates this point. Some people even believe that if a few bribes or kickbacks are necessary to conduct business, then bribery is not immoral, especially if the bribes are given outside the United States. In a market economy, all economic behavior is evaluated in market terms, with individuals making decisions in order to cut the best deal for themselves. Anthropologists have been interested in the factors that determine how decisions are made and whether these decisions are based exclusively on expectations of economic gain or loss. Such studies often assume that individuals make "rational" choices for themselves and that their purpose is always to maximize their own position.

In a market economy, labor also operates according to the laws of supply and demand. Workers go to places where employment is available. If a factory closes, its workers are expected to freely move to other places where work is available. In Europe, this sometimes means moving to another country. If an industry like the steel industry in the United States loses out to foreign competition, the workers in that industry are expected to retrain themselves for positions in other industries.

Much of the world today operates as a single market. However, what is good for workers in the modernized economies of Taipei or Hong Kong creates hardships for workers who have lost their jobs as a result of a plant closing in Elizabeth, New Jersey. The world system of money and markets has penetrated even the most remote societies. In some of them, it coexists with reciprocity and redistributive systems.

The market principle, which is based upon the law of supply and demand, assumes that nothing exists within our society which cannot be purchased with money. However, in our society other kinds of exchanges continue to coexist with the market system. Our society has cultural rules about reciprocal gift exchange. People who give you gifts expect them to be reciprocated with a gift that is roughly equivalent. Our rules do not require the recipient to return like for like, as the Abelam do. People often bring gifts when invited for dinner. It is appropriate to bring wine or flowers, but not considered appropriate to bring a pound of ground sirloin or to give the hostess a ten dollar bill.

Consumption

The end point of producing and distributing is consuming. Every aspect of consumption is determined by cultural rules. Consumption means more than eating. However, we will deal with the consumption of food first. When, where, how, and what you eat is determined by culture. Animals may feed, but humans eat meals. The number of meals per day and the time during the day when one eats vary from society to society. Where you eat is also culturally determined. For example, in many New Guinea societies, men eat in a men's house separate from women. Each wife brings her husband's food to the men's house, but she and her children eat separately in their own house. As we pointed out in the description of the

American funeral in Chapter 2, when wakes were held in the home, it was appropriate to serve food, but now that funerals are held in a chapel or funeral home, food is no longer appropriate. Nor is it appropriate to eat food in the lecture hall of a university, even though the anthropology professor may be talking about food.

How you eat is also determined by cultural rules. In India it is appropriate to eat with your fingers, though only with the fingers of the right hand. This is because other bodily functions are carried out with the left hand. In our society only "finger food" may be eaten with one's fingers. Otherwise, everything must be eaten with a fork or spoon. In China meals are taken with wooden sticks called chopsticks. To have a knife on the table is considered barbaric.

What people eat is not determined solely by what is available as a resource in the environment. What is considered to be edible is, in addition, determined by cultural rules. Cultures rank food in terms of what is highly desirable and what is minimal food. The Kwakiutl distinguish between "rich" food, such as olachen grease, and food used for everyday consumption. Only the former is suitable to serve guests at a potlatch. Frogs and snails are found in both France and England. However, the French eat escargots (snails) and frogs' legs, while the English do not consider these items to be food. This eating practice of the French so shocks the English that they use the word *frogs* as a derogatory term of reference for the French. Horses, dogs, and cows are raised in our society, but only the meat of the cow is used for human consumption. The anthropologist Marshall Sahlins has noted that though many dogs are raised in our society, we view eating them with abhorrence. However, the ancient Mexicans and ancient Hawaiians raised dogs to be used as food. While we have an aversion to eating horse meat, we do feed it to our dogs. However, horse meat is considered a desirable food by the French, as well as by nomadic pastoralists such as the Kazak and Kalmyk Mongols.

As we have noted in Chapter 4, a few societies also have rules that state that individuals cannot consume the pigs or yams they have raised themselves but must exchange them with others. They then eat the pigs and yams raised by someone else. This is true of the Abelam, whose exchange of long yams we have described above. The Abelam cannot eat their own long yams or pigs but must exchange them with their exchange partners, or *tshambura*. The Arapesh have the same practice. In fact, the Arapesh have the aphorism cited in Chapter 4 that states that you can't eat your own pigs and yams and you can't marry your own sister. You can only eat other people's yams and pigs and marry other people's sisters. Thus, this cultural rule about consumption is directly linked to the distribution and exchange of the goods produced by the society. Production, distribution, and consumption must be seen as interrelated parts of a larger economic system.

Consumption has a wider meaning than simply eating. Consumers in industrial societies like our own buy and use cars, appliances, and many other things in addition to food. In our own society, we talk about "guzzling gas." In nonindustrial societies, people may be said to "consume" such things as ceremonial objects and clothing.

Economic organization has always played a pivotal role in anthropological theorizing. The evolutionist Lewis Henry Morgan used technology as the basis for defining the stages of human cultural development, and contemporary Marxist anthropologists see the economy, defined as the mode of production, as strongly influencing other aspects of culture. Each of the theories of culture discussed in Chapter 1 has a particular perspective of or approach to the economic organization or economic aspect of society. Some stress the function of economic activities, others stress the structure of groups engaged in economic activities, and still others emphasize the role of the individual as an entrepreneur in the economic sphere. The economy as a system of symbolic meanings is the focus of some theories, while the economy as the means by which society adapts to the environment is the major thrust of others.

CHAPTER 8

Political Organization: Politics, Government, Law, and Conflict

 What is politics? Does politics always involve the use of power? What does it mean "to get an offer you can't refuse"? In American society, that phrase represents the exercise of power in a variety of contexts. It may be a way of getting a competitor to remove himself from the competition, or a way of forcing someone to do something he doesn't want to do. How does this idea, or other ideas about power and politics, operate in different societies? A Trobriand man aspiring to chiefly office will seize the opportunity of his mother's brother's death to organize the latter's funeral *sagali*. In this sense, a Trobriand funeral *sagali* is a political event. So too is the funeral of a Mafia boss, and the funeral of the secretary general of the Soviet Union. In all these examples, though the successor can come only from a small circle of eligible individuals, there is no fixed rule regarding this succession. The politics of power is an important aspect of the tapestry of culture.

We will begin to answer these questions about politics and power by looking first at small-scale noncentralized societies, where the processes of political organization may be seen more clearly. In order to understand the politics of Trobriand chiefdomship, we must examine the political organization of the society. Among the Trobrianders, the main island of Kiriwina is divided into a number of districts, each of which contains several villages. Four Trobriand matrilineal clans are dispersed throughout the districts. These clans are, in turn, divided into localized subclans. Within a particular

155

district, one subclan will rank higher than all the others, and its chief will be the paramount chief of the district. The other villages will have village headmen who are subordinate to the chief. The headmen give their sisters to the chief as wives and, as we pointed out in the previous chapter, each year furnish him with yams—*urigubu*—as tribute. When a chief dies, one of his real or classificatory sisters' sons succeeds to the position of chief, since there is no rule of succession like primogeniture. The contenders for the position of chief compete with one another. Before the man who succeeds can make the funerary *sagali* for his predecessor, he must demonstrate that he has many followers who will support him as the new chief and assist him at the *sagali*. The chiefly position among the Trobrianders is one that involves control over resources as well as over labor. The chief is titular owner of all the land in the district, although the garden magician and actual users of the land also have some rights in it. When the chief decides the time is propitious, he declares a *kayasa*, a period of feasting and competitive games, such as cricket, between his own village and another to be held at harvest time. As a result of this decision of the chief, all the people of the village are bound to work their hardest so the *kayasa* will be a success.

The chief can also marshal communal labor to perform tasks such as building a canoe. He gives food to the workers in return for their labor. The chief gives orders to people in his village, and these must be carried out. Malinowski stated that the chief has "special henchmen" to punish people who do not obey his orders. They may even inflict capital punishment. Frequently people obey the chief because they are afraid that he may command that evil magic be used against them. Special signs of deference are also shown to the chief. These are all symbols of authority of the type we discussed earlier. No man's head may be higher than that of the chief. Either the chief sits on a high platform, or people walk past him in a bent position. Only the chief may have a large, elaborately decorated yam house, where the *urigubu* yams given him as tribute are displayed. Members of the chief's subclan, the highest-ranked subclan, as "owners" of the village, are entitled to certain prerogatives. Only the members of this subclan may wear a certain kind of ornament, red spondylus shell disks, on their foreheads. Certain house decorations are used exclusively by this subclan. There are also certain food taboos that must be observed by people of rank. When the chief needs the support of his headmen and their villagers in warfare, he summons them with gifts of valuables. He must feed all those warriors who are mobilized.

In contrast, among the Yanomamo, there are no chiefs. Every Yanomamo man is his own boss, and no other Yanomamo can give him orders. The villages in which the Yanomamo live are each completely independent units. One village will entertain and feast another village in order to win its support as an ally. Villages that are enemies to one another will raid each other to capture women. Each Yanomamo village has a headman. The position is not hereditary but is held by individuals who have demonstrated ability as leaders. These leadership qualities include fearlessness in war and wisdom and judgment in planning the course of action for the village, in making alliances with other villages, in planning attacks on other villages, and in moving the village when the gardens are depleted. The headman does not make the decisions on his own; consensus among the men of the village must be obtained before any course of action is adopted. The headman does not direct individuals to do things; first he does them himself and thereby sets an example for the others to follow. No headman is completely secure in his position. He is constantly challenged by others who aspire to it. He is headman only as long as the villagers have confidence in his judgment. Another individual with supporters can begin to oppose the headman in his decisions. As this opposition grows, the headman, if the people lose confidence in him, may be supplanted by his rival, or the headman may inspire his villagers to use force to drive out the opposition. A third possibility is that the opposition leader and his group of followers may leave the village to form a new village of their own. Since there is no fixed rule of succession, the younger brother or son of a headman is no more likely to succeed as headman than any other adult man in the village. No one performs labor for the headman; he works his own garden. The headman has no special magical knowledge. There are shamans in Yanomamo society who have special access to the spirit world. However, the shaman is usually a different person from the headman. The shaman's special powers, though, may be utilized against enemy villages. There are no rank differences among the Yanomamo—all adult males are equal. Therefore, there are no outward signs of rank, no special deference, and no special food customs to differentiate aristocrats from commoners or those with power from those without it.

These two descriptions represent not merely differences between two societies. The Trobriand and Yanomamo examples represent two types of political organization that differ in the degree in which some members of the society control the actions of others in the society, as well as in a number of other features.

Concepts Used in Political Anthropology

The Trobriand and Yanomamo cases can be used to explore some of the concepts employed to examine the political systems found in all human societies, including our own. The key concept used in defining political organization is *power.* Power is the ability to command that others do certain things and to get compliance from them. On this point, one can immediately see the contrast between the Yanomamo and Trobrianders. The Yanomamo headman does not have the power to compel villagers to act in a particular way, whereas the Trobriand chief demonstrates his power in a whole range of activities. A distinction must be made between power and *authority*. When power becomes institutionalized, we say it has been transformed into authority. This means that there is a recognized position or *office*, the occupant of which can issue commands that must be obeyed. It is apparent that the Trobriand chief has authority, since the power he exercises derives from his office of chief and his commands are obeyed. What about the Yanomamo headman? Does he have any authority? The headman among the Yanomamo is a recognized position or office, but since the headman has no power to compel people to obey him, he has no authority. Nevertheless, he is a leader. Though he cannot compel others to obey his will, others will follow him if he has influence with them. Influence is the ability to persuade others to follow one's lead. They will continue to follow him and he will have influence over them as long as they have confidence in his leadership. Leadership is a type of social behavior found in a range of human groups, from informal assemblages to political states. When leadership is not vested in a formal institutionalized position and is based solely on influence, as is the case of the Yanomamo headman, loss of confidence means loss of followers and loss of leadership position.

Anthropologists studying political organization have also made a distinction between *politics* and *government*. Government is the decisions made by those in office on behalf of the entire group in carrying out common goals. This may involve implementing decisions about holding public festivals to maintain the prestige of the group, going to war to maintain the defense of the group, and dealing with the day-to-day matters of law and order. Thus, the Trobriand chief carries out important administrative functions. His decision to hold a *kayasa* involves the organization of production of those under him. Commoners in his district must work hard in the gardens to produce as much as possible in order to maintain the prestige of their village. The chief is also the initiator of overseas *kula* exchange and the owner of the canoe used. *Kula* deals with foreign affairs, literally overseas relations between Trobrianders and other peoples. In contrast, government among the Yanomamo is always a matter of the consensus of the group, even though they have a headman as their leader.

Politics is concerned with an entirely different aspect of political organization. Whereas government involves the carrying out of shared goals, politics involves people competing for power. A focus upon politics concentrates upon manipulation of people and resources, maneuvering, the rise of factions that compete for power, and the development of political parties with differing points of view. The study of politics does not emphasize common goals. Of course, it should be noted that in our own society as well as others, those vying for power in the political arena may claim that they are operating for the common good and not just for their own personal aggrandizement. They may actually believe this to be true. Politics emphasizes opposing points of view and conflict. It operates in both the Trobriand and Yanomamo examples. When a Trobriand chief dies, the rules of succession to the position of chief throw the choice of a new chief open to political maneuvering and competition among the individuals in the group of people eligible to succeed. These candidates must demonstrate their abilities as politicians to followers who are their fellow subclansmen. At this point, potential claimants to the chiefly office make promises and point to their demonstrated skills in organizational leadership and their wealth. The man who eventually succeeds to the position of chief makes the decisions of government.

Politics is constantly present among the Yanomamo, since Yanomamo headmen regularly face the potential opposition of those who also aspire to leadership in their village. Even the decision to hold a feast may be the basis for political maneuvering. A rival for the position of headman may himself try to organize a feast. He tries to convince others in the village that this is politically a wise decision. If he succeeds in enlisting the support of the majority of the villagers, then he has in effect become the new headman. If he can only mobilize partial support, he will have developed his own faction in the village, and he may try again in the future or even lead his faction off to found a new village. He may also fail to get any support, in which case he retires to the sidelines and sulks.

In the discussion to follow, it will become clear that a society's political structure is always interrelated with its economic structure. This is because the exercise of political power is based upon the control of economic resources. This close relationship is recognized by the use of the term *political economy*.

Types of Political Organization

In all human societies there is some form of authority and leadership. The simplest form of political organization is one in which leadership is manifested intermittently. This type of political organization may be called *situational leadership*. The Igluligmuit, an Eskimo group of eastern Canada, illustrate this type of political organization. The name given to the group means the people (*muit*) of Igluliq, who are all those living in that area. There are no fixed political offices, and a number of men, but never women, exert leadership in certain situations. Igluligmuit never come together as a single group, and there is no political structure for this entity. There are winter villages along the coast where a number of families related through various kinds of kin ties come together to spend the winter, exploiting the resources of the ocean. The same families do not winter together every year. The men of influence who exercise leadership in the winter village are the "boat owners." The boats are used by groups of men to hunt seals, and the boat owner is the senior male of the kin unit that owns the boats. Leadership is also exhibited in connection with the inland summer hunting of caribou. Numbers of families again come together. The hunting of caribou is conducted under the leadership of a man with expert knowledge. At the end of the hunt, the families scatter, and the leader is no longer a leader. Leadership operates only through influence, and different men exercise their influence in those areas where they have special expertise or abilities. These temporary leaders do not have the power to compel people to obey them. This kind of political organization was found among peoples whose subsistence was based exclusively upon hunting and gathering.

There are hunting and gathering societies that have more complex forms of organization. These are societies with what is known as *band organization*. The distinction between this and the previous type is that bands have a more fixed membership that come together annually to carry out joint ritual and economic activities. The Ojibwa—hunters and gatherers of the forests of the eastern subarctic in Canada—are an example of this type of society. During most of the year, small groups of related families move from one hunting area to another. In the summertime, the whole band frequently comes together on the shores of a lake and remains as a unit for the summer. Several men have influence and are leaders of the group.

The Yanomamo, though dependent on horticulture, a completely different mode of subsistence, have structurally the same type of political organization as the band. Each village is an independent unit equivalent to the band with a delimited membership and an office of headman, who has influence over his fellow villagers, but not authority. In Ojibwa and Yanomamo societies, the unit that acts as a political entity has more cohesiveness than political organizations with situational leadership. The political entity in societies with band organization acts as a unit under recognized leadership. However, that leadership is based on influence, not on authority.

A more complex political organization is the *Big Man* structure, which was first identified and analyzed in Melanesia. There is usually a native term for the Big Man position, and frequently it literally means "big man." In comparison with the Yanomamo headman structure, the Big Man structure represents sharper delineation of the leadership position. As leadership becomes more clearly defined, so does the group of followers. This group of followers is usually composed of the members of the Big Man's descent group, though the Big Man may also attract other kinsmen to that group. In Melanesia, the followers of a Big Man consist of ordinary men and some "rubbish men." The latter refers to men who do not participate in exchanges independently. Ordinary men are men who fulfill their obligations in exchanges with affines and kinsmen but do not take initiative in exchanges with other groups, as Big Men do. Instead, ordinary men contribute to what is accumulated by the Big Man of their group. Rubbish men are men who do not fulfill any of their obligations with regard to exchange. They are unmarried and dependent upon the wife of the Big Man to feed them in exchange for the labor they contribute to him. Men who do not fulfill male gender roles in economics and politics are called male women or male wastrels among the Arapesh of New Guinea. This indicates that, with regard to the exchange system, they are men who play political and economic roles like those of women. The Big Man organizes his group's production, which is geared to the accumulation of goods that will be distributed ceremonially in exchanges with other Big Men, also acting on behalf of their groups. Big Men are the nodes in the exchange system. They accumulate the goods of their group, ceremonially distribute those goods on behalf of their group to another Big Man, and then re-distribute to the members of their group what the other Big Man and his group have given in exchange. The Big Man derives his power from his di-rection of the ceremonial distribution of the goods accumulated by his group and the decisions he makes in the redistribution of goods within his own group. When another Big Man gives to him on behalf of his group, he decides how much each of his followers receives.

Earlier we pointed out that leadership can be exhibited in various areas of life. In the first type of political organization, situational leadership, dif-ferent individuals are leaders in different activities. Within the Big Man structure, the Big Man directs activities in a range of areas. For example, the Abelam exchange of long yams is between two Big Men, each acting on behalf of his patrilineal clan hamlet. Not only does the Abelam Big Man organize the labor involved in the production of these yams, but he also acts as the ritual expert, since he alone knows the magical spells that make the yams grow so long. On behalf of his entire group, he maintains sexual abstinence for the whole growing period. Prowess in warfare and artistic ability as a carver or painter of designs are also desirable characteristics in an Abelam Big Man, but the most important characteristic is his ability to produce the long yams on which the prestige of the entire group depends. Throughout New Guinea, oratorical skill of the Big Man is essential, since he must deliver speeches at ceremonial distributions as the representative of his group. The Big Man's involvement in warfare is usually in the orga-nizational area. Prowess as a warrior alone is not a sufficient qualification to become a Big Man, since the role of the Big Man in warfare primarily involves strategy and planning. The Arapesh and the Abelam are both soci-eties with patrilineal descent, and in neither of these societies are women permitted to carry out the role of Big Man. Since women cannot be near any phase of the growing or exchange of long yams among the Abelam, they cannot possibly be Big Men.

The position of Big Man is dependent on personal qualifications and individual ability. Anthropologists refer to this position as an *achieved status,* in contrast to an *ascribed status,* which is a position one inherits. At the prime of his life, a Big Man can carry out all the activities necessary to maintain his influence within his group. However, as he ages, he may no longer be able to do so. In that case, his leadership position may be challenged by other aspiring Big Men. Competition between challengers requires political skills and maneuvering. If the Big Man should die in the

An Abelam political leader sits before his men's house, wearing emblems and ornaments signifying that he is a Big Man.

prime of life, there is no rule of succession to his position. Though in a patrilineal society the Big Man's son may have an initial advantage, he will not be able to become a Big Man himself if he lacks the necessary abilities. A man who has leadership qualities, although he may be from another family in the clan, may surpass the Big Man's son in influence in gaining followers and, in time, be recognized as the new Big Man. Similarly, a real sister's son need not succeed his mother's brother to the position of Big Man in a matrilineal society.

Though women have influence and play an important role in exchange in many matrilineal societies of Melanesia, they rarely occupy the Big Man position. The women of the island of Vanatinai in the Coral Sea, one of the islands in the *kula* ring, are an exception. The term *giagia*, which literally means "giver," is a gender-neutral term which refers to Big Men and Big Women (Lepowsky, 1990). These Big Women are central nodes in the exchange of goods and valuables. They lead *kula* expeditions, organize mortuary feasts, and orate at ceremonies, just like Big Men do.

With this type of Big Man structure, political groupings and their boundaries are largely determined by the nature of the descent system; hence they tend to be more fixed than in the other types of political organizations we have discussed—situational leadership and band organization. In Melanesia, as well as elsewhere, the Big Man political structure can be found with patrilineal, matrilineal, and cognatic descent systems.

The introduction of fixed positions of rank and some method of succession to these positions leads to a fourth type of political organization—the *chieftainship*. Kin groups of the descent system are ranked in chieftainships. The Trobriand case, with which we began this chapter, exemplifies this type of organization. The position of Trobriand chief is fixed, since there is only one chief in the district who occupies the highest-ranked position. The chief does not merely exert influence over others but has real authority, which means that he has the power to enforce his decisions. The power and authority are vested in the office, and whoever occupies that office exercises this authority. In the Big Man structure, any man can become a Big Man if he has the abilities and works hard. In chiefdoms, the chiefly

Dancers at a Trobriand harvest festival, or kayasa, *dance in front of the chief's yam storehouses.*

position is restricted to certain high-ranking individuals. For instance, among the Kwakiutl, who are another example of a chieftainship, the oldest child, regardless of sex, inherits the chiefly position through primogeniture. This position is the highest-ranking name in the *numaym* or kin group. Though a female may inherit the name, a male kinsman usually carries out the duties of the office. The Trobriand case is somewhat different. The successor to the chief must be a male member of the highest-ranking matrilineal subclan of the district. No matter how able members of other subclans in the district may be, there is no possibility for them to succeed to the position of chief. However, within the chiefly subclan, as we noted earlier, there is no fixed rule like the primogeniture rule of the Kwakiutl, and members of the chiefly subclan compete with one another for the position.

In chieftainships, there is a hierarchy of offices in addition to the chiefly position. These offices are ranked with regard to one another. Whereas the Big Man has influence over a group of people—his followers, who are members of his kin group or clan or even others not of that clan—in the chieftainship, the chief exercises control over an area and the kin groups contained within that area. For example, the Trobriand chief heads a district containing a number of villages. Each of these subordinate villages has a headman who pays tribute to the chief in the form of *urigubu*. The *urigubu* is paid to the chief because the headmen have given the chief their sisters in marriage. Since Trobriand matrilineal subclans and clans are exogamous, these village headmen are not of the chiefly subclan but of other subclans lower in rank than the chief's. This illustrates the hierarchy of political offices in the chieftainship.

Just as the Big Man structure is associated with an economic system characterized by the redistribution of goods, the chieftainship is characterized by a more complex redistribution. In a chieftainship, because there are more levels of political organization, villagers give to their village headmen, who in turn give to the chief. This is exactly what happens at a Trobriand *kayasa*, when two villages compete with one another, for example, in the size of the yam harvests. The yams are presented to the chief by the heads of the two villages. The chief then redistributes what he has received in feasts to reward the villages in his district for various services.

Segmentary lineage structures, such as those described in Chapter 5, can be found in combination with the Big Man type of political organization or with chieftainship. When Big Men operate within a segmentary lineage structure, there are Big Men at each of the levels of the structure. Minor Big Men head lineages, and important Big Men head clans composed of several lineages. All lineages in the segmentary lineage structure are equal in rank. It is very simple to envisage how this kind of structure can develop into a chieftainship. In fact, it occurred among the Kachin, a hill people of northern Burma with patrilineal descent and a segmentary lineage structure. In some Kachin areas, the political organization is that of a chieftainship, while in other areas it is a Big Man type of segmentary lineage system. The ethnographer of the Kachin, Edmund Leach, in his analysis of the political system (1965), shows how the Kachin Big Man type can develop into the chieftainship and how chieftainship can collapse into the Big Man type. The Kachin example demonstrates the process of political transformation at work. In its Big Man form, which the Kachin call *gumlao,* a number of Kachin make up a domain. The villages are tied together by a patrilineal genealogy, but all are equal. Each village has a headman, but there is no strict patrilineal inheritance of this leadership position. Each lineage is headed by the eldest male, and there is a Council of Elders (from each lineage) for every village. Each village holds its own ceremonies and sacrifices independently, and at village festivals, the heads of lineages sacrifice to a variety of spirits. All the Kachin follow a marriage rule that favors marriage with mother's brother's daughter. This, as noted in Chapter 5, divides lineages from the point of view of one's own lineage into those who take women (wife-takers) and those who give women (wife-givers) (Chapter 5, Figure 10). In the *gumlao* form of the Kachin there are no differences in rank between wife-givers and wife-takers, bride price payments are low, and a number of lineages in the same village tend to marry in a circle in such a way that Lineage A gives wives to Lineage B, which gives wives to Lineage C, which returns wives back to Lineage A.

If one lineage in a village grows wealthier or stronger than the others, it can try to raise its status by offering to pay a higher bride price and by seeking wives from high-ranking lineages in other villages. If it is able to do this, it can succeed in transforming itself into a chiefly lineage that will dominate the other lineages in its own village. The rising lineage also uses its increased surplus to sponsor village feasts, which will further raise its prestige. The head of this lineage becomes the village headman, since his lineage is deemed to be the highest-ranking and the aristocratic lineage of the village. Succession now becomes fixed by a rule, with ascribed rather than achieved leadership as in the Big Man structure. In the case of the Kachin this rule is ultimogeniture. The youngest son in the lineage succeeds to the position of chief. The line of the youngest son is superior to the line of descendants of other sons, and the chief always comes from the superior line. The aristocratic lineage of a village may succeed in gaining control of one or more other villages. All the villages of the newly formed domain are subordinate to the chiefly lineage. At this point, the Kachin would say that the political form is of the *gumsa* type. It has become a chieftainship.

In the *gumsa* form, the position of chief, whom they call the *duwa,* is both a political and ritual position. Though there is still a council of lineage heads, only the chief can make sacrifices on behalf of the domain to his ancestral lineage spirit, which is now taken to represent the ancestral spirit of all the lineages in the domain. The chief is referred to as the "thigh-eating" chief because he is entitled to receive a hind leg of all animals killed either in hunting or for sacrifice from everyone in his domain except his own lineage. This right to the hind leg has little economic importance but great symbolic value. There is a range of other symbolic manifestations of chiefly office, including the erection of a special kind of house post. A concrete indicator of his authority is the right to have the people in his domain build his house and work on his agricultural land. In some cases, the chief is even able to exact a portion of the rice harvest from each household in his domain every year. Whereas formerly, under the *gumlao* system, all lineages were equal in rank and there was no rank difference between wife-givers and wife-takers, in the *gumsa* form, a lineage that gives women to another lineage is superior to it. Instead of the lineages marrying in a circle, the system has been transformed into a ranked series of lineages, with women moving down like water over a cascading waterfall. This ranked series of lineages is the same as that of the segmentary lineage genealogy. There is also a series of gradations in bride price to match the ranking of lineages. The men of the chief's lineage, since women move down the ranking order, must get their wives from the aristocratic lineages of other domains.

Not only can the unranked *gumlao* turn into the *gumsa* chieftainship, but the reverse process also occurs among the Kachin. A point may be reached when the *gumsa* structure places such great economic strains upon the people that there is a revolt. When a chief attempts to expand his domain and extract goods from the people until the limit is reached and there is nothing left to extract, they will revolt and overthrow the chief and reestablish the egalitarian *gumlao* system. Thus the process can go in either direction, from *gumlao* to *gumsa* and back again to *gumlao*.

The primary factor in the transformation of political organization is the development of ranking of groups within the segmentary structure, which is paralleled by the ranking of leadership with the chief on top. In the Kachin case, it appears that their marriage pattern has the potential for the development of rank differences in a situation in which all lineage groupings exchanging women are equal. When that rank differentiation occurs, there is the development of chieftainship.

The fifth and last type of political organization that we will discuss is that of the *state*. Archaeologists have been interested in the conditions that produced the earliest states in Egypt, Mesopotamia, the Indus Valley, China, Mexico, and Peru. In these areas, states developed for the first time in the history of human life on earth concurrently with the earliest appearance of cities and civilization. Though these early states can be studied by archaeologists, clearly they are no longer available for cultural anthropologists to study. Instead, cultural anthropologists have focused upon still-functioning indigenous states. Many of the well-studied examples are found in Africa and Southeast Asia. Under the influence of British social anthropology, the concern was how these states were organized and how they functioned. These indigenous states were still in existence in the early twentieth century. Under their policy of indirect rule during the colonial period, the British retained the structure of these indigenous states and governed through them.

The state differs from the other types of political organization in a number of significant ways, the most important of which is a difference in scale. Though some states may be quite small, the state has the potential for encompassing within its orbit millions of people. It has a delimited territory and is organized on a territorial basis, made up of villages and districts, rather than on the basis of kinship and clanship. Though in the chieftainship there was a differentiation between the chiefly lineage, which controlled power and wealth, and other lineages made up of commoners, the system was still tied together by kinship. In the state we find social stratification—rulers from a particular kin group or lineage, aristocrats, commoners, and various low-status groups. These strata may also take the form of social classes. In both instances, there is differentiation between the strata in wealth and in political power, and there is no longer the idea that kinship ties the entire political community together. All those under the control of the state are its citizens or its subjects. Frequently, today, states contain not only small-scale societies like the Yanomamo but also multiethnic populations who speak different languages and are of different cultures.

The governing of the state is in the hands of a ruler. The ruler has legitimacy in that his right to govern and command others is acknowledged by the members of the society. Of course, in a democratic state, the government is headed by a chief executive. Many of the early states were theocracies; that is, the ruler was head both of the religious hierarchy and of the state. The same symbols were used for the merged religious and political structure. The state had a single bureaucracy, and the ruler was a semi-deity. In many indigenous states, the ruler is the religious symbol of the whole society. This is particularly true in East African states, where the ruler's state of health and ritual purity affect the welfare of the entire kingdom.

The administrative functions of the state are carried out by a bureaucracy, which is delegated authority by the ruler. The bureaucracy grows in size and increases in the number of areas it controls as the state expands. Customary law becomes formalized into a legal code. The adjudication of disputes by the leader grows into a court system, which now has the power to enforce its decisions through the police. This growing bureaucracy is supported by the state from revenues it collects from its subjects or citizens. The tribute given to the chief in the chieftainship is transformed into taxes paid to the state. Tax collection demands a bureaucracy of its own. The boundaries of the state are subject to change. The state expands by conquering neighboring peoples, who become subject peoples, and their territories are incorporated within the state. For this purpose, the ruler maintains an army, mobilized from among the subjects. The army also protects the state from attack by external invaders.

The powerful, ever-present hand of the state might also be involved in economic endeavors. In the ancient states, which were located in river valleys in the Old World, the state bureaucracy managed and controlled the large-scale irrigation works on which the economic subsistence base depended. States also may control trade and exchange and administer the marketplace. They may license buyers and sellers, adjudicate market disputes, and even fix and control prices. To facilitate trade, the state also coins money. In Mesopotamia, before the invention of money, taxes were collected in grain, which was stored by the state in warehouses and used to feed the populace in lean years.

How an indigenous state functioned in the twentieth century can be seen from a description of the Empire of Bornu, the Kanuri state on the borders of Lake Chad in northern Nigeria, studied by one of the authors of this book, Abraham Rosman, in 1956, when it was still under British colonial rule. When the British entered this area at the turn of the century, they found the indigenous state in a condition of partial collapse. They resurrected it and used the state structure to govern, which was in line with their policy of indirect rule. A single ruler, the Shehu of Bornu, was the head of state. The society was highly stratified. In addition to the ruling family, there were aristocratic families, commoners, and slaves. The Shehu granted the aristocrats titles, which tended to remain in the same families over the generations. Land, including entire villages, might be granted along with the titles. The bulk of the commoner population consisted of villager-farmers. The remainder included people with a variety of occupations. Some were craftsmen of different sorts; others were tradesmen; still others pursued low-status occupations such as butcher, tanner, and musician. Slaves were either persons captured in war or those whose ancestors were slaves. Most war captives became the personal property of the Shehu himself, and these individuals could become titled aristocrats, though they remained the slaves of the Shehu.

The Empire of Bornu was located at the southern end of a strategic caravan route that led from the Mediterranean Sea across the Sahara Desert to the populous states of West Africa. Caravans brought manufactured goods from Libya, in North Africa, to the capital of Bornu and returned to Libya with slaves, ivory, and other raw materials. There was an enormous market in the capital city controlled by the government in which these and many other items were bought and sold. The government of Bornu did not issue its own currency, but Maria Theresa silver dollars from Austria, brought in by the caravan trade, served as a medium of exchange.

Muskets, which had been introduced through the caravan trade, were monopolized by the state and used in Bornu's conquests of surrounding peoples. The army of Bornu was completely controlled by the Shehu, and its generals bore high titles signifying that they were slaves of the Shehu. Besides conquest and the raiding of neighboring tribes for slaves, the army also defended the borders of Bornu from incursions by other states, particularly Bornu's enemies, the Hausa states to the west.

In the fourteenth century, Islam spread to Bornu, following the same path as the caravan routes, and as happened with Christianity and the Roman Empire, Islam was adopted in Bornu when the ruler of Bornu converted and the entire population rapidly followed suit. The Islamic legal code, as practiced in North Africa, became the law of the land. Judges appointed by the Shehu, who had training in the Koran and in Islamic law, heard criminal cases. But the Shehu and his appointed administrators, the heads of districts, heard and arbitrated personal and family disputes that were brought before them. The Kanuri believed that persons in authority at every administrative level up to the Shehu must be available every day to hear the disputes and complaints of their people.

The administrative structure of the state was composed of a capital city in which the Shehu and his personal court resided and from which the state of Bornu was governed, along with a number of districts. Each of these had its district capital, in which the district head or his representative resided. The district head was a titled aristocrat, whose title, position, and district tended to be inherited along family lines, but whose appointment was ultimately at the discretion of the Shehu. The district head could also

Mounted retainers of a Kanuri district head in northern Nigeria demonstrate their allegiance to their leader. This photo was taken in 1956, when Nigeria was a British colony.

be deposed by the Shehu. The district included many villages, each of which had its village headman, who was appointed by the district head. Though the village headship tended to be inherited in family lines, the village headman had to demonstrate loyalty to the district head, who could appoint or depose him. The Shehu delegated authority to each district head to collect taxes and to administer his district. The district head had his own retinue—some retainers who were freemen and others who were his slaves. One or two men of the retinue were assigned to collect taxes from each village and from the nomadic pastoral peoples in the district. The pastoral peoples, who were Fulani, not Kanuri, paid their taxes by patrilineage according to the number of cattle that they owned. In earlier times, the Kanuri, too, had paid their taxes by patrilineage, but in the nineteenth century they shifted to a territorial basis of village and district. Today, the Kanuri do not remember their lineages at all. Because they are part of a state, Kanuri social groupings are no longer based primarily on patrilineal kinship, but rather on territoriality. The present-day Kanuri do not have a rule of patrilineal descent.

Though the Bornu government was a hierarchical structure with the Shehu at the apex, there were areas in which politics operated. The rule of succession for the position of Shehu was that only the son of a man who had been Shehu could himself become Shehu. Since the Shehu had many wives, including slave wives, there were always many contenders for the position. The council of aristocrats decided which one would become Shehu. After the death of a Shehu, the eligible contenders vied for support among the council members, and politics were rife until a successor was chosen. Absence of a rigid rule, such as primogeniture or ultimogeniture, prevented incompetents from succeeding to office and assured that individuals with political skills would become Shehu. District heads competed with one another to retain the favor of the Shehu, but they could not spend all their time and attention at court since they had to make sure that their districts were well administered. When a new Shehu came to power, the district heads had to shift their loyalty to him or else lose their positions. On the other hand, the new Shehu would appoint as many of his own supporters to district head positions as he could. In the same way, a reshuffling of power at the district level led to the appointment of new village heads. In a hierarchically organized state like that of Bornu, opposition to those in positions of power could be expressed only in indirect and subtle ways.

Until 1960, when Nigeria achieved its independence, the state of Bornu was the northeasternmost province of the British colony of Nigeria. As noted above, Bornu was governed under the system of indirect rule, formulated by Lord Lugard, the first governor-general of Nigeria. This system was used for all the other British colonies of the time. A small group of British expatriates was thus able to rule an enormous colonial empire. While Kanuri officials of the indigenous state structure carried out the actual administration of districts, applied native law, and collected the taxes, they were supervised by British officials under a lieutenant governor who resided in the provincial capital. Real authority was in the hands of the colonial masters. Where indigenous political state institutions did not exist, colonial officials in many parts of the world created "chiefs" through whom they governed.

After gaining independence, Nigeria had a democratic government for a time, and since 1966 it has been ruled by military governments. The anthropologist Ronald Cohen (1987), who has returned to Borno, as it is now officially spelled, several times since independence, has commented on the changes that have taken place. After 1966, the capital, Maiduguri, became capital of a much enlarged Northeast State, which encompassed three of the former colonial provinces. With the influx of people from other places, it soon became a larger, more heterogeneous and cosmopolitan city. The structure of the Shehu's government continued but much reduced in its autonomy. The formal structure of titled aristocrats—district and village heads—is still present but is now part of an enlarged municipal and state governmental organization.

Law and Social Control

At various points in this chapter, we have touched upon the subject of law. Anthropologists, in their ethnographic fieldwork among various peoples in the world, have often been interested in the way in which disputes have been settled in the particular society they have studied. In the absence of any written legal codes or formal courts before which lawyers argued cases, the anthropologist in the field would listen to and record the manner in which disputes were aired and conflicts resolved. By doing this, the anthropologist could get at the rules, what constitutes proper behavior in light of those rules, what is the acceptable range of deviation from the rules, and what is unacceptable behavior that would be punished in some way. This is known as the case method, and it is the way law is taught in American law schools. Anthropologists who have studied law in particular societies have recorded a body of cases from which they have abstracted the legal principles that act as precedents and upon which decisions are based. Law is not simply the regularity abstracted from what most people do. For instance, many people at some time or other may manipulate financial figures on their income tax statements in a way not in accord with the law. No matter how many people do this, it is still against the law.

The law in societies with writing is usually codified in a written legal code. However, where writing does not exist, as was the case in many of the societies studied by anthropologists, the legal principles or bases upon which disputes are resolved are usually not explicitly verbalized by the people in those societies. They emerge only through the analysis of cases.

The broadest anthropological approach to law considers that whenever conflicts or disputes arise and a cultural mechanism for resolving them exists, or behavioral infractions occur that are punished in some way, we are dealing with law. Societies have a variety of ways to settle conflicts or disputes. Sometimes the two parties may thrash it out themselves; the solution may be a fair one, or the stronger party will force the weaker to capitulate. At other times, a third party will be called in to resolve the dispute. Third parties can play a number of different roles. They can be judges and decide cases on their merits, or they can play more of a mediating role and bring the two parties to a compromise.

A somewhat narrower anthropological approach to law insists on the presence of some third-party authority who acts to resolve disputes. Such authorities must have political power or influence in order to force the disputants to accept their decisions or recommendations. They may be the political leaders of a group, such as the district heads in Bornu, or someone appointed as a judge. The legal principle applied in a particular case becomes the legal principle for all such cases. This idea of universal application is what makes it a principle of law, rather than simply a political decision of someone in authority. When a legal decision is made after a violation of the law has occurred, some sort of sanction must be applied. This may involve the use of force, but it need not. A punishment just as severe

The traditional Yoruba ruler of Akure, in western Nigeria, holds court and renders judgment in his palace.

may result if the community avoids someone or shames a person by public flogging, for example. These are just two of the various means of social control that are employed in societies over the world. Other methods of social control include gossip and accusations of witchcraft, a topic to be discussed in greater detail in Chapter 9.

There are also anthropologists who argue that law should be strictly defined and recognize it as being present only when it exists as a codified system with courts, judges, and a penal system. In fact, this combination of institutions is only found within a state. These anthropologists argue that small-scale societies have customs but not law. As we pointed out above, many of the early states were theocracies. In such a situation, legal codes grew out of religious codes.

Anthropologists in the field have studied the methods employed in different societies to resolve conflicts and disputes. Such methods include each side mobilizing support from people among whom they have economic relationships (the Ndendeuli of southern Tanzania); application of pressure by cross-cutting interest groups to resolve the dispute (the plateau Tonga of Zambia); song contests, in which an audience decides the winner (both the Inuit and the Tiv of Nigeria); and the simple dispersal of the disputants (the Hadza of Tanzania).

In complex societies, a distinction is made between civil or private law and criminal or public law. Criminal law deals with crimes against society as a whole, and the wronged party in a crime is not allowed to punish the offender himself. Civil law deals with private disputes between individuals in which society acts as an arbitrator. This kind of distinction is not found in small-scale societies. Since private disputes in small-scale societies rend the fabric of the social structure, they are dealt with as actions against society as a whole.

Law is also associated with morality and value systems. When viewed as a series of statements of what constitutes proper behavior, the law differentiates right from wrong, good from bad. In our own legal system, some of our laws are, in effect, the carrying over of religious commandments such as "Thou shall not steal." For most members of the society, laws of this sort have been internalized. That is, most people do not break such laws, not because they are afraid of being punished, but because if they did break such laws, they would feel guilty. The enforcer of the law is the person's own conscience.

Anthropologists have examined behavior involving violation of norms and rules, crimes and punishments, and settlement of disputes in an enormous variety of societies. Newer nation-states like the Sudan and Papua New Guinea have been very interested in anthropological studies of customary law because they have sought to take into account the various forms of customary law found within their borders in creating legal codes for their nations, rather than to simply adopt a Western-oriented legal system. From their studies, anthropologists have attempted to generalize about social control in human societies and that which constitutes law in its most general and abstract form.

War and Peace

Warfare is also a subject that anthropologists have investigated. Decisions about going to war are among the most important decisions made by those in positions of authority in the political structure. Warfare, and other kinds of hostile actions such as feuds and revenge-seeking, is resorted to where no lawful, mutually acceptable means of peaceful resolution of conflicts exist. Under such conditions, one group will make the decision to take hostile action against the other group to force it to submit. Anthropologists have attempted to distinguish between warfare and feuding by defining feuding as hostile action between members of the same group and warfare as hostile action between different groups. This distinction is generally accepted. The problem with this separation is that, in a segmentary lineage type of structure, subclans within the same clan may fight each other on one occasion but join together as a single clan when fighting another clan. It is then hard to say which is feud and which is war, since the clans themselves are part of the same larger society. The Enga, whom we have discussed earlier, have such a segmentary structure, and Mervyn Meggitt, the ethnographer of the Enga, does not make the distinction between feud and war, calling fighting between subclans warfare, since the nature of the fighting and the reasons for it are identical in both (1977).

Contrary to the belief that warfare is a no-holds-barred action aimed at exterminating one's foe, it operates according to cultural rules, like all other forms of cultural behavior. Since explanations of warfare in complex societies still elude us, anthropologists have attempted to comprehend warfare in small-scale societies to try to cope with it in today's uncertain world. By understanding the relationship between warfare and other institutions in small-scale societies, we can perhaps grasp its role in more complex societies. Unfortunately, by the time most anthropologists got to the field to do their research, those small-scale societies they came to study were under colonial rule or were parts of nation-states. Pacification was the first step in these conquests. It is only from field descriptions of societies in Amazonia and New Guinea, where warfare continued despite contact with Europeans and colonial rule, that we have some understanding of indigenous ideas about warfare, its causes, and how it is conducted. However, there are also accounts of warfare in the past, for example, that of the Plains Indians of North America.

One of the fullest accounts is that of the warfare of the Yanomamo in Amazonia. There are several levels of hostility among the Yanomamo, each of them representing a distinct phase in the escalation of conflict, but hostilities can terminate at any level. The chest-pounding duel is the most innocuous form of fighting, halfway between a sporting contest and a fight. It can take place between two individuals of the same village or between the men of two villages on the occasion of a feast. In a chest-pounding duel men are paired and take turns striking each other on the pectoral muscle of the chest with a bare fist. The chest-pounding duels arise from accusations of cowardice, stinginess with food, or gossip. The next more intensive level is the side-slapping contest, when the blow is administered with a hand to the side of the body between the ribs and pelvis. The provocations are the same as for the chest-pounding duel. The third level is the club fight, which can also take place within or between villages. Two men attack one another with wooden clubs eight to ten feet long and attempt to hit each other on the skull. Such fights arise as a result of arguments over women, or more rarely, food thefts. These contests end when one opponent withdraws. The most intensive kind of hostility is the raid, which is conducted by one village against another. Villages that have a history of being enemies raid one another to take revenge for past killings. However, even when there is no immediate history of enmity between villages, hostile relations can build from a club fight to raiding if one or another individual

The side-slapping duel among the Yanomamo represents a low level of conflict, but one that can escalate.

has been seriously injured or killed. The Yanomamo say that fights over women are the primary cause of raids. Though raiding may be precipitated by motives of revenge, women are frequently captured in the course of a raid, and this becomes another reason to continue to raid.

Maring warfare has been described in detail, and a similar set of cultural rules defines the levels of hostility. There are two kinds of hostilities among the Maring. The simpler is the "small" or "nothing" fight, which takes place between two clan-clusters that may, on occasion, be joined by their allied clans. The clan-cluster is the politically autonomous unit among the Maring, which holds the *kaiko* ceremonial distribution described in Chapter 7. The group that feels itself wronged calls out to its enemy to prepare to fight in several days on land that has been designated as a fight ground. Ceremonial rituals are performed on the night before the fight. The antagonistic groups line up opposite one another and take shots at each other with bow and arrow and sometimes throw spear. The "nothing" fight can end if the aggrieved group feels it has obtained satisfaction, but it can also escalate into the ax fight, or true fight.

The rituals preceding the ax fight are different from and more elaborate than those for the "nothing" fight. Allies are always involved on both sides. Formations of the opposing sides meet on the fight ground with axes, shields, and also spears and bows and arrows. Engagements of this type may continue for weeks or months. Ax fights usually end in a truce, when the numbers of fatalities are considered to have been evened up or the initially aggrieved side feels it has obtained revenge. Occasionally the stronger side routs the weaker, which then retreats to find shelter with allies. Sometimes warfare breaks out between groups that have been ongoing enemies, but at other times, groups that were formerly friendly may fight each other. These fights break out because individuals in the two groups are in unresolved conflict over abduction of women, rape, marauding pigs, crop theft, game poaching, and sorcery accusations. Rules define appropriate behavior at each level of conflict. If two sides do not accept a mutually agreeable resolution of the conflict at one level, the conflict escalates to a more violent level.

Just as rules exist for making war, so too do rules exist for making peace. Among the Maring, a truce is facilitated when the number of killings is roughly equal. When a truce has been agreed upon, each side returns home and plants a cordyline plant, which is a symbolic indication that a truce has been formally established, and the ritual cycle, which will end in the *kaiko* pig festival, is begun. At the *kaiko,* allies and ancestral spirits are repaid for their assistance in the previous fight. Until this is carried out, the group cannot initiate new fighting, nor can it occupy the territory of a routed enemy for fear of the ancestral spirits of the vanquished group. Enemy land can be taken over at one point in the *kaiko* itself if the land has not been reclaimed by its owners through the planting of their own cordyline.

Anthropologists have been very concerned with offering explanations for warfare. Their explanations for warfare must be distinguished from those of the combatants. Most anthropologists find the explanation that warfare is due to instinctive human aggressiveness unsatisfactory. Warfare is prevalent at certain times and not others, and under certain conditions and not others. The task of the anthropologist is to explain why warfare occurs when and where it does. Proposing a universal human aggressive instinct cannot explain this variability.

The Yanomamo say that they go to war to avenge a previous killing, and as a result of conflicts over women. Chagnon, the ethnographer, has concluded that Yanomamo villages go to war in order to maintain their political autonomy (1983). Harris offers a competing cultural materialist explanation, indicating that Yanomamo villages need large forest areas for hunting in order to ensure their supply of protein, and warfare results when villages are in competition for hunting territory. Chagnon strongly disagrees with Harris's explanation of Yanomamo warfare, arguing that the Yanomamo have more than an adequate supply of protein and are not competing over hunting territory.

Rappaport's (1984) explanation for Maring warfare is that with increased population density on the land, pressure for desirable agricultural land results in conflict which leads to warfare, with the weaker group being pushed from its land. Warfare functions to redistribute dense populations of militarily superior people over the less densely populated land of militarily weaker people. Koch (1974), who worked on warfare among the Jale in New Guinea, offers another kind of explanation—that warfare breaks out when no third party exists to settle disputes. In his view, war is just another means of dispute settlement. If accepted means for resolving disputes exist, then wars will not break out. The Maring material supports this view. Not every dispute escalates into a war; some are resolved by direct negotiation between the two parties.

Many of the points made about warfare in small-scale societies are also applicable to complex societies. The motives of those who carry out the war, both the fighters and the planners, are different from the causes of war as seen by analysts. For example, the United States declared war on Japan after Pearl Harbor was bombed. We, as natives, explain the war as a result of Japan's aggressive act. A disinterested analyst might explain the war as a result of the fact that Japan, an increasingly more powerful and industrializing state, needed to expand its sphere of influence to obtain more raw materials, such as oil from Indonesia (then the Dutch East Indies), and thereby impinged on the U.S. sphere of influence in the Pacific.

Like the wars fought by the Maring and the Yanomamo, our wars are also conducted according to rules. After World War I, the use of poison gas in warfare was outlawed by international agreement. The Korean War was conducted as a limited war—limited in that nuclear weapons were not used. When certain unspoken agreements about the geographical extent of the war were violated and the United States moved its troops north of the Yalu River, the Peoples' Republic of China entered the war and the level of conflict escalated.

Ecological explanations of warfare seem to be as applicable to modern complex societies as they are to small-scale societies. The desire to obtain more land, or other important strategic resources such as mineral wealth or oil, has often caused warfare in modern times. Sometimes modern states carry out preemptive strikes, that is, attacks on the enemy when they believe that the enemy is about to launch an attack. This is like Chagnon's explanation of Yanomamo warfare, which is conducted in order to maintain the political autonomy of a group. Just as Koch offered an explanation of the prevention of warfare by the presence of third parties to arbitrate disputes between potential combatants, so, too, in the modern world the International Court of Justice and the United Nations exist for such a purpose, but there is nothing to force countries to bring their disputes before these third parties.

Politics in the Contemporary Nation-State

Many political anthropologists are interested in the modern nation-state. Local-level politics and the competition for power in communities and how these relate to the policies and goals of the nation-state are among the kinds of problems that anthropologists investigate. They focus primarily upon politics rather than upon administration.

The distinction between social structure and social organization referred to in Chapter 1 has been particularly useful to anthropologists interested in contemporary politics. While not denying the presence of political structure, they have focused instead upon the organizational dimension—how individuals go about making choices and decisions in the political arena. After all, the relationship between power and decision making is at the heart of politics. Choosing to support one leader over another and deciding how to vote in an election are decisions that will determine who will have power. The person who gains power makes administrative decisions and also rewards supporters and punishes the opposition. Thus, political choices and political power are interrelated and reinforce each other.

One of the recurring themes in the study of local-level politics today is *factionalism.* Many of the studies of peasant communities in the Old and New Worlds explore the operation of political factionalism as it relates to the way in which national politics is played out on the local level. Leaders of factions vying for power may build their followings in a number of different ways, depending upon the structure of the village community. For example, Ralph W. Nicholas, in a study of two villages in India (1968), points out that followers of a faction leader may be related to him as kins-

men, may be his economic dependents, may be residents of the neighborhood, may be in the same caste, or may even become supporters by seeking his protection in escaping from an opposition leader. Factions are
always organized around a leader. Followers give the leader support; in
return, with the political power the leader amasses, he gives his followers
economic assistance, minor positions of power, and other kinds of support.
Individuals join a faction. They are not members of a faction by birth as
they would be members of a patrilineal lineage.

The faction consisting of the leader and his followers is much like the
Big Man and his followers. Like the Big Man, the leader of a faction is in
opposition to other faction leaders. The faction leader vies with other leaders to attract followers, as does the Big Man. There is an exchange relationship between the faction leader and his followers, as there is between the
Big Man and his followers, and both types of leaders need to continue supporting and rewarding followers in order to hold onto them. When the
leader in either case loses power or dies, the faction or group of followers,
as the case may be, dissolves. In this, factions contrast with political parties,
which continue to exist though individual leaders may come and go.
However, within political parties, factions may be found on a local level, as
party leaders and their supporters compete for control of the party appara-
tus at that level.

A recent study of the Mafia in Sicily and in Detroit explicitly likens the
Don to a Big Man (Louwe, 1986). The Big Man in the Mafia family provides for a source of income for his "family" and protection against the
risks of making money illegally, and in return family members pay him
respect, give him complete obedience, and give him a share of their profits
from the criminal enterprise. His status is achieved through the demonstration of his ability. The Don maintains his influence by manipulating his
connections with the police, politicians, and judges. Loyalty of followers to
him is paramount. The greatest threat to the family is the member who is
"turned" into an informer by the police.

The relationship between *patron* and *client* has also been the focus of
political anthropologists. Patrons, who are frequently landowners, play
roles as intermediaries between the peasants of the village and the provincial or national government at a higher level. The patrons are always of a
higher class than the clients. Problems with tax collectors and the court
system bring clients to their patrons for assistance. The patrons can help
clients because of their wide social contacts with other members of the
upper class who are the patrons' social equals in the towns and cities. The
social contacts of clients usually are turned entirely inward within their
own villages. There are no links of kinship between patrons and clients.
However, ties in the form of compadrazgo may be created as the patrons
become godparents to their clients' children. This tie between patrons' families and those of the clients may therefore be perpetuated over generations.
The social class distinctions between patrons and clients are frequently par-

alleled by the economic distinctions between landlords and tenants. Unlike the faction leader, whose group of followers will disintegrate when the leader either dies or loses influence, the positions of patron and client are different and are relatively fixed. When patrons are landlords and clients are their tenants, the social distinctions are based on their differential access to land and on the class differences between gentry and peasants. These social and economic differences are the basis for a difference in political power that can even be expressed in the political maneuvering of contemporary elections. In other political arenas, where patron-client relationships are absent, the different interests of the socioeconomic classes serve to separate and oppose them. In a revolutionary situation, the link between patron and client can turn overnight into class opposition.

Colonialism and the emergence of new nation-states in Africa and Asia have brought about great changes in the nature of traditional leadership. In the highlands of Papua New Guinea, according to Paula Brown (1987), new kinds of Big Men have emerged among the Chimbu. Since 1965, government councils have governed local areas. Though councillors are elected officials, limited to one per clan, the authority structure is similar to that of a Big Man in that it is strongly embedded in the consent and approval of kin and community (Podolefsky, 1990). All elected councillors are Big Men, though not every Big Man may become a councillor. Some Big Men operate beyond the local level, on the provincial level as well as on the national political scene (Brown, 1987). They are elected officials, government employees, and businessmen. They speak and write English, value education, are well-to-do, and have widespread business interests and a network of personal contacts beyond their home area that may even be nationwide. Back home, among their clansmen, they operate as Big Men in arranging marriages, organizing local ceremonies and feasts, and contributing to compensation payments, but they are different from purely local Big Men, who do not have the characteristics noted above. These new Big Men must satisfy much larger constituencies than the Big Men of old.

Sir Iambakey Okuk had been Minister of both Civil Aviation and Primary Industry in the Papua New Guinea government when he died precipitously at age forty-two. His business interests in coffee, garages, liquor outlets, and trade stores had made him wealthy and successful, and he used the system of gift exchange lavishly in attempting to gain political support. One hundred thousand people are reported to have paid their respects as his body was taken through the highlands. After his funeral, his mother's clan destroyed his property in the traditional manner, and this was followed by widespread destruction of property beginning with his liquor store, "as a mark of respect" to Sir Iambakey. The newer generation of leaders, as described above, found his behavior old-fashioned. Sir Iambakey Okuk was a transitional figure between the traditional Chimbu Big Man and the emerging multiethnic elite class in the nation that the new leaders represent. Brown points out that as long as members of this elite group are tied to their local constituencies for support, a true social class system will not develop.

Today's nation-states contain culturally diverse populations. The newly emerged nations of Africa and Asia were successors to colonies that were arbitrarily carved out by the colonial powers. These colonies brought together as single political entities tribal groups that often were very diverse culturally. After independence was gained, tribalism was seen as a problem to be overcome in forging a new national identity. However, tribalism does not die; rather, it is transformed and then maintained as ethnic differences, despite conscious attempts to forge a national culture. Ethnic differences become the basis of political competition. The drive to establish a national culture may be (or is often seen as) an attempt by the dominant and most powerful group or the numerically superior group to establish its culture as the national culture. This was the case with the Javanese, who dominate Indonesia. In the Soviet Union there have been efforts to Russify the distinctly different Central Asian peoples, with opposition but little overt conflict. With "glasnost," ethnicity asserted itself, and many republics such as the Baltic states, Moldavia, the Ukraine, and the Russian Republic itself have made moves toward political independence from the Soviet Union. For the non-Russian republics, this has meant moving out from under the domination of Russian culture. With the collapse of the Communist political structure in Yugoslavia, the central government is losing its struggle to hold together the various ethnic provinces. In Sri Lanka ethnic conflict has exploded into prolonged warfare between the dominant Sinhalese and the Tamil ethnic minority, which is demanding cultural autonomy. The attempt to submerge the Sikh ethnic and religious minority in India has resulted in guerrilla warfare and a demand for Sikh autonomy. The Kurdish ethnic minority, which straddles the borders between Turkey, Iran, and Iraq, has been fighting an unending war of independence in order to establish its own state.

Even after hundreds of years of existence as independent nation-states, "tribalism" and ethnic differences continue to be manifested in conflicts between Flemish and French speakers in Belgium. Anthropologists have applied the methods and concepts of their discipline to investigate the phenomenon of ethnic conflict and how and why it develops. They are interested in the relationship between ethnic conflicts and class conflict. They attempt to answer the question of why open hostility between ethnic groups erupts at particular points in time, after years of lying dormant.

Our discussions of how leadership operates in terms of power and exchange, politics and administration, the emergence of leaders through political maneuvering, factionalism, and patron-client relationships are as applicable to political situations in our own society as they were in the situations in which they were described. For example, in the past, the ward boss in big American cities was like a New Guinea Big Man in redistributing patronage in the form of material benefits among the "ward heelers."

Factions representing different political positions and coalitions operate at every level of our political system. They may coalesce around individuals or around an issue, such as abortion, equal rights for women, or civil rights for minorities. Ethnic politics are as active today in American cities as they are in any nation-state in Asia or Africa. Mayoral elections pit Poles against blacks in Chicago and Cubans against blacks in Miami.

––––––––––

At the beginning of this chapter we noted that political organization and economics were intimately interwoven and that this was referred to as political economy. As we have shown throughout this chapter, the various types of political organization are associated with different forms of distribution and often different forms of production. For example, chieftainship is interwoven with redistribution systems, described in Chapter 6, where surplus goods funnel into a central political position, that of the chief, and are distributed on a ceremonial occasion to other chiefs, who in turn redistribute to their followers. The maintenance of political control by the chief is dependent upon the control and disbursement of economic goods, while the economic system is dependent upon the establishment of fixed positions of authority. In contrast, the only kind of political structures with which markets are associated are state structures. The state as a political system, as we have pointed out, operates on a territorial basis beyond the level of kinship and clanship, and the less personal relationships of a market are in accord with this.

Ortner's discussion of political economy as a framework of analysis points out its advantages (1984). She notes that an approach in terms of political economy is very open to symbolic analysis. Throughout this chapter, we have indicated how symbols are used to express rank and authority—as, for example, among the Trobrianders. In a situation like that of the Kachin, who oscillate between two forms of political structure, the Big Man of the *gumlao* type and the chieftainship of the *gumsa*, symbols are used in different ways to express these opposing structures. In the context of the modern nation-state, symbols become powerful means of constructing ethnic identity, and they are employed to express ethnic conflicts as well as class struggles.

Instead of thinking of particular societies as isolates, political economy tends to promote a view in terms of a regional focus. As we pointed out, systems of ceremonial exchange such as the *kula* demonstrate how societies with differing political systems are joined together in a system of regional exchange. An emphasis on political economy shows how societies have increasingly been drawn into a world system, a topic to be explored in much greater detail in Chapter 13.

CHAPTER 9

Religion and
the Supernatural

 Many people in the world believe in the supernatural, in an order of existence beyond the observable universe. For example, the Trobriand Islanders believe that when a person dies, his spirit splits in two. One part goes to live on the island of Tuma in the village of the dead, to remain there until it is reincarnated in the spirit of a newborn child. The other part of the spirit haunts the favorite places of the deceased, and its presence is frightening to the living villagers. More frightening still is the suspected presence of sorcerers, especially flying witches, who are thought to have caused the death in the first place.

Sorcery, spirits, and witchcraft are not unexpected in a society like that of the Trobriand Islanders. However, imagine one's surprise, when riding along a country road in England, at the sight of a billboard announcing an impending meeting of a local witches' coven to be held the following week. Meetings of American witches' covens are announced in the newspaper. There are people in England and America today who believe in witchcraft as a religion. To them, the witchcraft trials were an example of religious persecution. How can witchcraft and Christianity coexist as sets of religious beliefs? Believers in witchcraft, like the believers of many other faiths in America today, are protected by the fundamental right to religious freedom.

Black witches (the term refers to the use of "black magic"—harmful or injurious magic) celebrate the summer solstice in Oldham County, Kentucky, in 1972.

Although our country is founded on freedom of worship and belief, one periodically finds accounts of religious communities that run afoul of the law in the practice of their religious rites. Some of these rites involve the handling of venomous snakes. Believers, while in an ecstatic state, pick up large rattlesnakes, a practice based on the belief that if they are free of sin, worshipers will not be bitten by the snakes. This belief derives from the Scriptures, in which it is stated that "they shall speak with new tongues; they shall take up serpents." These people take the Bible literally. Some people are bitten during the ritual and subsequently die. The worshipers believe that those who die in this way are being punished for their sins. The snake, in this instance, is seen as acting as an agent of God. Causation here is seen as supernatural. Whether a person is pure or sinful determines if the snake will bite that individual. This is not an empirical explanation of why rattlesnakes bite, but is dependent on belief. Though their beliefs may be considered extreme by some Americans, the Snake Handlers are a religious sect that is part of a larger religious community—that of Christianity. Despite beliefs that seem aberrant, the sect is a historical offshoot of the Christian tradition in which one aspect has been developed to an extreme.

Shortly after holding the rattler, this woman fell to the floor in an ecstatic state.

The Trobriand belief in the power of sorcerers and the snake handlers' belief that, because of the purity of their character, God will protect them from the snake's bite, are both explanations that deal with phenomena beyond the observable universe. Such phenomena are seen by some analysts as falling into the category of the supernatural. A variety of explanatory frameworks are utilized in different societies. We categorize empirical explanations of the observable world as scientific. Explanations that do not depend on empirical evidence are categorized as religious. Such explanations depend on strongly held beliefs in nonempirical or supernatural forces. This distinction between natural and supernatural is clearly culturally ordered and comes out of our Western orientation. People in other societies consider their spiritual culture heroes and the ghosts of their ancestors as absolutely real. They are no more supernatural to those people than wind, rain, and thunder. In our society, science is more than an acceptance of empirical evidence; it is a matter of strongly held belief.

How can we distinguish between religion as a belief in the supernatural and the other parts of culture? This is a problem similar to the one encountered in the discussion of economics and political organization. Religious phenomena involve the use of symbols that evoke powerful emotional responses. One has merely to consider the difference between water and holy water and the emotional response invoked only by the latter to realize this. Water is transformed into holy water by the blessing of a priest. However, symbols that invoke strong feelings are to be found in parts of culture not labeled religious. Political symbols, such as the flag and the national anthem, produce such sentiments. Memorial Day, which is a national day of commemoration, has a similar effect. Sometimes the emotion evoked by these secular symbols is as strong as a religious response.

Religion is the cultural means by which humans deal with the supernatural. Humans also believe that the reverse is true—that the supernatural deals with humans. In this interaction, the supernatural is usually seen as powerful and human beings as weak.

If religion involves the interaction of humans with the supernatural, then it is necessary to pose the question: Why do human beings propose the existence of the supernatural in the first place? What is it about human life and the world in which that life is lived that seems to compel human beings to propose that the world is governed by forces beyond their empirical observations? Many theorists have attempted to answer this age-old question. Some, like Max Weber (1930), have said that since life is made up of pain and suffering, human beings have developed religion as an attempt to explain why they were put on earth to suffer. Others, like Sigmund Freud (1928), propose that religious institutions represent society's way of dealing with childish needs of dependency on the part of individuals. What would otherwise be a neurotic trait thereby finds expression in the form of all-powerful gods and deities who control the individual's destiny. More recently, Melford Spiro (1966) has attempted to deal with the problem of religion by suggesting three kinds of needs that religion fulfills. The first need is called the *cognitive need,* that is, the need to understand. This is the need for explanations, the need for meanings. The second need is the *substantive need*—to bring about specific goals, such as rain, good crops, and health, by carrying out religious acts. The third need is the *psychological need* to reduce fear and anxiety in situations in which these are provoked. Émile Durkheim (1915) and others who have followed Durkheim's approach saw religion as the means by which society inculcated values and sentiments necessary to the promotion of social solidarity and the society's ultimate survival.

From these different considerations of why religion exists, we can make some tentative conclusions. Human beings are part of a social world as well as a natural world. They are dependent upon the actions of others around them as well as upon the forces of nature. They can control some of these actions and forces through their own behavior. However, they are helpless in the face of other actions and forces. Humans attempt to understand and at least influence or control what is otherwise uncontrollable and unexplainable through a belief in the supernatural. As Spiro suggests, by doing this they alleviate their anxieties about their helplessness in the situation. The shape of the supernatural world that is constructed by human beings has a relationship to the society in which they live (Durkheim, 1915). The structure of the supernatural and the sentiments and emotions generated by it are an important force in the enhancement of social solidarity.

Religion, Science, and Magic

There is a distinction between the explainable parts of the universe and those aspects that are unexplainable. In the modern world, we would say the aspects of the natural world that can be explained are accounted for by means of science. Judeo-Christian belief states that humans were created, along with all the other species, by God. The seventeenth-century clergyman Bishop Ussher determined for Christians that creation should be dated as occurring in the year 4004 B.C. Until the beginning of the twentieth century, this was Western man's belief about creation. In the mid-nineteenth century, Darwin proposed his theory of evolution. This theory, based upon scientific evidence from comparative anatomy, geology, and paleontology, proposed an alternative explanation for the development of all the species in the world and the appearance of human life. For a time, the religious and scientific explanations of creation competed with one another. However, today, most people accept the scientific theory of evolution, which can itself be incorporated as part of a divine plan. Religion has not ceased to be important, but it is not used to explain this phenomenon because the creation of humans is no longer in the realm of the unexplainable. Recently, fundamentalists in the United States have attempted to transform their religious belief in divine creation into a theory called *creationism*, which they claim is scientific and which they would like to have given an equal status with evolutionism in school curricula. However, the United States courts have ruled that, while creationism is a religious belief, evolutionism is qualitatively different, and, as a field of study, open to question and thus teachable in United States public schools.

People in Western society as well as people in less complex societies have scientific knowledge based upon their observations of the world, which support hypotheses they have developed. The Trobrianders have a body of scientific knowledge about the displacement of objects in the water and about wind currents, which they put to use in the construction of their complex outrigger canoes. But they have no scientific explanation based on empirical evidence for why the wind blows or why storms come up, and therefore they have recourse to supernatural explanations. They attempt to control the wind through the use of wind magic. We have little scientific evidence for why some children contract leukemia, while others do not. If such a disease strikes a child in a family, the family may have recourse to nonscientific explanations and a search for nonscientific cures through faith-healing or religious mysticism.

Magic, science, and religion are all ways of understanding and influencing the natural world. Magic and religion are different from science in that what is unexplained in the natural world is explained in magic and religion by recourse to the concept of the supernatural. However, magic and science are similar in that the aims of both are specific, and both are based upon the belief that if one performs a set of specific actions, one will achieve the desired result. Magic and science differ in that they are based on different theories of knowledge—magic is based on the belief that if spells or rituals are performed correctly, the supernatural will act in such a way that the desired end within the natural world will result. Magic is based on the idea that there is a link—the supernatural—that will compel the natural world to act in the desired way if the spell is performed as it should be. Science, on the other hand, is based on logical connections between aspects of the natural world. Its hypotheses concerning these logical connections are subject to change if new empirical data suggest better hypotheses. One difference between magic and religion is the fact that people attempt to manipulate the supernatural through magic. If the right formula is used, success is inevitable since magic is seen as being able to bend the supernatural to the will of the practitioner. Religion, on the other hand, is not as specific in its aims. Religious rites emphasize the degree of human beings' powerlessness and do not compel direct results in the way that magic does. Religious rites involve people making appeals to the gods, which the all-powerful gods may or may not choose to grant. Magic is therefore manipulative and religion supplicative. Religion and magic also differ in that magical knowledge is known, controlled, and used usually on behalf of individuals, whereas religion is the belief system and ritual practice of a community.

Conceptions of the Supernatural

People see the supernatural world as inhabited by a variety of superhuman creatures, agents, and forces that act upon them to bring about good fortune or misfortune, rain or drought, famine or fertility, health or disease, and so forth. Since these superhuman creatures are the cultural creation of human minds, the real world serves as a model, though not an exact one, for their conceptualizations of the supernatural. It would be too simplistic to say that the supernatural world is simply a mirror image of people's life on earth. Nevertheless, there is a direct relationship between the social structure of a society and the way in which its supernatural world is organized. Similarly, the power relationships in the supernatural world are related to the kind of political organization the society has.

We may group the kinds of spirits that populate the supernatural into types using English terms that analysts have developed to describe them. There are several different categories of spirits of the dead that are recognized by various societies. These types usually include the ghosts of the recent dead, the ghosts of those more remote dead of previous generations who are considered ancestor spirits, and the ancestral spirits of the ancient past who were founders of the group in mythological times. In societies with totemic clans, founding ancestors may be represented as animal spirits, not human spirits. The belief in totemic animal spirits as ancestors of human groups serves to link humans with the natural world.

In addition to totemic animal ancestor spirits, some peoples believe that all animal and plant species have both physical and spiritual components. The natural world is then seen as having its spiritual counterpart. These spirits represent another large category in the spirit world. Inanimate forces such as rain, thunder, lightning, wind, and tide may also be seen as motivated by spirits or controlled by deities or gods. If the spirit is directly perceived as having human characteristics as well as supernatural power, then it is referred to as a god or deity and not a spirit. The population of gods and deities recognized by a society is referred to as a *pantheon*. The relationships between the gods of a pantheon are frequently conceived of in human terms. The gods show jealousy, have sexual intercourse, fight, and live much like human beings. Human characteristics of this sort are also attributed to ghosts and ancestral spirits in many societies. The origins and activities of supernatural beings are depicted in myths, a topic we will discuss in the next chapter.

In some societies, individuals go out alone to seek a vision of an animal spirit, who then becomes their protector and *guardian spirit* throughout life. There is also a widespread notion that particular individuals acquire special supernatural powers that enable them to perform evil deeds. A societal means always exists to undo the evil magic. Finally, there is the belief in an impersonal supernatural force or power that can be found that is inherent in people or things, to which the Polynesian term *mana* is applied.

Ideas about ghosts and human spirits are part of a larger category of beliefs about the spiritual or noncorporeal counterparts of human beings. Tylor (1874), the nineteenth-century evolutionist, termed this *animism*. He saw this idea as the seed from which all other forms of religion grew. He hypothesized that primitive people saw all living things, including the forces of nature, as composed of a corporeal or bodily form and a spiritual aspect. This was an extension of the idea that each person has a body and a separable other self or soul. This other self was seen in the person's shadow, or in the reflection in a pool, and it traveled far and wide in the person's dreams. Tylor saw this belief in a separable spirit projected onto the natural world. All the forces of nature and all the natural world were similarly possessed of spirits. He referred to this as the theory of animism. It was the cornerstone for the development of his evolutionary theory of religion, which evolved from animism into a pantheon of deities and finally into monotheism.

Any particular combination of different kinds of spiritual entities may be found in a given society. Since the supernatural world conforms to its own logic, it is pointless to look for complete consistency in its ordering. This will become apparent as we examine the supernatural worlds of several different societies. We shall see that it is even possible for people to believe in a monotheistic god, such as occurs in Judaism, Christianity, and Islam, and still maintain beliefs in ghosts, witches, and spirits of nature as parallel systems. Indeed as we have observed, this occurs in our own society.

The people of Wogeo, an island off New Guinea, studied by the Australian anthropologist Ian Hogbin (1970), provide an example of a sorting of the supernatural world in their traditional belief system, which illustrates a combination of spiritual entities. To the Wogeo, this supernatural world is just as real as the natural and cultural world around them. Their supernatural world is made up of three kinds of beings. The first of these is called *nanarang,* or culture heroes. These culture heroes are the founders of the Wogeo natural world and the givers of all cultural inventions. The Wogeo believe that the earth is a huge platter under an upturned bowl, which is the sky. The island of Wogeo, the home of mankind as well as of the culture heroes, is at the center, and radiating out are other islands, the moon, and the stars. The culture heroes are said to have formulated all of the customs of Wogeo society. These are related in myths that provide the story of how all of this came about. Most of the culture heroes have disappeared. These departed heroes left black basalt columns as reminders of their deeds. The culture heroes who have remained dwell in certain sacred places, in particular territories on earth. They guard the land against intruders, injure trespassers, and are responsible for bringing about what is desired by those who perform present-day magic rites. Culture heroes keep spirit pigs, just as the people of Wogeo keep pigs.

A second and quite different category of supernatural beings is the ghosts of the dead. The spirits of the dead are generally not harmful to people unless they are spirits of men killed in a raid or women who have died in childbirth. These latter may try to steal the spirit of a living person. Persons who have lost part of their spirit become unconscious or delirious. They are deemed to be in a cold state and are fed hot curry so their spirit will return. The soul of a dead person may appear to the living in a dream and try to take the soul of that living person to the land of the dead. Dreamers may even imagine that they have made a trip to the land of the dead in their dream.

The last category of spirits in Wogeo is that of the spirit monsters. There are two types of spirit monsters: one represented by flutes, called *nibek,* and the other by masks, called *lewa.* These spirits must be summoned to enable men to carry out their ceremonial distributions. When the spirits are called

Men in Wogeo perform a dance, wearing masks in their impersonation of the lewa *spirit monster.*

in, people are not allowed to collect certain crops so that large quantities will grow, and they are not allowed to kill pigs so that a sufficient number of them will mature. These crops and pigs will be used later in the large-scale ceremonial distribution. Men put on the masks to impersonate the *lewa* spirit and blow the flute to impersonate the *nibek* spirit. The impersonation of spirits places men in a ritual state, which is considered dangerous and in which they are said to be cold. The *lewa* are offered hot curry, which the men then consume to warm themselves. The *nibek* spirits are said to have "eaten" the pigs distributed at the ceremony before they are sent back to the spirit world.

The three kinds of Wogeo spirits do not form a consistent interrelated whole. They do different kinds of things and deal with different kinds of problems. The category of culture heroes, who created the things that make up the natural world and brought to people the important inventions in their lives, is similar to such supernatural individuals found in other societies. Accounts of such individuals usually form the basis for mythologies. These myths are an attempt to provide explanations for the unexplainable and justifications for why the present-day world is the way it is. The spirit monsters are that part of the supernatural and the sacred which is involved in large-scale ceremonial distributions that have political and economic aims. These monsters are called forth to lend their sacred presence to the ceremonial to promote the well-being of the society and are given offerings of food and pigs. Lastly, the Wogeo concept of ghosts is a good example of a kind of supernatural belief that is very widespread and that led Tylor to develop his theory of animism.

A somewhat different conceptualization of the supernatural is found among the Kachin, a hill tribe of Burma discussed in Chapter 8. Kachin social organization consists of a patrilineal segmentary lineage structure with a preferential marriage rule for mother's brother's daughter so that there is a division between wife-givers, known as *mayu,* and wife-takers, known as *dama.* The Kachin supernatural world is made up of spirits called *nats.* The world of the *nats* is hierarchically ordered like the hierarchical *gumsa* world of Kachin political organization. The chief of all the *nats* is Shadip, who is the reincarnation of the creator of everything. Shadip is responsible for all forms of good fortune and fertility. Beneath him are his children, the sky spirits. The senior-most sky spirit is Madai, the youngest of the sky spirits. It should be recalled that the Kachin have a rule of succession of ultimogeniture: the youngest son succeeds his father in the position of chief. *Nats,* like people, belong to lineages. Madai's daughter is said to have married a human being who was the first ancestor of all Kachin chiefs. The Madai *nat* gave a woman to the first Kachin chief and is therefore *mayu* to the most senior Kachin line of chiefs. This links the world of the supernatural and the world of human beings through marriage alliance. Below the sky spirits are the ancestor *nats.* These are the spirits of the ancestors of the various Kachin lineages. To approach the sky *nats,* one must first make offerings to one's ancestor *nat,* who acts as an intermediary. Only the senior chief can make offerings to Madai directly, because his ancestor was *dama,* or wife-taker, to Madai, and only he makes offerings through Madai to Shadip. The sky spirits are superior to humans because they are wife-givers to humans.

Another category of *nats,* or spirits, is seen as inferior to humans. They are the offspring of a human girl and an animal. These inferior spirits are said to cause all kinds of misfortunes to humans, such as death in childbirth and fatal accidents. There is also a category of human beings who are witches. This human characteristic is inherited in a particular lineage, and the people in the lineage themselves are unaware that they possess this attribute. They may unknowingly cause misfortune and illness to others. Witches cause misfortune to people who are their affines, those to whom they give wives.

It is apparent that the Kachin picture of the supernatural world is an extension of and directly correlated with their own social organization. The relationships among the spirits and between the spirits and human beings are the same as the relationships between individuals and social groups on the human level, with wife-takers always lower in rank than wife-givers.

Like human beings, the spirits are also organized into lineages. This close connection between the organization of the spirit world and the organization of human society among the Kachin is also found in other societies. These kinds of conceptions of the spirit world were the basis for the formulation of Durkheim's theory of religion which we discussed earlier. Not only did the supernatural world mirror the real world, but human propitiation of that supernatural world through prayers and sacrifices was seen as having the function of reinforcing the human society and reinforcing social solidarity. Human worship of the supernatural was, in effect, the worship of a projection of society. The relationship between the social structure and the organization of the world of the supernatural is often not a simple one-to-one relationship. Sometimes the supernatural world is an inversion or distortion of the real world. For example, the Kaguru of East Africa believe that witches walk upside-down, on their hands.

Ritual Approaches to the Supernatural

Generally speaking, human beings approach the supernatural by carrying out ritual acts, usually involving a combination of speech and patterned behavior which have the effect of altering the emotional states of the participants. What are called *hortatory rituals* by Firth (1951) consist of exhortations to the supernatural to perform some act. Just before a shipwreck, the captain of a Trobriand canoe will exhort the supernatural powers to send the marvelous fish to guide the drowning victims to a friendly shore. The Trobrianders have a native term for this category of exhortation. It is "by the mouth only." The voice alone must be projected toward the supernatural. *Prayer* is another kind of ritual involving words only. It differs from hortatory ritual in its method of approach and intent. Prayer emphasizes people's inferior position to the gods since they beseech the gods to act on their behalf.

Sometimes, the gods can be approached only by going into a self-induced or drug-induced trance. For example, the hallucinogenic substance *ebene* is blown up the nose by the Yanomamo to induce a trance and contact with the spirit world. In the trancelike state produced by the drug, individuals may hallucinate that they are flying to the spirit world. Sometimes trances may be induced without the use of any drugs at all. Many North American Indian societies have the *vision quest*, in which a man, through starvation, deprivation, and sometimes even bodily mutilation, attempts to induce a trance in which a supernatural being will visit him and thenceforth become his guardian spirit and protector. The Crow of Montana were famous for their vision quest. An adolescent boy would go out into the wilderness and fast and thirst for days in order to induce the vision to visit him. He might even mutilate himself by cutting off a joint of a finger on his left hand if the vision was not forthcoming. The vision usually came on the fourth night, since for the Crow the number four has magical significance. Supernatural visitors came most frequently in the form of animals, sometimes powerful ones like buffalo and eagles, or at other times animals like dogs or rabbits. The Crow believed that the supernatural spirit adopted the individual who saw him, and the spirit in the vision repeated the Crow formula for adoption. Henceforth, the spirit acted as a protector. It taught its protégé a sacred song, instructed him in special medicines to use, and imposed special dietary restrictions. The man wore tokens of his vision and accumulated a medicine bundle consisting of sacred objects connected to his first and subsequent visions of his spirit protector. Part of the man's power could be used to protect others whom he adopted for this purpose, as his spirit protector had adopted him.

Still another way of approaching the supernatural is by making *sacrifices*. The supernatural world of the Kachin can cause good or bad fortune to people. Sickness and misfortune are attributed to the acts of the *nats,* or spirits. The Kachin attempt to intercede by making sacrificial offerings. There is a relationship between the size and value of the sacrificial offering and the importance of the spirit to which it is offered. The inferior *nats* are offered the most insignificant sacrificial animals, including rats, dogs, pigs, and chickens, but never cattle. When offerings are made to the ancestral spirits of each household, they usually consist only of chickens. Ancestral *nats* of the village headman are given offerings of pigs. Sky *nats* are given offerings of pigs and buffalo. Shadip, the creator, is given a sacrifice of a whole pig, which is buried. In the previous cases, the essence of the sacrificial animals is given to the *nats,* while the meat is consumed by the human participants. Only Shadip's offering is not eaten. These sacrifices need to be made on ritual occasions, since the *nats* must be "remembered" or else they will cause misfortunes. The sacrifice constitutes the giving up of something of value. However, this is part of an exchange with the spirits. Expected in return are fertility and the supernatural protection of crops. The eating of the meat from the sacrificial animals is the eating of sacred food, which brings the humans into contact with the gods. W. Robertson Smith (1889), another nineteenth-century theorist on religion, took the communal eating together of god and man in the sacrifice to signify the bond of kinship between them, just as eating together among men symbolically signifies kinship, as noted in Chapter 4. Sacrifices and offerings of food, vegetables, incense, and even money, as well as live animals, are widespread. It is a way of approaching the supernatural by bearing gifts. Since the relationship between humans and the supernatural is one that emphasizes the subordination of the humans, people can only hope for something in exchange for their gift. What they hope for is supernatural support in fighting wars; in warding off misfortune, sickness, and death; and in providing fertility. The sacrifice of live animals is the sacrifice of life itself.

Anthropologists have identified at least two kinds of rituals or rites: *rites of passage* and *rites of intensification*. Rites of passage are communal ceremonies held to mark the changes in status an individual goes through as he or she progresses through the life cycle. The beginning of life—birth—and the end of life—death—are always marked by some kind of ritual. In addition, one or more points between life and death at which one's status changes, such as girls' first menstruation or marriage, may be marked with a ceremony. Rituals of this type were described in Chapter 2, and in Chapter 6 we discussed the cultural construction of gender as expressed in such rituals. Sometimes, in their rites of passage, cultures emphasize a biological change, but in other instances the changes are purely culturally determined, like the first catch of a fish, the piercing of ears and nose for ornamentation, or a child's first haircut. This arbitrariness is demonstrated in the variation in the age at which a male child is circumcised in societies over the world. Where there are age grades such as those discussed in Chapter 6, the ages at which males are initiated into the successive age grades are also more or less arbitrary, though in general tied to the life cycle. In these societies, each boy does not have his own separate rites of passage. Instead, the male population is sorted into age grades that go through successive initiatory rites of passage as a group.

Van Gennep (1960), in his analysis of rites of passage, drew attention to certain universal characteristics that rites of passage exhibit. All rites of passage involve three stages. The first stage marks the separation of the individual from the category or status previously occupied. Next is a period of transition in which the individual is in a kind of limbo. During this period, all individuals in the same state are frequently secluded from the rest of the society. Victor Turner (1967) has characterized this period as a particularly sacred one, a *liminal period* in which the individual is literally "in between," no longer in one status and not yet in another. The last stage is one of reincorporation, in which the individual is ceremonially incorporated back into society, but this time in the new status. Frequently, this three-stage process is represented by means of the metaphor of death and rebirth. The individual in the former category "dies" and is "reborn" into the new category. In the third stage of the ceremony, the person is often given a new name and is decked out in a type of clothing different from that worn previously. The name and clothing mark the birth of a different kind of person.

Typical of the kinds of occasions that are marked as rites of passage are those celebrated by the Arapesh of New Guinea. As we noted in Chapter 4, though the Arapesh have a patrilineal rule of descent, they believe their blood comes from the mother while the father contributes the semen. When one's blood is spilled, the mother's group must be recompensed by the payment of shell valuables. It is this idea that underlies all rites-of-passage ceremonies, as well as other aspects of Arapesh culture. After the birth of a child, the child's father "pays for the blood" by giving shell rings to the mother's brother of the child. Through this act the child now belongs to the father's group, though the mother's lineage is still said to "own" the child's blood. Ear and nose piercing are minor rites of passage that take place during childhood and are performed by the mother and the mother's sister.

At puberty, a boy goes through an initiation in order to become a man. This is usually done for several boys at the same time. The rites involve isolation from females, the observance of a series of taboos, and the incision of the boy's penis. He is also introduced to the Tamberan Cult, the secret cult of men. He learns that the Tamberan spirit is really only the sounds of the drums and the flute secretly played by the adult men. Women and children do not know this. During initiation, the boy also goes through an ordeal in which his mother's brother beats him. After the incision of his penis by a man designated as the Cassowary, representing the spirit of the large flightless bird found in New Guinea, who acts on behalf of all the men, the initiate drinks blood that has been contributed by all the old men of the group. At the end, the initiate is bathed, puts on new clothing, and is reincorporated into society in his new status at a feast made by his father to honor the boy's mother's brother, who must be paid. Finally, the boy, who is now a man, goes on a trip and meets all of his father's trading partners as a sign of his new status.

The three stages of the rites of passage Van Gennep described may be seen in the Arapesh boy's initiation rite. During the boy's childhood, he is often in the company of women. At the beginning of the initiation, he is separated from female society and is secluded. Becoming a man involves learning the mysteries of the Tamberan Cult from which women and children are excluded. The boy's tie to women is represented by his blood, which comes from his mother. This female blood is "removed" by the incision of his penis during the initiatory rite. He then takes in male blood by drinking the old men's blood. He is thereby reborn as a man, the old men having given birth to him. As a result of this initiation ceremony, the boy is no longer a child but has become a man, and as a man he is now separate from women.

The Arapesh have child betrothal, and a girl, while a child, frequently goes to live with the parents of her future husband. At her first menstruation, she is secluded and does not eat. After this period of seclusion and fasting, she is scarified on the shoulder and buttocks by her mother's brother. This represents an initiation for a girl into the status of an adult woman. She is ceremonially fed by her new husband. He then hunts for meat, which is used to make a feast for the girl's mother's brother, since her blood was shed by the scarification process.

The final Arapesh rite of passage occurs at death. Once again, the mother's lineage of the deceased is paid in shell rings in compensation for the death. The same kind of ceremonial payment that marked all the other Arapesh rites of passage marks the death.

   The American wedding and funeral described in Chapter 2 are also examples of rites of passage. There are other rites-of-passage ceremonies in American society, such as the Jewish circumcision rite, Christian baptism, bar mitzvah, confirmation, and, in a sense, the retirement party. The same stages of separation, transition, and reincorporation can be seen in these rites of passage as in all the others.

   The other major kind of ritual—rites of intensification—is celebrated communally by the whole group either at various points in the yearly cycle, such as spring, fall, or the winter and summer solstices, or at times when the society is exposed to some kind of threat. Societies may hold rites of intensification to mark planting, in hope for a good crop, or to mark the harvest, in thanks for what has been given. The Kachin ceremonial sacrifices known as *manau,* which are carried out by the chief on behalf of the whole community, are rites of intensification. One such occasion occurs during the growing period when there is anxiety about whether the crop will be satisfactory. The sacrifices to the whole series of *nat* spirits,

Contemporary mortuary rite of passage in New Ireland involves payments to members of the opposite moiety of the deceased who erected the cement grave marker.

which are part of the ceremony, serve to reiterate the social structure. The major sacrifice made by the chief serves to reinforce the solidarity of the group.

Another example of a rite of intensification comes from Wogeo. The *nibek* spirit monsters of Wogeo are summoned when the large-scale ceremonial distribution known as the *warabwa* is to take place. This ceremony is held when an event of importance to the whole community occurs. Such an event may be the appointing of an official heir to the chief. The community as a whole sponsors the *warabwa* and hosts many other villages. One of the distinctive occurrences at a Wogeo *warabwa* is the free-for-all that takes place on the last day before the great distribution of food and pork. On this occasion, the rules regarding the respect relationship between certain categories of relatives are suspended, and these relatives may insult and humiliate each other. The suspension of rules in this case serves to emphasize the rules of the group in a negative fashion. The rites allow the expression or release of tension in a ritual context that could not be permitted in the everyday course of events. A similar reversal of everyday behavior occurs at Mardi Gras, just before Ash Wednesday, which marks the beginning of the forty-day period of penance leading to Easter. Mardi Gras rites are marked by great exhuberance and individual freedom, in contrast to the restraint and somberness that follows.

Thanksgiving, the "giving of thanks," is an American rite of intensification though it does not usually involve church or synagogue ritual. Thanksgiving has a historical basis in the Pilgrims' celebration, when they gave thanks to God for their safe survival during their first year in the New World. Today, most Americans participate in a Thanksgiving meal and, by their participation, give thanks in a way that may be completely secular. The religious aspect, if present, may only involve saying grace at the start of the meal. Despite the great range of performance of this rite, it nevertheless is a rite of intensification. Its communal aspect demands that particular foods be eaten to symbolize Thanksgiving. It is turkey, not lamb chops or meatballs, that symbolizes Thanksgiving.

Religious Specialists

In many societies, people approach the supernatural indirectly, through an intermediary. These intermediaries have access to the supernatural because they possess some special gift, because they have been through some training, or because they have inherited this knowledge or ability. Even in small-scale societies, this kind of specialization can be found. In complex, hierarchically organized societies it may be represented by an entire class of priests. We have sorted these religious specialists according to their primary functions, such as curing illness or predicting the future. Most often the English labels directly reflect the specialist's function (e.g., diviner, oracle, magician). Since they use the supernatural for curing purposes, such native specialists are popularly known as "witch doctors" or "medicine men." The anthropological term for this kind of curing specialist is *shaman*. Though the English labels imply that these specialists perform only a single function, in most cases these people carry out other functions as well.

Shamans

Shamans are part-time specialists who use their powers primarily to diagnose and cure illness and also sometimes to cause illness. The shaman is usually the only religious specialist in small-scale societies. Shamanism was widespread in Asia at an earlier period. The word is from the Tungus of Siberia. Shamanism continues in both small-scale societies and complex ones like Korea, Japan, and Thailand, where it coexists with world religions, such as Buddhism. Shamans were also found among a great many indigenous societies of North and South America.

Kwakiutl shamans and the way in which they traditionally operated are typical of shamans elsewhere. Kwakiutl shamans are classified on the basis of the level of their expertise or power. The least powerful are those who are able only to diagnose and locate the disease, that is, determine the place in the body where the object causing the disease is lodged. But the most powerful not only can cure diseases but also have the power to cause illness in others. Kwakiutl men and women both can become shamans. One becomes a shaman as a result of an initiation by a supernatural spirit who comes to the person while he or she is sick. The most common spirits that appear are the spirits of the wolf, killer whale, and toad, though a great variety of others may also appear. The spirit teaches the novice songs and dances and gives the shaman a new name, which is always used by the shaman when acting in that capacity. The shaman wears certain paraphernalia—a neck ring of shredded red cedar bark to which is attached a pouch bearing small objects, which represent the diseases the shaman can cause. The shaman also employs a special rattle and a ring made of hemlock branches, which is used for purifying patients. The curing of a patient takes place at a public ceremony with many other people present. The first step is to diagnose the disease, which is caused either by loss of the soul or by some foreign object that has entered the body. The shaman makes a diagnosis through contact with the supernatural spirit. If the cause is loss of the soul, the shaman uses the purification ring to call back the soul. If the cause is some foreign object, the supposition is that it has entered by accident or been "thrown" by another shaman acting on behalf of an enemy of the patient. The shaman must remove the foreign object by sucking it out or squeezing it out of the body of the patient. Shamans resort to a variety of tricks to produce the removed object. The common one is for the shaman to conceal bird down (tiny bird feathers) in his upper lip and then to bite his lip and spit out the bloodied bird down as if it were some worm-

A Tlingit shaman, wearing ritual paraphernalia including a horn crown, shakes his shaman's rattle while dealing with a witch.

like object. In keeping with the ranked social structure of the Kwakiutl, great chiefs have their individual shamans who protect the chief by throwing disease into their enemies. The Kwakiutl expression is that "the chief owns the shaman." Kwakiutl shamanistic practices must be set within a cosmology consisting of myriad spirits of nature and of the flora and fauna of the Northwest Coast environment in which they live. Hortatory rituals are used to exhort the supernatural to allow men to have success in hunting and fishing endeavors. For example, after an animal has been slain, its spirit is asked to tell all its relatives that they will be treated with respect and that they, too, should come to the hunter.

Kwakiutl shamanism is an example of how shamanism operates in a ranked society. In simpler societies like the Inuit and the Yanomamo, shamanistic activity is not limited to curing or causing disease. The Inuit shaman in former times also intervened with the supernatural in attempting to control the forces of the environment that directly affected the life of the community. When game was unavailable, shamans were asked to call on their spirits to indicate where animals were located. Shamans were also said to control thunder and stop snowstorms and the cracking of the ice. Shamans were called in to protect the community against malevolent spirits and monsters. The Inuit believed that sickness was caused by the sufferer's loss of his soul or by evil ghosts and spirits who were usually angered by the breach of some taboo. The shaman, who was called to act in either case, invoked the supernatural spirits with which he was in contact. An Inuit boy became a shaman by joining the household of an elderly shaman as a novice, where he observed special taboos, had visions, and was taught special shamanistic techniques. The novice also had to refrain from sexual relations.

The Yanomamo shaman achieves his power through contact with the small humanlike supernatural creatures called *hekura*. Any man can become a shaman, and since the procedure is simple, half the men in a village may be shamans. To become a shaman, a man fasts, abstains from sexual relations, and, as mentioned earlier in this chapter, takes a drug that causes hallucinations for several days. The most powerful shamans keep the *hekura* spirits in their chests. Among the Yanomamo, illness can be due to two causes—the loss of the soul or the intrusion of evil spirits into the body. The shaman, in the latter case, will try to suck out the evil spirits from the patient. The shaman also acts aggressively toward enemy villages when he tries to lure away and capture the souls of their children.

Among the Wana of Sulawesi, Indonesia, whose ideas about the cultural construction of gender we have discussed in Chapter 2, though gender is not a qualification for becoming a shaman, most shamans are male since only they are brave enough to go into the forest to obtain the requisite spiritual knowledge. The major shamanic ritual is a dramatic performance that brings the coresidents of a swidden settlement together. The primary purpose of the ritual is to cure illnesses resulting from loss of soul parts or the intrusion of foreign objects. This healing ceremony also articulates Wana cosmology and acts as a forum for establishing political authority.

As can be seen from these examples, shamans function primarily as healers. Illness is very commonly attributed to either the intrusion of foreign objects into the body or loss of the individual's soul, both of these brought about by external supernatural forces. Through his close contact with these supernatural forces, the shaman attracts the wandering soul back into the body, or removes the foreign object that has come to be lodged there.

Diviners

Another type of part-time religious specialist is involved in divining—providing information about the future from supernatural sources to enable people to make decisions concerning future actions so that they will be successful. In some cases, as in the Inuit example, the shaman has a dual function of curing and divining the future. Diviners use a variety of methods to gain their information. Sometimes chickens or other animals are killed and their entrails inspected to determine what action to take in the future. Roman diviners, or augurs, inspected the entrails of sacrificial animals for good or bad omens. Julius Caesar was advised not to venture forth on the Ides of March because the sacrificial animal, when examined, had no heart. Similar techniques of divination were used in the past by hunters in northern North America and Siberia. They took the shoulder blade, or scapula bone, of animals such as reindeer, moose, elk, otter, and seal and placed it on a fire until cracks appeared, which formed a pattern. The pattern of cracks was then interpreted to locate the place where animals were to be found. Omar Moore (1957), a sociologist, has pointed out that since the cracks appear in a random fashion, the hunter following the omens will pursue game in a random fashion, avoiding overhunting in one area and the possibility that game will flee that area. The Chinese, as archaeological information has revealed, used tortoise shells in the same manner to foretell the future. The Chinese, in general, have always placed great emphasis upon omens. Fortune-telling and geomancy—the interpretations of the future from cracks in dried mud—are two of the methods they use. In some places diviners are referred to as oracles.

In our own society, there are several examples of divination. Water witching—the use of a branch of a tree or a stick as a dowsing rod to indicate the presence of groundwater, enabling people to dig wells and hit water—is one such example. Water witching is carried out by a specialist who has a special talent in this regard. Similarly, Gypsy fortune-tellers in city storefronts and at rural fairs read palms, tea leaves, and Tarot cards to divine the future for their clients.

Witches and Witchcraft

Another kind of specialist concentrates upon doing evil things, causing illness and death rather than curing it. These specialists are known as sorcerers or witches. Since there is a logical connection between curing illness and causing it, in many societies the same specialists who cure illness can also cause it. In terms of anthropological usage, sorcery is something that is learned, whereas people are born with a propensity toward witchcraft. As pointed out in the discussion of the Kachin, Kachin witches are unaware that they have this power. Witchcraft and sorcery involve the use of supernatural means to cause bad things to happen to one's enemies. These enemies may be persons outside one's own group or persons within one's own group with whom one is in opposition. Both Kwakiutl and Yanomamo shamans could use sorcery against enemy groups. Among the Trobrianders, as noted in Chapter 8, the people of a district fear that their chief will use sorcery against them if they go against his commands. There sorcery is being used as a means of social control.

In many societies, when a person in the prime of life becomes sick or dies, it is necessary to ascertain what caused the illness or death. This means going beyond the immediate cause of, say, a death, such as the tree that fell or the lightning that struck, to the more important underlying reason for why the person was chosen to die. This was the case in the death of Sir Iambakey Okuk, the Papua New Guinea politician referred to in a previous chapter, who died suddenly at age forty-two. The underlying reason usually involves the evil intentions of other people, and a hypothesis that the death was caused by sorcery is forthcoming. British social anthropologists working in Africa, especially E. E. Evans-Pritchard and Max Gluckman, adopted an approach in which they saw such sorcery and witchcraft accusations as the product of tensions and conflict within the community. When a person in the prime of life dies, an investigation into the cause must be conducted. The investigators try to divine through supernatural means who caused the death. Like a "whodunit" in our own society, the diviner—detective—asks who has the most to gain, who is the most likely suspect. When individuals fall ill, accusations of witchcraft may also be forthcoming. Claims of witchcraft are usually made in such a way that they reveal the cleavages in a society.

In many Old World societies, the institution of the evil eye operates in the same way as witchcraft. If misfortune occurs, it is assumed to have happened because of the operation of the evil eye by some enemy. Any auspicious event or good luck is said to attract the evil eye. Because of this belief, people take precautions against the evil eye. People believe that it is dangerous to praise a child as beautiful, strong, or healthy, since this will create jealousy on the part of others and cause them to invoke the evil eye. Various protective devices and verbal ritual formulas are used to ward off the evil eye. Among the Basseri, a nomadic pastoral society of Iran, a mirror is placed on the back of the horse on which the bride is taken to her groom, since a joyous occasion like a wedding is likely to promote envy on the part of onlookers, and the mirror is used to reflect the evil eye back to its sender.

Magicians

Magic is another kind of religious specialization, as we have noted above. Magic, witchcraft, and sorcery all involve the manipulation of the supernatural. While witchcraft and sorcery are directed toward evil ends, magic is directed toward a positive goal—to help individuals or the whole community. In parts of Melanesia one frequently finds societies in which there are several part-time religious specialists who carry out magical rites to bring rain, promote fertility in the gardens, and ensure successful fishing. The garden magician among the Trobrianders is one of the most important people in the village. He recites his magical spells and performs his rituals at every stage of the process of growing yams, and what he does is seen as being as essential to the growth and maturation of crops as weeding and hoeing. He officiates at a large-scale ceremony involving all the men of the village that takes place before any gardening begins. He carries out specific rites at the planting and weeding and in assisting the plants to sprout, bud, grow, climb, and produce the yams. This is done at one time for all the people of the village. Malinowski (1935) pointed out that the garden magician, through spells at each stage of production, acts, in effect, to coordinate and regulate the stages of work throughout the entire village. This is because the garden magician must perform his rites before the next stage is initiated. Each village has its own special system of garden magic, which is passed on by matrilineal inheritance, so that a sister's son succeeds his mother's brother as garden magician.

Priests

With the evolution of more complex forms of society, in earlier and later states, religion becomes more elaborated and more differentiated as a separate institution. Despite this, religion is still interwoven with other institutions. In contrast to the shaman and magician, who operate as individual practitioners and part-time specialists, are religious specialists who come to be known as priests. They operate in concert in carrying out a more codified series of rituals, and their activities are associated with a shrine or temple. Priests eventually become full-time specialists. In order to become a priest, one must learn the rituals and how to use them. The body of ritual knowledge, which is the priest's method of contacting the supernatural, must be learned over a lengthy period of time. Archaeological data on Mesopotamia reveal that in societies that were the forerunners of full-fledged states, there was a single figure who was both the political and religious head of the community, and there was a priestly class. Subsequently, as the state evolved, there was a separation of political and religious positions. In Chapter 8 it was noted that formal legal codes evolved out of religious codes in early states. These religious codes comprised moral statements that have remained an integral part of the universal religions. The development of full-time religious specialists in these early states is usually paralleled by social stratification and economic complexity. The class of religious specialists was but one of a number of social classes in an increasingly more hierarchically organized society.

Priests were intimately associated with development and control of the calendar in the early civilizations of the Maya and the Aztec and in Egypt and Mesopotamia. It is not known whether the priests invented the calendar, but it is clear that it was used for religious purposes and for determining when communal rites should take place. In ancient Egypt, the flooding of the Nile was absolutely regular; its onset could be dated 365 days from the last onset. The development of a solar calendar, in place of the more widespread lunar calendar, enabled the flooding to be predicted.

The development of this solar calendar was based upon a certain amount of astronomical knowledge. In these early civilizations the priesthood seems also to be associated with scientific observations of the heavens. The ability to predict natural phenomena, such as the yearly flooding, was connected, in the eyes of the people, to priestly proximity to the supernatural. This in turn gave the leader of the theocracy—the priest-king—great power over the ordinary agriculturalists.

Aims and Goals of Religious Activity

The previous sections were concerned primarily with ways to approach the supernatural and with religious specialization. This section is directly concerned with the aims and goals of religious activity. First we must distinguish the aims and goals of the participants in the religious activity that they themselves articulate from the latent functions; that is, we must identify the consequences brought about by the activity that may be unforeseen or unconscious on the part of the participants. The motives of the people carrying out religious behavior relate to the fulfillment of substantive needs. Much of religious behavior has as its goal the control of natural phenomena. Those who carry out the rites and perform the spells desire to produce results such as stopping a storm, bringing rain, or bringing fertility to their crops. The Kwakiutl hunter repeats the magical formula to convince animals to come to him. The Trobriand garden magician recites the particular spells that will make the yams grow. The Kachin sacrifice to the *nats* to ensure that their crops will successfully grow to maturity. The goals of religious practitioners in all these cases are very similar, as their motives in carrying out these acts are to bring about quite specific results in such a way as to make natural forces and processes respond to human needs.

Some religious behavior is directed toward guiding human action. Such religious practices enable people to make decisions about how to act. For example, decisions about where to hunt are made as a result of divination. Oracles and fortune-tellers are consulted to determine which course of action to take when faced with a choice. It is reported that even the wife of a president may consult an astrologer to determine the course of action that the president should take. Omens may be interpreted to decide whether to do something now or to delay that action. Whenever individuals are uncertain about what they should do, what course of action to take now or in the future, they often use one of these procedures to enlist the assistance of the supernatural to enable them to make a decision. What are the motives of the individual in doing this? When filled with doubts about one's ability to make a decision, one is provided with a means for obtaining an answer.

In many societies religious behavior is directed toward curing illness. The purpose of this kind of religious behavior is to find the cause of the illness and to remove that cause and thereby cure the individual. Ascertaining the cause involves seeking answers from the supernatural. The cause of the illness is often seen as the manipulation of the supernatural by evil people for evil purposes. The cure, of necessity, also involves supernatural means.

Sometimes, worshipers and religious practitioners may say that the purposes of the religious rite are to emphasize communal values and to inculcate these values in the young. At this point the conscious purposes are close to the latent functions. Rites of passage specifically have this purpose. Such rituals serve not only to teach those involved the specifications of their new roles, but also to reinforce the structure of the society, as people are moved from one social position to another. Rites of intensification tied to the yearly calendar also provide order, structure, and meaning for the organization of society as well as for the life of each individual.

Latent Functions of Religious Behavior

In contrast to the goals and purposes of the participants themselves, the latent functions of religious behavior are those results usually unknowingly caused by the actions of the participants. Thus the hunter examines the cracks on the animal's shoulder blade (the process is called scapulimancy), and the pattern tells him where to hunt. The latent function of this technique is to randomize the direction in which the hunter looks for game. It is like spinning a roulette wheel and deciding to hunt in accordance with where the ball falls. This randomizing of the choice of where to hunt is functional. Hunters who operated according to these randomizing principles in theory should be more successful than other hunters who did not use such procedures. The latter might consistently hunt the same area until it is exhausted of game and would then have to move far away. Besides preventing overhunting, two other latent functions are at work here. One is the reduction of indecision and uncertainty about where to hunt. Such indecision makes hunters anxious, but scapulimancy reduces such anxiety since it provides clear answers relatively rapidly. When men hunt in groups, there may be differences of opinion on where to hunt. Scapulimancy provides an independent opinion from the supernatural that the group can then follow, avoiding conflict within the group.

The Trobrianders believe yams will not grow unless the garden magician recites his spells at particular stages during the production process. Each of the different work stages commences after the garden magician has performed the necessary rite. The purpose of the garden magic is to make the yams grow better, but although the people may not be aware of it, it also has the effect of coordinating work activity involved in gardening. This is a latent function.

Some of the latent functions of religious behavior involve effects upon the psychological state of the participants. Being in a dangerous situation produces anxiety. Malinowski pointed out that when Trobrianders fished within the safe confines of the protected lagoon, they did not use magical formulas. However, when on the open sea, where their small canoes were in danger of being smashed against the barrier reefs, they relied on a series of magical formulas to protect them in this hazardous situation. Malinowski argued that the real physical dangers might arouse their anxieties to such a point as to incapacitate them. The recitation of magical formulas reduced their anxiety and gave them the confidence necessary to handle the situation. The magic is not used in lieu of established fishing procedures but as an adjunct to these in dangerous situations that generate anxiety. George Gmelch (1971) has pointed out the way in which baseball players use magic rituals and formulas in areas of the game most fraught with uncertainty—hitting and pitching. The same explanation that Malinowski advanced for Trobriand fishing magic applies, since anxiety is involved in both situations. Reducing anxiety for the pitcher or the hitter and giving the individual a sense of confidence, even if it is false confidence, will improve performance.

Malinowski's argument could be turned on its head. One might argue that anxiety itself has important functions in dangerous situations. Under such circumstances adrenalin should be flowing and all one's senses should be alerted to potential danger. Performing magical rites just before such situations produces anxiety. This anxiety is said to be advantageous since it makes people alert. How can these two opposed positions be reconciled? One might say that the resolution lies somewhere between the two. Excessive anxiety may be paralyzing, but overconfidence may also lead to bad performance. When a person is faced with uncertainty in important and possibly dangerous situations, a combination of alertness to the real dangers and confidence in one's ability to cope with the situation is the most desirable mix. This synthesis can be brought about by performing some magical or religious ritual. It is said that there are no atheists in foxholes.

It should also be noted that religious ritual is a dramatization that functions to reinforce and standardize a world view among the members of a congregation.

At the beginning of this chapter, we noted the existence of witchcraft side by side with Christianity in England and the United States. In these same societies, we also find that some people still wear amulets to ward off the evil eye, seek advice from fortune-tellers, and go to faith healers to be cured by the "laying on of hands." Various pagan beliefs and local spirits were incorporated into Christianity when it spread through Europe and into Islam as it moved through the Middle East and parts of Africa. The same process occurred when Christian missionaries carried Christianity throughout the world. This missionary activity, which continues today, did not result in the eradication of earlier traditional beliefs and activities described in this chapter. Instead, a syncretism, combining Christianity and local beliefs, has produced many different forms of Christianity throughout the world. This has also occurred with Islam. We will discuss this in greater detail in Chapter 13.

We have pointed out that religious institutions respond to changing conditions and to contact with other religious ideas. This process has occurred in the United States. America has produced its own new forms of Christianity and Islam, for example, Mormonism, or the Church of Jesus Christ of the Latter Day Saints; Christian Science; and the Nation of Islam. These religious groups represent responses to the distinctly American scene. Although the forms of religious expression may change, the functions they fulfill remain constant.

CHAPTER 10

Myths, Legends,
and Folktales

 If people attempt to explain the unknowable by constructing a supernatural world, they also talk about that world. They tell folktales about supernatural creatures. They relate legends about the distant past of unrecorded history in which knights slew dragons. They tell myths about the origins of the world and of people and their social groups. They tell stories about the exploits of supernatural animals that talk; about big bad wolves that swallow grandmothers; about the brother of the wolf, the coyote, who acts as a trickster. They tell stories about fairies, elves, and the Little People. What these different types of stories have in common is that they deal with certain kinds of universal themes. These themes include birth, growing up, male-female relations, and death.

We are treating myths, legends, and folktales together because they form a continuum. Though these categories derive from our own culture, they provide a useful framework for organizing this material. All three deal with times past. Myths deal with the remote past, often with the time of the origin of things, both natural and cultural—how the world and its people were created, how fire was discovered, and how crops were domesticated. As the time period becomes less remote, myths fade into legends, which are sometimes thought to have a basis in historical fact. Folktales deal with an indeterminate time. In European folktales, this is demonstrated by the standard opening—"Once upon a time. . . ." In the sections that follow, we will be discussing various anthropological explanations of myths, legends, and folktales. To the tellers of these stories they constitute accounts of real people and real events.

Myths

The people of Wogeo, whose cosmology was described in the preceding chapter, have a myth that tells how the flutes that represent the *nibek* spirits came to be. As is typical of myths, this myth takes place in the distant past when the culture heroes and heroines who created everything in the world lived. Two heroines dreamed the idea of making flutes. They cut two sticks of bamboo and bored a hole in each, forming flutes that immediately began to play. They were overjoyed with the self-playing flutes. When they went to work in the gardens, they stoppered the holes to make the flutes stop playing. An adolescent boy stole the flutes from the two women. He tried to blow them, which caused the women to return to the place where they left the flutes. Seeing that the boy had stolen the flutes, the women told him that the flutes would never again play by themselves. Though the flutes were intended for everybody, since a male had stolen them, no female would ever look at the flutes again. The women told him that it would be hard to learn to blow the flutes. However, if boys did not make the effort, they would never grow up to be men. The two women then set off, leaving the island of Wogeo in disgust. The two islands where they eventually settled, Kadovar and Blupblup, and the mainland of New Guinea, where they passed some time, are the only places where bamboo for flutes can currently be found.

This myth can be interpreted in a number of ways. Anthropological approaches to the interpretation of myth are directly related to different theoretical frameworks. One approach would interpret this myth as literal history. People who use this approach view myths about great floods that inundated the world as based upon actual floods. Myths about the disappearance of the lost continent of Atlantis are seen as based upon the actual disappearance of a real civilization located on an island. In such an approach, the Wogeo myth would be interpreted as signifying an earlier period of matriarchy, when women controlled those parts of society men now control. Nineteenth-century evolutionists, such as Lewis Henry Morgan and Johann Jakob Bachofen, would have interpreted this myth as demonstrating an earlier stage of matrilineal organization and matriarchy. They hypothesized that all societies went through such a stage as they developed. This stage was followed by patrilineal organization and patriarchy.

This method of interpreting myths as literal history has been discredited by anthropologists, as was the unilineal theory of evolution of societies

Wogeo flutes, which can be seen only by men, are played by initiated men and represent the voices of the nibek *spirits.*

through a fixed succession of stages. Twentieth-century approaches to the interpretation of myth include the Freudian approach, which has been adopted by people interested in psychoanalysis, including anthropologists like Alan Dundes. The Wogeo myth lends itself readily to a Freudian interpretation. The flutes are masculine objects, associated only with males, and are obvious phallic symbols. What happens to the flutes in the myth seems to involve penis envy on the part of the women and anxiety about castration on the part of the men. Just as individuals express unconscious fears and anxieties in symbolic form through dreams, myths are seen as reflecting the collective anxieties of a society. Myths in this approach function to give cultural expression to these anxieties. Freud considered certain repressed anxieties and frustrations to be universal—that is, connected to universal pan-species characteristics related to growth and development.

Still another approach to myths is provided by Malinowski, who was antievolutionist and anti-Freudian. He insisted on the necessity of analyzing a myth in relation to its social and cultural context. Myth to Malinowski was a charter for how and what people should believe, act, and feel. Just as our Declaration of Independence states that "all men are created equal," a body of myths lays out the ideals that members of a culture should use as a guide to behavior. Myths may also be charters for the organization of social groupings like clans, containing statements about their rights to land and other clan possessions, their relations to totemic ancestors, and their relative rank and relations to other social groups. The Malinowski approach to myth as charter would require that the Wogeo myth be examined in the context of Wogeo culture. To interpret the myth from this point of view, one needs additional cultural facts. It is necessary to understand that there is a men's cult that revolves around the men's house where the sacred flutes are kept. At adolescence, boys are initiated into this cult. The initiation involves the scarification of the tongue so they can be rid of the effects of their mother's milk. Only after this is done can they learn to play the flutes. Boys are also taught to incise their penises at the same time. They stand knee-deep in the ocean, and each makes an incision in his penis with a sharpened clamshell so that the blood flows into the ocean and not on his body, which would be dangerous and polluting to him. Subsequently they do this periodically to rid themselves of the pollution resulting from sexual intercourse with women. Both men and women are seen as polluted by sexual intercourse. Women get rid of this pollution through menstruation, but men have to be taught to incise their penises to accomplish the same end. Women are kept away from the men's house and are never allowed to see the sacred flutes. When the *nibek* spirits appear prior to the large ceremonial distribution, their voices are the flutes. The people of Wogeo say, "Men play flutes, women bear infants." When the men play the flutes, they are in a ritual state that is considered dangerous, and they must abstain from sexual intercourse. Malinowski's approach to myth would interpret the Wogeo myth as providing the justification and rationale for men performing certain ritual and ceremonial roles from which women are excluded.

The American anthropologist Clyde Kluckhohn stressed the interdependence of myth and ritual. In many instances, myths provide statements about the origins of rituals as well as details of how they are to be performed. However, Kluckhohn saw ritual and myth as fulfilling the same societal needs. The same kinds of emotional feelings are aroused in the telling of the myth and in the performing of the ritual. There is a direct connection between the myth and the ritual in Wogeo. The flutes have a central role in ritual activity, and they are said to be the voices of the *nibek* spirits. The initiation ritual of boys, which involves their learning how to play the flutes, is directly connected to the mythic statement about a boy's not growing up until he learns to play the flute.

More recently, Lévi-Strauss has pursued a large-scale, detailed analysis of myths from North and South American Indian societies. According to Lévi-Strauss, myths provide explanations for contradictions that are present in a culture and that cannot be resolved. The Wogeo myth emphasizes the separation of women from men, after men obtained possession of the flutes. In Lévi-Strauss's terms, the myth attempts to resolve the contradiction between the ideal of keeping males and females apart and the need for them to come together in order to reproduce society. Like all myths, this myth, too, fails to provide a permanent solution to this contradiction.

The theoretical approaches to myth are complementary to one another. Each examines myths from a different point of view. Only the approach that interprets myth as literal history has been completely discredited. The analysis of the Wogeo myth will show that the sexual symbolism that Freud would emphasize is significant, the myth as charter for male-female relations that Malinowski would stress is evident, the close connection between the myth and rituals of male initiation that Kluckhohn pointed out exists, and finally the myth deals with an irreconcilable contradiction, which is the focus of Lévi-Strauss's concern.

As noted above, this myth must be understood not by itself, but in connection with other cultural facts. The aphorism "men play flutes, women bear infants" is very important. Male and female are seen as separate but complementary. Women bear children as part of a natural biological process. Flutes are cultural objects manufactured by men. Men have to learn how to play the flutes through the difficult process of initiation. Women are therefore associated with natural things and men with cultural things. When men play the flutes, they are associating with the *nibek* spirits, whose voices are the flutes, and they must practice sexual abstinence. As we mentioned, the people of Wogeo believe that when men and women have sexual intercourse, each becomes polluted by contact with the other. Both men and women must be ritually cleansed. The woman does this in a natural way, through menstruation. But men must do this through culturally learned behavior—the incising of their penises. Once again, women are associated with nature and men with culture. Wogeo culture erects symbolic barriers in order to keep men and women apart. Ideally each sex should lead its life separately, but in order for women to bear children, as the aphorism says they should, the sexes must come together. This is the only way that society can continue.

Boys' initiation consists of a series of ceremonies. Young boys are associated with women and are not permitted to see or play the flutes. The several initiation ceremonies they go through serve to separate them symbolically from the women and turn them into men. In the course of the initiation rituals, the *nibek* monsters, which are associated with the flutes, are called forth. When very young boys have their ears pierced, they are told that the *nibek* monsters, the "big things," have bitten them and will come back later and eat them up. When the boys are ten years old, a ceremony is held during which they are admitted to the men's house. The boys are symbolically swallowed by the *nibek* monster, pass through his bowels, and are "reborn" through his anus. When they are reborn at initiation, they are not born from women, but from the *nibek,* which are associated with men. Several years later each boy's tongue is scarified. This is to allow the pollution resulting from nursing and drinking mother's milk to flow away and to permit him afterward to play the flute, since scarifying the tongue makes it more pliable. The *nibek* monsters are summoned when the boys play the flutes for the first time. Initiation is therefore a process through which boys, who are associated with women, are separated from them and are reborn as men from the *nibek* spirits.

With this background, let us return to the myth. The first part of the myth deals with a time when women dream and then make the flutes, which play by themselves. No cultural learning is involved. At this time men and women are not separate. After the boy steals the flutes, men must learn to play the flutes and are separate from women. In the aphorism "men play flutes, women bear infants," in the initiation ceremonies, and in the myth the same pattern is repeated. Men, representing culture, are separated from women, representing nature. Boys, who are associated with their mothers and have not yet learned the secrets of their culture, learn those secrets at initiation, and in the process they acquire culture. But the myth says more than that. It says that, at one time, women were superior to men. They bore the children and were given the flutes. The present domination of men rests upon their having stolen what was once women's. Women are naturally superior because they can bear children, because they can cleanse themselves naturally through menstruation, and because for them the flutes played by themselves. Men have to do everything the hard way, which is through learned cultural ways. But their control of culture enables them to dominate women. Ultimately, the myth is about the tension inherent in male-female relations.

This theme of the tension in male-female relations is universal in all human societies and, as such, is expressed in their mythologies. On the other side of the world, the Mundurucu of the Amazon forest of Brazil have a myth that is strikingly similar to the Wogeo myth. The Mundurucu have sacred trumpets that are kept from the women. In the myth, the trumpets were discovered by the women, who then owned them. At this time, men performed all the women's tasks, such as getting firewood and water and making manioc cakes, and women were dominant over them. The trumpets had to be fed meat, which only the men could provide through hunting. Finally the men took over the trumpets, as well as control of the men's house. The women were no longer allowed to see the trumpets, were no longer permitted into the men's house, and were henceforth subordinate to the men. Like the Wogeo myth, the Mundurucu myth is a justification for male domination over females, and Yolanda and Robert Murphy (1974), the ethnographers of the Mundurucu, use the myth as a starting point in their discussion of male and female roles in Mundurucu society. As in Wogeo, the myth begins with a reversal of roles and the attribution of superiority to females in mythic times. Tension in the relationship between males and females in Mundurucu and in Wogeo, and male insecurity about domination over females, leads to the common occurrence of such a myth.

In ancient Greek mythology, which is an integral part of our Western civilization, there are echoes of the same theme. In his introduction to the Greek myths, Robert Graves (1955) links the myths to what he believes to be an earlier matriarchal stage in the development of European society. Both the Amazons, superhuman women who controlled their society, and the Fates, women who, through their weaving, determined the destiny of all humanity, are supposedly evidence in the myths for this matriarchal stage of society. But the Greek myths should not be taken as evidence of literal history any more than the Wogeo or Mundurucu myths should. These Greek myths tell us about contradictions and tensions in ancient Greek society. Myths deal with universal themes, and one such theme is male-female relations, which may be handled in very similar ways in very different societies.

Legends

Myths treat the ancient past and the origins of things, while legends deal with the less remote past, just beyond the fringe of history. Frequently legends are about heroes who overcome obstacles, slay dragons, and defeat conquering armies to establish the independence of their homelands. Such legends are retold to justify the claim of a people to their land and their integrity as a people. The traditions of Polynesian societies, as they have been retold over the generations, illustrate the way in which myths fade into legends. For example, the Maori, who are the original Polynesian population of New Zealand, have a myth of how Maui fished up the island of New Zealand from the ocean depths and later became a culture hero who obtained fire. Kupe, another culture hero, subsequently rediscovered the island while chasing a supernatural octopus and reported back to the other Maori living in their original legendary homeland. The first settlers set sail and reached the island by following Kupe's directions. The Maori have a tradition of remembering and repeating lengthy genealogies. These genealogies, which go back forty generations, link the present population to the first settlers and to Kupe. The legends of the Maori are concerned with their migration to the island of New Zealand and the manner in which each tribe and kin group occupied its land. The traditions of the native Hawaiians, who are also Polynesians, are similar to those of the Maori. Like the Maori, the Hawaiians are great genealogists, with traditions of migrations by canoe from Tahiti to the islands of Hawaii. The genealogy of the Hawaiian royal family, the Kumulipo, is a prayer chant and goes directly back to the gods. The gods appear to be like men in their form and

The fierce god of war, Kukailimoku, is portrayed by Hawaiians in their sculpture.

actions, and it is hard to separate them from chiefs who lived and were later deified. Thus the world of myth imperceptibly becomes the world of legend, and finally the known world of history.

Folktales

Folktales are set within a timeless framework. They are concerned with morality and usually take the form of demonstrating what happens to individuals who violate the moral code of the society. Often animals freely interact with humans as heroes or villains, and at other times tales may be about animals who talk, act, and think like human beings.

One of the most common folktale motifs is that of the Trickster. Among many North American Indian societies the Trickster takes the form of the Coyote, though among the Kwakiutl he is a Raven. There are many sides to the character of the Coyote, the Trickster. Sometimes he is depicted as being very cunning—he feigns death in order to catch game; he tricks birds into a bag; he cheats at races and wins. Other times he is singularly stupid, as when he joins the swaying bullrushes, thinking they are dancing, and drops from exhaustion, or when he dives into the lake for something reflected on the surface. In some tales he is a glutton, and in others he is involved in amorous and ribald adventures.

Typical of the Coyote tales is "Coyote and Bullhead," collected by Harvey Pitkin (1977) from the Wintu Indians of northern California. Coyote, while traveling north, encounters a swarm of small black bullhead fishes and is able to roast and eat all but one by tricking them into swarming onto hot stones over a fire. Subsequently he meets a rotten tree stump creaking in the wind who refuses to answer him. Thinking himself teased, Coyote punches at the stump until he is stuck fast. The people who had been traveling by earlier come along and free him. Later Coyote again encounters the sole surviving bullhead. Coyote teases and provokes the bullhead, insulting him by implying that his relatives are all dead, until the fish eats Coyote up. The fish then rolls into the water under a big rock. The people come looking for Coyote and see the fish. They are able to spear the fish only when they get a magical sky-spear. They slit open the fish's belly and Coyote pops out. On emerging Coyote pretends that he has dozed off and doesn't know how he came to be in the fish's belly. The people then sew up the bullhead and return him to the water.

In this Wintu tale about Coyote, he is revealed, as he characteristically is in other tales, as a strange combination. He is the clever deceiver and teaser, as well as the dupe and victim of his own actions. Though he is referred to as "uncle" by the "people" in the story, he is really more like a child. His actions get him into difficulties from which he must be extricated by the grown-ups—the people in the story. They then lecture him not to behave in this way anymore. Like a mischievous child, he of course does the same thing again. This sequence of events has a twofold function—it is hilarious to the listeners, while at the same time it imparts the moral that insulting, provoking, and teasing are bad.

A structural analysis of this Coyote tale will enable us to understand its message more clearly. It can be broken down into three distinct episodes: (A) Coyote eats the little bullheads, (B) Coyote fights with the stump, and (C) the last bullhead eats Coyote. By arranging the three episodes in columns, the relationships among the three can be more clearly seen.

Episode	I	II	III
A	Coyote tricks bullheads.	Coyote eats bullheads.	One bullhead escapes.
B	Coyote is provoked by the stump.	Coyote is stuck to the stump.	Coyote escapes with the people's help.
C	Coyote teases the last bullhead.	Bullhead eats Coyote.	Coyote escapes with the people's help.

When lined up in this way, the three episodes are seen to be very similar. However, episode B is diametrically opposed to episode A. In A, Coyote successfully tricks the bullheads, while in B he himself is tricked by his own stupidity. In A he wins and eats all but one of the bullheads; in B he loses and is trapped, though he ultimately escapes. Episode C reconciles and unites the seemingly unrelated episodes A and B into a single story. Episode C refers back to episode A in that the bullhead has his revenge on Coyote for eating his relatives. Episode C is a reversal of episode A, since the bullhead eats Coyote (in C), while Coyote eats the bullheads (in A). Episode C is very similar to episode B in that Coyote's teasing leads to his entrapment in both episodes.

What is the meaning of this Coyote story? What message does it convey? The structural analysis we have presented reveals the message of the tale. In Wintu culture Coyote represents the child. This story is an attempt to teach Coyote the rules of the society, though Coyote will never really learn. Though Coyote succeeds as a trickster in the first episode, he fails in the second and third episodes and must be extricated by the people, the larger community. The message conveyed is that, though a trickster may seem at first to be successful, one must ultimately conform to the rules. One can only succeed by being a member of a group and conforming to its rules. The Wintu rules that Coyote violates are striking out on one's own, teasing, and insultingly referring to the dead. The gathering of food is a communal activity, and striking out on one's own, as Coyote did, violates this. Teasing and being provoked by teasing are not considered proper adult behavior by the Wintu. But worst of all, Coyote breaks the Wintu taboo against referring to the dead by teasing the last surviving bullhead. The message to the listeners is that if you violate these rules, you will end up like Coyote, a child who can survive only if he is constantly rescued by adults from dilemmas.

Originally myths, legends, and folktales were transmitted orally, and each telling was a performance. They were retold from generation to generation, to the awe and amusement of successive audiences. Each time a story is retold, it comes out slightly differently. Variations are introduced, different episodes are included, and eventually different versions of the same story develop. A story may spread from one society to another over a wide area, and in each of these societies a somewhat different version of the story will be found. Anthropologists are interested in collecting all the versions of a single story told in a particular society. By comparing these different versions, the anthropologists are better able to ascertain what is significant in the story and what its meaning is. In similar fashion, the same and related stories in different societies over a wide area are collected and compared by anthropologists. Lévi-Strauss, after he had developed the structural method applied in the analysis of the Wintu folktale about Coyote, used this method in his analyses of different versions of the same myth and related myths in different South American Indian societies.

Ultimately, by the conclusion of the fourth volume of *Mythologiques* (1971), he had analyzed hundreds of South and North American Indian myths. His analysis revealed the presence of the same themes and contradictions in mythologies throughout this large area. His aim in this enormous endeavor was to attempt to reveal the innate structuring of the human mind.

When myths, folktales, and legends are written down, an oral literature becomes a written literature. The stories may form the basis for the literary tradition of the society. The legends of King Arthur and the Knights of the Round Table cease to be stories told by bards, or professional storytellers, and become part of the poetic tradition of English literature. The fact that the story is now written down does not mean that it will not continue to change. The story may be rewritten by poor storytellers and by good storytellers and may change with each retelling. The characters, motifs, and central themes of these stories may often be used by poets, novelists, and dramatists in their own works.

Legends and Folktales
in American Culture

A logical question is: Does our culture have myths, legends, or folktales? Since myths deal with the remote past and with the origins of things, American culture does not have myths; however, legendary figures abound.

Some were real people, such as Davy Crockett, Daniel Boone, Kit Carson, Annie Oakley, and Buffalo Bill. The stories of their lives became the subject of legends, to which were added other legends about them that had no basis in fact. Other legendary heroes, such as Pecos Bill, John Henry, and Paul Bunyan, probably never existed. The setting for these legends was the expanding American frontier. The stories about these men usually involved a demonstration of how they conquered natural obstacles and made the frontier livable. They were scouts who led the wagon trains across the dangerous and endless plains. They were rivermen who opened up the rivers to settlement and commerce. They were railroad builders who laid the steel track across an expanding nation. They were the sheriffs and marshals who made the frontier safe.

Sometimes the heroes of the legends assumed superhuman proportions, as did Paul Bunyan. Bunyan was a legendary lumberjack and logger. As the lumber industry moved across America from Maine to Michigan and Minnesota, and then later to Washington and Oregon, the Bunyan stories moved with it, and Paul Bunyan changed from a regional to a national hero. The Paul Bunyan stories all have a distinctive character. Bunyan, his ax, and his blue ox Babe are of enormous and superhuman size. Bunyan's feats are distinctive because of both his cleverness and his great strength, and many of the stories are humorous. In some of the stories he creates natural landmarks, like Puget Sound. Many stories demonstrate his ability to conquer nature. In one story he makes a river run backward in order to break up a log jam. Paul Bunyan stories are also told in the oil fields of Texas and Oklahoma. In these stories Bunyan is an oil man, who even invents the tools and methods of drilling for oil. The Bunyan stories had an obscure beginning in the tales told in the lumber camps of northeastern Michigan. The tales reached a maximum popularity and audience when they became the subject of newspaper columns and advertising copy in the second decade of the twentieth century. At this point they were no longer folktales; they had become popular literature.

In American legends, the theme is a characteristically American one— that of the conquest of the frontier and the settlement of the land. As occurs in legends in general, American heroes, by their bravery, their ingenuity, and their labor, assert the claim of a people to their land. This, of course, totally ignores the claim of an earlier native population to that same land and the contributions to the development of our country of other groups, such as blacks, Asians, and Mexican Americans.

While the legends of Paul Bunyan and other tall tales seem to be indigenously American, folktales and fairy tales associated with American society are largely derivative, coming from other countries, as did the population originally, except of course for Native Americans. Fairy tales like "Cinderella," "Little Red Riding Hood," and "Jack and the Beanstalk" were part of the large body of European tales written down by the Brothers Grimm in the nineteenth century. These stories continue to be told in America for the amusement of children, but at the same time they convey moral lessons to them. Joel Chandler Harris recorded a series of stories from blacks living on former plantations in the American South in the latter part of the nineteenth century. These stories, revolving around the characters of Uncle Remus and Br'er Rabbit, were also derivative; they had their origin in African folktales, which were brought to America by black people who came as slaves. West Africa, the area from which the majority of slaves were taken, is particularly known for its animal tales, such as the stories of Ananse the Spider, a trickster figure similar to Coyote. It is interesting to note that the theme of the Rabbit as a trickster also appears in the tales of the Creek, Natchez, and other southeastern Indian groups. Scholarly analysis indicates that the tales were borrowed from slaves by these Native American groups.

In present-day American society, a change of major proportions has taken place. Myths, legends, and tales are rarely told by storytellers and are infrequently read in books—except by parents to small children and, perhaps, in required courses in English literature. The major themes, however, continue to be repeated, but now in the new media of mass communications. It is in movies and television that these same themes appear. One has only to think of the Western film to understand this point. The hero of

The character of Uncle Remus was modeled after Remus Banks. The boy in the picture is the grandson of author Joel Chandler Harris, who recorded the stories.

the classic Western, like the heroes of American legends, is a rugged individualist who tames the frontier. But Americans have an ambivalent attitude about taming the frontier. They look back with fondness to the time when the frontier represented escape from the constraints of society—a time when individuals took the law into their own hands. The cattlemen who used the open range for cattle grazing represent the beginning of law and order. But they fought the farmers who wanted to fence in the range, and who represent a further step in the process of control over nature. In the film *The Man Who Shot Liberty Valence,* director John Ford captures the ambivalence between the wilderness of the frontier, represented by the outlaw Liberty Valence, civilization, represented by Senator Ransom Stoddard, and Donovan, the real hero, who straddles both worlds. The story of the killing of Valence, the villain, is told in a series of flashbacks from a civilized present time to an earlier frontier time. But a sense of loss and nostalgia for that earlier period is pervasive.

Will Wright, in his book *Sixguns and Society* (1975), analyzes the way in which Western film plots have changed over time in response to changes in American society. In phase one, the classic Western, the hero is a stranger who stands outside of society, rescues it from the threats of the villains, and is reincorporated into society. The transitional Western represents phase two, in which the hero begins as a member inside the society and ends up outside, because he is now fighting society itself, which is identified with the villains. In phase three, the hero begins and ends up outside of society. He is part of a professional group undertaking to defend a weak and ineffectual society against a gang of equally professional villains, who are ultimately defeated. Wright sees this development of the Western as reflecting the growth of disinterested professional elitist groups in an increasingly technocratic American society beginning in the late 1950s.

The same ambivalent attitude about someone who takes the law into his own hands is represented in other kinds of films today. Clint Eastwood portrays the cop who takes things into his own hands in *Dirty Harry*. There is an obvious continuity in the moral values of the character he portrays in *Pale Rider* and the character of Dirty Harry. The structure of the *Rambo* films is a recapitulation of Wright's transitional structure, in which the hero is fighting society, which is the villain.

Cartoonists frequently portrayed former President Reagan as Rambo, or as a cowboy on a horse. President Reagan himself often quoted from movie scenes and has used Clint Eastwood's most famous line, "Go ahead, make my day." With this phrase, Dirty Harry conveys how eager he is to waste the villain. A popular American myth is that of the moral individual who stands outside a society that is either ineffectual or corrupt, and fights the forces of evil. Both the president and the actor played out the same myth.

Like the films discussed by Wright, television situation comedies are constantly being transformed in response to changes in American society. Fifteen years ago, no situation comedies focused in a central way on middle-class black people. Today, a very popular television program, *The Cosby Show*, is about the Huxtables, a middle-class black family. In this program, universal themes such as relations between different ethnic groups, relations between the sexes, intergenerational conflict, and ways to inculcate proper moral conduct into the young are portrayed in their particular American cultural context. For example, Dr. Huxtable, who requires frankness from his children, must then contend with his adolescent daughter's teasing him about her having stayed overnight at her boyfriend's house while the parents of the boy were away.

A program like *L.A. Law* ostensibly portrays the way in which lawyers as a profession deal with dispute settlement in our society (the program is about the daily activities of a law firm). However, the significant underlying theme of the program is about relations between the sexes. This theme is manifested in the sexist behavior toward secretaries and junior female associates. The marriage of two senior partners created difficulties because each felt it necessary to maintain a separate career identity. We saw this in the Shriver-Schwartzenegger wedding described in Chapter 2. The lawyer in the firm who handles divorces is an opportunist who can't resist taking advantage of women in his own personal life, to the point that his own marriage eventually fails. The managing partner repeats his father's behavior as he himself searches for a sex partner. *L.A. Law* recapitulates the same universal theme of the Wogeo myth discussed earlier, the tension inherent in male-female relations.

Narratives with universal themes, embodied in myths, legends, tales, and contemporary forms of mass media, are found in all societies, including our own. They reflect problems and contradictions with which all cultures wrestle. They embody the values of the culture and point out what has significant meaning in that culture. In this sense, what we as Americans see in the movies and watch on television, and how we respond to it— whether we love it or hate it, accept it or reject it—is revealing about the nature of our own culture.

CHAPTER 11

The Artistic Dimension

 Every culture, universally, produces what we of the Western world label as art. Objects not only are shaped and formed to meet utilitarian needs, but also are frequently embellished and decorated. Such embellishments are referred to in the West as the decorative arts. Though everyday language is capable of communicating information, thought, and emotion, poetry and song are heightened and more expressive ways of communicating the same things. From this, one can conclude that some kind of universal aesthetic impulse exists and is manifested in all cultures in what we call the arts.

Beyond this universal aesthetic impulse, which enables us to identify cross-culturally a category called art, cultures differ from one another with regard to the nature of their artistic expression. Some societies, such as the Tikopia, stress poetry but have little in the way of visual arts. In some societies people decorate their bodies, while in others they decorate their houses. Still others seem to stress each of the arts equally. The interpretation of the meaning of a work of art in its culture can only be made in terms of the symbolic system of that society. Of course, someone from another culture can appreciate a work of art in terms of its aesthetic qualities, without understanding its meaning in the culture that produced it. Art represents the style with which a particular culture expresses its symbols. Each culture has its own style, in the same way that a tapestry does.

Only in the Western world is art produced for art's sake, to be hung in museums, galleries, and homes or to be performed in concert before large audiences. In the societies that anthropologists typically study, art is embedded in the culture. It is actively used in the performance of ritual, and the meanings the art is communicating relate to the meaning of the ritual and the mythology associated with it.

The Visual Arts: Sculpture and Painting

Masks are a special kind of sculpture, found in a number of societies over the world, but certainly not universally. We have chosen to examine masks as an exemplification of art in culture because they have certain intrinsic features, and yet their meaning and use differ from one culture to the next. The two stone masks pictured have been acclaimed as works of art. What makes them works of art? What do we know about their place in the culture that made them? These two masks were collected from the Tsimshian of British Columbia in the late nineteenth century. They were found in two different locales by two different individuals and ended up in two different museums, one in Ottawa and the other in Paris. An anthropologist, Wilson Duff, thought they matched. In 1975 he brought them together for an exhibit at Victoria, British Columbia, and found that the

Tsimshian stone masks, one with eyes open and another with eyes closed, fit together as a set.

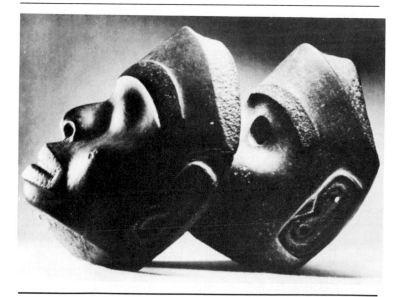

sighted mask fit snugly into the back of the unsighted one, the two forming a single entity. The inner mask had holes drilled in it for the wooden
harness with which it was attached to a human head. We know, therefore,
that they were used as masks, but this is the only direct information on
their use that we have. Now that we know that the two masks form a set,
their meaning must be interpreted in that light. The alternation of sighted
and unsighted may mean something to us, but what did the masks mean
in Tsimshian culture? In addition to conveying emotion, does all art also
convey meaning?

We do know a good deal about the meaning of masks and how and
when they were used in ritual and ceremonial life among the Kwakiutl,
who are southern neighbors of the Tsimshian. Using these data, in addition
to what we also know about Tsimshian culture, we gain some insights into
their uses among the Tsimshian. In the Kwakiutl wedding potlatch,
described in Chapter 2, many chiefs come to help the groom symbolically
"move" the bride. These chiefs wear masks and costumes that depict the
supernatural ancestors who are the mythological founders of their
numayms. Each chief makes a speech in which he relates how his privileges,
including the right to wear a particular mask, have descended to him from
mythological times. The names and privileges of each *numaym* are embodied in its ancestral myth. Two different masks are described in Chapter 2.
One is called "The Devourer of Tribes" and represents a sea bear, a mythological monster combining characteristics of the bear and the killer whale.
The father of the bride is able to call forth this supernatural creature because his *numaym* is descended from it, and only that *numaym* has the right
to make a mask representation of it and personify it in a ritual. Similarly,
another chief, "Made-to-Be-Tied," wears the great wolf mask of Walking-
Body, the chief of the wolves. The chief is descended from the original
mythological owner of the wolf mask and the great wolf ceremonial. The
Kwakiutl masks, which now hang on museum walls, were used in ritual
performances to enact the myths of the spirits they represented.

Use of masks among the Tsimshian, carvers of the twin stone masks, is
very similar to that among the Kwakiutl. Tsimshian masks represent supernatural spirits. They were used at potlatches and at supernatural dance
society rituals. Contact with supernatural spirits operates along lineage
lines, and at initiation, power from the supernatural spirits associated with
a boy's own lineage is "thrown" into him. Somewhat later he is initiated
into a secret society. He now has the right to sing the song of his spirit and
wear its mask at ceremonies. When a chief wears his mask, the supernatural spirit is in him. Its presence is also indicated by whistles, which represent the voice of the spirit. Among the Tsimshian, carvers of masks, artists,
song composers, and dramatists were all men who had received supernatural power. Returning to the stone masks, we can imagine these masks, now
in museum cases, being used in a Tsimshian ceremony. It is dead of winter
in a village on the Skeena River, and the *hala'it*, the sacred dance of the

Tsimshian, is being held. Whistles announce the approaching spirit, and before the entranced audience the chief appears with the face of the sightless stone mask. As he slowly dances, the stone mask miraculously opens its eyes. The great power of the spirit residing in the chief has caused this miracle.

The two stone masks represent a single face, which opens and closes its eyes. What does this mean? Wilson Duff (1975) suggests that the sighted/sightless states represent looking outward and looking inward or self-recognition, sight and memory, seeing and imagining, looking ahead and seeing the past.

Let us now look at the use of masks in another part of the world, West Africa, an area where masks also play a central role in the art of societies. These masks are associated with the Poro, the secret society found among a group of tribes in Liberia and adjacent Sierra Leone, which we discussed in Chapter 6. One of these masks, a Poro Society mask from the Mano of Liberia, is shown on page 229. George Harley, a missionary doctor, amassed a great deal of material on the Poro Society among the Mano to enable him to better understand the significance of the masks he collected during the many years of his medical practice there.

Though the masks portray different things, all of them represent some kind of spirit. In fact, the same word, *ge,* is used for both spirit and mask in Mano. When a person dons a mask, the spirit is said to be present in him. Among the Mano, as among the Tsimshian, whistles and horns symbolize the voice of the spirit. As we noted in the previous chapter, the people of Wogeo believed that the flutes were the voices of the *nibek* spirits. Mano women are not permitted to see masks or anything else associated with the Poro Society spirits, except for special masked dancers who perform on stilts and entertain a general audience. There are basically two different kinds of masks. The first are portrait masks. When an important leader dies, his portrait mask becomes the repository for the spirit of the dead man. Other portrait masks represent more ancient tribal heroes, who are also ancestor spirits. The spirit of the mythical founder of the Poro Society is also embodied in a sacred mask. The other kind of mask is a grotesque half-animal, half-human associated with the spirits of nature and other spiritual beings, such as the god of the dance, the god of fertility, and the god of war. Ritual sacrifices of chickens or sheep were made to the masks on a regular basis in order to enable the masks to sustain their power. The masks were smeared with the blood of the sacrificed animal.

The Poro Society, with which these masks were associated, was a secret society, a male cult. All of its activities were kept from women and uninitiated boys. There were several initiatory grades, and men wishing to gain access to the higher grades had to pay large sums of money to go through the rites that earned them these high positions. At the top were the old men who, through a combination of inheritance and payments to the Poro Society, achieved the right to wear the most powerful masks. Among the

*A Poro Society mask from
the Mano of Liberia.*

activities of the Poro Society was the ritual for determining whether an individual accused of a crime was innocent or guilty. After discussion by the powerful elders, the masks were said to make the judgment. Since the wearer of the mask assumed its spirit when he put it on, the Mano would say that the mask punished or even executed someone when the wearer "carried out" the mask's decision. In addition to their judicial function, the masks and their wearers also stopped village quarrels, controlled fighting warriors, promoted fertility of the fields, presided at various public functions and life crisis rituals, and taught young boys the proper ways to behave in the bush schools of the Poro where they were first initiated. People conformed to the rules of the society because they feared the power of the spirits, including ancestral spirits, which were contained in the wooden masks of the Poro Society. Here spirits, which are physically represented by artistic means, were used as a means of social control.

How the masks came to be poses an interesting problem in the light of their role in the Poro Society. Warren d'Azevedo (1973) has studied woodcarvers among the Gola and Vai peoples, who are neighbors of the Mano in Liberia. The Gola and Vai also have the Poro Society and are similar in many respects to the Mano. The link between the carvers and the masks that they manufacture is denied in these societies. Young children are punished if they ask who made a particular mask. Adults, if questioned, simply say that the masks must have been made long ago and were passed on by the ancestors. But there are always carvers who continue to make masks. D'Azevedo found that parents try to dissuade their children from becoming woodcarvers. Carvers, like professional singers, dancers, and musicians, were regarded by the community as irresponsible and concerned more with their own creativity than with communal well-being. Boys intent on becoming carvers frequently ran away and apprenticed themselves to master carvers. Many carvers have a direct relationship with a particular spirit, and inspiration for masks comes to them from that spirit through dreams. Since they carve masks for the Sande Society, the secret women's society, as well as for the Poro Society, carvers are the only younger men who have direct contact with women in the Sande and know the secrets of their society. Because he is a man with access to women's secrets, the carver is in an ambiguous position. In his negotiations with the Sande Society, the carver shows reluctance to take on the task, and the women try to induce him to make the mask by offering him sexual favors. The carver of the mask and the women of the Sande Society, who own the mask, never fully terminate their relationship. He has special access to the group, and they jokingly use the term *lovers* for one another. The carver in these West African societies is someone who, through his creativity and artistic skill, produces an object with supernatural power. But the relationship between the carver and his artwork is not even formally recognized. Like his work—the mask, which is a combination of the natural and the supernatural—the artist who creates this thing is himself somewhat outside of society. Artists in a great many societies, including our own, are frequently considered marginal people who are not bound by the norms of usual behavior.

Masks have some special characteristics that make them different from other forms of art. A mask is worn by a person. The mask is always a face. It can represent the face of a human being or the face of an animal. It can also represent the face of an imaginary creature, such as a monster or a supernatural being, in which human and animal features are combined. There is a relationship between the faces of wearers of masks and the faces of the masks, which cover the wearers' own faces and stand between them and the outside world. In Bali, Indonesia, the face itself is considered a mask. While the Balinese do wear masks in ritual performances, donning a mask and leaving the face bare are equivalent. The masks in Kwakiutl, Tsimshian, and Mano societies represent statements about the nature of the individual in each of these societies. Each society has a particular view of the individual—what his or her relation is to others in the society, where he or she came from, how he or she came to be, what his or her place is in the natural world. Thus, Tsimshian clan masks make a statement about the connection between the individual wearer and the mythical clan ancestor that the mask portrays.

Among the Kwakiutl, there are masks called *Dzonokwa* and *Xwexwe*, each representing a different supernatural creature. Lévi-Strauss (1979), who has studied these masks, has pointed out that stylistically one is a reversal of the other. The eyes in both are emphasized. In the *Dzonokwa* mask they either are deeply recessed or are deep holes, while in the *Xwexwe* they protrude extraordinarily, as can be seen in the illustrations. Both masks are used during the course of the winter ceremonial. This emphasis on eyes runs throughout Kwakiutl art, as well as through the art of other societies of the Northwest Coast, including the Tsimshian. Lévi-Strauss has suggested that the protruding eyes of *Xwexwe* indicate extraordinary visual abilities, such as clairvoyance—the ability to see the future. Masks therefore have an additional dimension of vision beyond the two dimensions already discussed for the sighted and sightless stone masks. In addition to the normal vision exemplified by the sighted stone mask, the *Xwexwe* mask has the capacity to see the future and the sightless stone mask to see the past. Eyes as a recurrent theme in the art seem to relate to the great importance placed on shaming in these societies. When an important man trips and falls or accidentally overturns his canoe, he is shamed and must give a potlatch in order to wipe out the shame. Thus it may be said that eyes are constantly watching and observing everyone's behavior. Kwakiutl individuals believe that their behavior is always in public view, and they must avoid actions that will shame them. The theme of eyes in the art, especially in the masks, reflects this view of the individual. If an American painter constantly used eyes in his or her art, we would say that the paintings reflect a

A Kwakiutl Dzonokwa mask (left) *and a Kwakiutl Xwexwe mask* (right).

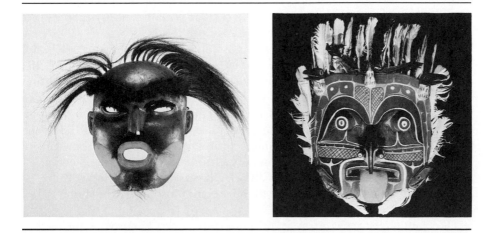

slight paranoia. What eyes mean in Northwest Coast art still remains to be investigated by anthropologists.

Masks are not simply objects that are carved to be looked at and admired. Rather, masks are used in rituals of different sorts. Masks are embedded in culture; that is, they play a significant role in religious, kinship, and political activities. This is true not only of masks but also of all objects or things we define as art in the kinds of societies anthropologists have usually studied. Among the Kwakiutl, summer and winter are clearly separated as the secular and sacred periods, and the art employed in the different rituals in summer and winter is contrasting in style (Rosman and Rubel, 1990). Summer is the time for potlatching, such as the wedding potlatch discussed earlier in this chapter, and on these occasions claims to rank are demonstrated. Chiefs wear masks illustrating their mythological ancestors, such as the wolf mask of Walking-Body, the chief of the wolves, in order to show his ancestry and high rank. The secular art style characterizes the portrayal of the wolf in this mask, as illustrated in the picture on page 233. There is a ritual period of transition between the secular world of summer and the sacred world of winter when the spirits come into the village and the Winter Ceremonial is held. The Kwakiutl Winter Ceremonial dances, which last several months, parallel the *hala'it*, the sacred dance of the Tsimshian discussed earlier. Young people are seized and devoured by the spirits, are initiated into secret societies, and then subsequently emerge. The spirits are portrayed by individuals wearing masks that represent particular spirits. The initiated members of the secret society are considered to be shamans, and they cross the border from the natural world into that of the supernatural and become dangerous cannibal spirits. The art style used in these winter ceremonial masks is an exaggerated and distorted style, in contrast to that used in the masks of secular summer rituals, and it is appropriate to the supernatural world of the shaman. As can be seen in the picture, the strongly curved beak of the eagle in the secular potlatch mask becomes the greatly distorted beak of the "Crooked Beak of Heaven," and the pronounced snout of the wolf in the secular potlatch mask becomes the exaggerated mask worn in the Winter Ceremony.

In our own culture, much of what is labeled art is created solely to give aesthetic pleasure, to be admired. This point has so influenced the definition of art in our society that we make a distinction between that which is useful or utilitarian and that which is art and has no practical use. Sometimes utilitarian objects are recognized as art at a later point in time and valued for their aesthetic beauty. Examples of this are furniture and other objects made by the Shakers and quilts made by the Amish. The decorative arts is a general category embracing utilitarian objects that are admired for their aesthetic qualities. In small-scale societies there is no such thing as pure art, and therefore in those societies there is no point in making this distinction.

Like language, art is a mode of communication. It conveys messages.

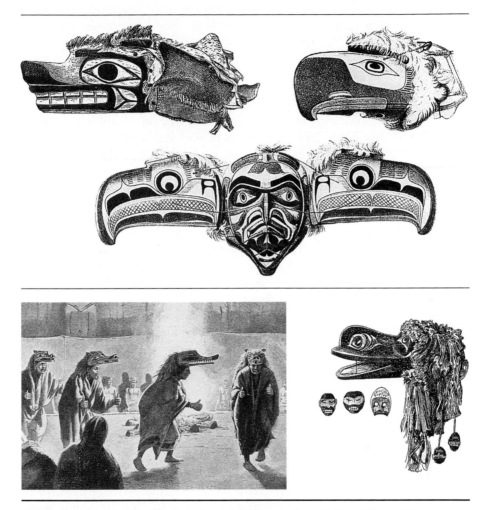

On top are the masks of wolf and eagle worn during secular potlatches. The eagle is a transformation mask that opens up to reveal another mask, representing the face of a man (middle). These masks contrast in style with the wolf and Crooked Beak (eagle) of the sacred Winter Ceremony (bottom).

Some anthropologists, like Anthony Forge and Nancy Munn, see art as a system of visual communication. Forge (1973) also includes dance and gesture, along with painting, sculpture, and architecture, as part of this system of visual communication. Nancy Munn (1973) has studied the art of the Walbiri, a society in Australia, and has analyzed it in terms of the fundamental graphic elements of which it is composed. Each element has a range of meanings, and the elements combine in regular ways according to rules. In this approach, art is much like language and has rules of combination like grammar. The artistic products of the Walbiri, such as sand drawings or decorated objects used in ceremonials, contain representations of totemic myths known as "dreamings." These are stories about the mythical totemic ancestors of the Walbiri and their travels.

On the Northwest Coast, in addition to the masks we have discussed, totem poles, sculpted house posts, painted house fronts, decorated ceremonial bowls, and other utilitarian objects contain the designs that represent particular clans. (Such a totem pole is illustrated in Chapter 4.) These designs depict the mythological ancestors of the clan, such as the wolf, the grizzly bear, the sea bear, the raven, the eagle, and the killer whale. The message conveyed here is that the art object represents the kin group and that the kin group and its representation are one. The art object may be used at a ritual, such as the masks worn by individual chiefs at a Kwakiutl wedding potlatch, at which time myths recounting the adventures of the mythological ancestor will be told or the dance or song associated with that myth will be performed. Forge points out that in Arnhem Land in Australia, art, myth, and ritual are completely interlocked and interdependent. They are three different ways of expressing the same thing—in words, in actions, and visually. The art of the Northwest Coast illustrates the same point.

Art also communicates emotion. The emotion may be awe, as is the case when statues represent powerful supernatural spirits such as the Hawaiian god pictured in the previous chapter. It may be terror, as when the Poro masks are invoked. It may be laughter and pleasure, as when masked dancers carry out their antics or when satirical art caricatures pomposity.

Sometimes, the aesthetic appreciation of art objects extends only to the members of the society within which they are made. Each society has particular standards by which it judges its art. However, there are some masterpieces that people of very different cultures can appreciate aesthetically. In some instances, the emotional impact of the object appeals to some universal sense and does not require particular cultural knowledge in order to be appreciated. In an experiment carried out by Irvin Child, a psychologist, and Leon Siroto, an anthropologist (1965), photographs of BaKwele masks from Central Africa were shown to BaKwele elders, including carvers, all of whom were knowledgeable about masks. These men ranked the masks in terms of their aesthetic value, from the best mask to the worst. The same photographs of the masks were then shown to a group of art history students at Yale University, and they too ranked the masks according to their opinion of the aesthetic value of each mask. There was significant agreement between the two groups of judges. Though the American students knew nothing about the masks or about BaKwele culture, they tended to agree with the BaKwele experts about which masks were good and which masks were mediocre. This is an area in which investigation is just beginning, but research seems to indicate that there is some universal aesthetic sense.

Beyond its communicative function, art can also be examined in terms of style. If the function of art is the role it plays in society, its use in ceremonial rituals, and the information and the aesthetic pleasure that it communicates, then its structure is the component parts of which it is formed. *Style* refers to a consideration of the component elements of art and how the elements are put together. For example, the art of the Northwest Coast is said to be characterized by a particular style, as is apparent from previous illustrations. What are the characteristics of that style that make it easy to identify art coming from that area? The typical art form of the Northwest Coast area is three-dimensional carving in wood. This undoubtedly relates to the fact that the societies of the Northwest Coast are located in the northern coastal rain forest, where massive trees like cedar and spruce provide excellent raw material for the carver. The colors used in Northwest Coast art were predominantly yellow, black, red, and green-blue, with the unpainted natural wood as a background color. The pigments were made from natural materials—fungus, berries, ochre, moss, charcoal. The distinctive green-blue used was produced by allowing native copper to corrode in urine. Because of the emphasis on sculpture, round, oblong, oval, circular, and curvilinear forms predominate. The interlocking of animal and sometimes human forms, such as that found on totem poles, is typical. Franz Boas has noted that the depiction of animals in Northwest Coast art is characterized by the emphasis of certain features—eyes, mouths, ears, fins, feathers, and tails. Each animal species, from killer whale to dragonfly, can be distinguished by the distinctive representation of these features. Thus, as we have pointed out above, the curved beak is the distinctive feature of the

Painting from a Tsimshian house front representing a bear.

eagle, and the snout is the distinctive feature of the wolf. The same techniques for carving the wood were adapted for use in other media, such as stone, bone, and metal. Besides carving in the round, Northwest Coast artists also worked on two-dimensional flat surfaces. The change from three dimensions to two dimensions required a transformation of design. The technique adopted on the Northwest Coast is called *split representation*. The painting from a Tsimshian house front (page 235) illustrates this technique. The bear has been sliced in half and the two sides placed next to each other to make up the house front. This represents a bear—the two sides in profile—but together they form a bear looking frontward.

Two other features of Northwest Coast art should also be noted. Design elements cover an entire surface, leaving no blank spaces, and eyelike shapes are used as fillers and in place of joints. Earlier, we discussed the significance of the portrayal of eyes in masks, and indicated the great importance of eyes in Northwest Coast society. All these features, taken together, form the distinctive style of the art of the Northwest Coast.

The concept of style also has a hierarchical aspect. One can speak of the style of the individual artist, that is, the small features that are characteristic of the work of a particular artist. Sometimes the art style of a village can be identified. It is more frequent to refer to the art style of a single society, such as Kwakiutl. Certain general features delineate the art style of a larger area, made up of a number of societies, as we have shown above for the Northwest Coast. Contemporary Northwest Coast artists, such as the remarkable Haida carver Bill Reid, use the traditional content and the distinctive style of Northwest Coast art, but the style of each artist is different, as is the case for European and American contemporary artists. The sculpture in wood by Bill Reid (page 237), entitled "The Raven and the First Men," exemplifies the combination of traditional themes from Haida mythology and the genius of a creative artist. The same concept of style applies to the art of complex societies. One can speak of the style of Renaissance art, of the Italian Renaissance in particular, of the schools of Venice or of Florence, and of the particular style of Raphael. The concept of style is applicable at each of these levels.

This leads directly into the question of whether one can speak of the style of the individual artist in small-scale societies as comparable to the style of Raphael in terms of its uniqueness. As we have noted, art in small-scale societies is embedded in social, ritual, and ceremonial contexts, and therefore it must be produced within a set of constraints, since it must convey certain messages. The artist who carves a Poro Society mask operates under such a set of constraints, but beyond that he can show some degree of inspiration and individualism. After all, he does not merely copy a previously existing mask. He carves a representation of a known spirit in terms of his conceptualization of that spirit. He gets his inspiration in dreams. Accounts from other societies indicate that there, too, inspirations are said to come from dreams. William Davenport (1968) reports that woodcarvers

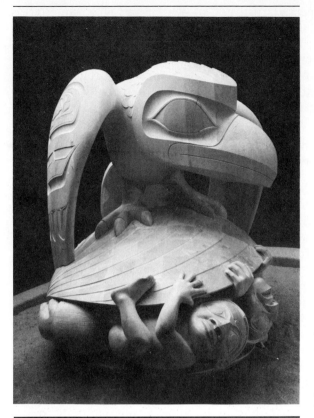

Modern Haida sculpture by Bill Reid depicting the mythic incident in which Raven, the culture hero, discovered the first Haida men in a giant clamshell.

in the Solomon Islands also receive their inspiration from the supernatural, which comes to them in dreams. Creativity in some people and not in others is a difficult phenomenon to explain, and people the world over resort to external factors like divine inspiration from the supernatural, or the Muses, to account for it. In addition to inspiration, the artist must also have the technical skills to translate a vision into a work of art. Craftsmanship is also a part of creativity. All carvers, and all artists, are not the same. Some are better than others and some are worse, and all people in all societies distinguish between good and bad art. They do this by applying a set of aesthetic standards.

It has been argued that one of the characteristics of the art of small-scale society is that it is the product of a communal tradition and that the artist remains anonymous, whereas our society exhalts the creativity of the individual artist. This erroneous idea is a construct of Western society (Price, 1989). Within the cultural context and in the community in which the art is produced, the creativity of the individual artist is recognized and rewarded, and the names of superior artists are known far and wide. Such art is made anonymous when it is extracted from its original cultural context and transported to Western society.

The removal of artifacts from "exotic" places began with the Age of Exploration. Captain Cook brought back many specimens that people in Europe saw as representative of the way of life of the people he encountered. He also brought back a "living specimen"—Omai, the Tahitian—referred to in Chapter 1. "Artificial Curiosities" as well as "Natural Curiosities" like fossils, rocks, and shells found homes in the collectors' cabinets of royalty and aristocracy. Such collections were the nuclei around which museums like the British Museum began to be formed during the nineteenth century. At the height of colonialism, the latter part of the nineteenth century, large quantities of such objects were taken by traders, missionaries, and government officials from small-scale societies that had become parts of colonial empires and sent to museums in all the capitals of Europe. In the course of this process, the masks that now hang on museum walls were removed from the cultural context in which they were created and used, and their creators were reduced to anonymity.

At the turn of the century, European artists who created what is called modern art were seeking new ways to depict the world about them, in particular the human form. Some, such as Vlaminck, Matisse, and Picasso, began to appreciate and to collect what Westerners then called "primitive" art. Much of this art came from the French colonies in Africa. In these carvings and sculptures the Western artists saw what was for them a completely new way of conceiving of and depicting the human figure, and they used these conceptualizations in their own sculpture and paintings. This is an example of the borrowing of culture traits from small-scale societies by specialists from more complex societies.

Examples of borrowing going in the opposite direction, this time of content but not of style, are to be found in Julius Lips's book written in 1937, *The Savage Hits Back*. Lips provides numerous examples from all over the world of how the art of subject peoples reflected their views of their colonial masters. As can be seen from the illustration of the Yoruba sculpture, this art makes pointed political comments and is both humorous and satirical in nature.

A rather special kind of art involves the decoration of the human body. Among the peoples of the central highlands of New Guinea, this is the most important type of art, since these people do little carving, painting, or mask making. In these societies, the decorations people wear and the painting of the body at cult performances and exchange ceremonies, like the *kaiko* of the Maring (discussed in Chapter 7), convey messages about the social and religious values of the people and also demonstrate the relationship of the people to clan ancestral spirits. Certain ideals and emotions are evoked for audience and participants by the wearing of the decorations. An extensive work dealing with this subject is by Andrew and Marilyn

Yoruba sculpture portraying a European on horseback.

Strathern (1971) on the Melpa of the central highlands. The use of particular colors in body painting and certain combinations of colors in feathers, shells, and beads unite to display abstract qualities like health and vitality. Similarly, darkness and brightness relate to the opposition between men and women. The Wahgi, another society of highland New Guinea not very far from the Melpa, also express their aesthetic impulses entirely through the decoration and adornment of the human body. Michael O'Hanlon points out that these displays of feather adornments and painting of the face and body during dances carried out at the Wahgi pig festivals serve to communicate the strength and health of the clan hosting the festival. But the most important part of the message conveyed is the moral strength of the host group. This derives from absence of friction within the group and from its sense of security in having fully fulfilled its obligations to others. The moral strength or weakness of the host group directly affects the brightness and quality of their adornment and the success of their performance during the ceremony (O'Hanlon, 1989).

The *malanggan* mortuary art of northern New Ireland, now part of Papua New Guinea, was so striking that European explorers of the early nineteenth century, who spent only a short time on the island, were sufficiently captivated to bring back examples to Europe and America. The carvings were part of the local religious ritual held to commemorate the deaths of several individuals of a single clan and simultaneously to initiate the boys of that clan. When the missionaries brought Christianity to the people of New Ireland in the late nineteenth century, they tried to suppress the *malanggan* ceremony and its associated carvings, since these represented earlier "pagan" beliefs. However, the *malanggan* ceremony persisted and continues in a modified fashion today. Now, for example, the Catholic Church no longer sees a conflict between the *malanggan* rite and Catholicism, and has even incorporated *malanggan* sculpture into church architecture. The *malanggan* ceremony of today often includes the erection of a cement cross in addition to the carvings.

A contemporary malanggan *carver from New Ireland holding his carving adze, beside an unfinished carving.*

As in the past, today the designs for *malanggans* are owned and are sold by one clan to another. The owner of the design tells the carver the myth embodying the design and what it should look like. The carver then translates the words into a visual image. Sometimes the process of translation for the carver involves dreaming the image, which he will then carve. As we have noted earlier, dreams play a role in providing inspiration to artists in other societies as well. Like the carver of masks for the Poro Society, not only does the carver on New Ireland work within a set of constraints such that the design can immediately be recognized as a member of a particular named category of images, but further the owner of the design must be able to recognize it as his particular design. Since the carver does not use a sculpture from a previous *malanggan* ceremony as a model, a degree of artistic creativity is also involved. Carvers are evaluated in terms of how successfully they express the design, and several have islandwide reputations.

Earlier, after the *malanggans* were used in a ceremony, they were burned or left to rot. After European colonization, *malanggans*, since they were no longer valued, were given or sold to Europeans. Large numbers of them wound up in museums all over the world. Today, after they are used in ceremonies, *malanggans* may sometimes be sold to tourists and collectors. One contemporary carver has carved a *malanggan* on a post for the National Museum in Port Moresby. Modern carvers use steel chisels and commercial paints. When shown pictures of *malanggan* carvings 100 years old and now in the Australian Museum, modern carvers admired the workmanship of the earlier carvers, particularly since the latter had only stone tools to use. However, they felt their own carvings were superior.

The three-dimensional *malanggan* art of New Ireland has provided the inspiration for the New Ireland printmaker David Lasisi. This translation of a sculptural style into modern graphics has also taken place on the Northwest Coast, as, for example, in the prints made by Tony Hunt. Traditional styles of what were small-scale societies like those of New Ireland and the Northwest Coast continue today, vibrant and alive, translated into new media. In these new forms, the art has become part of a commercial art market that includes buyers from all over the world.

When tourism develops in an area, frequently simplified versions of traditional art objects, and objects embodying traditional motifs in new media, begin to be manufactured as tourist art. In the mid-nineteenth century, the Haida of British Columbia began to carve miniature totem poles, platters, and boxes, with traditional designs, out of argillite, a soft, black, easily carved form of coal, a medium that the Haida had not used before European contact. These items were carved for sale to tourists. Sometimes argillite carvings were made that portrayed Europeans, such as ship captains and their wives. What has been called "airport art" can be found from Nairobi to Port Moresby. When style and content are dictated by what tourists buy, and Navajos make crosses and Stars of David out of silver and

Contemporary malanggan *carvings, which utilize traditional designs, displayed at mortuary rites held at Tabar Island, off New Ireland.*

turquoise to be sold in Albuquerque, then it is impossible for the art style to retain its characteristics. In fact, silver-working was introduced by the Spaniards several centuries earlier, and silver jewelry is itself an introduced art form. Sometimes the designs of tourist art become so popular that miniature ivory totem poles are made in Japan and sold in Vancouver and Navajo silver and turquoise jewelry, mass-produced in Hong-Kong, is sold in Santa Fe. This tourist art is clearly distinct from creative translations of traditional forms by artists like Reid and Lasisi.

Music and Dance

Like painting and sculpture, music and dance are commonly considered among the arts. These four categories constitute arts in that they all evoke emotion and can be evaluated in terms of aesthetic qualities. However, music and dance differ from painting and sculpture in a number of ways.

Music and dance are like spoken language in several important respects. All three unfold through time. Every sentence, every musical composition, every dance has a beginning, a middle, and an end. This is not true of a painting or a carving, which has no beginning or ending. Once made, it continues to exist. Musical compositions and dances are ephemeral. They find expression in performances, but once the performance is over they no longer exist. The musical instrument upon which the composition was performed is still there, and an idea of how the piece should be performed persists; however, the performance of the piece dies away, unless it has been recorded on tape or film, a modern phenomenon. Like the retelling of a tale or a legend by a bard, the musical piece exists as a concept in people's minds, and each performance is a slightly different manifestation of that idea. This conceptualization of a piece of music is just like the mental template a potter uses to make and decorate a certain kind of pot. In complex societies, musical compositions are written down, using some form of musical notation, and there are systems of dance notation for recording dance as well. These systems of notation are analogous to written language. Ethnomusicologists and anthropologists, when they study music and dance in small-scale societies, are studying a tradition that is transmitted orally and by performance. In these societies, music and dance, like oral literature and folktales, are taught and learned without benefit of written notational systems.

The anthropological emphasis has always been on the relationship between music and dance and other aspects of culture. In our discussion of the other arts, we saw that art was not produced simply to be admired, but was an integral part of other aspects of culture in small-scale societies. The same is true of music and dance. In fact, when anthropologists first began to study dance, they were more interested in the cultural context of the dance than in the dance itself. There is a great range of ritual and ceremonial settings in which music and dance play important roles. Birth, initiation, weddings, and funerals are typically occasions for music and dance.

The Kwakiutl and American weddings we described in Chapter 2 both included music and dancing. These two examples illustrate the contrasting ways in which music and dance function in the two societies. The dances and songs performed at the Kwakiutl wedding were owned by the *numayms* of the chiefs who performed them, as were the crests on the masks worn by the performers. The ancestral myths recount how the mythical ancestor spirit gave these songs and dances to the ancestor of the *numaym* to be transmitted down through the generations. In Kwakiutl culture, music and dance are forms of communication that convey messages. In addition to the message of ownership, the songs and dances of the groom's side convey the power based on supernatural contacts that is intended to move the bride.

The music at an American wedding also conveys a message. When the organ plays as the bride marches down the aisle, the audience silently repeats the words: "Here comes the bride, all dressed in white." The mes-

Dancers at a Mae Enga funeral.

sage conveyed is the ideal of the purity and virginity of the bride. This message is carried by the whiteness of the bride's gown, by the words of the song, and even by the melody of the music.

Music also plays a role in funerals. In this instance, music can convey the emotions of grief and sadness better perhaps than any other medium. In some societies dance also accompanies funerals. For example, among the Mae Enga of the western highland of New Guinea, the matrilineal relatives of the deceased as a group dance onto the plaza where the body is displayed, as pictured above. They wear white body paint and carry spears. The aggressive dance movements express their anger at the loss of their sister's child. Thus it can be seen that music and dance convey meaning as well as express emotion.

Ethnomusicologists and anthropologists also investigate music and dance in complex societies, from Iran, Japan, and Bali to the urban barrios of New York and Los Angeles. Adelaida Reyes Schramm (1986) has analyzed the way in which certain aspects of the music and dance of recent Vietnamese immigrants to New Jersey persist, while new elements from the American scene have been introduced. The maintenance of ethnic identity by the New Jersey Vietnamese centers on the celebration of Tet, the Vietnamese New Year. At the event that Schramm describes, a piece by a well-known émigré Vietnamese composer was performed, which incorporates many regional Vietnamese folk songs within an overall symbolic theme of Vietnamese unity. In the social dancing that followed, the dance forms were Western (tango, rumba, bebop, and twist), while the lyrics were sung in Vietnamese and the music was considered Vietnamese. The performance of music and dance is a sensitive indicator of the dialectic between continuity and adaptation of immigrant groups in America. The Vietnamese are only one of many immigrant groups who demonstrate this.

While the function of music and dance is similar to that of the visual arts, each is characterized by a different kind of structure. The elements of music are sounds and their characteristics, such as pitch and duration. Sounds produced consecutively form what is called a melody. Sounds produced simultaneously form harmony. Melody, harmony, and rhythm, which is a steady succession of beats, represent the basic concepts for analyzing the structure of music. The music of different cultures varies in terms of its structure. For example, the music of our society is based upon a system of eight tones within one octave—usually taught as do, re, mi, fa, sol, la, ti, do. Other societies in the world base their music on a scale in which there are only five tones within the range of an octave. This is called a pentatonic scale, and in fact it is more common in the world than our eight-tone scale. Rhythm is also subject to cultural variation. In our own society, each musical composition is characterized by a single rhythm. A waltz has one kind of rhythm and a march another kind of rhythm. Recent pop music in American culture may shift rhythms throughout the piece. This is in contrast with other societies, such as those in Zaire in Africa, where a single musical composition can have two different rhythms carried on simultaneously. Such variations make the music of other cultures sometimes sound strange to our ears. In addition, the instruments created to produce musical sounds are enormously varied.

The basic elements used to analyze the structure of dance are body movements. A formal description of dance would include the steps, spatial patterns, relationships to music, and postural positioning. The focus of the analysis is on the isolation of patterning in the dance.

In discussing the arts, we must also consider the role of the artist, the musician, or the dancer. There is a great range of variation, even within societies, regarding the degree of specialization involved in the performance of music and dance. Sometimes, as is the case among the Kwakiutl, songs and dances are privately owned and may be performed only by their owners. There are dances that may be performed only at a particular stage in life, such as dances for a male initiation. Within all societies, there are always some songs or dances everyone, regardless of age or sex, may perform. In many societies, men and women have two rather differentiated spheres of expressive activity. Concurrent with the increased interest in gender roles, researchers have begun to more systematically explore women's musical practices (Koskoff, 1987). Since a woman's identity is believed to be embedded in her sexuality, frequently women's role in music expresses this. Musical performance is seen as enhancing sexuality, and female court musicians in the past in India, Indonesia, and Tunisia were associated with sexuality and profane pleasures. In many societies, the genre or type of music performed, the style of the performance, and the location of the performance are different for males and for females.

As societies become more complex, dancers and musicians often become full-time specialists. For example, Kanuri musicians are a highly trained and specialized group who occupy a particular position in the social structure. The performers play as a group, which includes a vocalist, drummers, and a player of an oboelike reed instrument. The musicians are male, but the vocalist may be female. They frequently are attached to a patron, an aristocrat, who supports them in exchange for singing his praises on ceremonial occasions. They can also travel and perform as a group, living on the money they receive from their audiences. They are generally considered to be of low status by the rest of the Kanuri populace, since the way they earn their living is considered to be begging by the Kanuri. Nevertheless, virtuoso performers are greatly admired by everyone. Though the performers are aware of what other people think of them, they consider themselves to be artists. They value their own talents and thrive on the admiration of the audience. Thus the musician in Kanuri society is ambiguous in a way similar to that of the carver in Mano society. In general, artists are in an ambiguous position in most societies, including our own. Artists' talents are admired; yet the creativity that makes them different from other people also makes them suspect. The Kanuri musician wears an earring in one ear, unlike ordinary Kanuri males. Like the unconventional dress of the artist or jazz musician in our society, this marks him as different. Sometimes performers are of a different ethnic group from the rest of the people in the society. Gypsies of Afghanistan and Pakistan, who are traveling performers and musicians, differ from the rest of the population and are considered a low-status group, completely outside of the existing social structure. The Gypsies of Romania, distant relatives of those in Afghanistan, are also professional musicians who play the Gypsy violin which is so closely associated with Romania.

The various arts we have discussed in this chapter usually operate within a set of traditional constraints. Yet every carver, painter, musician, and dancer adds his or her individual conceptualization, his or her own interpretation to the final product. It is in this aspect of art that creativity is to be found, and this creativity forms the basis for the audience's judgment of the aesthetic worth of the art produced.

CHAPTER 12

Culture and the Individual

 The last chapter closed with a discussion of the relationship between the creativeness of the individual artist and the constraints of cultural style. Artists must conform to the art style of their particular culture in order for their work to be significant and meaningful to the people of that culture. Yet certain aspects of the art produced are uniquely the product of the artist's individuality. The latter is an expression of the artist's personality. The relationship between each artist's style and the art style of the culture is an example of the relationship between culture and the individual personality. Individuals make decisions and take risks. There has been a revival of interest in anthropology in the everyday experience of individuals. This is the result of the work of Bourdieu and his theory of practice. The emphasis is upon how people make choices from a set of cultural alternatives, given the cultural "rules of the game." These distinctions parallel Firth's distinction between social structure and social organization which was presented in Chapter 1. In Chapter 4 we distinguished private symbols, which have meaning only for each particular individual, from public symbols, which have shared meanings throughout the culture. In Chapter 10, we pointed out that dreams express the unconscious anxieties of individuals, while myths reflect the collective anxieties of a society. At the individual level, persons have dreams that are symbolically meaningful only in terms of

their own life experiences and that provide important insights into their personalities. However, the dreams of individuals utilize cultural materials and can be fully interpreted only with a knowledge of the dreamer's culture. On the other hand, myth and the meanings of public symbols represent shared cultural knowledge. This cultural knowledge is handed down from generation to generation and constitutes an entity beyond the individual bearers of the culture. The opposition we have set up between culture and the individual is, in some ways, overstated, as we shall see below.

In all societies, people exhibit individual personality differences as a result of upbringing and particular life experiences. Each individual has a certain personality, a certain character, which is more or less stable over his or her lifetime. This is not to say that individuals never change. An individual's personality can change, sometimes through his or her own efforts and sometimes with the assistance of someone like a therapist. But most frequently individuals demonstrate stability of personality. They act consistently in different kinds of situations. Stable patterns of personality are the result of the interaction of genetic, biological predispositions and the individual's life experience from birth on. There are individuals with different kinds of personalities among our acquaintances and friends, in the classroom, where we work, among our neighbors. A range of personality types exists in our society, as well as in every society in the world.

Though there is a range of personality types in every society, there are personality differences from one society to the next. In any one society a preponderance of individuals with a particular kind of personality is to be found. The attempt to characterize the dominant personality types of different societies and tribes goes back to ancient times. Tacitus, the Roman historian, in his work *Germania: On the Origin, Geography, Institutions, and Tribes of the Germans,* written at the end of the first century A.D., characterizes the Germans as "a race without either natural or acquired cunning, they disclose their hidden thoughts in the freedom of the festivity." He also notes that they represent a strange combination of idleness and sloth and readiness to go to war. Tacitus tried to capture what was distinctive about the personality characteristics of the Germans as a people. Throughout history, such characterizations of different peoples have been made. One must always be wary of stereotypes based on prejudice, as distinguished from accurate characterizations based on data and observations.

Earlier anthropological studies of personality and culture focused on personality differences between various cultures, the measures for determining and verifying these differences, the investigation of the cultural institutions that bring about the development of these particular personality types through time, and the other aspects of culture to which these personality differences were related. Anthropologists were also interested in how children were socialized into the cultures into which they were born, and as we shall see below, this continues to be a subject of great interest. Rather than talk about personality types, anthropologists talk about the structure of emotion, the notion of the person and the self in particular cultures and how these relate to other aspects of culture, sometimes going on to make cross-cultural comparisons.

Culture and Personality Studies

Early investigations in American anthropology of the relationship between personality and culture were strongly influenced by the ideas and concepts of Sigmund Freud. Freud's concept of personality was an outgrowth of his development of psychoanalysis, a therapeutic technique for dealing with mental illness. Anthropologists who were interested in Freud's ideas became especially concerned with child-rearing techniques and the socialization of the child, and the way in which these affected the development of the adult personality.

Margaret Mead and Ruth Benedict, both students of Franz Boas, took Freud's emphasis on early childhood experiences and combined it with Boas's theoretical point of view of cultural relativism. In separate works, Mead and Benedict applied this point of view to personality, maintaining that cultures varied in terms of patterns of child rearing, personality development, sex-role behavior, and type of mental disorder. They took from Freudian psychoanalytic theory the basic premise that early childhood experiences were fundamental determinants of personality, but modified it by focusing upon the ways in which child-rearing techniques differed from one culture to the next, thereby producing different kinds of personalities. Thus, they moved away from Freud's proposed universal stages of development. In her first important work on Samoa, Mead demonstrated that while adolescence in America involves a period of crisis and search for identity, in Samoa there is no equivalent period of crisis. In her subsequent fieldwork in the Admiralty Islands off New Guinea she focused upon the specific ways in which children were reared, how they were weaned and toilet trained, how and when they learned to walk and to swim, how infants were handled, and how children were taught and encouraged to become adults and develop the kind of personality valued by the Admiralty Islanders. In *Sex and Temperament*, published in 1935, she demonstrated how male and female roles in three New Guinea societies were culturally determined. She showed that aggressiveness and assertiveness were not always associated with the male role, nor were passivity and sensitivity always associated with the female role. In some societies, such as the Tchambuli, the females were assertive, and in others, such as Arapesh, Mead claimed that the males were passive, gentle, and sensitive. In *Sex and Temperament*, which was written for the general public, Mead went beyond her ethnographic data to strengthen her argument, and some of her interpretations have been challenged by anthropologists working in the same societies.

After Mead's death, Derek Freeman (1983) raised issues concerning her research on Samoa. On the basis of his own fieldwork there, he called into question Mead's emphasis on the role that learning and cultural factors play in child development, "nurture," in contrast to his own stress on biological factors, or "nature." He accused Mead of distorting the data on Samoa, claiming she was carrying out a Boasian political agenda that emphasized that differences between people were the product of cultural factors, rather than due to biological differences. This is part of an ongoing controversy concerning the relative weighting of biological and cultural factors.

Ruth Benedict, in her most famous book, *Patterns of Culture* (1934), sought to characterize each culture in terms of a dominant configuration or pattern to which corresponded a particular personality type. She characterized societies like the Zuni, in which the typical personality was one in which order, restraint, and control over emotions were valued, as Apollonian. Others, in which the valued personality type stressed emotionality and expressiveness, were characterized as Dionysian.

The anthropological research method used by Benedict in *Patterns of Culture* involved the analysis of ethnographic materials collected by the field anthropologist. From these materials she derived the typical personality of the people of the society, as deduced solely from looking at the culture. This was referred to as the *basic personality type*. This was based upon an assumption that there is a correspondence between a culture and the personality of individuals that make up that culture. In particular, this will be expressed in the motivations that impel individuals to act in ways valued by the culture. This concept dealt only with the typical individual. The concept of *modal personality type* was developed to portray the range of variation as well. Modal personality is a statistical statement giving the frequency distribution of different personality characteristics in a society. This kind of information is dependent upon measurement of actual personality characteristics of individuals in the society, rather than observations made about the culture. Projective tests were developed in Western countries as a means for assessing personality. Anthropologists have tried to adapt these tests for use in non-Western societies as a means for assessing personality characteristics of individuals in those societies.

In Chapter 1 we discussed a concern of contemporary anthropology with the methods used by the fieldworker in going about the task of understanding and interpreting meaning in another culture. This has involved a reflexive process in which both informant and fieldworker become more aware of themselves in the continuing interpretive process. The psychoanalytic theory of personality is similar to anthropology in this respect. The method in both involves the interaction between two individuals (fieldworker/informant, therapist/patient) that raises issues of self-awareness and reflexivity. The goal in both is to help construct a narrative through the interpretation of symbolic material which results in understanding the present. It is not surprising, therefore, that there continues to be an interest in Freudian psychoanalytic theory in anthropology.

Socialization of the Child

As we noted above, Freud's stress on the relationship between experiences in early childhood and later personality development was taken up by anthropologists interested in culture and personality. Anthropologists interested in child development and socialization concentrate on gathering data on child-rearing practices, paying particular attention to interaction between mother and child, the way in which the child acquires language and learns the categories, rules, knowledge, and values of his or her culture. As noted above, Mead had devoted an entire monograph to the socialization of the child in the Admiralty Islands.

Culture is transmitted from generation to generation as children are taught the ways to behave in their society. It is not transmitted as part of the biological inheritance. This process by which children acquire their culture through learning is called *enculturation.* Through this process, the child learns the rules of his or her culture. The child learns the values of the society and increasingly becomes motivated to act according to those val-

An Ifugao son practicing on a modern flute in imitation of his father's actions in Mountain Province in the Philippines.

ues. Every society has its rules, and most people conform to the rules most of the time. The motivations that have been built in during the enculturation process are what lead most people to conform to those rules. To act otherwise—to violate rules—produces guilt in the individual. As the psychoanalyst Erich Fromm (1944) has noted, stable individuals in a well-integrated culture will want to do the things that they have to do. This applies not only to cultural behavior, but to emotion as well, which is also culturally determined. The Trobriand funeral described in Chapter 2 shows how emotional response is culturally learned. When a man dies, his wife and children weep ostentatiously, while close relatives, such as his mother and his brothers, who are members of his own clan, must appear reserved and stoic, no matter how emotional they feel about his death. Though the form in which emotion is expressed varies from one culture to another, there are certain universal aspects of emotional states like happiness and grief.

The psychoanalytic approach conceives of personality development as proceeding through a series of developmental stages. Eric Erikson (1963), a psychoanalyst strongly influenced by anthropologists, broadened Freud's stages of psychosexual development in order to make it applicable to non-Western cultures. He was impressed by the cultural differences among the Yurok, the Sioux, and the American patients whom he was treating, and he saw these differences in culture and in child rearing as being related to differences in the adult personality. Instead of talking about an oral stage of development, Erikson talked about the development of an attitude of basic trust that will grow if there is a successful interaction between mother and child during the period of nursing and its termination in weaning. The second stage, Freud's anal stage, during which toilet training takes place, he characterized as the period of developing autonomy. Failure, or partial failure, to negotiate successfully the struggle over toilet training during this period results in the development of attitudes of shame and doubt, rather than of autonomy, according to Erikson.

Among the Sioux of South Dakota, children are freely breast fed up to age three, and there is no systematic weaning. The Sioux child is toilet trained by imitating older children, and the matter of toilet training is treated in a very relaxed fashion. Erikson sees a clear relationship between the way in which the Sioux handle these two developmental stages and the value that the Sioux place on the generous adult individual. Generosity among the Sioux is expressed in the economic institution of the "give-away," when someone with a surplus of goods ceremonially distributes them to others. In contrast, among the Yurok of California, a child is breast fed for only six months. Autonomy is encouraged very early, and weaning, which is called "forgetting the mother," may be brought about by the mother leaving the house for a few days. With respect to toilet training, the Yurok are particularly concerned that the child not urinate into the Klamath River, which each year brings them salmon on which they

A Fulani mother from northern Nigeria nurses her infant daughter.

depend. In Erikson's view, these aspects of child rearing are tied to an adult Yurok personality characterized by retentive hoarding, suspicious miserliness, and compulsive ritualization. It was Erikson's interpretation that the Yurok, who had their own kind of money in the form of shells, adapted well to American economic institutions. Their personalities and their own economic system were already very similar to that of American culture. Sioux culture and Sioux personality were quite different, and they did not adapt well.

Another approach to the study of differences in child rearing and in personality was adopted by John Whiting and Irvin Child (1953) in their cross-cultural study of seventy-five societies. They rated the child-rearing practices in each of these societies in terms of the age and severity of weaning, the age at which toilet training is carried out, the severity of toilet training, sex training, the age and severity of independence training, and the way aggression is handled. Whiting and Child saw a sequence of causation. Variations in child-rearing practices are caused by variations in "maintenance systems"—that is, the economy and the sociopolitical structure through which the group directly adapts to its environment. Child-rearing practices, in turn, bring about the personality processes that characterize each society. These typical personality processes in each culture lead to other expressive aspects of culture, such as religion, art, folklore, and belief systems, which Whiting and Child refer to as "the projective systems." They directly correlate the ratings of child-rearing practices with characteristics of the projective system, specifically with different theories about how disease is caused in these societies. While the typical personality exists as a variable in their formulation, they do not assess its characteristics directly. Among their findings, for example, they demonstrate that societies that produce high oral anxieties through their child-rearing practices, such as early and severe weaning, are much more likely to attribute disease to agents that enter through the mouth than societies that are more relaxed about weaning. The methodology Whiting and Child use is based upon statistical correlations. Such correlations tell the degree to which two variables are related, but they cannot tell which one is the cause and which one is the effect.

More recent research into how a child learns his or her culture has moved beyond the early interest in nursing, weaning, and toilet training. Today, much research is devoted to topics such as cognitive development and learning the appropriate emotional responses in a particular culture. In a study of Venda children in South Africa, Blacking (1988) investigated how they learn to understand and eventually perform the music and dances of their culture, and how this relates to learning how a Venda should think, act, feel, and relate to others. During infancy, a Venda child spends most of the time on his or her mother's or a sibling's back, hearing the songs and feeling the movements as the latter dances and sings during ritual performances and other social contexts. When a child starts spontaneous banging with an object, the adult converts this behavior into musical action by adding a second part in a different rhythm. As is characteristic of the music of many African societies, Venda music is polyrhythmic. The Venda view of personhood is that it is created through interaction with others. When Venda children sing as they play together with adults and later with other children, the polyrhythms in which they sing both assert their own person and create a sense of community at the same time.

The Relationship of Personality to Culture and Social Structure

Various studies continue to explore the nature of the relationship between cultural characteristics and the structure of emotion. Differences in the expression of emotions such as anger have been related to differences between what Rosaldo (1984) called bride-service societies—those societies that are loosely hunting and gathering societies—and bridewealth societies—more complex sedentary agricultural societies. In foraging bride-service societies, anger, if expressed, is quickly contained or forgotten. It is not allowed to fester. People in these societies see the expression of anger as destructive to social relationships. In a society like the foraging Hadza, discussed in Chapter 8, if anger cannot be contained, disputes can be settled only by the dispersal of the disputants. In bridewealth societies, it is expected that anger will be publicly expressed in words, since holding anger within can only lead to its expression in other ways, such as witchcraft. The implication of Rosaldo's suggestion is that small-scale foraging societies do not have the social mechanisms to deal with overt expressions of violence and anger, while more complex societies have a variety of institutions to deal with this. This is not to say that these institutional devices in more complex societies are successful in dealing with violence and anger. The failure of our own court and prison system attests to this.

Individuals who make up a society occupy different social positions, different statuses in the society. In all societies, people are minimally differentiated according to age and sex. Beyond this, there are many other bases for differentiation. Individuals who occupy different statuses within the same society are likely to have different personality characteristics. Ralph Linton referred to these personality differences as *status personalities.* For example, shamans in a society will have somewhat different personalities from nonshamans in the same society. Big Men, whom we discussed in Chapter 8, will have somewhat different personalities from their followers. There are two ways to view this relationship between social status and personality. In the first view, individuals with certain kinds of personality characteristics will gravitate toward those social roles or occupations that suit their personalities. For example, in our own society, individuals who are self-confident, assertive, and willing to take risks often gravitate toward positions in the business world. Others, with different personality traits, such as a tendency to intellectualize and a curiosity about the world but a sense of uneasiness in dealing with other people, are more likely to become scientists and to do research. In the second view, people moving into particular social roles will undergo personality changes brought about by the demands of the role. A classic example of this is Thomas à Becket, who, as Chancellor of the Exchequer in the twelfth century, was a free spirit and caroused with King Henry II. When Becket was appointed archbishop of Canterbury, he proceeded to behave according to that role. He changed from a frivolous, pleasure-seeking individual to the committed defender of a moral cause who chose martyrdom at the hands of his former friend, the king, rather than surrender his principles.

Culture and Mental Illness

If, in our society, a man said one day that a guardian spirit had come to him and told him that it would protect and watch over him throughout his life as long as he would follow certain commands and obey certain taboos, we would consider him to be mentally ill. If he reported that he had actually seen and spoken to the spirit, we would say that he was having hallucinations. However, as noted in Chapter 9, adolescent boys among the Crow of the Plains were expected to go on a Vision Quest to seek such a spirit. Seeing visions was very common among the Crow, as well as among many other Native American societies that also had the Vision Quest. What is regarded as a symptom of illness in one society may be merely one aspect of normal, healthy life in another.

The anthropological definition of mental illness takes the normal, expected, and acceptable behavior in a culture as a baseline and views unconscious or uncontrollable deviance from this baseline as abnormal behavior or mental illness. Seeking a vision was normal and expected behavior for Crow boys, and they might torture themselves and undergo deprivation until the vision came to them. But visions of spirits are not considered normal behavior in our society. Someone who sees them and hears them is exhibiting abnormal behavior. Another instance of this is the belief in witchcraft. Among the Navajo and the Basseri, individuals who believed that someone was practicing witchcraft on them would not be considered abnormal. However, in most segments of our society, individuals who came into the emergency room of a hospital complaining of internal pains because they had been bewitched would be considered mentally ill.

This approach to abnormal behavior and mental illness is essentially a relativistic one. Nevertheless, anthropologists who study forms of mental illness cross-culturally use certain general categories. They distinguish between disorders caused by brain damage and behavioral disorders where there is no apparent brain damage. The latter category is subdivided into psychoses, such as schizophrenia, depression, and paranoia, and neuroses of a variety of types. Recently, depressive illness has been examined cross-culturally (Kleinman and Good, 1985). Bereavement is experienced in all societies, and grief is the emotion that accompanies it, as we noted in the example of the Trobriand funeral. The relationship between the normal experience of grief and pathological grieving or depression has yet to be investigated. Depression as an emotion or affect seems to be similar experientially in many different cultures. However, the boundary line between a depressed state as normal behavior and abnormal depressive disorder has not yet been established. Depressive illness has a psychophysiological syndrome of behaviors that can be recognized by clinicians cross-culturally. At the same time, the cultural meanings of depressive illness and the cultural expression of the symptoms differ from one culture to another. Universal aspects of other mental illnesses, such as schizophrenia, neuroses, and personality disturbances, have also been recognized (Draguns, 1980). However, these illnesses are also culturally shaped. Variations in their manifestations are related to social, economic, technological, religious, and other features of the societies in which they are found.

Some kinds of symptoms seem to be specific to a particular culture. These culturally shaped symptoms have been viewed in two quite different ways. One view is that there are universal psychopathological disease categories (such as schizophrenia and depression) that are manifested in different kinds of behavior from one culture to another. The opposing view is that universally stressful situations produce different kinds of diseases in different cultures. The Windigo psychosis, which occurred among Algonquian Native Americans in the Northeast, was characterized by feeling persecuted by supernatural spirits and having cannibalistic fantasies. Though its symptoms were specific to Algonquian culture, Windigo psychosis is much like paranoid schizophrenia. In Western society, the symptoms of paranoid schizophrenia include ideas of persecution by other human beings, such as people in the government, people in the telephone company, or men from Mars, and anxiety over homosexual impulses. Amok is another mental illness, found in Malaysia and Indonesia, that has a specific set of symptoms. The central feature of amok is that the victim kills people while in a temporarily deranged state. Some researchers consider amok to be a disease specific to these particular cultures, while others consider it to be a culturally determined form of depression psychosis produced by extreme stress. We get our expression "to run amok" from this mental illness of Southeast Asia. Arctic hysteria is a form of mental illness found in Central Asia and among Siberian peoples in which the victim shouts obscenities, acts in an immodest fashion, and senselessly imitates the behavior of others. An illness similar to arctic hysteria, latah, is found in Malaysia. These forms of abnormal behavior are recognized as abnormal by the peoples of the cultures themselves, and the terms *amok* and *latah* are the native terms used to describe them.

Mental illness has been defined as abnormal behavior, that is, behavior that is different from the cultural norm. It is important to differentiate deviant behavior that represents mental illness from deviant behavior that does not. Not all those who violate the rules of a society are, by definition, mentally ill. Some are criminals; some are rebels; some are innovators.

Rebels and Innovators

From time to time, individuals appear who renounce important aspects of their own culture and propose that a radically different way of doing things be substituted for the old way. When they are successful in attracting followers and overthrow the old order, they are called innovators and revolutionaries. These individuals are central in bringing about changes that result in significant transformations in the design of the tapestry of culture. Their conceptualization is often a new organization for society. When they first expound on the wrongs of the existing society and the need for change, they may be considered mentally deranged. In 1917 Russian society underwent a revolution. The revolution was successful, the leaders moved into positions of power, and at no time were they considered mentally ill. Now, over seventy years later, these revolutionary ideas have become the status quo. Up until recently, dissenters and rebels in the Soviet Union—those with a different view of how society should be—were placed in mental institutions as frequently as they were placed in prisons. During that period, Pyotr Grigorenko, a former war hero and major general in the Soviet army, was declared insane by Soviet medical authorities. A member of the establishment who had held a position of authority and enjoyed great prestige and respect would have to be insane, in the view of the authorities, to stand on street corners passing out petitions objecting to the way the Soviet government treated its minorities. Calling dissenters insane could be considered a political act on the part of the Soviet authorities, a way of threatening other dissenters.

The typical personality type of the well-adjusted individual in all cultures incorporates the motivations and values of the culture. Such an individual will want to do the things considered desirable in the society and will not think of changing them. This individual is very different from the rebel and innovator. The rebel, therefore, must differ in personality in some significant way from the typical person. These differences in personality between the rebel and the typical person reflect a difference in early life experience on the part of the rebel. Erik Erikson (1958, 1969) has explored the relationship between successful rebels and their culture in a series of biographical case studies of such individuals as Martin Luther and Gandhi. Erikson has stressed the significance of these individuals to the historical process of cultural change. The opposite position on this issue was long ago taken by anthropologist Leslie White. White (1949) argued that individual innovators are of no significance. Cultures change due to forces entirely within the culture. He demonstrated that, in Ancient Egypt, the pharaoh Akhnaton introduced monotheistic beliefs. However, after he died, Egypt reverted to its earlier polytheistic beliefs, demonstrating that the culture was not ready for change.

The Person and the Self

The socially constituted person, as distinguished from the individual self, is a concept with a long history in anthropology. Individuals learn to perform a repertoire of social roles, and these roles constitute a major component of the social person. The conception of the person varies from one society to the next. Each society has its own conception of what emotions persons can appropriately express and when they can be expressed, as well as its own ideas about what is right and wrong and what characterizes the good person and the bad person.

Clifford Geertz (1974) has examined differences in personhood in Java, Bali, and Western society. Geertz is particularly noted as an exponent of the interpretive approach in anthropology and is concerned with the methodology used by the anthropologist to see things "from the native's point of view." Rather than put himself in the place of the Other or conduct psychological tests, as did proponents of the earlier school of modal personality, Geertz prefers to analyze the series of symbolic forms that people in a culture use to represent themselves to themselves and to others. Like Margaret Mead, he begins his analysis with the Western conception of the person, which he describes as "a bounded, unique, more or less integrated motivational and cognitive universe, a dynamic center of awareness, emotion, judgment, and action organized into a distinctive whole and set contrastively both against other such wholes and against its social and natural background" (1984:126).

The sense of personhood in Java, according to Geertz, is different from the Western conception of the person. It is based on two sets of contrasts: inside/outside and refined/vulgar. The ideal for a person is, through religious discipline, to achieve a state of stilled emotion in the inner realm (he "thins out his emotional life to a constant hum"), while in the outer realm, the same kind of purity and refinement is achieved through elaborate etiquette. Refinement is desired both inside and outside, and vulgarity is to be avoided. The Javanese concept of person is a bifurcated one, in contrast to the Western concept, which emphasizes integration.

The Balinese view of the person is as an appropriate representative of a category, rather than a unique individual. People attempt to mute individual personal characteristics and to emphasize, in contrast, features of status. Geertz, who frequently uses the dramatic or theatrical metaphor to describe Balinese culture, likens Balinese persons to a cast of characters. This is consistent with the point made in Chapter 11 that in Bali the face itself is considered a mask. Geertz's point is that the Western concept of the person as an autonomous bounded entity operating in his or her own way vis-à-vis other like entities is not shared by other cultures. Since Geertz is a cultural relativist who emphasizes the unique features that differentiate cultures, he also views personhood as distinctive for each culture.

While the person may be conceived of in different ways in various cultures, there are certain universal characteristics of the person as well. These universal features are present in the early stages of the process of development of the person. Developmental psychologists are of the opinion that the boundedness of self and self-motivation are found universally in children in all societies. During the enculturation process in some societies such as Java and Bali, a different notion of self is inculcated. All infants share boundedness and act as autonomous entities that contrast with others. However, as the child develops in some non-Western cultures, he or she learns to suppress this autonomous self.

The people who inhabit the Kerkennah Islands twelve miles off Tunisia think of males and females as having sharply different ideas of self. Platt (1988) states that according to their traditional beliefs, males and females are basically different by nature. They think that a female fetus rides "in the lap" and a male fetus "astride the hips" during the mother's pregnancy. After birth, babies of both sexes are swaddled to avoid any external influences or dangerous forces. Beyond the first two months of birth, the Kerkenni treat males differently from females based on their belief that they are different by nature. The mother behaves toward the male child as if he were an adult male, playfully referring to him as "oh, Daddy" or "oh, Sir." This results in an earlier and fuller development of a sense of self on the part of male infants as compared with female infants. The female infant instead is treated as an extension of the mother herself. Male infants are seen as more demanding and requiring more attention. They are the foci of much more ritual activity. After circumcision, between the ages of three and four, the male child moves beyond the sphere of the mother and into the world of male peers. There is no equivalent sharp break for the female child, who remains close to her mother. Older boys are expected to express aggression outwardly, and they are teased to foster this, while girls turn their anger inward upon themselves. These differences in child-rearing practices produce two different kinds of selves for the males and females in this society. However, as we noted earlier, the Kerkenni see these differences in the expression of self as attributable entirely to nature.

Recently, there have been new attempts to integrate the approaches of anthropology and psychology which are somewhat different from the earlier debate concerning the relationship between culture and personality. This approach involves moving away from the idea that the fundamentals of mental life are fixed, universal, and abstract by nature to a concern with cultural psychology, which is "the study of the way cultural traditions and social practices regulate, express, transform, and permute the human psyche, resulting less in psychic unity for humankind than in ethnic divergences in mind, self and emotion" (Stigler, Shweder, and Herdt, 1990:1). A basic premise of cultural psychology is "intentionality." That is, individuals are perceived as actors who "seize meanings and resources" from their cultural environment and by this process are transformed. In turn, the socio-cultural world is a human product that is changed as a result of human action. Culture and human psyches are seen as interdependent and dialectically interrelated to one another. This point of view has been influenced to some extent by Bourdieu's theory of practice and its emphasis on everyday experience, mentioned at the beginning of this chapter.

Shweder, Mahapatra, and Miller (1990), in a study that focuses on cultural distinctions in moral development between Brahman and "Untouchable" families in Orissa, India, and Judeo-Christian families in Chicago, Illinois, illustrate how the Indian child is socialized regarding moral understandings relating to pollution and purity. Menstruating women must remove themselves from physical contact with other people. A menstruating mother exclaims, "I am polluted *(Mara)*. Don't touch me!" when her young child tries to sit on her lap. She will get up and walk away if he comes closer. They explain that their state of menstrual pollution is due to their having stepped in dog excrement. Children soon learn that when their mothers are *Mara,* they will avoid them, sleep alone on a mat on the floor, stay out of the kitchen, eat alone, and not groom themselves. According to the authors, "most six-year-olds think it is wrong for a 'polluted' *('mara')* woman to cook food or sleep in the same bed with her husband; most nine-year-olds think that *'mara'* is an objective force of nature and that all women in the world have a moral obligation not to touch other people or cook food while they are *'mara'"* (Shweder, Mahapatra, and Miller, 1990:196). In the social interaction and communication between the young child and his or her cultural world, the child learns about the moral tenet of pollution experientially.

The nature of the relationship between culture and the individuals who live according to its precepts and pass them on to future generations has always been of great interest. Most anthropologists see this as a dialectical relationship. As the field of cultural anthropology has changed in recent years, so too has its view of the relationship between culture and the individual.

CHAPTER 13

Fourth World Peoples in the Colonial and Postcolonial Periods

In the past, anthropologists have at times looked at cultures as if they were static, unchanging entities for the purposes of analysis. In one or two years of fieldwork, anthropologists record a series of observations on the cultures they are study-ing. Aside from seasonal changes, the cultural patterns dis-cerned may seem essentially the same from the beginning of the fieldwork to its end. In reality, cultures are constantly undergoing change, sometimes at a barely perceptible rate and sometimes at a very rapid rate. Today's anthropologists face the fact that any group, any society chosen for study, including our own, is in a situation of culture change. If we conceptualize cultures as having an overall design as a tapestry does, then in situations of change we see either a part of the design beginning to unravel and change or sometimes a transformation in the overall design itself. Under extreme or traumatic circumstances the tapestry of culture survives only in shreds.

The forces for change in the modern world are numerous and powerful. Colonialism is all but gone, and in its place is a series of new nation-states based on the geography of colonial empires rather than on sameness of culture. These nation-states are building national cultures that attempt to supplant and suppress the native cultures, in the same way that European nation-states in the past attempted to forge national cultures with varying degrees of success. However, despite political independence, the often continued economic reliance of one-time colonies on their former colonial masters constitutes a form of "neocolonialism." Over several centuries, economic changes have greatly altered traditional economies. These include the introduction of cash crops, the introduction of the desire for modern manufactured goods, the introduction of foreign exploitation of native resources, and the need for labor. With the enormous expansion of cities in these new nations in modern times, the economic and cultural inducements to be found there have attracted many migrants from the rural areas. When they return to their villages, they bring urban culture with them and introduce changes in the traditional culture.

Concepts in the Study of Culture Change

The development of new cultural ideas and traits through the processes of innovation and invention is one basic source of culture change. Innovations usually come about as a result of new ideas and discoveries or through the recombination of existing ideas into something new and creative. As indicated in the previous chapter, new ideas and innovations take hold and are accepted by the people in a society when they can be integrated into the culture. Evidence of this is the case of Gregor Mendel, whose significant discoveries in genetics took place in the 1860s but lay dormant and unrecognized until they were picked up by theoretical biologists at the beginning of the twentieth century. Not all innovations and inventions are accepted. Many are accepted for a short time and then discarded, some are never accepted, and only a few become part of the cultural repertoire. Sometimes inventions have a trivial impact, like the Roach Motel. Other times, an invention is one of a group of inventions. An example is the spinning jenny, one of a group of inventions involved in the manufacture of cloth made within the span of a single decade at the end of the eighteenth century. These inventions had a significant impact, as they marked the beginning of the Industrial Revolution. Their introduction formed the basis for the development of the factory system, which led, in turn, to significant social and economic changes.

Not all changes that are introduced involve material things. Sometimes they involve ideas. The democratic form of government developed in our country represented a different form of government from the monarchies under which the immigrants who came here had lived. It included the idea of religious freedom, which also differed from their previous experience. The change that has taken place in gender relations in America today, discussed in Chapter 6, also represents a significant change in cultural ideas.

An idea that has been developed in one society spreads to another through a process known as *diffusion*. Ralph Linton humorously pointed out how much American culture owes to the diffusion process, though the American natives may be unaware of this.

[At breakfast] a whole new series of foreign things confronts him [the typical American]. His food and drink are placed before him in pottery vessels, the popular name of which—china—is sufficient evidence of their origin. His fork is a medieval Italian invention and his spoon a copy of a Roman original. He will usually begin the meal with coffee, an Abyssinian plant first discovered by the Arabs. The American is quite likely to need it to dispel the morning-after effects of over-indulgence in fermented drinks, invented in the Near East; or distilled ones, invented by the alchemists of medieval Europe. Whereas the Arabs took their coffee straight, he will probably sweeten it with sugar, discovered in India; and dilute it with cream, both the domestication of cattle and the technique of milking have originated in Asia Minor.*

When a sizable group of people migrates, the group takes its culture with it. If the migrating group moves into an unoccupied territory, its culture will begin to change in adaptation to the ecological situation of the new territory. This is what happened when the first settlers of the New World crossed the Bering Strait tens of thousands of years ago and moved into North and later South America. If the migrating group moves into an area that is already occupied and conquers it, then the conquered peoples usually undergo more culture change than do the conquerors. However, this is not always the case. During the thirteenth century, the Mongol conquerors of China became Chinese in their culture within one generation. In this case it was the culture of the conquerors that underwent radical change.

Contexts of Culture Change

The major form of culture change is a result of contact with another culture. Contact between individuals of different cultures can occur in a variety of ways—migration, conquest, immigration, or slavery. *Context* refers to the setting within which contact occurs.

The contact between Native American societies and the developing American nation-state exemplifies one type of context. In the earliest period, these Native American societies were in contact with the British and French colonial empires. Over time, a large and more powerful immigrant population engulfed and often completely destroyed a great number of different native societies. This situation was one of grossly unequal power, and many of the changes brought about in Native American societies were the result of coercion.

Another, and different, context for culture change was that of the European colonial empires in Africa, South and Southeast Asia, and Oceania, where large numbers of European settlers were absent. Instead of

---

*Excerpt from Ralph Linton, "One Hundred Per Cent American," *The American Mercury,* April 1937, pp. 427–429.

a small indigenous society confronting waves of technologically advanced settlers, as was the case in America, in these colonial situations, usually, a large indigenous population was conquered and placed under the domination of a small colonial administration, backed by armed forces. These colonies endured in some cases from the sixteenth century to the end of World War II. The idea of colonies was not invented in sixteenth-century Europe. In ancient times, Persia, Greece, and Rome had conquered other lands and established colonies. Earlier we talked about how the Roman Empire conquered vast territories. As a result of this colonization, the people of the Iberian Peninsula and Romania speak Romance languages.

The initial motivation for the establishment of colonies was primarily economic gain, which frequently took the form of exploiting raw materials, as well as providing markets for the goods of the mother country. The Industrial Revolution led to shortages of resources locally and the need to find them further afield. Often, a single large trading company, such as the British East India Company, the Hudson's Bay Company, or the Dutch East India Company, held a monopoly on trade. Such trading companies were sometimes given political as well as economic control over a colony.

Differences in colonial government policy were also a factor affecting the context of culture change. For example, the British developed the policy of indirect rule, which was then applied throughout the British Empire. This model of political control was first used in India, where a handful of English controlled a subcontinent of Indians. In contrast, the French ruled directly, establishing military garrisons and large administrative staffs throughout their empire. The French had a policy of accepting an educated individual from their empire, who was then referred to as an *évolue*, as a citizen of France. The British never had such a policy and refused to accept the best-educated Indian, Pakistani, or African as an equal to an English native. Though the indigenous population was much larger than the foreign population, the power and wealth were all in the hands of the representatives of the colonial power. The context of these contacts was in every respect an unequal one.

Recent writings by anthropologists on colonialism indicate how complex were the dimensions of colonial life (Cooper and Stoler, 1989). The colonizers felt that it was constantly necessary to define the boundary between themselves and the colonized, whose "otherness" was perpetually subject to change. The European colonizers had varying intentions toward the indigenous population. Methodist missionaries hoped to turn the tribesmen of southern Africa into yeoman farmers modeled on the yeomanry of eighteenth-century England. Other colonizers attempted to transform the existing social organization to provide laborers who would work in the mines. The boundary between the European colonizers and the local population was sometimes eroded by sexual relations between European men and local women, which produced an intermediate population with an ambiguous identity in the European system of classification.

As in the case of the European colonization of North America, colonial situations often included the permanent settlement of migrants from the mother country in the colony. The proportion of foreign settlers to the indigenous population determined the nature of the context in which culture change took place. In Australia, the kinds of changes affecting the indigenous peoples, the Australian Aborigines, were similar to those found in the United States. A small native population was overwhelmed by the much larger settler population. In New Zealand, the indigenous Maori population was proportionately larger than its counterpart in Australia and the United States. The greater political influence of the Maori today may be due to this proportional difference. In Kenya and Zimbabwe, the settler population remained a minority in relation to the larger indigenous population, whom the settlers used as a labor force to exploit the natural resources of the area.

The colonial empires of the world have now almost all disappeared. Taking the place of these colonies are many new emerging nation-states. These new nations form a large part of what is known as the *Third World*. Within most of these Third World nations are the tribal people, who constitute the *Fourth World* peoples. Fourth World peoples are brought to public attention when they put up heroic struggles to preserve their autonomy and culture, as the Kurds of Turkey, Iran, and Iraq and the Nagas of India did and are still doing, or when they are being machine-gunned by helicopter, like the Indians of Brazil. Otherwise, the world today ignores their existence.

The process of culture change both in the colonies which later became Third World nations and among Fourth World peoples can be examined at several levels. The unit that anthropologists isolate for study in the field is at the *microanalytic level*. However, they do not study it alone, but in relation to like units and to the more inclusive political levels. The next more inclusive level of analysis is that of the nation-state, where the focus of the anthropologist has been on the construction of a national culture and the creation of a national identity. Since nation-states operate as independent, politically autonomous units, political decisions and economic planning take place at this level. Consequently, the unit of analysis of economic development is also the nation-state.

At a still more inclusive level of analysis is the world system. This concept, developed by Immanuel Wallerstein (1974), refers to the historic emergence of the economic interrelationship among most of the world in a single market system, in which the concept of the division of labor, usually seen as operative in a single society, is projected onto the world. Wallerstein sees the system developing after the breakdown of feudalism and the rise of capitalism and entrepreneurship and the succeeding Industrial Revolution. During and after the Age of Exploration, Europeans vastly expanded their search for sources of raw material and mineral resources, as well as for markets for their manufactured goods. These

European countries formed the core of a world system, and the colonies and protectorates that they dominated formed the periphery. The world system operates according to capitalist market principles, and the profits constantly revert to the investors of capital in the core. This requires that one adopt a processual point of view. In general, the gap between core and periphery was constantly widening, but, on the other hand, the system was constantly expanding in the search for new markets. Anthropologists have been particularly concerned with the effects of the penetration of the world system on tribal peoples all over the world. Eric Wolf (1982), in *Europe and the People without History,* has explored this topic, focusing, for example, on how the Kwakiutl and other native people of North America responded to the trade network set up by the Hudson's Bay Company in the eighteenth century. As in Wolf's work, anthropologists may look at problems that involve study not only at the microanalytic level, but at the national- and world-systems level as well.

The Study of Culture Change

The contexts of culture change are highly varied, and each case may appear to be different from any other case, particularly since the time of the contact can range from within the last decade to centuries ago. Nevertheless, the conditions of contact and the ensuing culture change can be described in terms of a number of variables. Some of these variables include land policy, resource exploitation, kind of labor recruitment, and intensity and kind of missionary activity.

Precontact Culture Change

Migrations of peoples and contact between different cultures did not begin with the appearance of travelers or explorers from the West, but goes far back beyond recorded history. Of course, information about this culture contact can come only from archaeology, not from cultural anthropology.

Sometimes cultural changes from the West reached tribal peoples even before the first physical contacts with outside agents of the Western world. An early example of this is the diffusion of horses among Native American peoples. In the 1500s, the Spanish explorers brought horses into Arizona and New Mexico. By the 1700s, horses had spread to peoples like the Blackfoot of Montana. The introduction of horses radically changed the subsistence pattern of these people. As mounted hunters, utilizing different techniques, they were much more successful than they had been on foot. The introduction of the horse had an effect not only on their subsistence pattern but also on their residential pattern and concepts of wealth and status. The effects of the introduction of the horse were so great that horticultural societies like the Omaha and the Hidatsa, who lived in the river valleys of the Missouri and its tributaries, became equestrian nomads for part of the year. Because of the close association of the horse and the Plains Indian in the popular mind, it is difficult for us to accept that this is a diffused trait and, furthermore, that this borrowing and many of the changes that followed it took place before sustained contact between Native Americans and the white man.

Diffusion of technologically advanced implements such as steel axes also frequently took place before actual contact between tribal peoples and agents of the Western world. Steel tools began to be traded to the Etoro of Papua New Guinea in 1955, about ten years before direct contact with Australian government patrols. The Etoro received the steel tools from other highland peoples to whom they had formerly traded stone tools. The trade in steel tools thus reversed the former flow of goods and disrupted traditional exchange patterns. The introduction of steel tools among the Etoro also had an effect on the traditional division of labor. Men's work in clearing the land for gardens was reduced by half, while women's work in sago processing, which was unaffected by steel technology, remained the same. Similarly, the Yanomamo, discussed in earlier chapters, received steel tools from the Yekwana, an intermediary group, who were in direct contact with the outside world at a time when the Yanomamo themselves had no contact with Europeans.

The Nature of Initial Contact

Initial contact and the establishment of Western sovereignty over areas inhabited by tribal peoples occurred in a number of ways. Sometimes, the tribal society was treated as a sovereign state with which treaties were made. The Treaty of Waitangi in New Zealand in 1840, between the British Crown and the assembly of Maori chiefs, is such a treaty. The British Crown received all rights and powers of sovereignty over Maori territory. The Maori chiefs thought they were giving the British only partial rights, and the British did not correct this mistaken interpretation. Such cession could only occur in societies that were chiefdomships or states like the princely states of India. Treaties could not be made with societies that were less complex politically because there were no leaders who could legitimately speak on behalf of large groupings and who could cede sovereignty.

Sometimes, outside administrative control was set up in the form of patrol posts in the native territory. This was the manner in which the Brazilian government established control over tribal people in the Amazon area. Though these patrol posts were often attacked at first, the hostile attitude soon changed as the attractiveness of the trade goods brought by the governmental representatives won people over. The same method was used by the Australian government to achieve control over the tribal peoples of New Guinea. Here, too, the initial response was frequently hostile. But gifts of trade goods such as the steel tools that eventually reached the

Etoro and the large number of ritually important shells brought in by the Australians succeeded in reducing overt expressions of hostility. The aims of pacification were to eliminate warfare between tribes and between villages and to introduce a police force that would transfer jurisdiction over serious crimes from the native population to the larger government. Wherever the process of government contact, pacification, and control occurred over the world, tribal peoples who had been politically autonomous and independent lost that autonomy and the ability to determine their own destiny.

The first contact was often peaceful, as illustrated in the picture of the mutually beneficial exchange between the Maori and a member of Captain Cook's crew on his first voyage on the *Endeavour* (1768–1771). Military resistance later usually occurred when people realized the significance of their loss of independence, autonomy, and cultural distinctiveness. The

An unknown artist's depiction of the first exchange of a crayfish for a piece of cloth between a Maori of New Zealand and a sailor from Captain Cook's crew.

Maori vigorously resisted the settlement of the English after this initially peaceful exchange, and the fighting culminated in the Treaty of Waitangi mentioned above. The Sioux uprising in the latter part of the nineteenth century and the Zulu War of 1879 are additional examples of this kind of active resistance to the establishment of colonial rule.

In some situations contact with traders preceded military and political control. When North America was being colonized, fur was in great demand in Europe for men's hats and women's coats. Ambitious traders ranged far and wide, purchasing furs in exchange for cloth, tools, beads, and whiskey. Some of them established trading posts in strategic locations. This was often far in advance of political control of the area by colonial governments. The Hudson's Bay Company, established in the seventeenth century, had a string of trading posts throughout the northern woodland area of North America. The people of this area were dependent upon hunting and gathering for their subsistence. The demand for furs that the traders introduced resulted in a shift from hunting for food to trapping for furs. Band hunting territories exploited for subsistence were often subdivided into individual family hunting territories exploited for furs only by members of that family. This economic change affected the residence pattern and the nature of social relationships, and people slowly became dependent on the trading post to supply them with most of their food.

Land Rights

Land is the basic resource, and how rights over land are handled is a crucial variable in the culture change situation. Different colonial empires had somewhat different policies with respect to the rights of native peoples over their land. Furthermore, these native peoples themselves had a variety of different conceptualizations about land rights. Both Australia and the United States illustrate very similar situations in which a large immigrant population of settlers grew to overwhelm the much smaller indigenous societies. In one respect, their policies toward native land rights were very different. In the Australian case, the government did not recognize that the native people had any rights to any of the land. The native Australians were hunters and gatherers and with their simple technology exploited the whole of the area. Though the colonial government understood the native pattern of land utilization and the claims of various Australian bands to ancestral homelands, it chose to ignore these and claim the whole of the continent as "unoccupied wasteland," recognizing neither the land rights nor the sovereignty of the natives. Reserves for the native peoples were later established, but these were set up at the discretion of state governments in the least desirable areas, and not even these areas were for the exclusive use of native peoples.

In America, the attitude toward land rights of Native Americans was totally different from that of the Australians. Though Peter Minuit's legendary purchase of Manhattan Island for twenty-four dollars' worth of trinkets may be the shrewdest real estate deal in history, it still was a recognition of Native Americans' rights in land. This recognition was the basis for British policy in the colonial period and was reaffirmed by the fledgling American government in the Ordinance of 1787 for the Government of the Northwest Territory. Treaty relationships were maintained with Native American tribes up to the beginning of the nineteenth century. As the immigrant population grew and the demand for land grew with it, the Indian land base began to be reduced by successive treaties that the Indians were forced to conclude with the United States government. Groups like the Iroquois gave up some land and sold other land to land speculators.

In the latter part of the eighteenth century, the Cherokee of Georgia were forced to begin ceding land to the government. By 1822, the white population had greatly increased and now demanded all the rich farmland owned by the Cherokee and Creek. These demands were not met; the Cherokee did not wish to cede any more land. Finally in 1830 President Andrew Jackson's Indian Removal Act was passed, which called for the removal of all southeastern tribes—namely, the Cherokee, Choctaw, Chickasaw, Creek, and Seminole—to "permanent" Indian country west of the Mississippi. As President Jackson informed these tribes, "Beyond the great river Mississippi . . . their father has provided a country large enough for them all, and he advised them to move to it. There their white brothers will not trouble them, and they will have no claim to the land and they can live upon it, they and all their children, as long as grass grows and waters run." The Florida Seminole resisted relocation and fought a six-year war at a cost to the United States of 1,500 soldiers and $20 million. The Cherokee fought the Removal Act up through the Supreme Court, won their case, but nevertheless had to surrender 17 million acres and were forced to go to Oklahoma. Fourteen thousand Cherokee left for the Oklahoma Territory, and four thousand died en route. The deceit of Jackson's promise was revealed when the Cherokee lost much of their land in Oklahoma which had been promised to them for "as long as grass grows and waters run." They had to surrender it forty years later after they made the mistake of siding with the South during the Civil War.

From the beginning, individuals within the dominant settler community in the United States agitated against traditional Indian communal use and ownership of land. In the view of these people, Indians would never be absorbed into the larger society unless each family lived on and owned its own plot of land in the European fashion. This culminated in the Allotment Act of 1887, which authorized the division of tribal lands into plots assigned to individuals. It also bestowed citizenship upon Indians who abandoned their tribes and adopted "the habits of civilized life." These successive changes in the nature of Indian land tenure had far-reaching effects on subsistence and ultimately on all other aspects of Indian culture. The fight over land continues today, but the positions are reversed. Tribes like the Passamaquoddy of Maine and Mashpee of Massachusetts have gone to court to lay claim to their traditional land, on the basis of their claims that the United States government broke treaties made with these tribes in centuries past. While the Passamaquoddy won their case, the Mashpee lost theirs. In Papua New Guinea and Nigeria, the native land tenure systems were legally recognized by the colonial governments. Unlike Australia and the United States, there were few foreign immigrants who came as settlers to compete with the indigenous population and drive them off the land.

Resource Exploitation

In some situations, exploitation of resources other than land were critical in defining the nature of culture change. In contrast to land rights, which are appropriately examined on the level of the nation-state, colonial exploitation of resources is better analyzed at the level of the world system. For example, the core nations of Europe during the nineteenth century used copra, the meat of the coconut, in the manufacture of soap and cosmetics. This copra market demanded large supplies of coconuts, produced either by native peoples who raised them as a cash crop or by large expatriate-run plantations. The Germans acquired the coconuts both ways in their colony of German New Guinea. A similar situation existed in the British colonies of West Africa, where oil palms were cultivated and the nuts sold to traders who were representatives of large trading companies. The palm oil was sold on the world market. The traders who bought raw materials like copra and palm oil also sold the indigenous population manufactured goods—metal tools, cloth, shotguns, kerosene lamps, matches. Once these goods had been introduced, they became highly desired, and the native population came to regard them as necessities of life. The only way to obtain the manufactured goods was with cash, and the only source of cash came from selling the crop that the trader bought. Cash was also necessary to enable people to pay taxes to the government. Many colonial governments used the imposition of taxes to force the native population to raise the cash crops necessary for the national economy.

Crops grown on plantations and cash crops raised on village or clan-owned land were cultivated to meet the demands of an international market that was part of the world system. The price received was not related to local conditions, but rather to supply and demand in the world as a whole. Under the plantation system a small number of settlers or foreign managers directed the enterprise, while a large pool of natives did the actual work, often under conditions of extreme hardship and exploitation. A great range of crops were, and continue to be, grown as cash crops. Besides the previously mentioned coconuts, they include cocoa, coffee, tea, sugar, peanuts, palm oil, bananas, and cotton. All these crops can be grown either on plantations or by villagers. There are some Third World countries, with little or no mineral resources to exploit, whose entire economy is dependent upon the export of a single cash crop. The fate of such a country is dependent upon the price of that cash crop on the world market, a price set by commodities dealers in New York, London, or Geneva. Fluctuations in the price of commodities on the world market have a dramatic and immediate effect on the internal economies of those nations without long-term price agreements. If the purchase of a country's sole crop, such as bananas, is by a multinational company, such as the United Fruit Company, then such a company has great economic and political power in the country. The result is a "banana republic," like Guatemala was until recently.

The demand for rubber, which is also a cash crop, by the core countries of the world system has had an interesting history. It illustrates the way in which the economic fates of people on three different continents were linked together. The natural stands of rubber trees in the Amazon and Congo river basins were exploited during the wild rubber boom of 1895–1910. In both places, tribal peoples provided the source of labor for the tapping of latex from the rubber trees in the tropical forest. British entrepreneurs took wild rubber plant seedlings and transported them to the British colony of Malaya where they established rubber plantations to provide a steady source of this raw material. Rubber from these plantations captured the world market, bringing to an end the boom in wild rubber from the Congo and Amazon basins. Subsequently, rubber plantations were developed in Liberia by the Firestone Rubber Company of America, and this rubber also gained a share of the world market. Since rubber was the dominant cash crop, the entire economy of Liberia at that time was controlled by this single foreign company. The shift to synthetic rubber, developed during World War II, signaled the great reduction in importance of plantation-grown rubber.

Exploitation of resources took forms other than the imposition of cash crops. Extractive industries, such as lumbering, fishing, and mining, for a world market were also very important. Recently, the increasing scarcity of lumber has led to a rise in price, especially for valuable hardwoods, and to a more intensive search for it in out-of-the-way places. In the Montaña region of Peru, tribal peoples like the Urarina, who were rubber tappers until the bottom fell out of the rubber market, now cut down rare hardwood trees and float them down the river. The trees are turned over to agents of the lumber companies, to whom the Urarina are in debt for shotgun shells and cloth purchased during the previous year. Small groups of kin-related men work together and sell their lumber together. The nature of social groupings and residence patterns has changed from an earlier form in response to the need for cooperative labor to carry out the logging. The earlier pattern of postmarital residence was uxorilocal. With the introduction of logging, a group of brothers and their wives may now come together to form a temporary residence unit for the purpose of logging. But brothers-in-law may also log together. The organizer of the logging group who makes direct arrangements with the agent is usually an ambitious younger man. For the Urarina this is a new means for establishing leadership.

Probably the most valuable natural resources to be found on the lands of tribal peoples are mineral resources—gold, copper, tin, oil, coal, uranium. Mineral rights are rarely controlled and exploited by tribal peoples themselves. However, in the United States sometimes reservation lands that had been set aside for tribal peoples were later discovered to have extensive mineral resources. This happened in many Western states. For example, the Ute tribe's reservation lands in Utah, though undesirable for agriculture, contain mineral resources, including coal, oil, natural gas, uranium, and oil shale. In fact, 25 to 50 percent of all uranium deposits in the United States are on lands owned by Native Americans. At first the Native American Tribal Councils gave concessions to private companies to extract the resource in exchange for a fixed royalty, for example, twenty-five cents per ton of coal. The Peabody Coal Company, one of the largest coal mining companies in the country, strip-mines coal on Black Mesa, in the middle of the Navajo reservation, in exchange for a fixed royalty that was negotiated between Peabody Coal and the Bureau of Indian Affairs. These royalties do not go to individuals, but rather are paid to the tribal council fund, to be used for the benefit of the entire tribe. Tribal leaders are very concerned that their tribes receive appropriate recompense for these concessions to mineral rights. Some tribes are seeking expert advice so they can exploit these resources themselves and get a fairer return. The Crow of Montana are trying to obtain financing for their own coal company. The Jicarilla Apaches of New Mexico are contemplating a propane gas plant and their own oil refinery. The Navajo are considering building a power plant using their own coal to supply the Navajo reservation with electricity. A consortium has recently been formed of tribes with extensive mineral holdings to share expertise and lobby the U.S. government.

The exploitation of mineral resources was also significant in the African colonial experience. Starting in the 1880s, important discoveries of gold and diamonds were made in South Africa. Cecil Rhodes and other financiers formed the companies that exploited these resources, and with the mines came urbanization and industrialization. Rhodes compelled the British colonial government to expand north into what is now Zimbabwe in order to exploit the mineral resources there. Meanwhile, Belgium mining interests—Union Minière du Haute-Katanga—were expanding southeastward into Katanga, the northern part of the copper belt. The mineral wealth in gold, diamonds, cobalt, copper, chrome, zinc, and later uranium was highly prized by the colonial powers because of the demand for these resources in the core countries of the world system. In the early twentieth century, exploitation of these resources was totally in the hands of

European-based and European-financed companies, operating under the umbrella of a colonial administration. Oil was discovered in Nigeria after the country became independent in 1960. Though European capital was involved in its development, exploitation of the oil is controlled by the Nigerian government, at the level of the nation-state. But the price of oil is controlled by OPEC, an international cartel, of which Nigeria is a member. Paradoxically, because Nigeria overextended its financial resources on expansion and development in the expectations of vast wealth earned from its oil, it is now deeply in debt. Its economy is barely able to pay its debts and support its large and expanding population. The mineral-rich Union of South Africa, with its large white minority, operates as both core and periphery. The white population controls the mining of gold and diamonds, and the black majority provides the labor. The rewards go to the white investors. Since a consortium of diamond producers controls the world supply of diamonds for sale, a free market does not operate.

Labor Exploitation

Exploitation of resources in the colonial areas and their successor nation-states required labor. This need for labor was met in a variety of ways, all of which had profound effects on tribal peoples, dislocating their economies and their traditional forms of family and social organization in varying degrees. In the earliest period of the colonization of the New World, the demand by the colonizers for a large-scale labor force in order to exploit resources was satisfied by the enslavement of native tribal peoples. The Portuguese did this with the Tupi-speaking coastal peoples of Brazil, whose population was decimated due to disease and the conditions of slavery. The Spanish did the same with the native Arawak-speaking peoples of the Caribbean islands, and they too perished in the same way. Slaves were then imported from Africa to fill the great need for labor in the sugar plantations of the New World. From the sixteenth century to the middle of the nineteenth century, some 8 to 10 million Africans were brought to the New World as slaves to furnish the labor for the plantations. Great dislocations took place in the African societies, primarily those of West Africa, from which these people taken as slaves came. While one kind of culture contact was taking place between the slave traders of various European nationalities and the enslaved Africans, another kind of contact was occurring in the New World between plantation owners and their slaves. As African slaves from different cultures and with different languages were forced to adapt to the new conditions of slavery and to the cultures and languages of their masters, new cultures were forged.

Labor for the plantations was also sometimes obtained by means of indenture. Contracts were signed between the laborers and the plantation owners for a fixed period of time. In the case of Trinidad, the period was five years. During this period the laborers were bound to the employers and forced to work for them. The laborers' passage from their homeland was provided by the owners, and they were not free to leave until the period of indenture was over. Many Indians from India signed on as indentured laborers to work on the sugar plantations of British Guiana (Guyana) and of Trinidad in the Caribbean after the emancipation of slaves in these British colonies. Other Indian laborers went to Fiji in the Pacific and to South Africa. They settled in these areas and form significant ethnic groups there today. Though derived from India, their cultures have changed and reflect the cultural conditions to which they have had to adapt.

Various forms of coercion were used to provide labor during the colonial period. King Leopold of Belgium personally owned the Congo from 1884 to 1908. He exploited the rubber resources of the Congo during the wild rubber boom referred to earlier by using local corvée labor, that is, by requiring that each adult male provide a certain amount of labor as tax. In other areas of the colonial world, such as Melanesia, corvée labor was used to construct roads and other public works. Another means of obtaining labor for the sugar plantations of Queensland in Australia and Fiji during the latter part of the nineteenth century was through "blackbirding." When there was a scarcity of laborers willing to work on the plantations, unsuspecting tribal men from various islands of Melanesia were tricked or shanghaied aboard ships and taken to the plantations. These kidnapped men were compelled to work for three years on the plantations for low wages, after which they were permitted to return to their tribal homelands.

In time, these various coercive means for acquiring cheap labor were either outlawed or reformed. Slavery was abolished, and blackbirding and indentured service were halted. These forms of labor recruitment eventually gave way to contract labor. From the beginning of the twentieth century, copra plantations in Melanesia employed contract labor. Contract laborers for the plantations of New Britain came from other islands, such as Buka. This pattern of leaving one's home island to do contract labor for one or more years on the plantations of another island was common throughout Melanesia.

Contract labor is also very important in meeting the demand for native labor to exploit the mineral resources of southern Africa. Men migrate from the tribal areas to the mines for a period of nine to eighteen months, according to their contract. In order to work as a wage laborer in the Union of South Africa a tribal person must have a contract. In the past, the government controlled the free flow of workers through the Pass Laws, preventing those without a contract from leaving the tribal areas for the towns and cities. This pattern of migratory labor, which involves men moving a thousand or more miles from their tribal homeland to work in the mines, has many negative effects. Most migrants, who range in age from twenty to forty, are men whose wives remain behind. This migration leaves the tribal areas bereft of men, children without fathers and wives without husbands. Women must bear the burdens of everyday subsistence, and the cycle of economic activities based on the traditional male/female division of labor is upset. Women alone raise the children, and family life is thereby disrupted. The precontact organization of the family has been undercut and weakened. During the time they work in the mines, the men become increasingly familiar with urban life. They begin to think of themselves as industrial workers, and they join labor unions as well as tribal associations. Most still maintain close ties with their tribal homelands, sending back money and returning there to retire. They have not given up the traditional values of their culture and can move back into it when they retire.

Missionaries and Culture Change

When a colonial administration was set up in a tribal area, concerted efforts were made to abolish those practices that violated the colonizers' moral code, which was a product of their own Western European cultures. Missionaries were the most zealous enforcers of these kinds of changes. As we have pointed out, pacification involved the immediate cessation of all warfare. Any cultural practice that emphasized the political autonomy of a tribal people was considered threatening by the colonial power and was

Missionaries taught Christianity to the people of New Guinea in the early 1900s.

forbidden. Since in Melanesia, as well as elsewhere, head-hunting and can-nibalism, where they occurred, were part of the complex surrounding war-fare, these two practices were actively suppressed at the outset. Cultural practices that seemed immoral or offensive to the Europeans were also out-lawed, and individuals who continued these customs were fined or jailed. In particular, sexual practices that differed from Western custom and that missionaries considered abhorrent were forbidden. By the time Malinowski arrived to do fieldwork with the Trobriand Islanders in 1914, the mission-aries had already been there for some time and had brought about changes. Trobriand rules and attitudes about what constituted proper sexu-al behavior and what was forbidden were quite different from Western missionary ideas. Young people were permitted free expression of sexual impulses. In the *katuyausi,* a group of young girls from one village would go to a neighboring village, where they took lovers for the night. The mission-aries disapproved of the custom, and a special regulation was instituted to put down this "abominable abuse." On the other hand, the Trobrianders had very strong feelings against sexual intercourse between people of the same subclan, or *dala,* which they considered to be incest and punishable by suicide when the individuals involved were caught. The missionaries put an end to this form of punishment. As a consequence, the Trobrianders saw this as weakening native customs about incest. The missionaries also brought their ethnocentric point of view to bear on other areas of social life involving marriage and the family. Frequently, they forbade child betrothal, bride price, and polygamy and enlisted the support of colonial administrators in enforcing these edicts. Among the Trobrianders, an important source of political power for the chief was the large number of in-laws that he acquired by taking many wives. In Malinowski's time, the colonial administrator prevented all chiefs and headmen from taking additional wives and from replacing those who died, though there did not seem to be any written ordinance that prohibited such practices. As noted in Chapter 5, the Trobrianders do not recognize the role of the father as having anything to do with the conception of a child. The missionaries repeatedly attempted to convince them of the importance of physical paternity, in order to convince them to accept the doctrine of the Holy Trinity. However, the Trobrianders would not accept the missionaries' arguments.

Sometimes an entire ritual or ceremonial complex was outlawed. This is what happened to the potlatch on the Northwest Coast. Some 100 years after the first contact, the Canadian Indian Act of 1876 prohibited Northwest Coast peoples—the Kwakiutl, the Tsimshian, the Haida, and the Tlingit—from potlatching or carrying out the winter ceremonials. Anglican and Methodist missionaries among the Haida considered the potlatch a heathen custom, because it was a significant native religious rite. They thought that it impeded the spread of Christianity among these people. Another objection was from an economic point of view. The amassing of material goods was a good thing, but the practice of inviting guests and giving away the goods to them at a potlatch seemed irrational since it violated Western ideas of capitalist economic behavior. The Protestant ethic of working hard, saving, and investing one's savings conflicted directly with the Kwakiutl and Haida ethic of generosity and giving away great amounts of goods to validate one's name and position. The potlatch reinforced the indigenous status system and the entire social structure in these Native American societies. It had to be done away with in order for these people to be turned into useful Canadian wage earners and productive citizens. This was the view of the Canadian administration. In fact, the Kwakiutl potlatch continued to flourish through the first two decades of the twentieth century, despite the law of 1876 abolishing it. Because they had entered into commercial fishing and wage work, the Kwakiutl were able to accumulate ever larger amounts of goods. However, the potlatch had to be held secretly, away from the government agency and missionary station at Alert Bay. One of the largest potlatches ever given among the Kwakiutl was held in 1921. Thirty thousand blankets were given away. The kinds of goods distributed at this potlatch in addition to blankets reveal the kinds of changes that were taking place in the potlatch as it accommodated to changing times. Besides five gas boats and twenty-five canoes, there were bracelets for women, gaslights, violins, guitars, shirts and sweaters for young people, three hundred trunks, two pool tables, sewing machines, gramophones, and furniture. At this potlatch, for the first time, the law was enforced, and the givers of the potlatch were arrested by the Royal Canadian Mounted Police. They were tried and sent to prison, and their carved masks, instruments, and costumes were confiscated and eventually ended up in the National Museum in Ottawa. However, this important ceremonial could not be abolished by fiat. It continued secretly, until finally the Canadian government, in the Revised Indian Act of 1951, no longer prohibited potlatching and winter dances. The potlatch is important today among the Native Americans of the Northwest Coast, and large-scale potlatches continue to be held. The masks and other ceremonial paraphernalia that had been confiscated in 1921 were returned to the Kwakiutl recently when they built a museum at Alert Bay to house this material.

New Ireland: An Example of Increasing Incorporation into the World System

It is useful to see how the analytical variables and the levels of analysis discussed above come together in a particular case. We will see how the peoples of New Ireland have been increasingly drawn into a world economic system and how they have responded to this.

New Ireland is a long and narrow island (225 miles long) located in the Bismarck Archipelago, close to the equator and east of the much larger island of New Guinea. From the time of its original settlement some 30,000 years ago, the island has never been isolated. It was always part of several regional trade networks, tying it to other islands in the Bismarck Archipelago and beyond.

The first Westerner known to have made contact with New Irelanders, in 1619, was the Dutch explorer Schouten. He was searching for trading opportunities in the Pacific outside the sphere over which the Dutch East India Company had a monopoly. Schouten tried to exchange beads with the New Irelanders for needed supplies. The New Irelanders had their own ideas about exchange, but neither understood the other. When the New Irelanders attacked the intruders with their slings and clubs, Schouten responded with cannon fire, killing ten or twelve of them. This initial contact with the West was a violent one, not easily forgotten by the New Irelanders.

After Schouten, seven other European expeditions, Dutch, French, Spanish, and English, came to New Ireland between 1619 and 1800. Five of these expeditions involved encounters and exchanges with the people of New Ireland, who were portrayed in the accounts of the explorers as "exotic, naked savages." The New Irelanders approached these encounters as they would those with people from another island, prepared to fight or to conduct ceremonial exchange, and were thus armed, painted, and adorned. The Europeans in each case sought to replenish their supplies. They offered trade goods, such as beads and cloth, which did not seem to interest the New Irelanders.

During the first decades of the nineteenth century, ships put in more and more frequently at New Ireland. By this time, the New Irelanders knew that the European ships anchoring in their harbors wanted to reprovision with coconuts, tubers, and pigs, and the Europeans had become aware of the New Irelanders' desire for iron. Iron hoops, manufactured in Europe and America, were used to hold casks together. Cut into three- or four-inch segments, they were given in exchange for supplies and were greatly prized by the New Irelanders to make adzes and axes. As in the case of the Etoro, discussed earlier, the introduction of iron had an effect on many aspects of life. Men's work in clearing trees for gardening was made easier, and the process of carving *malanggan* sculptures, mentioned in Chapter 11, was transformed.

Whaling had also become an important activity in the Pacific during the first decades of the nineteenth century. The oceans off New Ireland were good whaling grounds, and like the explorers before them, English and American whalers from New Bedford and Nantucket put in to the bays of New Ireland for fresh water and supplies. In return, the whalers gave hoop iron, along with buttons, bottles, and strips of cloth. By the middle of the nineteenth century, tobacco had become the important item of exchange. A number of seamen became castaways on New Ireland and surrounding islands and throughout the Pacific Ocean at this time. For example,

Thomas Manners, an English whaler, asked to be put ashore on New Ireland in 1825. There he lived with the villagers, took wives, and fathered children. From Manners, the New Irelanders probably learned a great deal about his culture. As a result of Manners's presence, the Big Man of that village seemed to have had more political power. For men such as Manners, the islands of the Pacific were a romantic escape from the alienation of industrializing society.

During this period, the island was visited by traders seeking tortoise shell to be sent to Europe for the manufacture of combs and other decorative items, which became the rage of fashionable Europe. Bêche-de-mer (sea cucumbers) were also collected and then dried and sold to the Chinese as a food delicacy. By this point a mutually agreed-upon barter system had been established, and some New Irelanders were able to communicate in Pidgin English. (This language is known today as Neo-Melanesian.) The New Irelanders, without being aware of it, had thus become part of the world system.

The first trading post established on New Ireland was set up in 1880 by the German trader Eduard Hernsheim to purchase coconuts. Hernsheim had left his native Germany as a young man to make his fortune in the Pacific. His base in the late 1870s was Matupi Island in New Britain, and from there he set up a network of trading stations, including a number on New Ireland. At these stations he established his agents, Englishmen, Scandinavians, and later mostly Chinese, who worked for him buying unhusked coconuts, and later only the nuts, from the New Ireland villagers in exchange for tobacco, beads, and ironware from Europe. The price the villagers received for coconuts varied, depending on the price of copra on the world market, the price of beads in Europe, and the number of competing traders in the area. These were factors from the world economic system of which villagers on the local level were completely unaware. In their own system of exchange, shell valuables and pigs did not fluctuate in value. The coconuts received from the villagers were dried and turned into copra, which Hernsheim then transported on his own ship to be sold in Hamburg. With capital raised in Hamburg, which was part of the "core," Hernsheim was able both to run and to expand his business in New Ireland, which was part of the "periphery," with the profits being returned to Hamburg. The success of his business enterprise depended on the world price of copra. Hernsheim had competitors in the area, among them some colorful South Sea Island adventurers such as His Majesty O'Keefe, Bully Hayes, and the notorious Queen Emma, the daughter of a Samoan mother and the American consul to Samoa.

Relying on villagers to bring in their coconuts did not produce a steady supply of copra. As Hernsheim notes in his memoirs, "It was impossible to make long-term agreements with these savages; there were no chiefs and no large villages" (1983). Because the New Irelanders had Big Men, rather than chiefs, there was no one in a position of central political authority with whom traders and later political administrations could make binding agreements and sign treaties. On the local level, villages were autonomous political entities, and there was no single political structure that unified the whole island. Warfare between neighboring villages was endemic in this area. When trading stations were established on New Ireland, these too became targets for attack. Punitive expeditions were mounted against entire villages when white resident traders were killed.

The alternative to the unpredictable supply of copra provided by the operation of trading stations was the establishment of a plantation system. Queen Emma was the first to establish plantations in the Bismarck area, initially in New Britain in 1883. Plantations were not established on New Ireland until the beginning of the twentieth century. Since matrilineal clans, rather than individuals, own land on New Ireland, the individuals who represented themselves as the sellers to the European purchasers did not have the right to sell land. Land sales were frequently disputed by other clansmen later on. The signers, who were unable to read, marked their Xs on deeds.

Labor recruiters began in the 1880s to call at locations in New Ireland for workers for plantations in Fiji. Sometimes these labor recruiters resorted to blackbirding. Captain Wawn, one of the first labor recruiters, or "blackbirders," on New Ireland, recruiting for the sugar plantations in Queensland, Australia, in 1883, reports that men eagerly scrambled aboard his ship without knowing the pay or the length of service. Within a week, when the opportunity presented itself, 14 of the 143 "recruits" jumped overboard and escaped, having realized what they had committed themselves to. The remainder were forcibly taken to Queensland to work as laborers.

When they returned three years later, the recruits brought back "boxes" filled with Western goods. Many came back to New Ireland speaking Pidgin English, and this enabled them to deal more successfully with the European traders on the island. They used the goods that they brought back with them to operate in the political arenas of their own villages to become leaders and Big Men. The sugar produced in Queensland and the copra from Fiji and Samoa where the New Irelanders worked were destined for sale on the world market. The Australians preferred this method of labor recruitment, in which laborers returned home after a fixed period of time, rather than bringing in indentured laborers from India who would remain in Australia or the permanent immigration of non-European laborers to Australia.

There was vehement European opposition to the excesses of the blackbirders. This was led by Methodist missionaries, who had begun proselytizing in New Ireland in 1875. The Reverend George Brown, an Englishman, moved to the Bismarck Archipelago from Samoa, where he had been for some years, and set up a station at Port Hunter, in the Duke of York Islands, which lay between New Britain and New Ireland. After an initial trip to New Ireland in 1875 to survey the possibilities for missionary work, Reverend Brown established two Fijian religious teachers on New Ireland. Fijian teachers were important to the Methodist missionary enterprise because it was felt that since they were more like New Irelanders than Europeans, they would more effectively spread the message of Christianity. In the following year, the first Methodist church on New Ireland was opened. The Methodist missionaries voiced strong opposition to the New Irelanders about their custom of wearing no clothing, about ritual dancing which the missionaries considered to be lewd, and about cannibalism. There was no colonial administration on New Ireland at this time. Other Fijian teachers were sent to various parts of the island. However, the progress of missionizing was impeded, according to Reverend Brown, by the absence of authoritative leadership and the many languages spoken on the island. When a king converts, an entire kingdom converts with him; Big Men do not have the same kind of authority over their followers. In time, the Fijian teachers married local New Ireland women who had converted to Christianity. In contrast, European Methodist missionaries did not marry local women; most of them brought wives with them from overseas. While the Fijians crossed the boundary between colonizers and colonized (perhaps because they were the colonized in another context?), the Europeans did not. Catholic missionaries visited New Ireland in 1882. The Catholic approach to missionizing represented a different point of view toward the New Irelanders from that of Reverend Brown. It involved setting up mission stations run by Europeans to which the local people would come for religious instruction and schooling.

There was an attempt at European settlement on New Ireland, sponsored by the Marquis de Ray, a French aristocrat who had never been in the Pacific. Four ships, with 700 settlers, left Europe for "New France" between 1880 and 1882. Unfortunately, the area chosen was the least suitable for the settlement envisioned. Completely unprepared for what they had to face in New Ireland, within two years most of the settlers died of tropical diseases and the survivors eventually were taken off the island to Australia. The Marquis de Ray was later tried and found guilty of fraud.

Although traders of several nationalities were operating in the Bismarck Archipelago in 1880, German companies dominated the area economically. Australia, then a British colony, was concerned about German influence on the island of New Guinea, and proceeded to annex the southern half of the island. This promoted action on the part of both Germany and Great Britain, and within a year an agreement was signed between them in which Germany took control over northern New Guinea and the Bismarcks. The German flag was raised over New Ireland in November 1884. While it had already been tied into the world system economically, New Ireland now became tied into the world system politically as part of the colonial empire of Germany.

It was not until 1900 that a government station was established at Kavieng, the present provincial capital, with Franz Boluminski as district commissioner. For the first time in its history, New Ireland constituted a single political entity, a district within the colony of German New Guinea, instead of many autonomous villages. Former employees of the large German trading companies applied for land to establish plantations in such numbers that shortly thereafter the colonial government had to enact regulations to prevent the New Irelanders from losing all of their land. The monument Boluminski left in New Ireland was the coastal road, stretching for over 100 miles from Kavieng, built by means of corvée labor extracted from the villages along its path. Corvée labor was a device used by colonial administrations to institute "development" projects over which local people had no control.

During the German administration, great efforts were made by the colonial government to end the state of perpetual feuding between local communities and to end the raiding and looting of trade stations by the New Irelanders. Beyond the retaliatory raids against the offending communities by the local native police organized and led by the Germans, pacification took the form of moving villages to the coast, where they could be more easily supervised. This movement of inland villagers to the coast tore whole communities away from their ancestral clan lands and brought these people into the coastal villages as intruders. This left the interior of New Ireland relatively deserted. Headmen, called *luluais,* were appointed for each village by the German administration. These men were not always the traditional leaders of the village. Sometimes the men who had worked in plantations overseas, had learned Pidgin English, and had become Big Men were appointed *luluais.*

In contrast to most of the earlier European traders, like Hernsheim, who went to Australia or returned to Europe after they had made their fortunes, the Chinese employed by the trading companies stayed on in New Ireland, intermarried with the local people, and eventually took control of the trade stores.

The Germans were stripped of their colonies, including New Ireland, after they lost World War I, and Australia took over the administration of New Ireland under a mandate from the League of Nations. The Australians expropriated German-owned plantations and sold them at favorable rates to Australian ex-servicemen. The Australian plantation owners began to use local New Irelanders from nearby villages as a source of labor, but otherwise not much changed for the New Irelanders when colonial control passed from the Germans to the Australians. When the price of copra rose on the world market, Australian plantation owners became quite successful, but when it fell during the depression, they lost money. Villagers often sold coconuts from their own trees to raise cash both to purchase trade goods and to pay the head tax. Patrol officers encouraged the local villagers to cut and dry the meat of the coconut kernels themselves so that they could sell it as processed copra and receive a higher price for it than for the kernels. The Australian plantation owners and traders tried to discourage this, since it cut into their profits.

The Australians extended their administrative control over the island by establishing patrol posts at various locations. Patrol officers periodically visited almost every village to collect head tax, to adjudicate disputes, particularly over land, to examine health conditions, to see that labor recruitment rules were adhered to, and to conduct censuses. In this way, the colonial masters increasingly penetrated many aspects of the daily life of the New Irelanders. The Australians continued to use the *luluai* system put in place by the Germans. By this time, Pidgin English had developed as the lingua franca for New Ireland, as well as many other areas of the southwest Pacific. In addition to its use by Europeans to communicate with the local people, it was also used by New Irelanders from different parts of the island, who spoke different languages, to converse across these linguistic boundaries. Like other pidgins, it borrowed freely from German and English, as well as from the Austronesian and Papuan languages spoken locally, and it is now spoken throughout most of Papua New Guinea.

In 1929 an outsider, Hortense Powdermaker, came into New Ireland not to trade, convert, or colonize, but to study the people. Previously others had done some ethnographic research on New Ireland. Hortense Powdermaker, an American trained by Malinowski, studied the village of Lesu (1933). We have pointed out earlier that anthropologists tend to work at the microanalytic level. Powdermaker selected Lesu, a Notsi-speaking village, as her unit of analysis and lived in the village. She described Lesu as if it were an autonomous entity, as had been the case in the nineteenth century. She made no attempt to discuss the changes affecting the village of Lesu, such as the neighboring plantation, or to study the links between Lesu and the larger units of which it was a part, including the world system.

During World War II, Rabaul, on nearby New Britain, was the main Japanese base in the southwest Pacific, and New Ireland was occupied by the Japanese. For the New Irelanders, the primary hardship arose from Japanese confiscation of pigs and foodstuffs. The expatriate Europeans and Chinese traders were dealt with much more harshly.

The Australians returned after World War II to administer Papua New Guinea as a United Nations Trusteeship Territory, with independence as the eventual aim. The Australian plantation owners reopened their plantations, and Australian ex-servicemen who had served in the area went into a variety of businesses, such as the salvage and sale of scrap metal and timber logging. The economy continued much as it had before the war, though new crops, such as cocoa, began to be grown alongside the coconut palms. In the 1950s, as a first step toward independence, the Australians introduced a system of elected local government councils, which took over some of the functions that had been carried out by patrol officers. A House of Assembly was established in Port Moresby, with representation from all over Papua New Guinea.

In 1975 the independent nation of Papua New Guinea was established. New Ireland was set up as a province, with its own elected Provincial Assembly and a provincial government headed by a prime minister. Representatives from New Ireland are also elected to a national parliament. Since independence, Australian expatriates have begun to withdraw from the economic system of New Ireland. However, Australians still own many of the plantations. Some of the plantation laborers are New Irelanders, while others have been brought in from the Sepik River area of New Guinea. The world price for copra has been very low in recent years, and many of the plantations are run at a minimal level since the owners do not wish to take a loss. Abandoned plantations revert to the local villages. Villagers still have a subsistence economy, supporting themselves, for the most part, through gardening, raising pigs, and fishing. The local villagers produce copra and cocoa to sell to government marketing boards, which then sell these products on the world market. Sometimes villagers have organized themselves into cooperatives to buy and operate a truck or a boat. The trade stores are almost entirely owned by the descendants of the Chinese traders. In recent

The weekly Saturday market at Kavieng, the provincial capital of New Ireland, attracts villagers from other islands. They come with their produce in traditional long canoes equipped with outboard motors.

years, Malaysian and Japanese companies have been exploiting the timber resources in the interior part of the island. This is similar to the type of resource extraction involving rubber tapping and mining that took place in the nineteenth century. Though fixed royalties are paid to national and provincial governments and to local people, no thought is being given to the replenishing of this resource through reforestation.

The legacy of the Reverend George Brown is the many Methodist congregations all over the island led by New Ireland religious leaders. The Catholic mission stations of the island are run by expatriate American priests of the Order of the Sacred Heart. The diocese of New Ireland is headed by a German bishop. Neo-Melanesian (Pidgin English) is the official language of Papua New Guinea, but many New Irelanders also speak English.

The significant unit for New Irelanders continues to be the village. The village had been politically independent before New Ireland became a colony. Today, though there are still Big Men and matrilineal clans, every village is part of an electoral district. In contrast to people elsewhere who have become wage laborers or others dependent exclusively upon cash crops, New Ireland villagers have resisted being completely absorbed into a market economy. Many prefer only to sell products when they need cash for economic needs. For the past hundred years, New Irelanders have not been able to think of themselves solely in terms of their clan or village membership. They are increasingly forced to view themselves in regional terms, as New Irelanders, and today in national terms, as Papuan New Guineans. Changes at the world level affect them economically and politically, and they see themselves as necessarily part of the world system.

Directed Culture Change

During the colonial period, administrators in colonies all over the world instituted many changes. They saw these changes as bringing "progress" to peoples, helping to make them modern—that is, civilized and Westernized. These changes may not have been desired by the peoples themselves, but their opinions were not sought. Changes may be introduced by government or private agencies of one kind or another. The peoples who will be affected by the changes may sometimes be consulted in the decision to introduce change. More often, they are not. In Third World countries, the tribal peoples who make up the Fourth World are not consulted when sweeping changes are instituted by economic planners and officials of the national government.

By and large, directed culture change concerns two areas. The first is technology and economics; the second is health. The role played by an-

thropologists in such projects is one in which he or she provides basic judgments about the most effective ways of achieving results. The anthropologist is rarely in the position of policymaker. The decision to build a dam for
hydroelectric power and irrigation is made by economic planners in the
central government. The lake created by the dam will flood dozens of tribal
villages. The anthropologist typically is brought in to help devise ways to
resettle the villagers with the least amount of dislocation. Because of this
role in assisting governments to achieve their ends, the anthropologist was
sometimes considered a tool of colonialism. This has been an area involving serious ethical questions for anthropologists, particularly during and
since the Vietnam war, when governmental policies sealed the fate of tribal
peoples and some anthropologists were involved in suggesting ways of carrying out these policies. The most important questions that the anthropologist who is involved in directed culture change must be concerned with
are: Do the tribal people themselves seek the changes and understand their
consequences? Have they been involved in a collaborative effort with the
anthropologist to plan the changes that will take place?

One kind of directed culture change has been the introduction of new
crops and improved varieties of older crops. New food crops have been successfully introduced to tribal peoples all over the world when they have
accepted the new crop as a desirable food or when they have been able to
sell it as a cash crop. However, sometimes an improved variety of an old
crop has a taste that is somewhat different from the old one and is not
acceptable. Sometimes a new method of processing food is introduced as a
labor-saving device, but if the taste of the food changes, the new method
may be unsuccessful. Traditionally, Kanuri women grind sorghum, the staple crop, by hand between two stones to make the basic food dish of the
Kanuri. Mechanization of the grinding process was attempted by setting up
a mill to grind the grain, which would have saved enormous amounts of
daily labor, but the mill-ground sorghum did not have the gritty taste that
the Kanuri liked, and they would not use it.

Directed culture change has also been applied in the field of animal hus-
bandry, where the results of Western science have been put to practical
application. Nomadic pastoralists like the Bakhtiari in Iran readily worm
their herds with pills distributed to them by the veterinary services of the
national government. In general, changes in veterinary practices whose
effects are perceived by the people themselves as increasing the productivity and fertility of herds are usually accepted. However, proposed long-term
changes, such as reduction in the size of herds, are frequently opposed by
tribal peoples. For example, among the Navajo, during the mid-1930s, the
United States government introduced a stock reduction program. The
Department of the Interior had made an extensive study of all the range-
land on the Navajo reservation, determining that soil erosion had taken
place as a result of overgrazing. It was clear that the total number of sheep,

goats, and horses kept by the Navajo tribe would have to be reduced, but this could be accomplished only by reducing the size of each Navajo family's herd. This caused great consternation among the Navajo since their livestock represented their wealth and was a source of great prestige. Navajo resentment toward the government simmered for many years after. There are many other reasons for reducing the size of herds in addition to preventing further erosion brought about by overgrazing. Reduced herd size by selectively culling the poorer-quality animals improves the entire herd. Furthermore, smaller herds are more easily managed and less subject to predation, and selective breeding can be more easily carried out. Attempts to reduce herd size among pastoral cattle-keeping peoples of East Africa have also met with little success, for very similar reasons.

Another and more drastic kind of directed culture change involving nomadic pastoralists are the programs to sedentarize them. Nomadic pastoralists are found all over the Middle East. Since they are highly mobile, it is difficult for the national government to control them. Their emphasis on tribal identity above national loyalties also constitutes a political threat. As a result of this, governments throughout the area have attempted to settle the nomadic pastoralists in villages. These plans have invariably been resisted by the tribal peoples. As noted in Chapter 7, a policy of forced sedentarization of the nomadic tribes of Iran was instituted in the period of 1925–1941. Among the Basseri, for example, most families were prevented from migrating. Since their herds of sheep and goats are adapted to the migratory cycle, large percentages of the herds died because the enforced sedentarization subjected the animals to extremes of temperature to which they were not accustomed. After 1941, most of these nomadic pastoral tribes resumed migration and continue to do so today. Attempts at sedentarization or partial sedentarization in other countries, as in the case of the Bedouins of the Israeli Negev, have been more successful.

Directed culture change has also been concerned with health. Western medical practices have been accepted in varying degrees in many tribal areas. Generally, spectacular curative measures are more quickly accepted than preventive ones. Charles Erasmus, a medical anthropologist specializing in Latin America, notes the great success of the campaign to eradicate yaws in the coastal areas of Colombia and Ecuador, where the disease had been endemic. Even the folk beliefs and the fatalistic attitude that had surrounded yaws have been altered because of the success of modern medicine in treating the disease.

The introduction of Western medicine and Western health practices has greatly reduced mortality rates in most Third World countries. In the past, although the fertility rates were high in these countries, the population was kept in check by equally high infant mortality rates, as well as by traditional population control practices such as abortion, infanticide, and the spacing of childbirths. Introduction of Western medical practices had the direct effect of increasing the population, and the same available resources

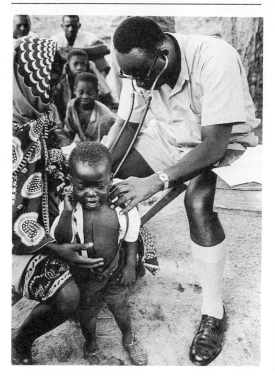

A Tanzanian doctor examines an unwilling patient for Kwashior Kor, a disease caused by malnutrition, in a mobile nutrition clinic.

now had to support a much larger population. The result is a parallel increase in hunger and malnutrition. These conditions make infants and young children, in particular, vulnerable to various forms of disease so that the infant mortality rate is again on the rise. In such countries, the question arises: Should directed culture change, in the form of technical assistance from another country like the United States, be aimed more at increasing the productive capacity of the country, which would enable the country to deal with the health problem itself, or should technical assistance be focused directly on improving diet and nutrition and saving the lives of children, which would mean even more mouths to feed? Logic would argue for increasing the capacity to produce food, but compassion would argue for saving the lives of children. In recognition of the problem of overpopulation, directed culture change has often been aimed at birth control. These programs have not been very effective since people are more concerned with their personal short-term goals of having children who will care for them in their old age, rather than the long-term goals of controlling the overall size of the population in their country, a distant goal that is hard to visualize. The goals for each family may be at variance with those of planners for the entire society. From this viewpoint, the opposition to family planning parallels resistance to herd reduction.

Assertion of Cultural Identity

Most people recognize that the introduction of changes from the industrialized world, which is itself constantly undergoing change, has had and will continue to have a profound effect on their cultures. Frequently people are ready and willing to accept those changes that they immediately perceive as useful, such as steel axes. Sometimes change is forced upon them, and sometimes they forcibly resist change. One form of resistance is to run away, as the Kreen-akore of the tropical forest of Brazil ran from attempts to contact and pacify them. But you can only run so far and for so long, and eventually even the Kreen-akore stopped running. Other tribal groups retain their tribal identity and uniqueness by conscious efforts to preserve the traditional and customary and to reject the new. As the Menomini man defiantly said to the former Commissioner of Indian Affairs, "You can make the Menomini reservation into Menomini County but you can't make a white man out of me!"

When a national identity is being built, political pressure is applied to suppress ethnic identity, as we noted in Chapter 8. Frequently this has the opposite effect. In response to such pressure, cultural identity is often reasserted. Malaysia has been dominated by Moslem Malay-speakers since it gained its independence. The non-Moslem Iban, who live in Sarawak, that part of Malaysia on the island of Borneo, have recently begun to reassert their cultural identity. In the past, the Iban had been headhunters and pirates in the South China Seas. Today, when Iban boys leave home to go to school, search for work, or join the military or the police, that is seen as symbolically equivalent to the traditional journey into the unknown that an Iban boy made as part of his initiation into manhood. Iban politicians talk about preserving their traditional lifestyle while at the same time fighting for a larger share of civil service and other government jobs for their people.

Tribal people have developed various ways to assert their continued identity. The ways in which they separate themselves from the dominant society are known as *boundary maintenance mechanisms.* For example, the Rio Grande Pueblos of New Mexico—Tewa and Keres—which were in contact with the Spanish missionaries and explorers in the seventeenth century, have divided their religious life into two separate domains: the indigenous one with its katchinas (religious figurines), priests, and kivas (underground religious chambers), which is operated in secret, closed off from the outside world and the eyes of the white man; and the village structure of the Catholic Church, which is in contact with the outside world. By preserving their language and much of their aboriginal ritual structure, the Rio Grande Pueblos have been able to maintain their culture

*A sign can mark
a social boundary
between groups as
well as between
areas of land.*

and identity for more than 300 years, despite their nominal conversion to Catholicism.

In contrast, the Navajo living in the same general area have been some-what more receptive to certain kinds of changes introduced from the dominant society. The reception accorded veterans returning from World War II gives some insight into the difference in attitude between the Navajo and Zuni toward those who have extensive contact with the outside world. Returning Navajo veterans had to undergo spiritual cleansing through the performance of rituals like the Enemy Way for combat soldiers who had come in contact with German or Japanese corpses on the battlefield. This was the traditional ceremony for dispelling the harmful effects of alien ghosts. Once back among their own people, the Navajo veterans introduced many new changes acquired in the army. They also took advantage of Veterans Administration programs. On the other hand, the Zuni maintained ever-greater control over returning veterans, requiring of them more ritual cleansing and ceremony in order to reintegrate them into Zuni society. They had to cut their ties with the outside and could not even accept terminal pay from the Veterans Administration.

As illustrated by the examples of the Rio Grande Pueblos, Zuni, and Navajo, boundary maintenance mechanisms frequently revolve around people's most strongly held beliefs, and these are usually in the area of religion. People resist the proselytizing onslaught of a dominant culture by insistently holding onto their own religious beliefs and ceremonies. The Amish, Hutterites, and Hassidic Jews carry this to an extreme, since their whole life, including the style of clothing from an earlier time that they wear, is part of their religion. The only way change can come into these groups is through religious edict. They fulfill within the group as many of their needs as possible, thus maintaining boundaries and reducing contact with the external world to an absolute minimum.

Often, after a certain amount of culture change has taken place, people recognize that they are in the process of being stripped of their own culture, but they have not been assimilated into the dominant culture. The uncertainty of their position makes them ready to follow a religious innovator, who has a more concrete vision of a better future. Out of these conditions, religious cults are born, which have been termed *nativistic movements* or *revitalization movements*. These religious movements synthesize many traditional cultural elements with elements introduced from the dominant society.

An example of this is the Handsome Lake religion of the Seneca, one of the six tribes that constituted the League of the Iroquois. By the end of the American Revolution, the Seneca had suffered partial devastation of their villages, decimation of their population, and the general dislocation of many aspects of their culture. In the 1780s, Handsome Lake, who was a sachem, or tribal leader, of the Seneca, had a series of visions, during which he had contact with the various Iroquois deities and foresaw what the life of the Seneca should be like in the future. What he saw was an amalgam of older Iroquois traditions and new ideas derived from the Quakers and from other missionaries. The Seneca had formerly emphasized matrilineal descent and uxorilocal postmarital residence. In contrast, Handsome Lake stressed the importance of the nuclear family and de-emphasized the matrilineage. Many of the economic values of the Quakers, such as thrift, were adopted by Handsome Lake. At the same time, much of the traditional Seneca ceremonialism was also maintained. Handsome Lake had many adherents during his lifetime, although there were other political leaders who opposed and competed with him. After his death, his doctrines were written down and formed the Code of Handsome Lake. Though it was revolutionary when it first appeared, the Handsome Lake religion, as it came to be called, gradually became a conservative force as more and more changes were accepted by the Seneca. Today the Handsome Lake religion is kept up by people who are among the more conservative members of the tribe. What began as a vision of Seneca accommodation to the culture of the white man was transformed over time into a bulwark resisting change.

A particular type of revitalization movement that has occurred repeatedly in Melanesia is the *cargo cult.* Cargo cults made their appearance early in the twentieth century. However, they proliferated after World War II, which was a period of more intensive contact with outsiders, particularly with American soldiers who drove out the Japanese and used the islands of Melanesia as a staging base. The Melanesians were astonished by the technological might of the Western world, as represented by the American armed forces. Like all revitalization movements, cargo cults revolve about a charismatic leader or prophet who has a vision. This vision usually involved conversations with the spirits of deceased ancestors, and the prophet foretold that the ancestors would rise from the dead. At this time, black Melanesians would get white skins, and white people either would become black or would be driven into the seas. The ancestors would arrive in a big ship or plane, bringing with them an inexhaustible cargo of steel axes, razor blades, tobacco, tinned beef, rice, and rifles. More recently, the expected cargoes include transistor radios, wristwatches, and motorcycles. People built piers into the sea, erected huge warehouses, and even prepared landing strips when planes were expected. They neglected their gardening and often killed off their pigs, since the expectation was that no one would have to work anymore after the cargo arrived. Sometimes elements of Christianity were included in the visions of the prophet, so that Jesus Christ was expected to arrive along with the cargo.

Sometime in the mid-1960s something akin to a cargo cult developed on Lavongai Island, an island off the north coast of New Ireland. It was called the Johnson movement because the people of Lavongai voted for President Lyndon Johnson in an election to the House of Assembly in Port Moresby. They continue to vote for Johnson in provincial elections today, though Lyndon Johnson is long dead and Papua New Guinea has been an independent nation for some time. Their votes are seen as a protest, though an ineffectual one, since, by voting for Johnson, they lose their voice in choosing their representatives. The Johnson movement supports economic development, and its people plant coconut trees. However, like other cargo cults, they think that by simply doing this all kinds of cargo will come to them.

Like all revitalization movements, cargo cults are a synthesis of the old and the new. In a situation of culture contact where tribal peoples find themselves helpless and overwhelmed by the power of the dominant society, a prophet appears who preaches turning to the ancestors to seek their help in acquiring the things that make the dominant society so powerful. The cargo is seen as the secret of the white people's power. Like all forms of religion that attempt to explain the inexplicable, cargo cults attempt to offer a supernatural explanation of what it is that makes white people so powerful. Converts to the cargo cult have faith that the secret of white people's power, the cargo, will come to them as a result of supernatural forces. Cargo cults are religious movements, though many of them are short-lived; but at the same time they make statements about power relations, for when the cargo comes, the present situation will be reversed, black will become white, and the powerless will become powerful.

CHAPTER 14

The Anthropology of Contemporary Life

 The small-scale societies studied by anthropologists of previous generations have all been caught up in a single communication network and an all-encompassing world economy. These societies are tied to market systems, which may be regional or worldwide. People from even the most isolated communities in the Fourth World go to cities to look for work. These topics—peasants in rural areas, migration, and urbanization—are considered in this chapter. We will be examining the process by which the tapestry of culture of peasants and migrants comes to include motifs of different urban styles.

Peasants

Some fifty years ago anthropologists turned from a preoccupation with small-scale societies of tribal peoples to the study of peasant societies and urban life. Field research has been carried out on peasant communities in every part of the world. Despite diversities of language, religion, and forms of government, one can isolate the characteristics of peasant society as a type.

Peasant communities arose with the development of cities in the Near East some 5,000 years ago. Such communities have always existed as *part cultures,* having a continuing relationship with the outside world. Part cultures are not self-sufficient and cannot exist by themselves. Peasant society as a type is characterized by the following set of features. The economic relationship between the peasant community and the city involves the sale of surplus grain and foodstuffs to city dwellers, who do not grow their own food. For the peasant community, the city is a source of specialized crafts and manufactured goods that are not made by the peasants themselves. The peasants are also part of a larger political unit, the state, which siphons off part of the peasants' surplus in the form of taxes. An asymmetrical relationship exists between the peasants, who produce the economic surplus, and the dominant group of rulers and elites located in the city, who control the surplus and make decisions about its use. All political decisions emanate from the capital, though the degree of political control over the peasant community varies. Peasant communities are never completely independent or autonomous. The peasants usually share a common language and culture with the city dwellers; they are an essential part of the civilization that the city represents. That civilization is sometimes referred to as the *Great Tradition.* The peasant community's variant of this, which includes folk belief, is known as the *Little Tradition.* If the Great Tradition is thought of as a tapestry, the Little Tradition or peasant variant of this is a folk version of that tapestry. Peasants have an intimate and reverent attitude toward the land that they farm. They place a high value on an agricultural way of life, as well as on hard work. Peasant communities tend to be culturally homogeneous and are not very tolerant of outsiders or of cultural differences. In the past, peasant communities seemed static and unchanging. While life in the city is constantly changing, life in the peasant village changes much more slowly. What is in fashion in the peasant village may have long since gone out of style in the city. We have described the characteristics of the peasant community as an ideal type. If one examines peasant communities over the world today, one will find that they vary to a greater or lesser degree from this ideal type.

Several different types of peasant communities have been described. One type is the closed corporate peasant community of Mexico, Guatemala, and central Java. Wolf (1955, 1957), who first described it, pointed out its distinctive features: communal ownership of the land, which is periodically redistributed; endogamy; the exclusion of outsiders; homogeneity of culture; pushing off of surplus population into newly formed daughter villages; and the presence of religious rituals like fiestas, which serve to level differences in wealth between community members. In such closed corporate communities, life risks were shared among all members through social relations that provide mutual aid and support. Closed corporate peasant communities developed in marginal areas as a result of conquest and the establishment of colonial empires. The colonial power demanded a labor force, which was supplied by the peasant community through part-time labor. At the same time the peasants had to provide for their own subsistence. The colonial authorities treated the community as a single entity, from which they extracted tribute and labor. The community was allowed to control its own internal organization. The distinctive characteristics listed were the peasant community's response to the demands made upon it by the larger society.

Other types of peasant communities were the result of somewhat different external conditions. In the open peasant communities of Latin America, there was individual rather than communal ownership of land, and the community accepted new members. Wealth differentials were present, since wealth was not redistributed in the way that it was in the closed corporate community. The introduction of cash crops brought about the development of such open peasant communities in Latin America. In prerevolutionary China, peasant communities were always of the open type; they were never endogamous or closed to outsiders, and free buying and selling of land was always possible. Chinese peasant communities were characterized by wealth and status differences between members. The peasant community was tied to the state since the state controlled the large-scale irrigation system. Still other types of peasant communities involve variations in the degree of dependence on cash crops and in ownership of land. There are also different forms of sharecropping, and relations with absentee landlords vary.

One important way in which the peasant community articulates with the larger society is through the market system. Markets are the places where peasants obtain the specialized goods that they neither grow nor manufacture. Markets have different kinds of structures. One kind of market structure links a number of different peasant communities to a central market town. In addition to its subsistence activities, each of these communities specializes in a different craft activity, such as weaving, manufacture of pottery, or manufacture of tiles. People from each of these communities periodically come into the market to sell their wares and to buy the goods that they require but do not make for themselves. Such markets are frequently held once a week. In some places markets are held in different villages and towns on successive days of the week. In northern Nigeria, a village may sometimes be labeled with the day of the week on which its market is held, as in the village called Saturday. Itinerant traders go from market to market with their goods. These kinds of marketing structures, where goods from industrial societies, as well as local products, are sold, define a region. They are found in Mexico, Guatemala, Peru, and areas of Indonesia.

Another topic that has served as a focus for anthropological research in peasant communities is kinship ties. In some peasant communities, extended kin ties play an important role. The patrilineal clan in prerevolutionary China had important economic and religious functions, as did the *zadruga,*

A contemporary Indian market in Ayacucho, Peru, showing the penetration of Western goods into the local peasant market.

the large virilocal extended family in Yugoslavia. In peasant communities in other parts of the world, such as in Mediterranean Europe and Latin America, kin ties were more attenuated, and godparenthood or compadrazgo relationships, whose important ritual and economic functions were discussed in Chapter 5, took their place. In our discussion of the patron-client relationship of peasants, we noted the way in which compadrazgo was used for political ends. Chapter 8 explored how factions coalesce and operate in local-level politics in peasant communities. The religious orientation of peasant communities is part of what was referred to earlier as the Little Tradition. Peasant communities usually hold their important religious rituals and festivals at times of the year that are significant in the yearly calendar—harvest, planting, the winter solstice. These rituals and festivals, which reflect the peasants' versions of the universal religions, serve as rites of intensification within the peasant community. In addition, they frequently reappear as the religious holidays of the universal religions that are the foci of Great Tradition. The Little Tradition of the peasant community also includes many folk beliefs. The evil eye described in the discussion of witchcraft in Chapter 9 is one such example. This belief is another mechanism that operates to minimize the development of wealth differences within peasant communities. The kind of folklore with which we are familiar—European fairy tales that are repeated to children to teach them morality—are part of the Little Tradition of European peasant communities.

Unlike tribal peoples, peasants, by definition, always had contact with both the city and the state. Though peasants were slow to accept change, and even resisted it, their continuing contact with urban centers meant that innovations were always accessible to them. From the time of the appearance of the first cities in the Near East, peasants have existed as a type of society. With the Industrial Revolution, the mode of production in the city changed. The factory system, which was centered in an urban environment, marked the appearance of the modern city. It required new sources of cheap labor and new markets for the great increase in the volume of goods produced. As the city industrialized, the peasant communities of the surrounding countryside were affected.

One of the peasants' first responses to the development of the modern city, in the nineteenth century, was an increase in migration into the cities. Peasants moving into the city and finding wage labor there were absorbed into the working-class population of the city. Two kinds of forces were at work in the movement of peasants into the cities. Shortage of land and lack of economic opportunities may have had the effect of "pushing" people out of their villages. At the same time, the promise of jobs and the bright lights of the city acted as factors that "pulled" these individuals into the city. From the modern city emanate powerful influences that are spread through a communication system involving radio and television programs in regional dialects, newspapers, and teachers trained in the urban centers and sent out into the countryside. The changes in peasant life brought about by the transformation of the preindustrial city into the modern industrial city were so great that people remaining in rural villages are now referred to as *postpeasants*.

Like tribal people who still maintain their positions in their tribal villages though they have taken jobs as migrant laborers in the city, some postpeasants have a way of life that combines the city and the countryside. They commute to nearby industrial plants, where they work for wages, and at the same time maintain their land and continue to work it with traditional, but by now outmoded, agricultural techniques. Farming is important for subsistence, but it is still more important as a symbol of a way of life that the people of the community wish to continue to pursue. Peasants can become involved in industrial enterprises without becoming urbanized and modernized.

In a study in Yugoslavia, Joel and Barbara Halpern (1972) describe a postpeasant community under a Communist government. The villagers of

Orasac commute to work in nearby mines and quarries, while still working their traditional agricultural holdings. The cash economy has influenced life in the village, since material items like cars have become important as status symbols. Even those peasants who have permanently migrated to the town come back to summer houses in the village. The peasant impact upon the town has taken various forms. Often villagers who move to the town build houses on its outskirts, and in furnishings and in design the houses are similar to the houses of the village. Water comes from a well in the yard, and there is no indoor plumbing. In Yugoslavia, peasant folk songs, dances, crafts, and literary themes have also had an influence on urban culture. This is an instance of the Little Tradition influencing the Great Tradition.

When rural villagers begin to concentrate on cash-cropping, they cease to produce food for their own subsistence. They are no longer peasants and become farmers dependent on a cash economy. Anthropologists have studied the ways in which agrarian societies in many parts of the world have been modernizing through the introduction of credit systems, cooperatives, and irrigation projects. Peasant rebellions and conflicts over land between peasants and landowners, as well as efforts leading to land redistribution and land reform, have also been the focus of study. Anthropologists have begun to concentrate on the process of development from the tribal agricultural community through agricultural peasantry to the development of a rural proletariat—peasants who have been alienated from the land. The plantation workers of Jamaica, described by Mintz, are an example of a rural proletariat whose lives are little different from their urban counterparts, since the plantation is the equivalent of a rural factory.

Anthropologists earlier dealt with peasant society as if it were a stable, unchanging way of life. One can see that such a vision was a myth and that, in reality, the same larger forces increasingly transforming the world into a single economic system are affecting peasants as well as urban dwellers.

Migration: The Mines and the City

We have observed how tribal people and peasants alike move from the rural area to the mines and the cities. In the post–World War II period, anthropologists followed these migrants from their original homes to the new locations where they worked or settled, and focused attention on the nature of their adjustment. A. L. Epstein (1958) studied the way in which Africans from a multitude of tribes, who flocked into the mining town of Luanshya in Zambia, developed a new form of urban organization. At first, tribal affiliation and tribal leadership were emphasized, but then gradually new associations such as unions developed, and leadership based on skill and on education superseded tribal leadership in most situations. Mitchell (1956) described a similar process in his study of a very different kind of phenomenon in the copper belt of Zambia, the *kalela* dance of the Bisa tribe. This was one of a number of tribal dances performed in towns in the copper belt that served to assert tribal identity. Mitchell contrasted the way in which tribal identity had meaning and was utilized in some contexts with the way class identity took precedence in other contexts.

Migration to work in the mines of South Africa continues to be a significant experience for men from the rural semiautonomous homelands of the Union of South Africa. Coplan (1987) has studied expressive poetry composed by Basotho migratory mine workers from the homeland of Lesotho, where 80 percent of the men work in the mines. This poetry, recited in the taverns and bars of border towns, expresses their sentiments about life in the mines and their continuing relationship with families and homes. In the miners' conceptualization, God rules above the ground while Satan rules the underground hell of the mines.

The Basotho see work in the mines as analogous to going to war and cattle raiding, the tests of manhood that their grandfathers carried out. Like the Iban in the previous chapter, the Basotho interpret the modern work experience in traditional terms. The migratory workers conceptualize their position as an exchange between the Basotho chief and the "chief" of South Africa. The Basotho chief sends men to work in the mines of South Africa, while the South African "chief" sends cattle (money) in exchange to the Lesotho homeland. Though 35 percent of their time is spent in the mines, the men consider their real life to be the time they spend at home. The poetry emphasizes their Basotho ethnic identity rather than their class identity as miners.

Oscar Lewis studied the Mexican peasant village of Tepoztlan in the late 1940s. He subsequently investigated the urban adjustment that people from Tepoztlan made when they migrated from their village to Mexico City. In his book *Five Families* he developed the concept of the culture of poverty. He argued that poor people in urban environments of industrialized capitalistic states, regardless of nationality, share a set of cultural characteristics. Poverty is the most significant element. Those able to work are unskilled and underemployed, finding work usually in marginal employment. When they make money, it is spent rather than saved. The people are said not to be future-oriented. Their living conditions are crowded, and physical violence is common. The male head of the house often disappears, leaving what is referred to as a matrifocal family. This kind of environment provides little security for the maturing children. While Oscar Lewis's descriptions of the culture of poverty in the barrios of Mexico City, and in Puerto Rico, are vivid, rich cultural accounts, the analytical concept of the culture of poverty as he developed it met with sharp critical attack. Lewis argued that the culture of poverty was a true culture in the meaning of the term as it has been used throughout this book and that it was perpetuated through its values being inculcated in the next generation. However, critics argued that the insecure and marginal existence of the poor was due to their lack of money and economic opportunity, and that if they had secure jobs and steady income, they would not exhibit the so-called cultural traits that are said to characterize the culture of poverty.

During the past few decades, Third World cities such as Mexico City, Cairo, and Rio de Janeiro have expanded enormously, surpassing the population of New York City. Most of the peasants who come to the city in Latin American countries are the more educated and skilled. They do not leave because land shortages have pushed them off the land, but because opportunities attract them to the city. They frequently come to friends in the city who help them to become established, and they continue to maintain ties with their home areas. They often end up living in what are known as squatter settlements, or *favelas*. Large-scale rural-urban migration soon exhausts the city's housing stock, and illegal housing begins to be built on unused land.

Perlman (1976) has described one such squatter settlement, Catacumba, located on a steep hill in the heart of a densely populated upper-middle-class and upper-class residential and commercial district of Rio, where world famous tourist spots such as Copacabana and Ipanema are located. Litigation over who owned this precipitously rocky bit of land began in the 1920s. Uncertainty over ownership allowed the squatters to settle there in the 1930s. The earliest settlers occupied the bottom of the hill, where they eventually built themselves cement and brick houses, and where urban amenities such as water, sewage disposal, electricity, and garbage collection became available. The better and larger groceries, bars, and shops were found at the bottom of the hill. As one went up the steep hill, the views got better, but the houses were less substantial and the services less dependable.

Unemployment was low, and most favela inhabitants worked in construction and domestic service in the areas surrounding the favela. The favela had a complex social organization. There were many voluntary associations, including a residents' association, which represented the inhabitants in disputes and demands for services, soccer clubs, youth clubs, and a samba school. There were also several churches and Afro-Brazilian spiritual centers. Since fear of eviction was a constant factor in favela life, the residential association was ever ready to petition the governor and inform the mass media of the favela's plight. However, finally the petitions didn't work; the favela of Catacumba was eradicated in the 1970s, and the people moved to housing projects elsewhere.

Immediately following World War II, the population of Lima, Peru, grew enormously. This increase was mainly due to migration of people from the rural mountain areas into the city: many migrants were Indians from the highlands of Peru. When they first arrive, most migrants move in with rel-

The Brazilian government constantly attempts to evict residents of these kinds of squatter settlements, or favelas, located on the outskirts of Rio de Janeiro.

atives or people from the same region, since they come with little money. Shortly after arrival, the new migrant, male or female, is likely to join a regional or ethnic association made up of people from the same home area. The officers of such associations are mostly men, although women play an important role. The association promotes learning how to act while in an urban environment and discourages the migrant from displaying rural or Indian customs, such as wearing Indian dress or chewing coca. It fosters interest in national culture through discussions of soccer, politics, and bullfighting. At the same time that the association emphasizes adaptation to life in the city, it also operates as a conservative force by reinforcing older regional customs. Regional solidarity is maintained, for example, by the annual club fiesta, with its regional food, music, and dance. When the stress of city life becomes great, the association is a familiar place to which one can retreat. Through the association one can meet eligible marriage partners. Members have an obligation to help one another. They exchange labor, borrow money from one another, and help each other when sick.

When members are seeking godparents for their children, it is common to select someone within the association. Membership in a regional association gives people access to persons of high status from the same area, such as lawyers, doctors, and politicians, whom they otherwise might never meet socially, and these individuals may be asked to serve as godparents. As the lower-class members acquire familiarity with the national culture within the association, they can exploit opportunities for social mobility. Leaders in the regional association can use it as a political base and as a stepping stone for getting ahead in national politics. They operate as leaders of immigrant associations did in the politics of American cities at the turn of the century. Association members also lobby with governmental agencies to obtain public services for their region.

While traditional West African cities typically had foreigners as permanent inhabitants, usually living in a ward set aside for "strangers," the modern West African city is completely diverse in its population. A large proportion of the migrants to the new city are young and work at jobs in industry. Many voluntary associations are found in these modern cities. Not only are there a great number of voluntary associations, but there are also a wide variety of types. One type, the tribal association, is based on membership in the traditional social organization, all members coming from the same lineage, clan, village, or tribe. The purpose of these tribal associations is to provide members with mutual assistance when they are out of work or ill, like the regional associations of Lima, Peru. They also operate, as immigrant societies in New York City formerly did, as burial societies, which assure members of a decent funeral. Tribal culture is fostered and kept alive in the cities by organized dances on festival days. Money is collected and sent back to the hometown for improvements there. The association also inculcates in the migrant new standards of dress, social behavior, and personal hygiene appropriate to life in the city.

Like the regional associations of Peru, the voluntary associations of West African cities assist the migrants from rural towns and villages in adapting to city life. In West Africa, however, many of the associations are based on traditional forms of social organization that are reworked within the urban context. The functions of the traditional kin groups, such as supernatural protection and social control, are taken over by the voluntary associations. The recent migrants into the cities gravitate toward tribal associations. Because these tribal associations emphasize ethnic differences between tribes, they maintain cleavages between peoples of different tribal origins in the cities. On the other hand, the most Westernized individuals tend to belong to associations that are European-derived, such as church societies, Masonic lodges, and soccer clubs, and which are pantribal in membership. The latter associations play down tribal differences and emphasize instead social class distinctions in the embryonic class structure. Their members either were born in the city or have lived there for a long time.

Another way to look at voluntary associations is to see how they develop and change in response to increasing urbanization and political change during the colonial and postcolonial periods. This approach is used by Claude Meillassoux (1968) in his study of the city of Bamako in the Republic of Mali. In 1888, Bamako was a small town of 800 to 1,000 people, the center of a small chiefdom of the Bambara tribe. When the French took over the town at the end of the nineteenth century, it became a colonial administrative center and continued to be important in trade. Bamako greatly increased in population, attracting many rural migrants to the city. This rise in population was paralleled by a great increase in the number of voluntary associations. There were tribal associations, cultural or theater associations, labor unions and mutual aid associations, and sports associations (the most numerous of all).

After Mali became independent, these associations were transformed. The new government emphasized national unity and tried to reduce the influence of regionalism and tribalism. Regional and tribal voluntary associations fell under suspicion and were restricted in their activities. The one-party government of Mali introduced a system of nonvoluntary organizations to which every citizen had to belong. Voluntary associations, particularly those dealing with mutual aid, continued to exist alongside the official, governmental ones. These remained because migrants continued to come into Bamako from different areas, and the mutual aid associations, which were based on the migrant's tribe or region of origin, still played an important function. By this time, however, a considerable number of young people had been born in Bamako, and they tended to join pantribal associations, youth clubs, and dancing groups, rather than the tribal associations favored by their parents' generation. Meillassoux's study of voluntary associations in Bamako demonstrates a process in which new forms of voluntary association, frequently based on European models and pantribal in membership, are constantly emerging, although tribal and regional associations continue to exist as long as there is a need for them.

Migration from a rural hinterland into the cities has also been an important social phenomenon in the United States. From the period of the depression in the 1930s, both whites and blacks migrated from the rural South to the cities of the North—Chicago, Detroit, and New York. Since the Civil War, the South had been like an underdeveloped colonial periphery in its relationship to the northern industrialized core area. The major cash crop was cotton, harvested by hand to be processed and woven into cloth in the North. Capital also came from the North to run the farms, while labor was provided by the resident sharecroppers and tenant farmers. According to figures compiled by Fligstein (1981), the South was still 82 percent rural in 1900. With the worldwide depression in cotton prices beginning in the 1920s and the government crop reduction and subsidy program, which allowed the larger farmers to mechanize in the 1930s, small landholders, tenant farmers, and sharecroppers were forced off the land. Many decided to migrate to the North, where there were better employment opportunities. Since the majority of the tenant farmers and sharecroppers were black, they formed the bulk of the migrants from 1930 to 1950. The black urban families studied by Carol Stack (1974) in *All Our Kin: Strategies for Survival in a Black Community,* discussed in Chapter 5, moved north as part of this migration. Stack's work reveals that job opportunities in the North, for unskilled men in particular, were rather bleak and that families developed strategies of pooling and exchange within kinship networks in order to survive in the city.

The methods of the anthropologist were originally developed in the study of small-scale societies, as noted in Chapter 1. When anthropologists began to study peasant communities, they had to pay attention to economic forces originating in the city, which were part of the larger system encompassing the peasant community. Since the anthropological method requires that the investigator study a culture by living it, one may pose the question: What should the unit of study in the city be for the anthropologist? The "parts" that make up the city are not neatly bounded like a village or an island. One kind of natural unit of study is the ward or neighborhood.

The gang as a subculture is studied today by contemporary anthropologists. A subculture consists of a body of cultural patterns peculiar to a certain group of people within a larger society. Suttles's book (1968) about a Chicago slum neighborhood uses the concepts of opposition and the segmentary lineage structure to analyze the relationships, behavior, and interaction among white Italian, Puerto Rican, Mexican, and black boys' gangs, as well as adults. Each boys' gang tends to remain within its own spatially delimited territory in the neighborhood. Adults cross the boundary streets of their ethnic territory to shop and go to work. The lowest level of opposition is between the boys' gang of one ethnic group (for example, the Italian) and a counterpart boys' gang of the same ethnicity, but from a different slum neighborhood. When Italian men join in on both sides, this represents a higher level of opposition in the segmentary structure. All the ethnic groups in the neighborhood may coalesce to oppose those of another slum neighborhood. Thus the interplay of ethnicity and territory in Chicago slum areas can be described and discussed in terms of a set of anthropological concepts derived from the study of small-scale tribal societies.

A methodology particularly suited to the study of urban life is the tracing of networks. When social groupings are not easily discernible, one can plot the relationships of one man, following the lines of his social connections, and thereby obtain a picture of the social world of that man, which is his network. Bott (1971), using network analysis with a small group of subjects, plotted the social relationships of husbands and wives in order to ascertain whether they had separate networks or the same network and how this related, in turn, to their class position. The structure of networks as they operate in different social conditions can be compared. One can also use the methodology of network analysis to study the functioning of kinship in urban conditions. Some of the studies of kinship in urban complex societies that we discussed in Chapter 5 utilized network analysis.

Anthropologists have isolated other kinds of units in the urban environment for study, as we noted in Chapter 1. These include organizations such as a mental health center, a school, an old-age home, a factory, and a union. The organization and its links to the larger system of which it is a small part become the focus of study. The anthropologist may choose to study an ethnic group, which frequently has territorial expression in one or more neighborhoods. The Hassidim of Williamsburg in New York City, the Japanese of Los Angeles, Samoans living in San Francisco, the Italians of Boston, and the Puerto Ricans of El Barrio have all been subjects of anthropological study. Other kinds of subcultures, such as the gay community, the drug-dealing community of a town in California, the Hare Krishna, and retirement communities have been investigated by anthropologists. These last few examples have focused upon urban life in our own society, but there are also many examples of similar studies in Third World nations.

It is apparent that the traditional subject matter of anthropology has given way to a focus upon the many-faceted and complex world of today. In the process, the methods anthropologists employ have been expanded to adapt to the new subject matter.

End of a Journey

 One of the goals of anthropology is to gain insight into one's own culture. This can be accomplished by repeating the anthropologist's journey to other cultures very different from our own. One acquires understanding of one's own culture by taking a journey to see how Yanomamo and Kwakiutl people or Besotho mine workers solve problems of living. By seeing things from the point of view of Others, we gain a new perspective on our own culture. This book is a guidebook, or a sailor's chart, for use by the novice traveler in the journey to other cultures. Each of the chapters has been an exploration of a particular area of life and the range of variation that different cultures exhibit in that area.

Anthropologists' journeys take them to worlds that are also psychologically very different, in the sense that people of other cultures may think and feel very differently from the way we do. We compared this to Alice's trip through the looking glass. When we look at other cultures that are very different from ours, we are also holding up a mirror to ourselves.

The Polar Eskimo of Greenland lived in the most northerly latitude of any people on earth. They believed that they were the only people on earth. When European explorers came upon them in 1820, the Polar Eskimo considered the white men to be the gods of their mythology. Their vision of the world was equivalent to the vision of people on earth looking out at the universe and assuming that they are its only intelligent beings. Just as the Polar Eskimo explained and categorized their Western visitors in terms of their own known world, we envision extraterrestrial beings either like pointed-ear versions of ourselves or similar to some other inhabitant of our world, such as insects or robots. On the other hand, the explorers who found the Polar Eskimos were merely encountering another Eskimo society, one of many such in the circumpolar region of the earth. If we are ever discovered by some more intelligent civilization, we would find ourselves in the same position as that of the Polar Eskimo. The anthropologists of that civilization would approach us with a set of concepts and a methodology that are beyond our imagination and theories that are beyond our comprehension. This true story about the Polar Eskimo is a parable that has a lesson for us. Because of the isolation of the Polar Eskimo and their separation from the rest of the world, they saw only themselves and had no idea of the range and variety of human cultures. Because they had no mirror of other cultures to hold up to themselves, they could not possibly develop an anthropological perspective, nor could they come to any adequate conclusions about the basic characteristics of human nature—that is, what is common to all human cultures, another goal of anthropology.

In this ever-changing world, decisions are constantly being made concerning the future direction of particular societies and ethnic groups. These decisions should be made by the people of these groups, and they should be informed decisions. People should make such policy decisions based on as much information as possible. This is where anthropology comes in. Basic anthropological knowledge can be provided by anthropologists from other places coming in to work with the members of a society. It would be better still if policymakers were also trained anthropologists from that culture who had an understanding of culture change. Jomo Kenyatta, the late president of Kenya, was such an individual, with training as an anthropologist and enormous respect as a political leader.

We have used the metaphor of the tapestry of culture. As we systematically examined the different aspects of culture, kinship, economics, political organization, religion, and the arts, we considered each independently for purposes of analysis. The metaphor of the tapestry emphasizes the interweaving of all the aspects to form a single, unified whole. People do not categorize the activities of their lives with labels such as "political" or "religious," nor do anthropological fieldworkers directly observe such categories of behavior in the flow of life that swirls around them in the community. Like the colors and designs of an enormous tapestry, every thread contributes to the pattern. In the same way, individual behaviors observed by anthropologists ultimately contribute to their picture of the culture. But not even the most elaborate medieval tapestry can approach the splendor and complexity of any single culture.

Cited References

Abu-Lughod, Lila. "Shifting Politics in Bedouin Love Poetry." In *Language and the Politics of Emotion,* edited by Lila Abu-Lughod and Catherine A. Lutz. Cambridge: Cambridge University Press, 1990.

Atkinson, Jane Monnig. "How Gender Makes a Difference in Wana Society." In *Power and Difference: Gender in Island Southeast Asia,* edited by Jane Fishburne Collier and Sylvia Junko Yanagisako. Stanford, Calif.: Stanford University Press, 1990.

Beattie, John. *Bunyoro: An African Kingdom.* New York: Henry Holt & Co., 1960.

Benedict, Ruth. *Patterns of Culture.* Boston: Houghton Mifflin Co., 1934.

Berlin, Brent, and Paul Kay. *Basic Color Terms: Their Universality and Evolution.* Berkeley: University of California Press, 1969.

Blacking, John. "Dance and Music in Venda Children's Cognitive Development: 1956–1958." In *Acquiring Culture: Cross Cultural Studies in Child Development,* edited by Gustav Johada and I. M. Lewis. London: Croom Helm, 1988.

Bloch, Maurice. "Ritual, History and Power: Selected Papers in Anthropology." *LSE Monographs on Social Anthropology,* no. 58. London: The Athlone Press, 1989.

Boas, Franz. Introduction to *Handbook of American Indian Languages,* 1911. Reprint. Lincoln: University of Nebraska Press, 1966.

———. *Kwakiutl Ethnography,* edited by Helen Codere. Chicago: University of Chicago Press, 1966.

Bott, Elizabeth. *Family and Social Network: Roles, Norms and External Relationships in Ordinary Urban Families.* London: Tavistock Publications, 1971.

Brown, Paula. "New Men and Big Men: Emerging Social Stratification in the Third World, a Case Study from the New Guinea Highlands." *Ethnology 26* (1987): 87–106.

Buckley, Thomas, and Alma Gottlieb (eds.). *Blood Magic: The Anthropology of Menstruation*. Berkeley: University of California Press, 1988.

Chagnon, Napoleon. *Yanomamo: The Fierce People,* 3d ed. New York: Holt, Rinehart & Winston, 1983.

Child, Irvin, and Leon Siroto. "BaKwele and American Aesthetic Evaluations Compared." *Ethnology 4* (1965): 349–360.

Cohen, Ronald. *The Kanuri of Borno.* Prospect Heights, Ill.: Waveland Press, 1987.

Cooper, Frederick, and Ann L. Stoler. "Introduction: Tensions of Empire: Colonial Control and Visions of Rule." *American Ethnologist 16* (1989): 609–621.

Coplan, David. "Eloquent Knowledge: Lesotho Migrants' Songs and Anthropology of Experience." *American Ethnologist 14* (1987): 413–433.

Davenport, William. "Sculpture of the Eastern Solomons." *Expedition 10* (1968): 4–25.

d'Azevedo, Warren. "Mask Makers and Myth in Western Liberia." In *Primitive Art and Society,* edited by Anthony Forge. London: Oxford University Press, 1973, pp. 126–150.

Douglas, Mary. *Natural Symbols: Explorations in Cosmology.* New York: Pantheon Books, 1970.

———. "Deciphering a Meal." In "Myth, Symbol and Culture." *Daedalus* (Winter 1972): 61–81.

Draguns, Juris. "Psychological Disorders of Clinical Severity." In *Handbook of Cross-Cultural Psychology,* vol. 6, *Psychopathology.* Boston: Allyn and Bacon, 1980, p. 174.

Duff, Wilson. *Images: Stone: B.C.* Seattle: University of Washington Press, 1975.

Dundes, Alan. "Into the Endzone for a Touchdown: A Psychoanalytic Consideration of American Football." *Western Folklore 37* (1978): 75–88.

Durkheim, Émile. *The Elementary Forms of the Religious Life,* 1915. Reprint. Translated by Joseph W. Swain. New York: Free Press, 1965.

Epstein, A. L. *Politics in an Urban African Community.* New York: The Humanities Press, 1958.

Erikson, Erik H. *Childhood and Society,* 2d ed. New York: W. W. Norton & Co., 1963.

———. *Gandhi's Truth: On the Origins of Militant Nonviolence.* New York: W. W. Norton, 1969.

Errington, Shelly. "Recasting Sex, Gender and Power: A Theoretical and Regional Overview." In *Power and Difference: Gender in Island Southeast Asia,* edited by Jane Monnig Atkinson and Shelly Errington. Stanford, Calif.: Stanford University Press, 1990.

Feinberg, Richard. "Market Economy and Changing Sex Roles on a Polynesian Atoll." *Ethnology 25* (1986): 271–282.

Feld, Steven. "Dialogic Editing: Interpreting How Kaluli Read Sound and Sentiment." *Cultural Anthropology 2* (1987): 193–210.

Firth, Raymond. *Elements of Social Organization.* London: Watts & Co., 1951.

Fishman, Pamela. "Interaction: The Work Women Do." In *Language, Gender, and Society,* edited by B. Thorne, C. Kramarai, and N. Henley. Rowley, Mass.: Newbury House, 1983.

Fligstein, Neil. *Going North: Migration of Blacks and Whites from the South: 1900–1950.* New York: Academic Press, 1981.

Forge, Anthony (ed.). *Primitive Art and Society.* London: Oxford University Press, 1973.

Freeman, Derek. *Margaret Mead and Samoa.* Cambridge, Mass.: Harvard University Press, 1983.

Freud, Sigmund. *The Future of an Illusion.* London: Hogarth Press, 1928.

Fromm, Erich. "Individual and Social Origins of Neurosis." *American Sociological Review 9* (1944): 38–44.

Geertz, Clifford. "Deep Play: Notes on the Balinese Cockfight." *Daedalus 101* (1972): 1–37.

———. *The Interpretation of Cultures.* New York: Basic Books, Inc., 1973.

———. "From the Native's Point of View—On the Understanding of Anthropological Understanding." *Bulletin of the American Academy of Arts and Sciences 28* (1974): no. 1.

Ginsburg, Faye D. *Contested Lives: The Abortion Debate in an American Community.* Berkeley: University of California Press, 1989.

Gmelch, George. "Baseball Magic." *Trans-Action 8* (1971).

Graves, Robert. *The Greek Myths.* New York: George Braziller, 1955.

Halpern, Joel M., and Barbara K. Halpern. *A Serbian Village in Historic Perspective.* New York: Holt, Rinehart & Winston, 1972.

Hammel, Eugene. *Alternative Social Structures and Ritual Relations in the Balkans.* Englewood Cliffs, N.J.: Prentice-Hall, 1968.

Harley, George W. *Notes on the Poro in Liberia.* Papers of the Peabody Museum of American Archaeology and Ethnology, Harvard University, vol. 19, no. 2. Cambridge, Mass., 1941.

Hernsheim, Eduard. *South Sea Merchant.* Port Moresby: Institute of Papua New Guinea Studies, 1983.

Hogbin, Ian. *The Island of Menstruating Men: Religion in Wogeo, New Guinea.* Scranton, Pa.: Chandler Publishing Co., 1970.

Huntingford, G. W. B. *The Nandi of Kenya.* London: Routledge & Kegan Paul, 1953.

Kaberry, Phyllis. "The Abelam Tribe, Sepik District, New Guinea." *Oceania 21* (1940): 233–258, 345–367.

Keenan, Elinor. "Norm-makers, Norm-breakers: Uses of Speech by Men and Women in a Malagasy Community." In *Explorations in the Ethnography of Speaking,* edited by Richard Bauman and Joel Sherzer. Cambridge: Cambridge University Press, 1974.

Kleinman, Arthur, and Byron Good (eds.). *Culture and Depression: Studies in the Anthropology and Cross-Cultural Psychiatry of Affect and Disorder.* Berkeley: University of California Press, 1985.

Kluckhohn, Clyde. "Myths and Rituals: A General Theory." *Harvard Theological Review 35* (1942): 45–79.

Koskoff, Ellen (ed.). *Women and Music in Cross-Cultural Perspective.* New York: Greenwood Press, 1987.

Kroeber, Alfred L. *Cultural and Natural Areas of Native North America.* Berkeley: University of California Press, 1939.

Leach, Edmund. *Political Systems of Highland Burma: A Study of Kachin Social Structure,* 1954. Reprint. Boston: Beacon Press, 1965.

———. "Magical Hair." *Journal of the Royal Anthropological Institute of Great Britain and Ireland 88* (1958): 147–164.

———. "Anthropological Aspects of Language: Animal Categories and Verbal Abuse." In *New Directions in the Study of Language,* edited by Eric Lenneberg. Cambridge, Mass.: MIT Press, 1964, pp. 23–64.

Lepowsky, Maria. "Big Men, Big Women and Cultural Autonomy." *Ethnology 29* (1990): 35–50.

Lévi-Strauss, Claude. *Tristes Tropiques,* 1955. Reprint. Translated by John Russell. New York: Atheneum, 1961.

———. "The Structural Theory of Myth." Chapter 11 of his *Structural Anthropology.* New York: Basic Books, 1963, pp. 206–231.

———. *L'Homme Nu: Mythologique 4.* Paris: Plon, 1971.

———. *La Voie des Masques.* Paris: Plon, 1979.

Lewis, Oscar. *Life in a Mexican Village: Tepoztlan Restudied,* 1951. Reprint. Urbana: University of Illinois Press, 1963.

Lips, Julius. *The Savage Hits Back,* 1937. New Hyde Park, N.Y.: University Books, 1966.

Louwe, Heleen. "Police-Reformers: 'Big Men' Failing Their Followers." In *Private Politics: A Multi-Disciplinary Approach to "Big Man" Systems,* edited by Martin A. Van Bakel, Renee R. Hogesteijm, and Pieter von de Velde, vol. 1, pp. 174–181. *Studies in Human Society.* Leiden: Brill, 1986.

Lutz, Catherine, and Lila Abu-Lughod (eds.). *Language and the Politics of Emotion.* Cambridge: Cambridge University Press, 1990.

Malinowski, Bronislaw. *Argonauts of the Western Pacific,* 1922. Reprint. New York: E. P. Dutton and Co., 1961.

———. *The Sexual Life of Savages in Northwestern Melanesia.* New York: Harcourt, Brace & World, 1929.

———. *Coral Gardens and Their Magic: A Study of the Methods of Tilling the Soil and of Agricultural Rites in the Trobriand Islands.* New York: American Book Co., 1935.

Mauss, Marcel. *The Gift,* 1925. Reprint. Translated by Ian Cunnison. London: Cohen & West, 1954.

Mead, Margaret. *Sex and Temperament in Three Primitive Societies,* 1935. Reprint. New York: Mentor Books, 1950.

Meggitt, Mervyn. "'Pigs Are Our Hearts!' The Te Exchange Cycle among the Mae Enga." *Human Ecology 1* (1974): no. 2.

———. *Blood Is Their Argument: Warfare among the Mae Enga Tribesmen of the New Guinea Highlands.* Palo Alto, Calif.: Mayfield Publishing Co., 1977.

Meillassoux, Claude. *Urbanization of an African Community: Voluntary Associations in Bamako.* Seattle: University of Washington Press, 1968.

Mitchell, J. Clyde. *The Kalela Dance: Aspects of Social Relationships among Urban Africans in Northern Rhodesia.* Manchester, England: Published on behalf of the Rhodes-Livingston Institute by Manchester University Press, 1956.

Moore, Omar Khayyam. "Divination: A New Perspective." *American Anthropologist 59* (1957): 69–74.

Morgan, Lewis Henry. *Ancient Society,* 1877. Reprint. New York: The World Publishing Company, 1963.

Munn, Nancy. "The Spatial Presentation of Cosmic Order in Walbiri Iconography." In *Primitive Art and Society,* edited by Anthony Forge. London: Oxford University Press, 1973.

Murphy, Yolanda, and Robert F. Murphy. *Women of the Forest.* New York: Columbia University Press, 1974, pp. 193–220.

Neville, Gwen Kennedy. *Kinship and Pilgrimage: Rituals of Reunion in American Protestant Culture.* London: Oxford University Press, 1987.

Newman, Katherine. *Falling from Grace: The Experience of Downward Mobility in the American Middle Class*. New York: The Free Press, 1988.

Nicholas, Ralph W. "Rules, Resources, and Political Activity." In *Local-Level Politics: Social and Cultural Perspectives*, edited by Marc J. Swartz. Chicago: Aldine, 1968, pp. 295–321.

O'Hanlon, Michael. *Reading the Skin: Adornment, Display and Society among the Wahgi*. London: British Museum Publications, 1989.

Ortner, Sherry B. "Theory in Anthropology since the Sixties." *Comparative Studies in Society and History 26* (1984): 126–165.

Perlman, Janice. *The Myth of Marginality: Urban Poverty and Politics in Rio de Janeiro*. Berkeley: University of California Press, 1976.

Peters, Emrys. "The Proliferation of Segments in the Lineage of the Bedouin of Cyrenaica." *Journal of the Royal Anthropological Institute of Great Britain and Ireland 90* (1960): 29–53.

Pitkin, Harvey. "Coyote and Bullhead: A Wintu Text." *Native American Text Series. International Journal of American Linguistics* 2.2, pp. 82–104. Chicago: University of Chicago Press, 1977.

Platt, Katherine. "Cognitive Development and Sex Roles on the Kerkennah Islands of Tunisia." In *Acquiring Culture: Cross-Cultural Studies in Child Development*, edited by Gustav Johada and I. M. Lewis. London: Croom Helm, 1988.

Podolefsky, Aaron. "Mediator Roles in Simbu Longfleet Management." *Ethnology 29* (1990): 67–82.

Powdermaker, Hortense. *Life in Lesu*, 1933. Reprint. New York: W. W. Norton and Co., 1971.

Poynton, Cate. *Language and Gender: Making the Difference*. London: Oxford University Press, 1989.

Price, Richard. *First Time: The Historical Vision of an Afro-American People*. Baltimore: Johns Hopkins University Press, 1983.

Price, Sally. *Primitive Art in Civilized Places*. Chicago: University of Chicago Press, 1989.

Radcliffe-Brown, A. R. *Structure and Function in Primitive Society*. Glencoe, Ill.: Free Press, 1952.

——— and Daryll Forde, eds. *African Systems of Kinship and Marriage*. London: Oxford University Press, 1950.

Rappaport, Roy A. *Pigs for the Ancestors: Ritual in the Ecology of a New Guinea People*, 2d ed. New Haven: Yale University Press, 1984.

Richards, Audrey. *Land, Labour and Diet in Northern Rhodesia: An Economic Study of the Bemba Tribe*. London: Oxford University Press, 1961.

Rosaldo, Michelle. "Towards an Anthropology of Self and Feeling." In *Culture Theory: Essays on Mind, Self and Emotion*, edited by Richard Shweder and Robert A. LeVine. Cambridge: Cambridge University Press, 1984.

Rosman, Abraham, and Paula G. Rubel. "Structural Patterning in Kwakiutl Art and Ritual." *Man 25* (1990): 620–640.

Sahlins, Marshall. *Stone Age Economics*. Chicago: Aldine-Atherton, 1972.

———. *Islands of History*. Chicago: University of Chicago Press, 1985.

Saussure, Ferdinand de. *Course in General Linguistics*, 1915. Reprint. New York: McGraw-Hill, 1966.

Schneider, David M. *American Kinship*, 2d ed. Chicago: University of Chicago Press, 1980.

————. *A Critique of the Study of Kinship.* Ann Arbor: University of Michigan Press, 1984.

Schramm, Adelaida. "Tradition in the Guise of Innovation: Music among a Refugee Population." *1986 Yearbook for Traditional Music,* pp. 91–101.

Sexton, Loraine. *Mothers of Money, Daughters of Coffee: The Wok Meri Movement.* Ann Arbor, Mich.: UMI Research Press, 1986.

Shweder, Richard, Manamohan Mahapatra, and Joan G. Miller. "Culture and Moral Development." In *Cultural Psychology: Essays on Comparative Human Development,* edited by James Stigler, Richard Shweder, and Gilbert Herdt. Cambridge: Cambridge University Press, 1990.

Smith, W. Robertson. *Lectures on the Religion of the Semites.* New York: D. Appleton & Co., 1889.

Spiro, Melford E. "Religion: Problems of Definition and Explanation." In *Anthropological Approaches to the Study of Religion,* edited by Michael Banton. A.S.A. Monograph no. 3. London: Tavistock Publications, 1966, pp. 85–126.

Stack, Carol B. *All Our Kin: Strategies for Survival in a Black Community.* New York: Harper & Row, 1974.

Steward, Julian. *Theory of Culture Change.* Urbana: University of Illinois Press, 1955.

Stigler, James, Richard A. Shweder, and Gilbert Herdt (eds.). *Culture Psychology Essays on Comparative Human Development.* Cambridge: Cambridge University Press, 1990.

Strathern, Andrew, and Marilyn Strathern. *Self-Decoration in Mount Hagen.* London: Gerald Duckworth, 1971.

Suttles, Gerald D. *The Social Order of the Slums: Ethnicity and Territory in the Inner City.* Chicago: The University of Chicago Press, 1968.

Tambiah, S. J. "Animals Are Good to Think About and Good to Prohibit." *Ethnology* 8 (1969): 423–459.

Turner, Victor. "Betwixt and Between: The Liminal Period in Rites de Passage." In his *The Forest of Symbols: Aspects of Ndembu Ritual.* Ithaca, N.Y.: Cornell University Press, 1967, pp. 93–111.

Tylor, Edward B. *Primitive Culture: Researches into the Development of Mythology, Philosophy, Religion, Language, Art and Custom,* 2 vols. London: John Murray, 1874.

Van Gennep, Arnold. *The Rites of Passage,* 1909. Translated by Monika B. Vizedom and Gabrielle Caffee. Chicago: University of Chicago Press, 1960.

Wallerstein, Immanuel M. *The Modern World System: Capitalist Agriculture and the Origins of the European World Economy in the Sixteenth Century.* New York: Academic Press, 1974.

Weber, Max. *The Protestant Ethic and the Spirit of Capitalism.* London: Allen & Unwin, 1930.

Weiner, Annette B. *Women of Value, Men of Renown: New Perspectives in Trobriand Exchange.* Austin: University of Texas Press, 1976.

West, C., and D. Zimmerman. "Women's Place in Everyday Talk: Reflections on Parent-Child Interaction." *Social Problems* 24 (1977): 521–529.

White, Leslie. *The Science of Culture.* New York: Farrar, Straus & Giroux, 1949.

————. *The Evolution of Culture.* New York: McGraw-Hill, 1959.

Whiting, John M. *Becoming a Kwoma.* New Haven, Conn.: Yale University Press, 1941.

————— and Irvin Child. *Child Training and Personality: A Cross-Cultural Study.* New Haven, Conn.: Yale University Press, 1953.

Wilson, Monica. *Good Company,* 1951. Reprint. Boston: Beacon Press, 1964.

—————. *For Men and Elders: Change in the Relations of Generations and of Men and Women among the Nyakyusa-Ngonde People 1875–1971.* International African Institute, 1977.

Wolf, Eric R. *Europe and the People without History.* Berkeley: University of California Press, 1982.

Wright, Will. *Sixguns and Society: A Structural Study of the Western.* Berkeley: University of California Press, 1975.

Young, Michael, and Peter Willmott. *Family and Kinship in East London.* Baltimore: Penguin Books, 1962.

Suggested Readings

Chapter 1: The Anthropological Point of View

Applebaum, Herbert (ed.). *Perspectives in Cultural Anthropology*. Albany: State University of New York Press, 1987.

A wide-ranging collection of articles on anthropological theory.

Bowen, Elenore Smith (Laura Bohannan). *Return to Laughter*. Garden City, N.Y.: Doubleday & Co., 1954.

The difficulties of doing fieldwork with the Tiv of Nigeria, related in the form of a painfully funny novel.

Crane, Julia, and Michael V. Angrosino. *Field Projects in Anthropology: A Student Handbook,* 2d ed. Prospect Heights, Ill.: Waveland Press, 1984.

A manual of field techniques in which data-collecting methods are illustrated by means of a series of student projects.

Ellen, R. F. (ed.). *Ethnographic Research: A Guide to General Conduct*. New York: Academic Press, 1984.

A general introduction to the procedures used in doing anthropological research and to the ethical issues raised.

Golde, Peggy (ed.). *Women in the Field,* 2d ed. Berkeley: University of California Press, 1986.

Female anthropologists' description of their experiences as participant observers and the problems of a woman doing fieldwork.

Hayano, David M. *Road through the Rain Forest: Living Anthropology in Highland Papua New Guinea*. Prospect Heights, Ill.: Waveland Press, 1990.

A narrative of fieldwork experiences among the Awa people of Papua New Guinea.

Jackson, Anthony (ed.). *Anthropology at Home*. London: Tavistock Press, 1987.
  The methodological and theoretical problems involved when anthropologists study their own culture, in this case in Great Britain.
Rabinow, Paul. *Reflections on Fieldwork in Morocco*. Berkeley: University of California Press, 1977.
  An anthropologist's account of the process of discovery involved in his Moroccan fieldwork, his penetration into the culture he is studying, and its effect upon him.
Sanjek, Roger (ed.). *Field Notes: The Makings of Anthropology*. Ithaca, N.Y.: Cornell University Press, 1990.
  Selections of articles by anthropologists on the problems of analyzing their field notes.

Chapter 2: Ritual in Small-Scale and Complex Societies: A Contrast

Bloch, Maurice, and Jonathan Parry (eds.). *Death and the Regeneration of Life*. Cambridge: Cambridge University Press, 1982.
  Analysis of rituals surrounding death in a number of different societies.
Codere, Helen. "Kwakiutl." In *Perspectives in American Indian Culture Change*, edited by Edward H. Spicer. Chicago: University of Chicago Press, 1961.
  An account of Kwakiutl culture change from the time of the Indians' initial contact with white society to the contemporary period.
Kottak, Conrad (ed.). *Researching American Culture*. Ann Arbor: The University of Michigan Press, 1982.
  The application of anthropological concepts to the study of American culture.
Malinowski, Bronislaw. *The Sexual Life of Savages*. New York: Harcourt, Brace & World, 1929.
  An ethnographic classic dealing with kinship and social organization, as well as sexual practices and love magic, of the Trobriand Islanders, a Melanesian society off the coast of New Guinea.
Spradley, James P., and Michael A. Rynkiewich. *The Nacirema: Readings on American Culture*. Boston: Little, Brown, 1975.
  A collection of articles dealing with various aspects of American culture.
Weiner, Annette B. *Women of Value, Men of Renown: New Perspectives in Trobriand Exchange*. Austin: University of Texas Press, 1976.
  A contemporary ethnography that not only brings Malinowski's account up to date but also focuses on the investigation of Trobriand society from the female point of view.

Chapter 3: Language and Culture

Chomsky, Noam. *Language and Mind*. New York: Harcourt, Brace, Jovanovich, 1972.
  The brilliant and provocative linguistic-philosopher's statement of his position on the relationship between mind and language.
Fishman, Joshua, et al. (eds.). *The Rise and Fall of the Ethnic Revival: Perspectives on Languages and Ethnicity*. Contributions to the Sociology of Language 37. New York: Mouton, 1985.
  Studies of the role language plays in the formation of ethnic identity.

Hickerson, Nancy. *Linguistic Anthropology*. New York: Holt, Rinehart & Winston, 1980.
A general introduction to linguistic anthropology.

Lutz, Catherine A., and Lila Abu-Lughod (eds.). *Language and the Politics of Emotion*. New York: Cambridge University Press, 1990.
Sociolinguistic analyses of the relationship between language and emotions.

Sapir, Edward. *Language*. New York: Harcourt, Brace and Co., 1949 (originally published in 1921).
The classic statement on language by a brilliant anthropological linguist.

Chapter 4: Symbolic Systems and Meanings

Douglas, Mary. *Natural Symbols: Explorations in Cosmology*. New York: Pantheon Books, 1970.
How different cultures use such natural symbols as the human body to speak about social relationships and social experience.

———— (ed.). *Food in the Social Order: Studies of Food and Festivities in Three American Communities*. New York: Russell Sage Foundation, 1984.
Studies of the eating patterns of Lakota, Italian-Americans, and rural Southern Americans, and their symbolic significance.

Firth, Raymond. *Symbols: Public and Private*. Ithaca, N.Y.: Cornell University Press, 1973.
An examination of the history of the study of symbolism and the scope of the application of symbolic analysis in contemporary anthropology.

Geertz, Clifford. *The Interpretation of Culture*. New York: Basic Books, 1973.
————. *Local Knowledge: Further Essays in Interpretive Anthropology*. New York: Basic Books, 1983.
Two collections of essays by the leading proponent of the culture-as-symbols school.

Guttmann, Allen. *A Whole New Ball Game: An Interpretation of American Sports*. Chapel Hill, N.C.: University of North Carolina Press, 1988.
A historical and sociological study of American sports, which relates it to its cultural context.

Leach, Edmund. *Culture and Communication: The Logic by Which Symbols Are Connected*. Cambridge: Cambridge University Press, 1976.
An extended essay on how meanings are communicated, presented from a structuralist point of view.

Turner, Victor. *The Ritual Process: Structure and Antistructure*. Chicago: Aldine Publishing Co., 1969.
A series of lectures by a leading proponent of symbolic analysis.

Chapter 5: Family, Marriage, and Kinship

Barnard, Alan, and Anthony Good. *Research Practices in the Study of Kinship*. New York: Academic Press, 1984.
A description of the procedures involved in the anthropological study of kinship.

Fox, Robin. *Kinship and Marriage: An Anthropological Perspective*. Baltimore: Penguin Books, 1967. Reissued by Cambridge University Press, 1983.
A clear and wittily written introduction to the field of kinship, social structure, and marriage.

Goody, Jack. *The Development of the Family and Marriage in Europe*. Cambridge: Cambridge University Press, 1983.
A historical study of changing kinship, family, and marriage patterns in Europe.

Radcliffe-Brown, A. R., and Daryll Forde (eds.). *African Systems of Kinship and Marriage*. London: Oxford University Press, 1950.
A series of detailed analytical essays about the kinship and marriage systems of nine different African societies, with a lengthy introduction by Radcliffe-Brown in which he expounds his theoretical approach to the subject.

Stack, Carol B. *All Our Kin: Strategies for Survival in a Black Community*. New York: Harper & Row, 1974.
An ethnographic analysis of kin and nonkin relationships of black families in a Midwestern urban ghetto and how these relationships constitute an adaptation to conditions of poverty.

Chapter 6: Gender and Age

Atkinson, Jane M., and Shelly Errington (eds.). *Power and Difference: Gender in Island Southeast Asia*. Stanford: Stanford University Press, 1990.
Articles about difference and power as they relate to men and women in island Southeast Asia.

Collier, Jane Fishburne, and Sylvia Junko Yanagisako (eds.). *Gender and Kinship: Essays towards a Unified Analysis*. Stanford: Stanford University Press, 1987.
Gender viewed from the perspective of a redefined approach to kinship. Articles from a conference.

Eisenstadt, S. N. *From Generation to Generation: Age Groups and Social Structure*. Glencoe, Ill.: The Free Press, 1956.
An interesting comparative study of age grades and youth movements, using examples ranging from small-scale societies like the Nandi and the Nyakyusa to complex societies like Israel and Germany, in an attempt to specify the social conditions under which they arise.

MacCormack, Carol, and Marilyn Strathern (eds.). *Nature, Culture and Gender*. Cambridge: Cambridge University Press, 1980.
Reconsideration of the categories of "nature" and "culture" and their association with gender symbolism in different societies.

Martin, Emily. *The Woman in the Body: A Cultural Analysis of Reproduction*. Boston: Beacon Press, 1987.
The relationship between women's views of menstruation, childbirth, and menopause and production metaphors in American culture.

Ortner, Sherry, and Harriet Whitehead (eds.). *Sexual Meanings: The Cultural Construction of Gender and Sexuality*. Cambridge: Cambridge University Press, 1981.
A series of essays dealing with how sex and gender are conceptualized and socially organized in various cultures.

Tiffany, Sharon. *Women, Work, and Motherhood: The Power of Female Sexuality in the Workplace*. Englewood Cliffs, N.J.: Prentice-Hall, 1982.
A consideration of anthropological contributions to the study of women from the feminist perspective.

Chapter 7: Provisioning Society: Production, Distribution, and Consumption

Firth, Raymond. *Primitive Polynesian Economy*, 2d ed. London: Routledge & Kegan Paul, 1965.
    A richly detailed account of the economic system of Tikopia, an island in Polynesia.

Gudeman, Stephan. *Economics as Culture: Models and Metaphors of Livelihood*. London: Routledge & Kegan Paul, 1986.
    An argument in favor of accepting the "native's" point of view of the economic system.

Maclachlan, Morgan (ed.). *Household Economies and Their Transformations*. Monographs in Economic Anthropology no. 3, University Press of America, 1987.
    How the household functions as a unit within the economic system, and how this has changed.

Plattner, Stuart (ed.). *Economic Anthropology*. Stanford: Stanford University Press, 1989.
    Coverage of the various subtopics of economic anthropology.

Rosman, Abraham, and Paula G. Rubel. *Feasting with Mine Enemy: Rank and Exchange among Northwest Coast Societies*. New York: Columbia University Press, 1971.
    An analysis of the potlatch in six Northwest Coast societies that shows the relationship between the social structure and the potlatch in each society.

Schire, Carmel (ed.). *Past and Present in Hunter Gatherer Studies*. New York: Academic Press, 1984.
    Hunter gatherer societies and their relationship to the outside world, viewed archaeologically, historically, and ethnographically.

Chapter 8: Political Organization: Politics, Government, Law, and Conflict

Fried, Morton H. *The Evolution of Political Society*. New York: Random House, 1967.
    A discussion of the evolution of political systems from simple egalitarian societies to states.

Leach, Edmund. *Political Systems of Highland Burma: A Study of Kachin Social Structure*. Boston: Beacon Press, 1965.
    An ethnography of a hill tribe of Burma, in which the political system is described in relation to kinship, social structure, and economic and religious systems.

Lewellen, Ted C. *Political Anthropology: An Introduction*. South Hadley, Mass.: Bergin and Garvey, 1983.
    A recent introduction to the concepts, theories, and methods of political anthropology.

Swartz, Marc J. (ed.). *Local-Level Politics*. Chicago: Aldine Publishing Co., 1968.
    A collection of papers dealing with how political power is acquired and used in small communities that are part of larger political entities.

Vincent, Joan. *Anthropology and Politics: Visions, Traditions and Trends*. Tucson: University of Arizona Press, 1990.
    A critical review of the anthropological study of politics from 1879 to the present.

Chapter 9: Religion and the Supernatural

Banton, Michael (ed.). *Anthropological Approaches to the Study of Religion*. Association of Social Anthropologists, Monograph no. 3. London: Tavistock Publications, 1966.

Durkheim, Émile. *The Elementary Forms of the Religious Life*, 1915. Reprint. Translated by Joseph W. Swain. New York: Free Press, 1965.
   The French anthropologist's classic study putting forth his general theory of religion, drawing many of his examples from native Australian societies.

Evans-Pritchard, E. E. *Witchcraft, Oracles and Magic among the Azande*. Oxford: Clarendon Press, 1937.
   A classic study of witchcraft in a Central African society by a British social anthropologist.

Hogbin, Ian. *The Island of Menstruating Men: Religion in Wogeo, New Guinea*. Scranton, Pa.: Chandler Publishing Co., 1970.
   A fascinating account of the religious system of an island society off New Guinea in which men ritually "menstruate."

Lehmann, Arthur, and James E. Myers (eds.). *Magic, Witchcraft and Religion: An Anthropological Study of the Supernatural*. Palo Alto, Calif.: Mayfield Publishing Co., 1985.
   A collection including classic and recent writings on religion, religious specialists, ethnomedicine, religious use of drugs, and other topics.

Lessa, William A., and Evon Z. Vogt (eds.). *Reader in Comparative Religion: An Anthropological Approach*, 3d ed. New York: Harper & Row, 1972.
   A broad-ranging compendium of writings on religion, symbolism, myth, ritual, magic, and witchcraft.

Malinowski, Bronislaw. *Magic, Science and Religion*. Boston: Beacon Press, 1948.
   Several essays by a pioneer anthropologist that discuss magic, science, and religion, using examples from the Trobriand Islands.

Stephen, Michele (ed.). *Sorcerer and Witch in Melanesia*. New Brunswick, N.J.: Rutgers University Press, 1987.
   Recent essays on the cultural contexts of witchcraft and sorcery in Melanesia.

Turner, Victor (ed.). *Celebration: Studies in Festivity and Ritual*. Washington, D.C.: Smithsonian Institution Press, 1982.
   A series of case studies of religious celebrations and rites of passage.

Chapter 10: Myths, Legends, and Folktales

Dundes, Alan. *Essays in Folkloristics*. Dehli: Folklore Institute, 1978.
   An anthology of some of the important essays on various aspects of the study of folklore by the outstanding American folklorist.

———— and Carl R. Pagter. *When You're Up To Your Ass in Alligators: More Urban Folklore from the Paperwork Empire*. Detroit, Mich.: Wayne State University Press, 1987.
   A sampling of urban office folklore, passed on by way of the office copier.

Lévi-Strauss, Claude. *The Savage Mind*. Chicago: The University of Chicago Press, 1966.
   An exposition of Lévi-Strauss's structuralist theoretical framework for the analysis of myth, symbols, and systems of classification.

Maranda, Pierre (ed.). *Mythology: Selected Readings*. Baltimore: Penguin Books, 1972.
   A broad-ranging compilation of essays and selections from books dealing with mythology and folklore.

Chapter 11: The Artistic Dimension

Boas, Franz. *Primitive Art,* 1927. Reprint. New York: Dover Publications, 1955.
A seminal volume on primitive art by a pioneer in the field, with emphasis on the art of the Pacific Northwest, where Boas did fieldwork.

Feld, Steven. *Sound and Sentiment: Birds, Weeping, Poetics, and Song in Kaluli Expression.* Philadelphia: University of Pennsylvania Press, 1982.
An innovative ethnography on the relationship between song and emotion among the Kaluli of Papua New Guinea.

Hatcher, Evalyn P. *Art as Culture: An Introduction to the Anthropology of Art.* Lanham, Md.: University Press of America, 1985.
A general introduction to the anthropological study of art.

Jonaitis, Aldona. *Art of the Northern Tlingit.* Seattle: University of Washington Press, 1986.
A creative analysis of the art of the Tlingit of the Northwest Coast.

Layton, Robert. *The Anthropology of Art.* New York: Columbia University Press, 1981.
A discussion of the ways of assessing works of art produced by cultures other than our own.

Lips, Julius. *The Savage Hits Back,* 1937. New Hyde Park, N.Y.: University Books, 1966.
A fascinating study of how colonized people portray their conquerors in sculpture and painting.

Nettl, Bruno. *The Study of Ethnomusicology: Twenty-nine Issues and Concepts.* Urbana, Ill.: University of Illinois Press, 1983.
A general work by the foremost American authority in the field of ethnomusicology.

Price, Sally. *Primitive Art in Civilized Places.* Chicago: University of Chicago Press, 1989.
A discussion of the relationship between Western viewers and non-Western art objects and their creators.

Chapter 12: Culture and the Individual

Bock, Philip K. *Continuities in Psychological Anthropology: A Historical Introduction.* San Francisco: W. H. Freeman, 1980.
An excellent introduction to the history of psychological anthropology.

Erikson, Erik H. *Childhood and Society,* 2d ed. New York: W. W. Norton & Co., 1963.
The theoretical approach of a contemporary Freudian psychoanalyst who has been much influenced by contacts with cultural anthropologists, containing case studies of the Sioux and the Yurok.

LeVine, Robert A. (ed.). *Culture and Personality: Contemporary Readings.* Chicago: Aldine, 1974.
A collection of articles that attempts to present a contemporary picture of research in the field of culture and personality.

Mead, Margaret. *Growing Up in New Guinea,* 1930. Reprint. New York: Mentor Books, 1960.
One of the earliest anthropological studies of how a child is socialized into a non-Western culture.

Valsiner, Jaan (ed.). *Child Development in Cultural Contexts.* Toronto: Hogrefe, 1989.
Selections examining child development in a number of different cultures.

Wagner, Daniel A., and Harold Stevenson (eds.). *Cultural Perspectives on Child Development*. San Francisco: W. H. Freeman & Co., 1982.
First-hand accounts of cross-cultural research on child development.

White, Geoffrey M., and John Kirkpatrick (eds.). *Person, Self, and Experience: Exploring Pacific Ethnopsychologies*. Berkeley: University of California Press, 1987.
Essays on indigenous concepts of self and person among various peoples in Oceania.

Chapter 13: Fourth World Peoples in Colonial and Postcolonial Periods

Deloria, Vine, Jr., and Clifford M. Lytte. *American Indians, American Justice*. Austin, Texas: University of Texas Press, 1983.
An exploration of the complexities of the present-day Indian situation, particularly with regard to legal and political rights.

Eddy, Elizabeth M., and William Partridge (eds.). *Applied Anthropology in America*, 2d ed. New York: Columbia University Press, 1987.
A broad-ranging collection of readings by some of the anthropologists who have been prominently involved in the applied field.

Grillo, Ralph, and Alan Rew. *Social Anthropology and Development Policy*. London: Tavistock Press, 1985.
Case studies of development in the Third World which discuss the fundamental issues of policy formation, implementation, and the ethics of collaboration with governments.

Handler, Jerome. *The Unappropriated People: Freedmen in the Slave Society of Barbados*. Baltimore: Johns Hopkins University Press, 1974.
A carefully detailed study of plantation slavery and its aftermath in the Caribbean island society of Barbados.

Jorgensen, Joseph G. *The Sun Dance Religion: Power for the Powerless*. Chicago: University of Chicago Press, 1972.
A study of the response of the Utes, which takes the form of a nativistic movement, to the increasingly oppressive domination of the larger American society.

Little, Peter D., and Michael M. Horowitz. *Lands at Risk in the Third World: Local Level Perspectives*. Boulder, Colo.: Westview Press, 1987.
Essays highlighting social, economic, political, and biological dimensions of environmental degradation in a number of Third World countries.

Spring, Anita. *Agricultural Development in Malawi: A Project for Women in Development*. Boulder, Colo.: Westview Press, 1987.
A description of the process by which women were successfully integrated into an agricultural development project in Malawi.

Stull, Donald D., and Jean J. Schensul (eds.). *Collaborative Research and Social Change: Applied Anthropology in Action*. Boulder, Colo.: Westview Press, 1987.
Case studies of long-term community research, involving close cooperation between researchers and representatives of the host community.

Wallerstein, Immanuel M. *The Modern World System: Capitalist Agriculture and the Origins of the European World Economy in the Sixteenth Century*. New York: Academic Press, 1974.
A historical account tracing the evolution and distinctive characteristics of capitalist world economy from the sixteenth century to the present, demonstrating how tribal peoples are increasingly integrated into a single world economy.

Wolf, Eric. *Europe and the People without History.* Berkeley: University of California Press, 1982.

An analytical history of the relationship between the West and the societies of Asia, Africa, and the Americas.

Worsley, Peter. *The Trumpet Shall Sound: A Study of Cargo Cults in Melanesia,* 2d ed. New York: Schocken Books, 1968.

A comparative analysis of cargo cults that examines their history and relates them to the changing economic and political situation.

Wulff, Robert, and Shirley Fiske (eds.). *Anthropological Praxis: Translating Knowledge into Action.* Boulder, Colo.: Westview Press, 1987.

In-depth studies demonstrating the way in which anthropological knowledge is applicable to real-life situations.

Chapter 14: The Anthropology of Contemporary Life

Harris, Rosemary. *Power and Powerlessness in Industry: An Analysis of the Social Relations of Production.* London: Tavistock, 1987.

A description of two manufacturing plants which are technologically similar but culturally different.

Klass, Morton. *From Field to Factory: Community Structure and Industrialization in West Bengal.* Philadelphia: ISHI, 1978.

A study of the effects of the introduction of a modern bicycle factory on the life of rural Bengali villagers in India.

Kugelmass, Jack. *The Miracle of Intervale Avenue: The Story of a Jewish Congregation in the South Bronx.* New York: Schocken Books, 1986.

A sensitive portrait of the last Jewish congregation, composed of elderly Jews, in the South Bronx.

Southall, Aidan (ed.). *Urban Anthropology: Cross-Cultural Studies of Urbanization.* New York: Oxford University Press, 1973.

A collection of readings in urban anthropology that presents a variety of ethnographic accounts as well as various diverse problem-oriented investigations, from regional associations to residential instability.

Taussig, Michael. *The Devil and Commodity Fetishism in South America.* Chapel Hill, N.C.: University of North Carolina Press, 1980.

How the peasants of Bolivia and Colombia conceptualize the Capitalist mentality in terms of a pact with the devil.

Wallace, Ben J., Rosie M. Ahsan, Shahnaz H. Hussain, and Ekramul Ahsan. *The Invisible Resource: Women and Work in Rural Bangladesh.* Boulder, Colo.: Westview Press, 1987.

A description of the economic activities of women in rural Bangladesh and the implications of their role for government policies and aid programs.

Wolf, Eric R. *Peasants.* Englewood Cliffs, N.J.: Prentice-Hall, 1966.

A brief but comprehensive analysis of the nature of peasant society as a type of organization by one of the outstanding authorities on the subject.

Glossary

acculturation   the process of culture change resulting from the contact between two cultures.

achieved status   position in a social structure dependent upon personal qualifications and individual ability.

adaptation   the process in which a population or society alters its culture to better succeed in its total environment.

affinal links   connections between kin groups established by marriage.

age grades   categories of individuals of the same age that are recognized by being given a name and that crosscut an entire society.

age set   a group of individuals of the same age that moves as a unit through successive age grades.

alliance   a linkage between kin groups established through marriage for the mutual benefit of the two groups.

allophone   a variant form of a phoneme.

ancestor-oriented group   a social unit that traces kin relationships back to a common ancestor.

animism   a belief in the spiritual or noncorporeal counterparts of human beings.

applied anthropology   the use of anthropological ideas to solve practical social problems.

ascribed status   an inherited position in the social structure.

authority   an institutionalized position of power.

avunculocal residence   a form of postmarital residence in which the bride goes to live with her husband after he has moved to live with his mother's brother.

band organization   a type of social group with a fixed membership that comes together annually for a period of time to carry out joint ritual and economic activities.

Big Man structure   an achieved position of leadership in which the group is defined as the Big Man and his followers.

bilateral cross cousins   cross cousins through both the mother's and father's side.

bilateral societies   societies with kindreds but without unilineal descent groups.

bilocal residence   a form of postmarital residence in which husband and wife alternate between living with the husband's relatives for a period of time and then with the wife's relatives.

boundary maintenance mechanisms   the ways in which a social group maintains its individual identity by separating itself from the dominant society.

bride service   a custom whereby the groom works for the bride's family before marriage.

bridewealth payments   payments made by the groom's family to the family of the bride.

cargo cult   a particular type of revitalization movement that first appeared in the early twentieth century in Melanesia and represents a synthesis of old and new religious beliefs.

caste system   a grouping of economically specialized, hierarchically organized, endogamous social units.

chieftainship   a type of political organization in which fixed positions of leadership are present along with a method for succession to those positions.

clan   a social group based on common descent but not necessarily common residence.

clan totem   an animal from which members of a clan believe themselves descended and with whom they have a special relationship that may prohibit the eating of that animal.

cognatic rule of descent   a rule of descent in which group membership may be traced through either the father or mother.

collateral relative   a relative not in the direct line of descent.

community   a naturally bounded social unit.

compadrazgo   ritual godparenthood found in Mediterranean Europe and Latin America.

components   the criteria used to characterize and differentiate any kind of category.

corporate descent group   a social group based upon common descent that owns property in common and extends beyond the lifetime of any one individual.

cross cousins   children of one's mother's brother or one's father's sister.

cultural relativism   the emphasis on the unique aspects of each culture, without judgments or categories based on our culture.

cultural rules   internalized rules of behavior covering all aspects of life.

culture   the way of life of a people, including their behavior, the things they make, and their ideas.

culture of poverty   the cultural characteristics of poor people in urban environments of industrialized societies.

dala   the Trobriand matrilineal subclan.

delayed exchange   the return of goods or of women a generation after their giving; associated with preference for marriage with father's sister's daughter.

demonstrated descent   descent in which kinship can be traced by means of written or oral genealogies back to a founding ancestor.

dialects   variations within a single language between one speech community and another.

diffusion   the process by means of which a culture trait that originates in one society spreads to another.

directed culture change   see *applied anthropology.*

distinctive features   see *components.*

distribution   the manner in which products circulate through a society.

double descent   the presence of matrilineal and patrilineal descent rules in a single society.

dowry   goods that are given by the bride's family to the groom's family at marriage.

duolocal residence   a postmarital rule of residence in which husband and wife live with their respective kinsmen, apart from one another.

ebene   hallucinogenic substance used by the Yanomamo.

ego-oriented group   a kinship unit defined in terms of a particular ego.

enculturation   the process by which culture is learned and acquired by particular individuals.

endogamy   a rule requiring group members to marry within their own group.

ethnocentrism   the idea that what is present in your own culture represents the natural and best way to do things.

ethnosemantics   the anthropological investigation of native systems of classification.

exogamy   a rule requiring group members to marry outside their own social group.

extended family   several related nuclear families living together in a single household.

favelas   squatter settlements in Latin American cities.

Fourth World peoples   oppressed tribal peoples living in Third World nations.

fraternal polyandry   a form of marriage in which a woman is simultaneously married to several brothers.

function   the way a particular unit or structure operates and what it does.

generalized exchange   a form of marriage in which women move from wife-givers to wife-takers, but never in the opposite direction.

government   the process by which those in office make and implement decisions on behalf of an entire group in order to carry out commonly held goals.

grammar   the complete description of a language, including phonology, morphology, and syntax.

Great Tradition   an elite version of an overarching historical civilization.

guardian spirit   among North American native peoples, an animal spirit that becomes the protector of an individual as a result of his quest for a vision.

gumlao   the egalitarian form of the Kachin political organization.

gumsa   the chieftainship form of the Kachin political organization, in which wife-givers are higher in rank than wife-takers.

hekura   small, humanlike supernatural creatures that are part of the Yanomamo religious belief system.

hortatory ritual   an exhortation to the supernatural to perform some act.

horticulture   a form of cultivation in which crops are grown in gardens without the use of a plow.

incest taboo   prohibition on sexual relations between certain categories of close relatives.

influence   the ability to persuade others to follow one's lead without the authority to command them.

innovation   the process of bringing about cultural change through the recombination of existing ideas into creative new forms.

joint family   a type of extended family in which married brothers and their families remain together after the death of their parents.

kaiko   a lengthy Maring religious ceremony.

kayasa   a competitive period of feasting, including a competitive giving of yams to the chief, and games like cricket among the Trobrianders.

kindred   a kin group oriented in terms of a particular individual.

kinship terminology   a set of terms used to refer to relatives.

kula   an exchange system involving one kind of shell valuables moving in a clockwise direction and another kind moving in a counterclockwise direction, which links the Trobriand Islanders to a circle of neighboring islands.

levirate   a rule whereby the widow of a deceased man must marry his brother.

lewa   Wogeo spirits represented by masks.

liminal period   the "in-between" stage in a rite-of-passage ceremony when the individual has not yet been reincorporated into society.

lineages   unilineal descent groups where descent is demonstrated.

lineal relative   a relative in the direct line of descent.

linguistic relativity   a point of view that emphasizes the uniqueness of each language and the need to examine it in its own terms.

Little Tradition   the folk version of a Great Tradition. The way in which the peasantry of each region interprets the civilization of which it is a part.

malanggan   term that refers to New Ireland mortuary ritual, as well as the carvings displayed at such a ritual.

mana   belief in an impersonal supernatural force or power that is found in all aspects of nature.

manau   a Kachin religious ceremony consisting of a feast and sacrifice to the spirits.

markedness   the process whereby a category (the marked category) is distinguished from a larger, more inclusive category (the unmarked category) by the presence of a single attribute.

matrilineal rule of descent   a rule stating that a child belongs to his or her mother's group.

maximizing   the concept in economic anthropology whereby individuals are seen as interpreting economic rules to their own advantage.

mayu/dama   Kachin lineage categories; wife-giving lineages are *mayu*, and wife-taking lineages are *dama*.

metaphor   an analytical concept in which one idea stands for another because of some similarity they are seen to share.

metonym   the symbolic substitution of one of the constituent parts for the whole.

moieties   a grouping based upon descent in which the entire society is divided into two halves.

monogamy   marriage with only one spouse at a time.

morpheme   the smallest unit of a language conveying meaning.

nativistic movements religious cults that develop in periods of drastic cultural change and synthesize traditional cultural elements with newly introduced ones.

nats spirits of the Kachin supernatural world.

neolocal residence a rule of postmarital residence in which the newly married couple forms an independent household.

nibek Wogeo spirits represented by flutes.

nomadic pastoralists societies completely, or almost completely, dependent upon herds of domesticated animals.

nuclear family a family consisting of husband, wife, and their unmarried children.

numaym cognatic descent group of the Kwakiutl.

office a recognized political position.

parallel cousins the children of two brothers or of two sisters.

participant observation the anthropological method of collecting data by living with another people, learning their language, and understanding their culture.

patrilineal rule of descent a rule stating that a child belongs to his or her father's group.

patron-client relationship a hierarchical relationship in which the superior (the patron) acts as an intermediary and protector of the inferior (the client) vis-à-vis the national government.

phonemes the minimal sound units that make up a language.

politics the competition for political positions and for power.

polyandry marriage in which one woman has several husbands at one time.

polygamy marriage with plural spouses, either husbands or wives.

polygyny marriage in which one man has several wives at one time.

Poro Society secret society associated with the use of masks, found in Liberia and Sierra Leone.

postmarital residence rule a rule that states where a couple should live after marriage.

postpeasants a term characterizing the life of peasants in contemporary industrial society.

potlatch a large-scale ceremonial distribution of goods found among the indigenous peoples of the Northwest Coast of North America.

power the ability to command others to do certain things and get compliance from them.

primogeniture a rule of inheritance of property or office by the firstborn child.

private symbols symbols that individuals create out of their own experience and that they do not share with other members of their society.

production the process whereby a society uses the tools and energy sources at its disposal and its own people's labor to create the goods necessary for supplying itself.

proto-language ancestral form of a language arrived at by reconstruction.

public symbols symbols used and understood by the members of a society.

reciprocal exchange a continuing exchange of like for like between two parties.

restricted exchange a marriage pattern in which sisters continue to be exchanged between two sides over the generations.

revitalization movement see *nativistic movements.*

rites of intensification communal rituals celebrated at various points in the yearly cycle.

rites of passage   communal rituals held to mark changes in status as individuals progress through the life cycle.

sagali   a large-scale ceremonial distribution among the Trobriand Islanders.

segmentary lineage system   a descent system, typically patrilineal, in which the largest segments are successively divided into smaller segments, like the branches of a tree.

serial polygamy   the practice of marrying a series of spouses, one after the other.

shaman   a ritual specialist whose primary function is to cure illness.

shifting cultivation   a type of horticulture in which new gardens are made every few years, when the soil is exhausted.

sister exchange   a marriage pattern in which two men marry each other's sisters.

situational leadership   a type of political organization in which there is no single political leader but rather leadership is manifested intermittently.

social role   the behavior associated with a particular social status in a society.

social status   the position an individual occupies in a society.

social structure   the pattern of social relationships that characterizes a society.

society   a social grouping characterizing humans and other social animals, differentiated by age and sex.

sorcery   the learned practice of evil magic.

sororal polygamy   the marriage of a man to several sisters.

sororate   the custom whereby a widower marries his deceased wife's sister.

squatter settlements   illegal housing usually built on wasteland on the outskirts of cities.

status personality   the characteristic personality associated with a social position.

stem family   a two-generation extended family consisting of parents and only one married son and his family.

stipulated descent   a social unit such as a clan, in which all members consider themselves to be related though they cannot actually trace the genealogical relationship.

structure   a description of parts or elements in relationship to one another.

style   a characterization of the component elements of art and the way those elements are put together.

suaboya   the single kinship term that the Yanomamo use for both female cross cousin and wife.

subcultural variation   cultural differences between communities within a single society.

swidden   see *shifting cultivation.*

te   the ceremonial distribution of pigs and pork among the Mae Enga of Papua New Guinea

technology   that part of culture by means of which people directly exploit their environment.

tschambura   among the Abelam, partners who exchange long yams with one another.

ultimogeniture   a rule of inheritance of property or office by the lastborn child.

unilineal descent group   a kin group such as a clan where membership is based on either matrilineal or patrilineal descent.

urigubu   a Trobriand harvest gift given yearly by a man to his sister's husband.

uxorilocal residence   a rule of postmarital residence whereby the newly married couple resides with the relatives of the bride.

virilocal residence a rule of postmarital residence whereby the newly married couple resides with the relatives of the groom.

vision quest the search for a protective supernatural spirit through starvation and deprivation

warabwa large-scale ceremonial distribution in Wogeo.

witchcraft a form of magic practiced by individuals born with this ability.

zadruga a Yugoslavian virilocal extended family.

Photo Credits

4   By courtesy of the Trustees of the British Museum
12   Abraham Rosman
27   By courtesy of the Rare Book Division, the New York Public Library, Astor, Lenox and Tilden Foundations
29   The American Museum of Natural History
31   By courtesy of the Rare Book Division, the New York Public Library, Astor, Lenox and Tilden Foundations
38   By courtesy of the Sterling Memorial Library, Manuscripts and Archives, Yale University
39   By courtesy of the Sterling Memorial Library, Manuscripts and Archives, Yale University
63   Abraham Rosman
68   Peter Buckley/Photo Researchers
69   Newberry Library
77   Abraham Rosman
83   Irven DeVore/Anthro-Photo
103 Dorka Raynor
112 Sussman/The Image Works
118 By courtesy of the Smithsonian Institution, National Anthropological Archive
124 By courtesy of the American Museum of Natural History
132 Abraham Rosman
137 Abraham Rosman
140 Abraham Rosman

143   By courtesy of the Bancroft Library, University of California at Berkeley
147   By courtesy of the Sterling Memorial Library, Manuscripts and Archives, Yale University
162   Abraham Rosman
163   Richard Harrington/Globe Photos
169   Abraham Rosman
172   Marc and Evelyne Bernheim/Woodfin Camp & Associates
175   Napoleon Chagnon/Anthro-Photo
184   Bill Strode/Black Star
185   James Holland/Black Star
191   By courtesy of Ian Hogbin
197   Abraham Rosman
200   By courtesy of the Department of Library Services, the American Museum of Natural History
211   By courtesy of Ian Hogbin
216   By courtesy of the Peabody Museum, Salem, Massachusetts. Photograph by Mark Sexton
221   By courtesy of the Print Collection, the New York Public Library
226   From *Images: Stone: B.C.* by Duff Wilson. By courtesy of Hancock House Publishers, copyright © 1975
229   By courtesy of the Peabody Museum, Harvard University. Photograph by F. P. Orchard
231   By courtesy of the American Museum of Natural History
233   *(Top)* Franz Boas, *The Kwakiutl of Vancouver Island,* 1909

        (Bottom) Franz Boas, *The Social Organization and Secret Societies of the Kwakiutl Indians,* 1897
235   Illustration from *Primitive Art* by Franz Boas (Oslo, 1927)
237   "The Raven and the First Men" by Bill Reid. Courtesy of the University of British Columbia Museum of Anthropology, Vancouver, B.C. Photograph by W. McLennan
239   By courtesy of the American Museum of Natural History
240   Abraham Rosman
242   Abraham Rosman
244   Abraham Rosman
251   Blair Seitz/Photo Researchers
253   Abraham Rosman
270   From *Drawings Illustrative of Cook's First Voyage,* fol. 11. Reproduced by permission of the British Library, London
278   Library of Congress
287   Abraham Rosman
291   Lynn McLaren/Rapho/Photo Researchers
293   Grunzweig/Photo Researchers
300   Victor Engebert/Photo Researchers
305   Christoph/Black Star

Index

Abelam (New Guinea), 3; Big Men, 161, 162; eating symbolism, 61, 152; exchange system, 136–138, 140, 141, 149, 152, 161; horticulture, 127; moieties, 92; *tshambura*, 136, 152
Achieved status, 161
Admiralty Islands, 249, 251–252
Adolescence: initiation of (*see* Initiation rites); personality studies, 249–250
Aesthetic impulse, 225
Affines and affinal links, 87, 94, 139, 142, 149
Afghanistan, 11
Age associations, 117–120
Age differences, 8
Age grades, 114–117, 195
Age of Exploration, 267–268
Agriculture, 125–129, 148; irrigation, 128–129; mechanization, 129
"Airport art," 241
Akhnaton, pharaoh, 258
Akure (Nigeria), 172
Albanians, 104–105
Algonquins (Northeast America), 257
Alliance, 94, 98
Allomorphs, 48

Allophones, 47
Allotment Act of 1887, 272
Amazon Indians, 267, 269
Amazons, 215
American culture, 6; bilateral society, 92; childbirth, 113; food in, 62; funeral in, 40–43, 74, 152, 197; gender roles, 112–113; generational conflict, 117; kinship relationships, 105–107, 112–113; kinship terminology, 98–101; language, 53; legends and folktales in, 219–223; marriage in, 32–36, 74, 79, 243–244; native culture and, 265; political factionalism, 181–182; religion and, 208; rites of intensification, 198; rites of passage, 197; sports symbolism, 70–71; witchcraft, 183 , 184
American Historical approach, 19–20
American Indians (*see* Native Americans)
American kinship, 22
Amish, 75, 232, 294
Amok, 257
Ancestor-oriented kindred, 92
Ancestral spirits, 189
Andaman Islanders, 20
Anger, 255

Animals: classification of, 64; domestication of, 129–133, 289; edibility of, 61, 64–65; farm, 64–65; game, 65; naming of, 50; pets, 64; societies, 8, 16; stock reduction programs, 289–290; symbolism of, 62–64, 67; totemic, 62–64, 86, 189
Animism, 189–190, 192
Anonymous art, 237–238
Anthropological linguistics, 15
Anthropological theory, 17–24; American Historical approach, 19–20; cultural evolution, 17–19; functionalism, 20–21; other approaches, 21–24; structuralism, 21
Anthropology: basic concepts of, 5–11; cultural, 15; discipline of, 15–16; ethnohistory, 22; fieldwork in, 11–15; informant's role in, 13–15; and insights to own culture, 311–312; interpretive, 22–23; Marxist, 153; method of, 1, 11–15; physical, 15; political, 157–159, 179; practice of, 16; symbolic, 21–22; units of analysis, 10–11
Anxiety: religion and, 207
Apache (Southwest U.S.), 55–56, 275
'Aqqara tribe, 91
Arabs: Marsh (Iraq), 131, 133. (*See also* Bedouin)
Arapaho, 117
Arapesh (New Guinea), 3; eating symbolism, 61, 152; gender roles, 111, 161, 249; patrilineal descent, 86, 161, 195; rites of passage, 195–196; sister exchange, 76, 94
Arawaks (Caribbean), 276
Archaeology, 15, 268
Arctic hysteria, 257
Arnhem Land (Australia), 234
Artistic expression, 225–246; as comunication, 233–234; music and dance, 242–246; visual arts (sculpture and painting), 226–242
Artistic standards, 234
Artistic style, 235–237
Artists: status and role of, 230, 245–246
Ascribed status, 161
Ashanti (Ghana), 3, 81
Associations: based on age, 117–120; ethnic and regional, 305–307; tribal, 306–307; voluntary, 306–307
Athapaskan language, 56
Atkinson, Jane M., 110
Atlantis legend, 210
Augurs, 202

Australia: labor exploitation, 277; and New Ireland, 284–287; settlement of, 267, 271
Australian Aborigines, 10; initiation rites, 71; and nation-state, 269–270
Authority, 158; symbols of, 67–70
Avunculocal extended family, 82, 83
Avunculocal residence, 80, 81, 89
Awlad 'Ali Bedouin (Egypt), 70
Ax fight, 176
Aztec priests, 204

Bachofen, Johann Jakob, 210
Bakhtiari (Iran), 132–133, 289
BaKwele (Central Africa), 234
Bali (Indonesia), 230; personhood in, 259
Baltic states: ethnic factionalism, 181
Bamako, Mali, 307
Bambara (Mali), 307
Banaro (New Guinea): body symbolism, 67
Band organization, 160, 163
Baraghith tribe, 91
Basic personality type, 250
Basotho (South Africa), 303, 311
Basque, 55
Basseri (Iran), 132, 203, 256, 290
Beattie, John, 148
Becket, Thomas à, 255
Bedouin, 3; Awlad 'Ali, 70; of Cyrenaican, 90–92, 98; Rwala, 3, 5, 131; sedentarization, 290
Belgium: ethnic factionalism, 181
Bemba (Central Africa), 126–127
Benedict, Ruth, 249, 250
Berdache, 111
Berlin, Brent, 51
Big Men, 160–165, 179, 180, 182, 255
Big Women, 162–163
Bilateral cross cousins, 95
Bilateral societies, 92
Bilocal residence, 81
Biological basis of culture, 16–17
Bisa (Zambia), 303
Bismarck Archipelago, 284
Black English, 15
Black folktales, 220, 221
Blackbirding, 277, 283–284
Blackfoot (Montana), 117, 268
Blacking, John, 254
Blacks: kinship relations, 105; migration in U.S., 307–308
Blood: menstrual, 110–112, 195, 212, 260–261; metaphor, 67; and rites of passage, 196

Boas, Franz: and American Historical approach, 19, 21, 249; and language studies, 50, 51; on Northwest Coast art, 235; study of Kwakiutl, 19, 26, 29, 30, 48, 49
Bodmer, Karl, 17, 118
Boluminski, Franz, 285
Bornu, Empire of, 168–172
Bott, Elizabeth, 308–309
Bougainville, Louis-Antoine de, 2
Bound morphemes, 47
Boundary maintenance mechanisms, 292–294
Bourdieu, P., 247, 260
Boys' gangs, 308
Brahmans, 62, 149, 260
Brazil: exploitation of Amazon, 274; Indians of, 267, 269
Bride service, 76, 94, 254–255
Bridewealth, 76–77, 79, 94, 254–255
British colonial rule, 170–171, 266–267, 284
British Guiana, 277
Brother exchange, 76, 77
Brown, Paula, 180–181
Brown, Reverend George, 283–284, 288
Buka (New Britain), 277
Bulmer, Ralph, 50
Bunyan, Paul, 219–220
Bunyoro (Uganda), 3, 148
Bureau of Indian Affairs, 275
Bureaucracy, 167
Burial societies, 306
Bushmen (Kalahari Desert), 123

Cairo, 304
Camelids, 129
Canadian Indian Act of 1876, 279, 280
Cannibalism, 284
Cargo cult, 294–295
Carvers, 229–230, 241, 246
Case method, 171
Cash crops, 273, 299, 302
Caste system: and distribution, 148–149; in India, 62, 148–149
Catacumba, Rio de Janeiro, 304, 305
Catholics: endogamy among, 75; kinship terminology, 107
Catlin, George, 124
Cavaliers, 69
Chagnon, Napoleon, 177, 178
Cherokee (Georgia), 272
Chest-pounding duels, 174–175

Chicago: boys' gangs in, 308
Chieftainship, 182; Kaochin, 165–166; Trobriander, 155–159, 163–166
Child, Irvin, 234, 253–254
Child betrothal, 196
Children: and self-concept, 260; socialization of, 248–249, 251–254, 260–261
Chimbu (Papua New Guinea), 180
Chin (Burma), 130
Chinese, 6; diviners, 202; marriage payments, 76; patrilineal clans, 104; peasant communities, 299
Choctaw (North America), 272
Chomsky, Noam, 49
Christian Science, 208
Christianity, 207–208; fundamentalists, 187, 207; funeral rite, 40–43; rites of passage and intensification, 197, 198
Circumcision, 115, 119, 197, 260
Cities, 298, 301; as unit of study, 308–309
Civil law, 173
Clairvoyance, 231
Clan totem, 62–64, 86, 189, 234
Clans, 74, 90–92; in complex societies, 104; land ownership, 128; patrilineal and matrilineal, 84–87; spirit of, 86; symbols of, 62–64, 234. (*See also* Kinship)
Class differences: in speech, 53
Client, 179–180
Clitoris surgery, 115
Closed corporate peasant community, 298–299
Club fights, 175
Cognates, 55
Cognatic descent, 87–89, 142; kinship terminology, 101; leadership and, 90
Cognition: language and, 49–50
Cognitive need, 186
Cohen, Ronald, 171
Collateral relatives, 100
Collaterality, degree of, 100, 101
Colonialism, 180–181, 263, 265–268; American, 271–272; anthropological study of, 11, 22, 289; and art, 238; closed corporate peasant community and, 298–299; evolution of, 266; functionalism and, 21; labor exploitation and, 276–278; missionaries and, 278–280; New Ireland, 284–286; peasants and, 298–299; resource exploitation, 273–276
Colors: in Northwest Coast art, 235; symbolism of, 72; terms for, 51–52

Community: study of, 10
Compadrazgo, 102–104
Complex societies: art in, 232; funerals in, 40–43; kinship in, 104–107; marriage in, 32–36; music and dance in, 243–245; rituals in, 25, 32–36, 40–43; study of, 10; warfare in, 177–178
Conflict resolution, 171–173
Congo, 277
Consonants, 47
Consumption, 151–153
Contemporary life: anthropology of, 297–312; migration, 302–309; peasants in, 297–302
Cook, Captain James, 1–4, 17, 22, 238, 270
Cooperative groups, 133–134
Coplan, David, 303
Copra, 273, 282–283, 285–287
Corporate descent group, 86
Corvée labor, 285
Cousins, 99–100; marriage between, 75, 95; parallel and cross, 95, 97–98
Coyote (folktale motif), 216–218
Craftsmanship, 237
Creationism, 187
Creativity, individual, 236–238, 247
Cree (Canada), 126
Creek (Georgia), 220, 272
Cremation, 42
Criminal law, 173
Crop introduction, 289
Cross cousins, 95, 97
Crow (Montana), 3, 275; kinship terminology, 101; and supernatural, 193–194, 256
Cults, religious, 294
Cultural anthropology, 15
Cultural borrowings, 238, 268–271
Cultural contacts, 269–271
Cultural differences: study of, 3–4
Cultural evolution theory, 17–19, 104
Cultural psychology, 260
Cultural relativism, 19, 49, 102, 249
Cultural rules, 6–7; food and, 60; individual behavior and, 7–8
Culture: biological basis of, 16–17; concept of, 5–6; and individual, 247–261; language and, 45–56; and mental illness, 255–257; part, 297–298; and personality types, 248–250, 254–255; of poverty, 303–304
Culture change, 263–264; concepts in study of, 264–265; contexts of, 265–268;

Culture change *(Cont.)*:
    directed, 288–292; example of New Ireland, 280–288; labor exploitation and, 276–278; land rights and, 271–273; missionaries and, 278–280; nature of initial contact, 269–271; precontact, 268–269; resource exploitation and, 273–276; study of, 268–270
Culture heroes, 190
Culture identity: assertion of, 292–295
Customary law, 173–174
Cyrenaican Bedouin, 90–92, 98

Dala (Trobrianders), 74, 75, 279
Dama (Kachin), 192
Dance, 242–246
Dani (New Guinea), 128, 129
Darwin, Charles, 17, 20, 187
Davenport, William, 236–237
d'Azevedo, Warren, 229
Debt repayment: in marriage, 28, 30–32
Decision making, 178
Delayed exchange, 97
Democratic government, 264
Demonstrated descent, 90
Depression, 256
Descent groups, 84–88; structure of, 88–92
Developmental theory, 252–253, 259
Dialect differentiation, 54
Diderot, Denis, 3
Diffusion, 19, 264, 269
Dispute resolution, 171–173
Distribution, 134–151; in egalitarian societies, 126–140; Kwakiutl potlatch, 27–32; market system, 141–149 ; in societies with rank, 141–149; Trobriander *sagali*, 36–40, 43
Diviners, 201–202
Divorce, 78–79; and downward mobility, 106
Dobu Islanders (South Pacific), 81, 145
Dominance: language and, 53
Double descent, 88
Douglas, Mary, 22, 60
Downward mobility, 106
Dowry, 76–77
"Dreamings," 234
Dreams: and art, 236–237; symbolism and significance of, 247–248
Drug trances, 193
Duff, Wilson, 226–228
Dundes, Alan, 71, 211
Duolocal residence, 81

Durkheim, Emile, 186, 187, 193
Dutch East India Company, 281
Duwa (Kachin), 165–166
Dzonokwa mask, 231

Eastwood, Clint, 222
Eating: culture and, 4, 6–7, 151–153; and
    sacrifice, 194; and sexual intercourse,
    6–7, 59–62, 64–65; symbolism of, 59–62
Ecology: balance, 125; and warfare, 178
Economic organization, 121–122;
    consumption, 151–153; distribution,
    134–151; politics and, 159, 182;
    production, 122–134
Economics: and directed culture change,
    288–290
Educational anthropology, 15
Egalitarian societies: distribution in,
    126–140
Ego, 92
Ego-oriented kindred, 92, 93
Egypt: pharaoh of, 68, 75, 258; priests,
    204
Embalming, 42
Emma, Queen, 282, 283
Enculturation, 6, 251–252, 259
Endogamy, 75–76, 98
Enemy Way ritual, 293
Enga (New Guinea), 3, 102; horticulture,
    127–128; pig breeding, 130; *Te* exchange
    system, 128, 139–141; warfare, 174
Engels, Friedrich, 18
Epstein, A. L., 21, 302
Erasmus, Charles, 290
Erikson, Eric, 252–253, 258
Errington, Shelly, 110, 112
Eskimo: dispute resolution, 173; kinship
    terminology, 100, 101; Polar, 3, 123,
    124, 311–312; shamans, 200–201;
    situation al leadership, 159
Ethnic associations, 305–306
Ethnic factionalism, 181–182
Ethnic identity, 292–295
Ethnocentrism, 4, 18; linguistics and, 48
Ethnographic present, 26
Ethnohistory, 22
Ethnomusicologists, 243, 244
Ethnosemantics, 50–52
Etoro (Papua New Guinea), 269, 270
Evans-Pritchard, E. E., 21, 203
Evil eye, 203, 300–301
Evolution: human, 16; specific versus
    general, 18

Exchange, 9; body painting at ceremonies,
    238; delayed, 97; and factionalism, 179;
    generalized, 96; reciprocal, 136–138;
    restricted, 94–95, 136
Exchange systems, 134–151
Exogamy, 75–76, 93, 97

Factionalism, 178–182
Factory system, 301
Faith healers, 207
Family planning, 290–292
Family types, 81–84
Famine, 129
Farmers, 301–302
Fates, 215
Favelas (Brazil), 304, 305
Feinberg, Richard, 114
Feld, Steven, 23
Female role, 109–114, 118–119, 124–125,
    214–215
Female speech, 53
Feminist movement, 113
Fertility rates, 290–291
Feuding, 174
Fictive kinship, 102–104
Fieldwork, 11–15, 250, 263
Fiji Islands, 277, 283, 284
Firth, Raymond, 9, 10, 193, 247
Fishman, Pamela, 53
Flag symbolism, 67
Fligstein, Neil, 307
Folktales, 209–210, 216–219; in American
    culture, 219–223
Food: cultural ranking of, 152; exchange
    systems, 136; symbolism of, 59–62. (*See
    also* Eating)
Ford, John, 221
Forge, Anthony, 233, 234
Fortune-telling, 202
Fourth world, 263–295, 297; defined, 267
Fraternal polyandry, 78
Freeman, Derek, 250
French colonial rule, 266
French food, 152
Freud, Sigmund, 186, 211, 249, 250, 252
Fromm, Erich, 252
Fulani (Nigeria), 3, 131–132, 170, 253
Function, 20; in anthropology, 9–10
Functionalism, 20–21
Funerals: in complex society, 40–43;
    enculturation and, 252; *malanggan*
    mortuary art, 240–242, 281; music in,
    244; as politcal events, 155; potlatch,

Funerals *(Cont.):*
143; as rite of passage, 196–197; in small-scale society, 36–40
Fur trade, 271

Games: symbolism of, 58, 70–71
Gandhi, Mahatma, 258
Garden magician, 203–207
Gathering *(see* Hunting and gathering)
Gay couples, 105
Geertz, Clifford, 22, 57, 259
Geidam, Nigeria, 11
Gender differences, 8; in artistic expression, 245–246; body painting and, 239; and idea of self, 260; myths and, 212–215; organization of work, 133–134; roles, 109–114, 160–161, 249–250; in speech, 53
Generalized exchange, 96
Generational conflict, 115–117
Geomancy, 202
German colonialism, 284–286
German New Guinea, 273
Germanic languages, 55
Germanic personality, 248
Ghosts, 189, 190, 192
Giagia, 162
Ginsburg, Faye D., 113
Giving, 135
Gluckman, Max, 203
Gmelch, George, 207
Godparenthood, 102–104, 107, 306
Gola (Liberia), 119, 229–230
Gold mining, 275, 276
Government: defined, 158
Grain cultivation, 128–129
Grammar, 48, 49
Gratification, 17
Graves, Robert, 215
Great Tradition, 298, 300, 302
Greek mythology, 215
Grigorenko, Pyotr, 258
Grimm Brothers, 220
Gros Ventre, 117
Guardian spirit, 189
Guatemala, 298, 299
Gumlao (Kachin), 165, 166, 182
Gumsa (Kachin), 166, 182, 192
Guyana, 277
Gypsies, 202, 246

Hadza (Tanzania), 173, 255
Haggling, 149

Haida (Northwest Coast), 236, 237, 241, 279, 280
Hair: symbolism of, 72
Halpern, Barbara, 301–302
Halpern, Joel, 301–302
Hammel, Eugene, 103
Handsome Lake religion, 294
Hare Krishna, 309
Harley, George, 119, 228
Harmony, 245
Harris, M., 177
Harris, Joel Chandler, 220, 221
Hassidic Jews, 294, 309
Hawaiian kinship terminology, 101–102
Hawaiians, 3, 22, 75, 152; legends of, 215–216
Headmanship: Kachin, 165–166; Yanomano, 156–160
Health: and directed culture change, 290–292
Hekura (Yanomano), 201
Hernsheim, Eduard, 282, 285
Hidatsa (North America), 117–119, 268
Historical approach: to anthropology, 19–20
Hogbin, Ian, 190
Homosexuality: *berdache,* 111; initiation rites and, 71; kinship relationships, 105; sports and, 71
Horses, 268–269
Hortatory rituals, 193
Horticulture, 127–128
Hudson's Bay Company, 266, 268, 271
Human body: decoration, 238–239; and kinship, 86; symbolism of, 66–67
Hunt, George, 19
Hunting and gathering, 122–126, 133–134; band organization, 160; colonization versus, 271; religious practice, 206
Huntingford, G. W. B., 115
Hutterites, 294
Hutu (Rwanda), 148

Iban (Borneo), 3, 292, 303; postmarital residence, 81
Idiolect, 7
Ifugao (Philippines), 251
Igluligmuit (Canada): situational leadership, 159
Incas, 75
Incest: eating and, 60–61; taboo, 74–75, 279
Indebtedness, 135

Indentured labor, 276–277
India: caste system, 62, 148–149, 260–261; child socialization, 260–261; colonial rule, 266; eating, 62, 152; factionalism, 178–179; indentured labor, 277
Indian Removal Act, 272
Indians, American (*see* Native Americans)
Indigenous states, 166–170
Individual behavior: and cultural rules, 7–8, 247–261
Individual creativity, 236–238, 247
Indo-European language, 48, 55
Indonesia, 181, 299
Industrial Revolution, 264, 266, 301
Industrialization: and gender roles, 113
Infant mortality rates, 290–291
Informant-anthropologist relationship, 13–15, 250
Initiation rites: homosexuality and, 71; myths and, 212–214, 227–230, 232; rites of passage and intensification, 26, 142, 195–198, 206, 256, 300; sports and, 71
Innovation, 264
Innovators, 257–258
Inspiration: individualism and, 236–238
Intensification: rites of, 195, 197–198, 206, 300
Intentionality, 260
International Court of Justice, 178
Interpretive anthropology, 22–23
Inuit (*see* Eskimo)
Invention, 264
Iran, 11; ethnic factionalism, 181, 267; nomadic pastoralists, 132–133; sedentarization, 133; women's roles, 114
Iraq: ethnic factionalism, 181, 267; Marsh Arabs, 131, 133
Ireland: stem family in, 84
Iroquois, League of the, 294
Iroquois kinship terminology, 100–102
Irrigation systems, 128–129
Islam, 207–208; fundamentalism, 114; legal code, 169

Jackson, Andrew, 272
Jakobson, Roman, 22, 52
Jale (New Guinea), 177
Jamaica, 302
Japanese, 6, 181, 199; language, 53; and Papua New Guinea, 286, 288; WWII, 177, 286
Java, 298; personhood in, 259

Jews: endogamy among, 75; rites of passage, 197
Jicarilla Apaches (New Mexico), 275
Johnson, Lyndon, 295
Johnson, Samuel, 1–2
Johnson movement, 295
Joint family, 82, 84
Judges, 172

Kaberry, Phyllis, 136
Kachin (Burma), 3; *duwa*, 165–166; generalized exchange, 96; *gumlao*, 165, 166, 182; *gumsa*, 166, 182, 192; political organization, 164–166, 191; and supernatural, 191–194, 197–198, 205; witches, 202
Kaguru (East Africa), 193
Kaiko exchange (Maring), 138–141, 176, 238
Kalela (Bisa), 303
Kalmyk Mongols, 11, 14, 152
Kaluli, 23
Kanuri (Nigeria), 3, 6, 11, 13, 289; family structure, 81; marketplace, 150; marriage prohibitions, 78; music, 246; political organization, 168–171
Karam (Papua New Guinea): language of, 50, 52, 64
Katanga, 275
Katuyausi (Trobrianders), 279
Kay, Paul, 51
Kayasa (Trobrianders), 71, 156, 163, 164
Kazaks (Central Asia), 5, 132, 133, 152
Keenan, Elinor, 53
Kenya: settlement of, 267
Kenyatta, Jomo, 312
Kerkennah Islands, 260
Khomeini, Ayatollah, 114
Kikuyu (Kenya): extended family, 83
Kindreds, 92–93
Kinship, 73–107, 121–122; American, 22; blood metaphor, 67; body metaphor, 66–67; in complex societies, 104–107; descent groups, 84–88; family types, 81–84; fictive, 102–104; land ownership, 128; by marriage, 93–98; terminologies, 51, 98–102, 107; in Trobrianders, 36–38, 74. (*See also* Marriage)
Kluckhohn, Clyde, 212, 213
Koch, K., 177, 178
Korea, 199
Korean war, 177–178

Korongo (Sudan), 3
Kosovo, Yugoslavia, 104–105
Kreen-akore (Brazil), 292
Kroeber, Alfred L., 19
Kukailimoku (god), 216
Kula ring exchange (Trobrianders), 121, 145–147, 150, 158, 162, 182
Kumulipo chant, 215
Kurds, 181, 267
Kwakiutl (British Columbia), 3, 19, 311; ancestral myths, 227, 232; artistic style, 236; chieftainship, 164; cognatic descent, 87–89; economic organization, 125–126, 141–144, 149, 268; folktales, 216; food ranking, 152; garden magician, 205; marriage, 26–32, 35–36, 43, 58, 74, 79, 98, 126, 141, 227, 243; masks, 230–232; *numaym*, 27–32, 73–74, 87–88, 90, 134, 141–142, 164, 227, 243; potlatches, 27, 28, 30, 32, 63, 121, 141–144, 147, 152, 227, 233, 234, 279–280; shamans, 198–200, 202; Winter Ceremonial Dances, 232
Kwoma (New Guinea), 3

L.A. Law, 222–223
Labor exploitation, 276–278
Lake, Handsome, 294
Land rights, 271–273
Landlords, 180
Language: borrowings, 56; change in, 54–56; and cognition, 49–50; and culture, 45–56; dialects, 54–55; ethnosemantics, 50–52; and evolution, 16–17; and experience, 49–50; and fieldwork, 12; linguistic relativity, 48–49; sociolinguistics, 52–54; versus speech, 52–53; structure of, 45–48; unwritten, 55–56
Lasisi, David, 241, 242
Latah, 257
Latin, 54–55
Latin America: peasant communities, 299, 300; urban poverty, 304–305. (*See also individual countries*)
Lavongai Island, 295
Law, 171–174
Laying on of hands, 207
Leach, Edmund, 22, 64–66, 72, 165
Leadership, 158; in patrilineal and matrilineal societies, 89–90; situational, 159–161, 163
Legal code, 171

Legends, 209, 215–216; in American culture, 219–223
Leopold, king of Belgium, 277
Lesbian couples, 105
Lesotho, 303
Lesu, Papua New Guinea, 4, 286; sex and eating in, 7, 59–60
Levirate, 78
Lévi-Strauss, Claude, 21, 23–24, 212–213, 218–219, 231
Lewa (Wogeo), 190–191
Lewis, Oscar, 303–304
Liberia, 274
Lima, Peru, 304–306
Liminal period, 195
Lineages, 90–92; marriage and, 93–98
Lineal relatives, 100
Linguistic relativity, 48–49
Linguistics: anthropological, 15
Linnaean classification system, 50, 52
Linton, Ralph, 255, 264
Lips, Julius, 238
Little Tradition, 298, 300–302
London: kinship in, 105
Love poetry: symbolism in, 70
Lovedu (southern Africa), 3, 98
Lugard, Lord, 170
Luluais (New Ireland), 285
Lumber exploitation, 274–275
Luther, Martin, 258

Madagascar, 53
Madai (Kachin), 192
Mae Enga (New Guinea), 111–112, 244
Mafia, 179
Magic: science and, 187–188; and sports, 71
Magicians, 203–204
Mahapatra, Manamohan, 260–261
Malagasy: female role, 111; language, 53
Malanggan mortuary art, 240–242, 281
Malaspina, 2
Malaya, 274, 292
Malaysia, 288, 292; mental illness in, 257
Male role, 109–114, 118–119, 124–125, 214–215
Male speech, 53
Mali, 307
Malinowski, Bronislaw: fieldwork on Trobrianders, 20, 37–39, 145, 147, 156, 203–204, 207, 279; and functionalism, 20–21, 286; on myths, 211–213

Malnutrition, 291
Mana (Polynesia), 189
Manau (Kachin), 197
Manchus (Manchuria): marriage among, 79
Mandan, 117
Manhattan Island, 272
Manners, Thomas, 282
Mano (Liberia), 3, 119, 228–230, 246
Maori (New Zealand), 3, 267; contact with settlers, 269–271; legends of, 215–216
Mara (pollution), 261
Mardi Gras, 198
Maring (New Guinea), 3; eating symbolism, 61; *kaiko* exchange system, 138–141, 176, 238; warfare, 176, 177
Marked category, 52
Markedness, principle of, 52
Market: meanings of, 150
Market mentality, 121
Market system, 141–149, 268, 299, 300
Marketplace, 150, 168, 299
Marri Baluch (Pakistan): eating in, 60
Marriage, 74–79; age grade and, 115; in complex society, 32–36; debt repayment in, 28, 30–32; delayed exchange, 97; dissolution of, 78–79; eating and, 7; endogamy and exogamy, 75–76; group relations through, 93–98; among Kwakiutl, 26–32, 35–36, 43, 58, 74, 79, 98, 126, 141, 227, 243; levirate and sororate, 78; number of spouses, 77–78; payments, 76–77; postmarital residence, 79–81; prohibitions, 74–75; sister exchange, 76; in small-scale society, 26–32; Thai space symbolism, 66
Marsh Arabs (Iraq), 131, 133
Marx, Karl, 17
Marxist anthropology, 153
Masai (East Africa), 116
Masculinity, 109–114
Mashpee (Massachusetts), 273
Masks, 226–234
Matrilineal clan membership, 85, 89, 142; among Trobrianders, 30, 37–38
Matrilineal descent, 84–88, 92, 96, 97, 142; kinship terminology, 101; leadership and, 89–90
Matrilocal residence, 80
Mauss, Marcel, 25
Maximilian, Prince, 17
Maximizing, 122
Maya priests, 204
Mayer, Philip, 21
Mayu (Kachin), 192

Mbuti (Zaire), 125, 134
Mead, Margaret: and gender roles, 109; personality studies, 249–251, 259; and sister exchange, 76
Meggitt, Mervyn, 139, 174
Meillassoux, Claude, 307
Melanesia: Big Man structure, 160–165; cargo cult, 294–295; labor exploitation, 277; magic, 203; missionaries, 279
Melody, 245
Melpa (New Guinea), 239
Mende (Sierra Leone), 3, 119
Mendel, Gregor, 264
Menomini, 3, 292
Menstrual blood, 110–112, 195, 212, 260–261
Mental illness, 255–257
Mesopotamian priests, 204
Metaphor, 22, 58, 312; of body, 66–67
Metonym, 22, 58; of authority, 68
Mexico, 298, 299; culture of poverty, 303–304; food, 152
Mexico City, 304
Michelangelo, 22
Microanalytic level, 267
Middle East: gender roles, 111; preferential marriage rule, 98. (*See also specific countries and societies*)
Migration, 265; contemporary, 302–309
Migratory cycle: in hunting and gathering, 123; of pastoralists, 131
Migratory labor, 277, 301–302
Miller, Joan G., 260–261
Mining, 275–277; migration and, 302–309
Mintz, S. W., 302
Missionaries, 208, 278–280, 284
Modal personality type, 250
Mohammad Shah, 133
Moieties, 92, 142
Moldavia: ethnic factionalism, 181
Money, 121, 149–150, 168, 273
Mongols, 265; body metaphor, 67; Kalmyk, 11, 14, 152
Monogamy, 77
Monotheism, 190
Moore, Omar, 202
Morgan, Lewis Henry, 17, 18, 102, 104, 153, 210
Mormonism, 208; endogamy, 75
Morocco, 4
Morphemes, 47, 57
Morphemic structure, 47–48
Movies, 220–223

Mundurucu (Brazil), 133; myths of, 214–215
Munn, Nancy, 233
Murphy, Robert, 214
Murphy, Yolanda, 214
Music, 242–246
Musil, Alois, 131
Myths, 209–215

Nagas (Burma), 130, 267
Nambikwara (Brazil), 24
Nanarang (Wogeo), 190
Nandi (Kenya), 3; age grades, 115–116
Natchez, 220
Nation of Islam, 208
Nation-state: political organization, 178–182; study of, 11, 263–264, 267
National culture, 181, 263, 306
National identity, 292–295
Native Americans: American Historical approach to, 19; and American settlement, 265, 271–273; folktales of, 216–218; languages, 48; and supernatural, 193–194. (*See also specific nations*)
Native culture: national culture versus, 263–264
Nativistic movements, 294
Nats (Kachin), 192, 194, 197, 205
Natural versus supernatural, 185–186
Navajos (Southwest U.S.), 3, 55–56, 241–242, 256, 273, 289–290, 293
Ndendeuli (Tanzania), 173
Near East: eating in, 60; evolution of communities in, 297, 301
Neighborhood: study of, 308
Neo-Melanesian, 282, 288
Neocolonialism, 264
Neolocal residence, 79, 80
Network tracing, 308–309
Neuroses, 256
Neville, Gwen K., 106
New Britain, 277, 286
New Guinea: animal domestication, 130; body painting, 238–239; contact with Australia, 269; culture and personality studies, 249–250; eating in, 151; gender roles, 111, 113–114; horticulture, 127–128; missionaries, 278; warfare, 174. (*See also* Papua New Guinea; *specific societies*)
New Ireland: Big Men, 282–283, 288; copra, 282–283, 285–287; culture change

New Ireland *(Cont.)*:
in, 280–288; *malanggan* mortuary art, 240–242, 281; settlement, 280–281. (*See also* Papua New Guinea)
New Zealand: settlement of, 267, 269, 271. (*See also* Maori)
Newman, Katherine, 106
Nibek (Wogeo), 190–191, 210–214, 228
Nicholas, Ralph W., 178
Nigeria: British rule of, 170–171, 273; fieldwork in, 11; independence, 171; markets, 299; oil, 276
Nomadic pastoralists, 5, 90–92, 125, 130–133, 148, 203, 289; kinship terminology, 102; sedentarization, 133, 290
Nootka (Canada), 3; house floor plan and ranking, 65–67
Northwest Coast: artistic style, 234–236, 241; missionaries and, 279–280; totem poles, 234
Northwest Territory, Government of, 272
Nuclear family, 81, 82, 106
Nukumanu Atoll (Polynesia), 114
Numaym (Kwakiutl), 27–32, 73–74, 87–88, 90, 134, 141–142, 164, 227, 243
Nupe (Nigeria), 3
Nyakyusa (Tanzania), 3; age grades, 116–117, 120

Observation, participant, 11, 13, 14
Office, 158
O'Hanlon, Michael, 239
Oil exploitation, 276
Ojibwa (Canada), 3; band organization, 160
Oklahoma Territory, 272
Okuk, Sir Iambakey, 180, 203
Omaha (North America), 268; kinship terminology, 101
Omai, 3, 238
Omens, 205
Onitsha (Nigeria): Obi of, 68
OPEC, 276
Open peasant communities, 299
Oral tradition, 216–219
Orasac, Yugoslavia, 302
Ordinance of 1787, 272
Organization of work, 133–134
Orissa, India, 260–261
Ortner, Sherry B., 182
Orwell, George, 121

Painting, 226–242
Pantheon, 189
Papua New Guinea, 4, 11, 14, 273; creation of, 287–288; food symbolism in, 59–60; *malanggan* mortuary art, 240–242, 281; political organization, 180–181, 286–288. (*See also* New Guinea; New Ireland; *specific societies*)
Parallel cousins, 95, 98
Paranoid schizophrenia, 257
Part cultures, 297–298
Participant observation, 11, 13, 14
Pass Laws, 277
Passage: rites of, 26, 142, 195–197, 206
Passamaquoddy (Maine), 273
Pastoralists (*see* Nomadic pastoralists)
Pathans of Swat: eating symbolism, 61
Patrilineal clan membership, 85, 89, 104, 123, 136, 299
Patrilineal descent, 84–89, 92, 96, 116–117, 138, 170; Big Man and, 162; kindred in, 93, 96; kinship terminology , 101, 102; leadership and, 89–90
Patrilocal residence, 80
Patron, 179–180
Pattern, 9
Peabody Coal Company, 275
Peace, 174–178
Peasants, 297–302
Penis incision ritual, 110, 196, 212, 213
Pentatonic scale, 245
Perlman, Janice, 304
Personality studies, 249–250; child rearing, 252–253; culture and social structure, 254–255
Personality types, 248–250; basic and modal, 250
Personhood, 258–261
Peru, 299, 300
Peters, Emrys, 90
Pharaoh of Egypt, 68, 75, 258
Phonemes, 46
Phonemic structure, 46–47
Physical anthropology, 15
Pidgin English, 282, 283, 286, 288
Pitkin, Harvey, 217
Plains Indians: age associations, 117–119; horse and, 268–269; warfare, 174
Plant domestication, 126–129
Polar Eskimo, 3, 123, 124, 311–312
Political anthropology, 157–159, 179
Political economy, 159, 182
Political leadership, 89–90

Political organization, 155–182; anthropological concepts, 157–159; band organization, 160; Big Man, 160–165; chieftainship, 163–166; in contemporary nation-state, 178–182; law and social control, 171–174; situational leadership , 159–160; state, 166–171; types of, 159–171; war and peace, 174–178
Political symbolism, 67–70, 186
Politics: defined, 158
Pollution: menstrual, 110–112, 195, 212, 260–261
Polyandry, 78
Polygamy, 78, 279
Polygyny, 77–78
Polynesia: legends in, 215–216
Population increases, 290–291
Poro Society, 119–120, 228–230, 236, 241
Postpeasants, 301–302
Potlatches: Kwakiutl, 27, 28, 30, 32, 63, 121, 141–144, 147, 152, 227, 233, 234, 279–280; outlawing, 144, 279–280; Tlingit, 142–143, 147, 279
Poverty: culture of, 303–304
Powdermaker, Hortense, 286
Power, 157–158, 178
Poynton, Cate, 53
Prayer, 193
Price, Richard, 23
Priests, 204–205
"Primitive" art, 238
Primogeniture, 164
Private symbols, 59, 247
Production, 122–134; agriculture, 126–129; animal domestication, 129–133; hunting and gathering, 122–126; organization of work, 133–134
Proto-language, 55
Provisioning, 121–153; consumption, 151–153; distribution, 134–151; production, 122–134
Psychoanalytic theory, 186, 211, 249, 250, 252
Psychological need, 186
Psychology, cultural, 260
Psychoses, 256
Psychosexual development theory, 252–253
Public symbols, 58–59, 247
Pueblos (Southwest U.S.), 292–293; uxorilocal residence, 80
Puerto Ricans, 303, 309
Puritans, 69

Pushtun (Afghanistan), 132
Pygmies (Zaire), 123, 134

Qashqai (Iran), 132
Questionnaires, 14

Radcliffe-Brown, A. R., 20–21, 78
Raids, 175–176
Rank: distribution in societies with,
    141–149; eating symbolism and, 61–62;
    shamanism and, 199–200; space
    symbolism and, 65–66
Raphael, 236
Rappaport, Roy A., 177
Ray, Marquis de, 284
Reagan, Ronald, 222
Rebels, 257–258
Receiving, 135
Reciprocal exchange, 136–138
Regional associations, 305–307
Reid, Bill, 236, 237, 242
Reincarnation, 183
Relatives: collateral and lineal, 100
Religion, 183–208; aims and goals of,
    205–206; latent function of, 206–208;
    and law, 173; needs and, 186; science
    and, 187–188
Religious community kinship, 107
Religious cults, 294
Religious identity, 293–294
Religious ruler, 167, 173, 205
Religious specialists, 198–205; diviners,
    201–202; magicians, 203–204; priests,
    204–205; shamans, 199–201; witches,
    202–203
Renaissance, 25, 236
Residence: postmarital, 79–81
Resource exploitation: and culture change,
    273–276
Restricted exchange, 94–95, 136
Returning, 135
Revenge-seeking, 174
Revised Indian Act of 1951 (Canada), 280
Revitalization movements, 294
Reza Shah, 133
Rhodes, Cecil, 275
Rhythm, 245
Richards, Audrey, 126
Riff (Morocco), 67, 98
Rio de Janeiro, 304
Rites of initiation (*see* Initiation rites)
Rites of intensification, 195, 197–198, 206,
    300

Rites of passage, 26, 142, 195–197, 206
Rituals, 25–43; and arts, 226, 240; defined,
    25; hortatory, 193; masks and, 228–233;
    music and dance, 243–245; rites of
    passage and intensification, 26, 142,
    195–198, 206; in small-scale society,
    25–32, 36–40; and supernatural,
    193–198
Romance languages, 54–55
Rosaldo, Michelle, 254–255
Rosman, Abraham, 11, 12, 13, 168, 232
Rubber industry, 274
Rubbish men, 160–161
Rubel, Paula G., 11, 13, 14, 232
Russian revolution, 257–258
Rwala Bedouin (Saudi Arabia), 3, 5, 131

Sa'ada genealogy, 91–92
Sacrifices, 194, 228; among Kachin,
    197–198
Sagali (Trobrianders), 36–40, 43, 86,
    144–145, 147, 149, 150, 155–156
Sahlins, Marshall, 17, 22, 125, 152
Samoa, 249–250
San (Kalahari Desert), 123
Sande Society, 120, 230
Sapir, Edward, 50
Saramaka, 23
Saussure, Ferdinand de, 45, 52
Scapulimancy, 206
Scarification, 119, 196, 214
Schizophrenia, 257
Schneider, David, 22, 102, 106
Schouten, Dutch explorer, 281
Schramm, Adelaida Reyes, 244–245
Schwartzenegger, Arnold, 33–35, 79, 222
Science: magic and religion versus,
    187–188
Sculpture, 226–242
Seasonal cycle: of agriculturists, 126–127;
    of pastoralists, 130
Secret societies, 119–120, 227–230
Sedentarization, 133, 290
Segmentary lineage system, 92, 164–165,
    192
Self. 258–261
Self-motivation, 259
Seminole (Florida), 272
Seneca (New York), 3, 294
Serial polygamy, 78
Service, Elman, 17
Settlement: colonialism and, 267
Sexton, Loraine, 114

Sexual behavior: culture and, 6–8; hair length and, 72; missionaries and, 279
Sexual intercourse: colonialism and, 266; eating and, 6–7, 59–62, 64–65; initiation rites and, 212–214; prohibitions, 75, 212, 279; shamanism and, 201; Thai space symbolism, 66
Shadip (Kachin), 192, 194
Shakers: furniture, 232; kinship terminology, 107
Shamans, 199–201, 232, 255; male, 110; Yanomano, 157, 200–202
Shehu of Bornu, 168–171
Shifting cultivation (*swidden*), 127, 128
Shriver, Maria, 33–35, 222
Shweder, Richard, 260–261
Siblings: equivalence of, 78; incest taboo, 75
Side-slapping contests, 175
Sinhalese, 181
Sioux (South Dakota): child rearing, 252–253; contact with settlers, 271
Siroto, Leon, 234
Sister exchange, 76, 93–95
Situational leadership, 159–161, 163
Siuai of Bougainville (Solomon Islands): eating taboos, 61
Slang words, 54
Slavery, 276, 277
Slavic languages, 55
Small-scale society: artists in, 236–238; customs as law, 173; funerals in, 36–40; marriage in, 26–32; rituals in, 25–32, 36–40; warfare in, 174–177. (*See also specific societies*)
Smith, M. G., 21
Smith, W. Robertson, 194
Snake Handlers, 184, 185
Social control, 171–174
Social Darwinism, 17
Social groups: and symbolism, 62–67
Social organization, 9, 178
Social relationships, 8
Social role, 8
Social status, 8; achieved and ascribed, 161; and personality, 255
Social stratification, 167, 168
Social structure, 8–9, 178; functionalism and, 20–21; personality and, 254–255
Socialization, 248–249, 251–254, 260–261
Society: concept of, 8–9
Sociobiologists, 15
Sociolinguistics, 52–54
Solomon Islands: dreams and arts, 237
Sorcerers, 183, 202, 203

Sorcery: and Trobriander funeral, 37, 39
Sororal polygyny, 78
Sororate, 78
South Africa: migratory labor, 303; mineral exploitation, 275–276
Soviet Union: 1917 revolution, 257–258; ethnic factionalism, 181
Space: symbolism of, 65–66
Spanish exploration, 268
Speech: class and, 54; communities, 54; geography/region and, 54; language versus, 52–53; male versus female, 53
Spirit: clan or ancestral, 86
Spirit monsters (Wogeo), 190–191
Spiro, Melford, 186, 187
Split representation, 236
Sports: symbolism in, 58, 70–71
Spouses: number of, 77–78. (*See also* Marriage)
Sri Lanka: eating in, 62; factionalism, 181
Stack, Carol, 105, 308
State, 166–171, 298, 301. (*See also* Nation-state)
Statistical analysis, 14
Status: achieved and ascribed, 161
Status personalities, 255
Steel tools, 269
Stem family, 82, 84
Steward, Julian, 18, 123
Stipulated descent, 90
Strathern, Andrew, 238–239
Strathern, Marilyn, 238–239
Stratification: social, 167, 168
Structuralism, 21
Structure: in anthropology, 9–10; family, 81–84; of language, 45–48; musical, 245. (*See also* Social structure)
Style, 235–237
Subclans, 90
Subcultures, 308
Succession: rules of, 158–159, 161–162, 165, 170
Sudanese kinship terminology, 102
Suffragette movement, 113
Supernatural: conceptions of, 188–193; ritual approaches to, 193–198, 232. (*See also* Folktales; Legends; Myths)
Supply and demand, law of, 151
Suttles, Gerald D., 308
Suvasova (Trobrianders), 75
Swidden cultivation, 127, 128
Symbolic anthropology, 21–22
Symbolism, 57–72; analysis of, 57–58; of authority, 67–70; of food, 59–62; politics

Symbolism *(Cont.)*:
  and, 67–70, 186; private, 59, 247; public,
  58–59, 247; religion and, 186; of
  sacrifice, 194; social groups and, 62–67;
  of sports, 58, 70–71; universal, 70 –71
Syntax, 48

Taboos: eating and sexual, 60–61, 116;
  marriage, 74–75
Tacitus, 248
Tahiti, 3, 4
Tamberan Cult, 196
Tambiah, S. J., 66
Tamil, 181
Tax collection, 167, 170
Te exchange (Enga), 128, 139–141
Technology, 123; agricultural, 128–129;
  and directed culture change, 288–290; of
  hunting and gathering, 123–124
Television, 220, 222–223
Temne (Sierra Leone), 119
Tenants, 180
Tepoztlan, Mexico, 10, 303–304
Teutonic tribes: body symbolism, 66–67
Thai, 3; house space symbolism, 66, 67
Thanksgiving, 198
Theocracies, 167, 173, 205
Third World, 267, 288; cities of, 304
Tibet: polyandry in, 83
Tikopia Island, 10, 225
Tiv (Nigeria), 173
Tlingit (Pacific Northwest), 3; moieties, 92,
  142; potlatches, 142–143, 147, 279;
  shamans, 200
Toilet training, 252–253
Tonga (Zambia), 173
Tools: and evolution, 16, 17, 269
Tor (New Guinea), 3, 127, 130
Totem: clan representation, 62–64, 86, 189,
  234; eating and, 60–61
Totem poles, 125, 234, 235
Totemic animals, 62–64, 86, 189
Tourism: and art, 241–242
Trading companies and posts, 266, 271
Trances, 193
Tribal associations, 306–307
Tribalism, 181, 267
Tribute, 148, 156, 164
Trickster (folktale motif), 216–218
Trinidad, 277
Trobriand Islanders, 3; avunculocal
  residence, 81; bachelor houses, 116;
  chieftainship, 155–159, 163–166; cricket,

Trobriand Islanders *(Cont.)*:
  71; *dala*, 74, 75, 279; distribution
  systems, 136, 144–147; eating
  symbolism, 59–60, 62; functionalism
  and, 20; funeral rite in, 36–40, 42–43,
  74, 144–145, 147, 252, 256; garden
  magician, 203–204, 206–207;
  horticulture, 128; *kayasa*, 71, 156, 163,
  164; kinship among, 36–38, 74; kinship
  terminology, 101; *kula* exchange, 121,
  145–147, 150, 158, 162, 182; marriage
  prohibitions, 78; matrilineal descent,
  85–87, 97, 144, 145, 155–156;
  missionaries and, 279; political structure
  of, 9–10, 155–159, 182; *sagali*, 36–40, 43,
  86, 144–145, 147, 149, 150, 155–156;
  and supernatural, 183, 185, 187, 193,
  202–204; *suvasova*, 75; *urigubu*, 144–145,
  147, 156, 164; work organization, 134
Truces, 176–177
Tsimshian (British Columbia): house front
  painting, 235, 236; masks, 226–228,
  230–231; potlatch, 279; totem pole, 63
Tungus (Siberia), 199
Tupi (Brazil), 276
Turkey: ethnic factionalism, 181
Turner, Victor, 195
Tutsi (Rwanda), 148
Twa (Rwanda), 125, 148
Tylor, Sir Edward B., 17, 189–190, 192

Ukraine: ethnic factionalism, 181
Ultimogeniture, 165
Uncle, 98
Unilineal descent groups, 87
Union Minière du Haute-Katanga, 275
United Fruit Company, 274
United Nations, 178
United States: colonization of, 271–272;
  land rights and, 271–273; migration in,
  307–308; WWII, 177. *(See also* American
  culture)
Unmarked category, 52
Untouchables, 149, 260
Uranium mining, 275
Urarina (Peru), 3, 274–275
Urban communities: studies of, 308–309
Urigubu (Trobrianders), 144–145, 147, 156,
  164
Ussher, Bishop, 187
Ute (Utah), 275
Uxorilocal extended family, 82, 83
Uxorilocal residence, 80, 89

Vai (Liberia), 229–230
Van Gennep, Arnold, 195, 196
Vanatinai Islanders, 162
Vancouver, George, 2
Venda (South Africa), 254
Vietnamese immigrants (New Jersey), 244–245
Virilocal extended family, 82, 83
Virilocal residence, 80, 89
Vision quest, 193–194, 256
Visual arts, 226–242
Voltaire, 3
Voluntary associations, 306–307
Vowels, 47

Wahgi (New Guinea), 239
Waitangi, Treaty of, 269, 271
Wake, 41, 152
Walbiri (Australia), 233–234
Wallerstein, Immanuel, 267
Wana (Indonesia), 110–111; shamanism, 201
Warabwa (Wogeo), 198
Ward: study of, 308
Ward boss, 181
Warfare, 174–178
Washo (California-Nevada), 123
Water witching, 202
Wawn, Captain, 283
Webber, John, 4
Weber, Max, 186
Weddings (*see* Marriage)
Weiner, Annette, 37
West, C., 53
West Africa: cities of, 306
Westerns, 221–222
Whaling, 281–282
White, Leslie, 18
Whiting, John, 253–254
Whorf, Benjamin Lee, 50
Wife-giver, 96, 192
Wife-taker, 96, 192
Willmott, Peter, 105
Wilson, Monica, 116, 117
Windigo psychosis, 257

Wintu (California), 3, 217–218
Wissler, Clark, 117
Witchcraft, 183, 184, 192, 202–203, 207, 256, 301; accusations of, 173, 203
Witches, 202–203
Wogeo (New Guinea), 3; eating symbolism, 60; male and female roles, 110, 111, 212–215, 223; myths of, 210–215, 223, 228; and the supernatural, 190–192, 198
Wok Meri, 114
Wolf, Eric, 22, 268, 298
Work: organization of, 133–134
World system: culture change and, 267–268, 297
Wright, Will, 221–222

Xwexwe mask, 231

Yako (Nigeria), 3; double descent, 88; *lejima*, 88
Yanomamo (Venezuela), 3, 311; bride service, 76; kinship terminology, 51, 95, 98–101; political organization, 156–160, 167; restricted exchange (*suaboya*), 95; shamans, 157, 200–202; and supernatural, 193, 200–201; warfare, 174–178
Yoruba (Nigeria): ruler, 172; sculpture, 238, 239
Young, Michael, 105
Yugoslavia: Albanians, 104–105; factionalism, 181; godparenthood (*kumstvo*), 103–104; postpeasants, 301–302; *zadruga*, 299–300
Yurok (California): child rearing, 252–253

Zadruga, 299–300
Zaire: music in, 245
Zambia, 302–303
Zimbabwe, 267, 275
Zimmerman, D., 53
Zulu War of 1879, 271
Zuni (Southwest U.S.), 250, 293